*ATP 3-90.1

Army Techniques Publication
No. 3-90.1

Headquarters
Department of the Army
Washington, D.C., 24 October 2023

Armor and Mechanized Infantry Company Team

Contents

*This publication supersedes ATP 3-90.1, dated 27 January 2016.

Figures

Tables

This page intentionally left blank.

Preface

ATP 3-90.1 provides techniques for the employment of Armor and mechanized Infantry company teams within combined arms battalions (CABs) in the Armored brigade combat team (ABCT). It provides the framework and technical employment principles for Armor and mechanized Infantry company teams within CAB in the ABCT. The techniques contained in this Army techniques publication are to be used as a guide and are not to be considered prescriptive. This Army techniques publication includes discussions of doctrine that are applicable to all Armor and mechanized Infantry companies.

This publication serves as an authoritative reference for United States Army Training and Doctrine Command personnel who develop doctrine material and force structure, institutional and unit training, and company team standard operating procedures (SOPs). It is a guide for Armor and mechanized Infantry companies to develop SOPs. This publication provides doctrinal guidance for commanders, staff, and leaders who plan, prepare, execute, and assess the operations of Armor and mechanized Infantry company teams. Specifically, it is directed toward the company commander, executive officer, first sergeant, platoon leader, platoon sergeant, fire support officer, master gunner, supply sergeant, signal support specialist, emergency care sergeant, field maintenance team chief, and all supporting units.

Commanders, staffs, and subordinates ensure their decisions and actions follow applicable United States, international, and, in some cases, host-nation laws and regulations. Commanders at all levels ensure their Soldiers operate according to the law of armed conflict and rules of engagement. (See FM 6-27 for more information.)

ATP 3-90.1 uses joint terms where applicable. Selected joint and Army terms and definitions appear in both the glossary and the text. Terms for which ATP 3-90.1 is the proponent publication (the authority) are italicized in the text and are marked with an asterisk (*) in the glossary. Terms and definitions for which ATP 3-90.1 is the proponent publications are boldfaced in the text. For other definitions shown in the text, the term is italicized, and the number of the proponent publication follows the definition. The techniques contained in this Army techniques publication are to be used as a guide and are not to be considered prescriptive. This Army techniques publication includes discussions of doctrine that are applicable to all Armor and mechanized Infantry companies.

ATP 3-90.1 applies to the Active Army, Army National Guard/Army National Guard of the United States and United States Army Reserve unless otherwise stated.

The proponent for ATP 3-90.1 is the United States Army Maneuver Center of Excellence. The preparing agency is the Doctrine and Collective Training Division, Directorate of Training and Doctrine, United States Army Maneuver Center of Excellence. Send comments and recommendations on DA Form 2028 (*Recommended Changes to Publications and Blank Forms*) to Commander, Maneuver Center of Excellence, Doctrine and Collective Training Division, ATTN: ATZK-TDD, 1 Karker Street, Fort Moore, GA 31905-5410; by email to usarmy.moore.mcoe.mbx.doctrine@army.mil; or submit an electronic DA Form 2028.

Introduction

ATP 3-90.1 has been updated and provided as an Army techniques publication per 2015 Doctrine Strategy. In addition to doctrine changes, a significant effort has been made to eliminate redundancies with parent doctrinal manuals. The result is a reduction of chapters from 11 to 8.

Chapter 1 discusses the operational overview for the company team and describes the role of the Armor and mechanized Infantry company team. It also includes the duties and responsibilities for key personnel.

Chapter 2 describes the basics of the offense, common offensive planning considerations, actions on contact, movement to contact, and attack.

Chapters 3 describes the basics of the defense, common defensive planning considerations, defensive techniques, engagement area development, and transitions.

Chapter 4 discusses the fundamentals of stability, stability operations at company level, and transitioning to the offense or defense.

Chapter 5 discusses principles of direct fire control, the fire control process, direct fire planning, and direct fire control.

Chapter 6 describes the provision of the logistics, personnel services, and the Army health system support necessary to maintain operations until mission accomplishment.

Chapter 7 establishes techniques and procedures that the company team can apply to these specialized missions (such as, linkup, passage of lines, relief in place, battle handover, assembly area operations).

Chapter 8 focuses on those elements with which the company team is most likely to work: fires, aviation, protection, and intelligence.

Appendix A describes the function of the company team command post (CP), locations for the CP, and resourcing the CP.

Appendix B focuses on the planning and preparation, troop leading procedures, rehearsals, and precombat checks and precombat inspections.

Appendix C provides an overview of combined arms breaching operation types and tenets at the company team level.

Appendix D discusses chemical, biological, radiological, and nuclear (CBRN) defensive measures to include the hazards of each threat, CBRN passive defense, and protection.

Chapter 1

Overview and Organization

The mission of the Armor and mechanized Infantry company team is to close with the enemy by means of fire and movement to defeat or capture them or to repel their assault by fire, close combat, or counterattack. Effective application of the company team as a combined arms force capitalizes on the strengths of the team's elements while minimizing its respective weaknesses. The company team must be aggressive, physically fit, disciplined, and well-trained. This chapter provides a brief operational overview but focuses primarily on the role, organization, capabilities, duties, and responsibilities within the company team.

SECTION I – OPERATIONAL OVERVIEW

1-1. An Armor and mechanized Infantry company team as part of a combined arms battalion (CAB) within an Armored brigade combat team (ABCT) is organized to conduct combined arms operations. An *operation* is a sequence of tactical actions with a common purpose or unifying team (JP 1, Vol 1). For the company team to fight as an effect member of this team, leaders within the company must understand how the operational environment, to include friendly actions, impact the company team and understand how key concepts are unchanging, no matter the circumstances.

OPERATIONAL ENVIRONMENT

1-2. An Armor and mechanized Infantry company team conducts combined arms operations within operational environments (OEs) across the globe. Operations occur in a variety of physical environments, including urban, subterranean, desert, jungle, mountain, maritime, and arctic. Although physical factors are important, there are other information and human factors that are relevant to the company team. An *operational environment* is the aggregate of the conditions, circumstances, and influences that affect the employment of capabilities and bear on the decisions of the commander (JP 3-0). For Army forces, an OE includes portions of the land, maritime, air, space, and cyberspace domains understood through three dimensions (human, physical, and information). The land, maritime, air, and space domains are defined by their physical characteristics. Cyberspace, a man-made network of networks, transits and connects the other domains.

1-3. The OE aids in accounting for all the factors, specific circumstances, and conditions that impact the conduct of operations. This understanding enables leaders to better identify problems, anticipate potential outcomes, and understand the results of various threat or friendly actions and the effect these actions have on achieving the military end state. A description of an OE includes all the factors that the company team needs to capture and understand to inform the conduct of operations.

1-4. To assist in understanding the OE, leaders in the company team use two tools, the operational and mission variables. Leaders continually assesses and reassesses the OE to understand how changes to the operational and mission variables affect not only the company team, but other forces as well.

OPERATIONAL AND MISSION VARIABLES

1-5. The operational and mission variables are tools to assist leaders in refining their understanding of the domains and dimensions of their operational environment. Leaders in the company team analyze and describe an OE in terms of eight interrelated operational variables: political, military, economic, social, information, infrastructure, physical environment, and time (PMESII-PT). Leaders use the operational variables to aid in understanding the land domain and its interrelationships with information, relevant actors, and capabilities in the other domains.

1-6.   Leaders in the company team use the mission variables to analyze and understand a situation in relationship to the unit's mission. The mission variables are: mission, enemy, terrain and weather, troops and support available, time available, civil considerations, and informational considerations. The mission variables are represented as METT-TC (I). The purpose of the mission variables is to provide a set of informational categories focused on what leaders need to know to achieve situational understanding once assigned a mission. This ensures Army leader understand the context in which they perform their missions and if necessary, take actions to modify their chosen tactic.

1-7.   *Informational considerations* are those aspects of the human, information, and physical dimensions that affect how humans and automated systems derive meaning from, use, act upon, and are impacted by information (FM 3-0). The pervasiveness of information and its applicability in different military contexts requires leaders to continuously assess its various aspects during operations. Information considerations are shown inside parentheses because they are not an independent consideration, but an important component of each variable of METT-TC that leaders must understand when developing understanding of a situation. (See FM 5-0 for more information on mission and operational variables.)

Various Actors

1-8.   To help classify actors that the company team will encounter in their assigned area, they can use the terms: threat, enemy, neutral, or friend. A *threat* is any combination of actors, entities, or forces that have the capability and intent to harm United States forces, United States national interests, or the homeland (ADP 3-0). Threats may include individuals, groups of individuals (organized or not organized), paramilitary or military forces, nation-states, or national alliances. Threats are, by nature, hybrid. They include individuals, groups of individuals, paramilitary for military forces, criminal elements, nation-states, or national alliances.

1-9.   When threats execute their capability to do harm to the United States, they become enemies. An *enemy* is a party identified as hostile against which the use of force is authorized (ADP 3-0). A *neutral* is in combat and combat support operations, an identity applied to a track whose characteristics, behavior, origin, or nationality indicate that it is neither supporting nor opposing friendly forces (JP 3-0). A friend is a contact positively identified as an actor that supports U.S. efforts.

1-10. Land operations often prove complex because threats, enemies, neutrals, and friendlies often intermix with no easy means to distinguish one from another. Leaders within the company team work to understand how threats, enemies, neutral, and friendly forces all of which include state and nonstate actors, interact in the context of their OE. With this understanding, the company commander develops a plan to accomplish the assigned mission. While all actors have impact on the company team, the most important to consider are threat and friendly actions.

Threat Considerations

1-11. Current and future enemies seek to counter U.S. advantage of information collection capabilities, long-range precision fires, armor protection and mobility, communications, and combined-arms integration by employing a series of integrated tactical and technical countermeasures. Enemy tactical countermeasures consist of deception operations, dispersion, concealment, and the intermingling with civilians in urban terrain. Complementing these tactical techniques, the enemy employs technological countermeasures such as cyberspace attacks and Global Positioning System (GPS) jamming to evade and disrupt U.S. forces' ability to develop the situation, seize the initiative, and consolidate tactical gains into favorable political outcomes.

1-12. The use of unmanned aircraft systems (UASs) and antitank guided missiles (ATGMs) by peer threats have increased. Understanding the capabilities of these systems and how they are employed are crucial to the success of the company team. Leaders must consider these threats throughout planning and execution of all operations.

FRIENDLY CONSIDERATIONS

1-13. A company's OE is part of a battalion's OE, and therefore, influenced by actions taken by that battalion commander, adjacent units, and the company team itself. Leaders within the company team need to understand how they contribute and are members of a larger friendly action. This includes concepts such as multidomain operations; offense, defense, stability, and enabling operations; large-scale combat operations; warfighting functions; combat power; combined arms, operational framework; and hasty versus deliberate operations.

Multidomain Operations

1-14. Company teams contribute to the Army's operational concept, multidomain operations. *Multidomain operations* are the combined arms employment of joint and Army capabilities to create and exploit relative advantages that achieve objectives, defeat enemy forces, and consolidate gains on behalf of joint force commanders (FM 3-0). Multidomain operations are the Army's contribution to joint campaigns. During conflict, the Army forces close with and destroy the enemy, defeat enemy formations, seize critical terrain, and control populations and resources to deliver sustainable political outcomes.

1-15. Armored and mechanized Infantry company teams provide complementary and reinforcing effects to their higher echelon and ultimately as part of a larger joint force. Company teams may not always notice the opportunities created by higher echelons or other forces that operate in other domains; however, leaders understand how the absence of those opportunities affects their concepts of operations, decision making, and risk assessments.

1-16. All operations are multidomain operations because every operation requires integrating capabilities from all domains to succeed. For example, company teams and platoons employ capabilities from other domains such as aviation (including UAS), joint fires, satellite communications, and the GPS. Even units that do not routinely integrate joint capabilities depend on the opportunities created by higher echelons creating effects in other domains. More importantly, every echelon on the battlefield must protect itself from enemy capabilities in all domains.

1-17. During combat, Armor and mechanized Infantry company teams execute offensive, defensive, and stability operations supported by enabling operations to achieve tactical objectives that support operational and strategic objectives. While higher echelons may possess the capability and capacity to conduct simultaneous offensive, defensive, and stability operations, armor and mechanized Infantry company teams are only capable of executing a single type of operation at a given time.

Offensive, Defensive, Stability and Enabling Operations

1-18. An *offensive operation* is an operation to defeat or destroy enemy forces and gain control of terrain, resources, and population centers (ADP 3-0). These types of operations impose the commander's will on the enemy. Even when conducting defensive operations, seizing and retaining the initiative requires executing offensive operations at some point. (See chapter 2 for more information.)

1-19. A *defensive operation* is an operation to defeat an enemy attack, gain time, economize forces, and develop conditions favorable for offensive or stability operations (ADP 3-0). Successful defenses are aggressive, and commanders use all available means to disrupt enemy forces. (See chapter 3 for more information.)

1-20. A *stability operation* is an operation conducted outside the United States in coordination with other instruments of national power to establish or maintain a secure environment and provide essential governmental services, emergency infrastructure reconstruction, and humanitarian relief (ADP 3-0). Commanders are legally required to perform minimum-essential stability operations tasks when controlling a populated area of operation (AO) in an area considered under military occupation as defined in the law of armed conflict. These include establishing security and providing for immediate needs such as access to food, water, shelter, and medical treatment. (See ADP 3-07 for a more detailed discussion on stability.)

1-21. An *enabling operation* is an operation that sets the friendly conditions required for mission accomplishment (FM 3-90). Enabling operations, by themselves, do not directly accomplish the end state, but are required to conduct offensive, defensive, and stability operations successfully. They are complex enough that they require either a deliberate planning effort or a well-developed and understood standard operating procedure (SOP) to execute. (See chapter 7 for more information.)

Large-Scale Combat Operations

1-22. *Large-scale combat operations* are extensive joint combat operations in terms of scope and size of forces committed, conducted as a campaign aimed at achieving operational and strategic objectives (ADP 3-0). In large-scale combat, multiple U.S. corps and divisions along with a substantial joint and multinational team will operate together to accomplish a mission.

Warfighting Functions

1-23. A *warfighting function* is a group of tasks and systems united by a common purpose that commanders use to accomplish missions and training objectives (ADP 3-0). Synchronizing the six warfighting functions through planning and preparation increases a unit's effectiveness when executing operations. The warfighting functions are:

- Command and control.
- Movement and maneuver.
- Intelligence.
- Fires.
- Sustainment.
- Protection.

1-24. The purpose of warfighting functions is to provide an intellectual organization for common critical capabilities available to the commander. Warfighting functions are not confined to single domain, and they typically include capabilities from multiple domains.

Command and Control

1-25. The *command and control warfighting function* is the related tasks and a system that enable commanders to synchronize and converge all elements of power (ADP 3-0). The primary purpose of the command and control warfighting function is to assist commanders in integrating the other elements of combat power to achieve objectives and accomplish missions. The command and control warfighting function consists of tasks and the command and control systems. (See ADP 6-0 for more information.)

Movement and Maneuver

1-26. The *movement and maneuver warfighting function* is the related tasks and systems that move and employ forces to achieve a position of relative advantage over the enemy and other threats (ADP 3-0). Movement is necessary to position and disperse the force as a whole or in part when maneuvering. Direct fire and close combat are inherent in maneuver. Effective maneuver requires some combination of reconnaissance, surveillance, and security operations to provide early warning and protect the main body of the formation. (See ADP 3-90 and FM 3-96 for more information.)

Intelligence

1-27. The *intelligence warfighting function* is the related tasks and systems that facilitate understanding the enemy, terrain, weather, civil considerations, and other significant aspects of the operational environment (ADP 3-0). The intelligence warfighting function fuses the information collected through reconnaissance, surveillance, security operations, and intelligence operations. Commanders drive intelligence and intelligence drives operations. (See ADP 2-0 and FM 2-0 for more information.)

Fires

1-28. The *fires warfighting function* is the related tasks and systems that create and converge effects in all domains against the adversary or enemy to enable operations across the range of military operations (ADP 3-0). These tasks and systems create lethal and nonlethal effects delivered from both Army and joint forces. Many of the capabilities that contribute to fires also contribute to other warfighting functions, often simultaneously. (See ADP 3-19 and FM 3-09 for more information.)

Sustainment

1-29. The *sustainment warfighting function* is the related tasks and systems that provide support and services to ensure freedom of action, extend operational reach, and prolong endurance (ADP 3-0). Sustainment determines the limits of depth and endurance during operations. Because the situation is always changing, sustainment requires leaders capable of improvisation. Because sustainment operations are often vulnerable to enemy attacks, sustainment survivability depends on active and passive measures and maneuver forces for protection. (See ADP 4-0 for more information.)

Protection

1-30. The *protection warfighting function* is the related tasks, systems, and methods that prevent or mitigate detection, threat effects, and hazards to preserve combat power and enable freedom of action (FM 3-0). Protection requires commanders and staffs to understand threats and hazards throughout the OE, prioritize their requirements, and commit capabilities and resources according to their priorities. The commander must balance the protection efforts with the need for tempo and resourcing the main effort. (See ADP 3-37 for more information.)

Combat Power

1-31. *Combat power* is the total means of destructive and disruptive force that a military unit/formation can apply against an enemy at a given time (JP 3-0). Commanders conceptualize capabilities in terms of combat power. Combat power has five dynamics: leadership, firepower, information, mobility, and survivability. Commanders' synchronization of all warfighting functions is essential to generating each dynamic of combat power. (See FM 3-0 for more information.)

Combined Arms

1-32. The organic composition, training, and task organization of an Armored and mechanized Infantry company team sets conditions for effective combined arms. *Combined arms* is the synchronized and simultaneous application of arms to achieve an effect greater than if each arm was used separately or sequentially (ADP 3-0). Complementary capabilities compensate for the vulnerabilities of one system or organization with the capabilities of a different one. For example, in an Armored and mechanized Infantry company team, the dismounted Infantry protects the armored vehicles from enemy infantry and antitank (AT) systems, while armored vehicles provide mobile protected firepower for the Infantry.

Operational Framework

1-33. CAB commanders and staffs use an operational framework and associated vocabulary, to help conceptualize and describe the concept of operations in time, space, purpose, and resources. An *operational framework* is a cognitive tool used to assist commanders and staffs in clearly visualizing and describing the application of combat power in time, space, purpose, and resources in the concept of operations (ADP 1-01). An operational framework establishes an area of geographic and operational responsibility for the CAB commander and provides a way to visualize how the CAB commander will employ the company teams against the enemy. (See ADP 3-0 for more information.) The three models used to build an operational framework are:

- Assigned areas.
- Deep, close, and rear operations.
- Main effort, supporting effort, and reserve.

1-34. While the operational framework has three components, the Armor and mechanized Infantry company team uses two of them. The company team commander is given an assigned area for the conduct of operations and designates the main and supporting efforts to designate the shifting and prioritization of resources. CABs and below conduct close combat and are often tasked to conduct rear operations such as securing fire or other capabilities that support division deep operations.

Assigned Areas

1-35. CAB commanders assign areas to company teams based on a range of factors, including the mission, friendly forces available, enemy situation, and terrain. An assigned area that is too large for a company team to control effectively or exceed a company team's area of influence increases risk, allows sanctuaries for enemy forces, and limits joint flexibility. An assigned area that is too small constrains maneuver, limits opportunities for dispersion, and creates congested lines of communication. There are three types of assigned areas that the commander uses:

- AO.
- Zone.
- Sector.

1-36. An *area of operations* is an operational area defined by a commander for the land or maritime force commander to accomplish their missions and protect their forces (JP 3-0). In operations, the commander uses *control measures*—a means of regulating forces or warfighting functions (ADP 6-0)—to assign responsibilities, coordinate maneuver, and control combat operations. Within an area of AO, the company commander integrates and synchronizes combat power. To facilitate this integration and synchronization, the company commander designates targeting priorities, effects, and timing within the assigned AO.

1-37. An AO may be contiguous or noncontiguous. When they are contiguous, a boundary separates them. When AO are noncontiguous, platoons do not share a boundary. The company commander retains responsibility for the area not assigned to platoons.

1-38. A *zone* is an operational area assigned to a unit in the offense that only has rear and lateral boundaries (FM 3-0). The nonbounded side of a zone is open towards enemy forces. Zones are best for front line units conducting high tempo offensive operations characterized by direct fire contact with the enemy and a fluid forward line of troops.

1-39. A *sector* is an operational area assigned to a unit in the defense that has rear and lateral boundaries and interlocking fires (FM 3-0). The nonbounded side of a sector is open towards the enemy. Sectors are best for front line units conducting a defense, making it easier for a higher headquarters (HQ) to conduct deep operations and for subordinate units to have mutually supporting fires.

Area of Influence and Area of Interest

1-40. OEs are larger than the assigned area a unit is given. They influence and are influenced by factors outside unit boundaries. To account for these factors, company commanders typically consider areas of influence and areas of interest.

1-41. An *area of influence* is an area inclusive of and extending beyond an operational area wherein a commander is capable of direct influence by maneuver, fire support, and information normally under the commander's command or control (JP 3-0). Understanding the area of influence helps the commander and staff plan branches to the current operation in which the force uses capabilities outside the AO. An AO should not be substantially larger than the unit's area of influence. Ideally, the area of influence would encompass the entire AO. An AO that is too large for a unit to control can allow sanctuaries for enemy forces and may limit joint flexibility.

1-42. An *area of interest* is that area of concern to the commander, including the area of influence, areas adjacent to it, and extending into enemy territory (JP 3-0). This area also includes areas occupied by enemy forces who could jeopardize the accomplishment of the mission. An area of interest for operations to support stability operations (see chapter 4) may be much larger than that area associated with the offense and defense.

Deep, Close, and Rear Operations

1-43. Within assigned areas, the commander organizes the operations in terms of time, space, and purpose by synchronizing deep, close, and rear operations. At the company team level, differentiating between close, deep, and rear may have less utility during large-scale combat operations because of the high tempo, narrow focus, and short planning horizons. However, the commander must understand the relationship among these operations and their combined impact on mission accomplishment. (See FM 3-0 for more information.)

Main Effort, Supporting Effort, and Reserve

1-44. The company commander prioritizes efforts by designating a main effort, supporting effort, and a reserve. The *main effort* is a designated subordinate unit whose mission at a given point in time is most critical to overall mission success (ADP 3-0). Company commanders weight the main effort with the preponderance of combat power. Designating a main effort temporarily gives that unit priority for support. Company commanders shift resources and priorities to the main effort as circumstances require. Company commanders may shift the main effort several times during an operation based on which platoon's actions is most critical to overall mission success at the time.

1-45. The company commander establishes clear priorities of support during planning and shifts priorities and resources during execution as the situation requires. A *priority of support* is a priority set by the commander to ensure a subordinate unit has support in accordance with its relative importance to accomplish the mission (ADP 5-0). Priorities of movement, fires, sustainment, and protection all illustrate priorities of support that commanders use to weight the main effort if the operation is phased.

1-46. A *supporting effort* is a designated unit with a mission that supports the success of the main effort (ADP 3-0). The commander resources supporting efforts with the minimum assets necessary to accomplish the mission. A main effort in an earlier phase can be a supporting effort for a main effort in a later phase.

1-47. A *reserve* is that portion of a body of troops that is withheld from action at the beginning of an engagement to be available for a decisive movement (ADP 3-90). It is the company team's main effort once it is committed. The company commander designates a reserve and bases the size on the level of uncertainty in the current tactical situation. The company commander must consider survivability, mobility, and the most likely mission when positioning the reserve. The primary purposes for a reserve are to—

- Exploit success.
- Counter tactical reverses that threaten the integrity of the friendly force's operations.
- Retain the initiative.

1-48. The commander gives the reserve a list of planning priorities. Typically, a reserve has no more than three planning priorities because of the time it takes to prepare adequately for each priority. Company commanders can also decide not to have a reserve but takes risk doing so.

HASTY VERSUS DELIBERATE OPERATIONS

1-49. Most operations occur somewhere between hasty operations and deliberate operations. A *hasty operation* is an operation in which a commander directs immediately available forces, using fragmentary orders, to perform tasks with minimal preparation, trading planning and preparation time for speed of execution (ADP 3-90). A *deliberate operation* is an operation in which the tactical situation allows the development and coordination of detailed plans, including multiple branches and sequels (ADP 3-90).

1-50. Generally, hasty operations take advantage of fleeting tactical opportunities that provide their formations a position of advantage over the enemy. In doing so, commanders accept the risk of reduced planning, preparation, and coordination. Some situations may require commanders to take more time to plan and prepare their formations to ensure detailed integration and synchronization of the combined arms team. Any type of operation can be characterized as hasty or deliberate.

SECTION II – ROLE OF ARMOR AND MECHANIZED INFANTRY COMPANY TEAM

1-51. The role of the Armor and mechanized Infantry company team is to fight and win engagements on any battlefield in any OE. The CAB commander may task organize the company team to execute close combat tactical missions as part of ABCT operations. Company teams are optimized to conduct offensive, defensive, and stability operations. Company teams can deploy worldwide and conduct operations across the range of military operations.

TASK ORGANIZATION

1-52. The company team is task-organized with mechanized Infantry and tank platoons based upon missions. Its effectiveness increases through the synergy of combined arms including tanks, Infantry fighting vehicles (known as IFVs), Infantry, engineers, and support elements. Typically, an Armor company team comprises two tank platoons with one mechanized Infantry platoon. A mechanized Infantry company team comprises two mechanized Infantry platoons with one tank platoon. However, the final task organization may include a variety of attachments. This determination is made to ensure that main and supporting efforts have the right elements at the appropriate time. Additional considerations include assigned tasks, terrain, and the nature of enemy forces. Effective application of the company team as a combined arms force can capitalize on the strengths of the team's elements while minimizing its respective limitations.

MECHANIZED INFANTRY COMPANY

1-53. The mechanized Infantry company consists of an HQ and three IFV platoons that are organized, equipped, and trained to fight with organic assets or as a task-organized company team. The HQ element comprises two IFVs and is under the command of the commander and executive officer (XO). (See figure 1-1.)

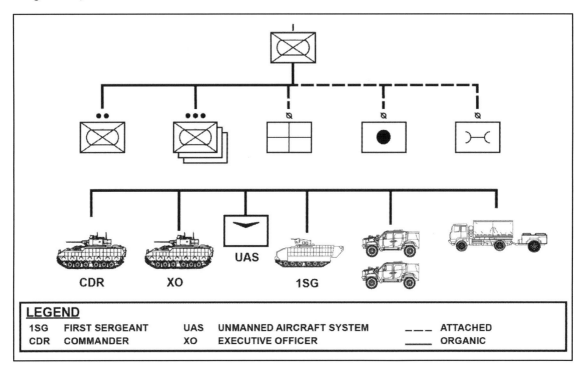

Figure 1-1. Mechanized Infantry company organization

1-54. The mechanized Infantry company is designed to fight and win engagements on any battlefield in any OE. Its design optimizes the mechanized Infantry company to conduct offensive and defensive operations. However, it is equally organized and trained to conduct operations focused on stability operations. The mechanized Infantry company can deploy worldwide and conduct missions in large-scale combat operations.

MISSION, CAPABILITIES, AND LIMITATIONS

1-55. The mission of the mechanized Infantry company is to close with the enemy by means of maneuver, to destroy or capture the enemy, repel the enemy's assault by fire, and engage in close combat and counterattack. The company maneuvers in all types of terrain, weather, and visibility conditions. It capitalizes on all forms of mobility, mechanized, motorized, foot patrols, as well as helicopters and tactical airlift. The inherent versatility of Infantry makes it well-suited for employment against asymmetrical threats.

1-56. The mechanized Infantry company is equipped with the IFV. The IFV provides the company the ability to assault rapidly through small arms and indirect fires to deliver the Infantry squads to an objective or critical point and continue the assault dismounted while being supported by the firepower of the IFV. It is best suited to less restrictive terrain and combat against an armored enemy.

1-57. The mechanized Infantry company has the following capabilities:

- Seizes and retains key terrain.
- Assaults enemy positions.
- Infiltrates enemy positions.
- Conducts combat operations under limited visibility.
- Clears enemy from restricted and urban terrain.
- Blocks mounted/dismounted avenues of approach.
- Conducts dismounted or mounted patrols.
- Conducts reconnaissance and security operations.
- Participates in air assault operations.
- Repels enemy attacks with close combat.
- Establishes strong points to deny the enemy key terrain or flank positions.
- Establishes battle positions (BPs) and engagement areas (EAs) as part of a larger defense.
- Operates in a chemical, biological, radiological, and nuclear (CBRN) environment.

1-58. The mechanized Infantry company has these limitations:

- High consumption rate of Classes III (petroleum, oils, and lubricants), V (ammunition), and IX (repair parts and components for equipment maintenance).
- Dependency on logistics packages (LOGPACs) from the forward support company (FSC) to maintain continuous operations.
- Lack of organic mortars.
- Built-up areas, dense woods, and other restricted terrain reduce the mobility of IFVs.
- Existing or reinforcing obstacles can restrict or reduce IFV mobility.
- IFVs pose a variety of challenges in gap (wet and dry) crossing operations. (The company may have trouble finding adequate fording sites or a bridge with sufficient weight classification.)

ARMOR COMPANY

1-59. The Armor company comprises an HQ and three tank platoons that are organized, equipped, and trained to fight with organic assets or as a task-organized company team. The HQ element comprises two tanks commanded by the commander and XO. (See figure 1-2.)

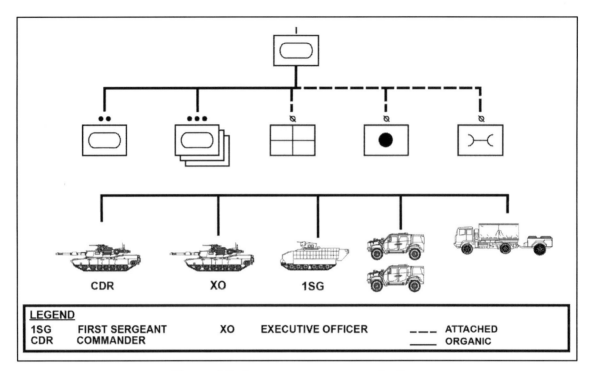

Figure 1-2. Armor company organization

1-60. The Armor company is designed to fight and win engagements through speed, firepower, and shock effect. As with the mechanized Infantry company, its design optimizes the Armor company to conduct offensive and defensive operations. However, it may be organized and trained to conduct operations focused on stability operations. The company can deploy worldwide and conducting large-scale combat operations.

MISSION, CAPABILITIES, AND LIMITATIONS

1-61. The mission of the Armor company is to close with and destroy enemy forces using fire, maneuver, and shock effect, or to repel assault by fire and counterattack. The company maneuvers within most types of terrain, weather, and visibility conditions. It capitalizes on long-range, direct-fire combat with enemy mechanized or armored units in open terrain with speed and shock effect.

1-62. The greatest benefits of the Armor company are its speed and power. Its main battle tanks provide a lethality, survivability, and mobility unmatched by any other ground combat platform. This provides the company the ability to assault rapidly through open terrain engaging enemy mechanized and armor units on the move and at long-range with devastating effects.

1-63. The Armor company has the following capabilities:
- Conducts operations requiring firepower, mobility, armor protection, and shock effect.
- Reduces mine and wire obstacles when equipped with mine rollers and mine plows.
- Employs a combination of fire and maneuver to destroy enemy tanks, fighting vehicles, antiarmor systems, and emplacements.
- Seizes key terrain.
- Assaults enemy positions.
- Provides support, in the form of armor protection and fires, to Infantry and engineer elements in restricted or urban terrain or during an assault.
- Conducts combat operations under limited visibility.
- Conducts mounted patrols.
- Blocks mounted avenues of approach.

- Conducts security, screen, and guard operations.
- Operates effectively as a counterattack or penetration force as part of a larger operation.
- Establishes BPs and EAs as part of a larger defense.
- Establishes strong points to deny the enemy key terrain or flank positions.
- The collective protection and overpressure systems in the M1 tank permit the crew to operate in a CBRN environment without individual protective equipment.

1-64. The Armor company has these limitations:

- High consumption rate of Classes III, V, and IX.
- Dependency on LOGPACs from the FSC to maintain continuous operations.
- Vulnerability to antiarmor when in built-up areas, dense woods, and other restricted terrain significantly reduce the mobility and maneuverability of tanks.
- Restricted, reduced, or ceased tank mobility when overcoming existing or reinforcing obstacles.
- Significant challenges in gap (wet and dry) crossing operations. (The company may have trouble finding adequate fording sites or a bridge with sufficient weight classification.)
- Limited capability to retain ground without Infantry support.

SECTION III – DUTIES AND RESPONSIBILITIES OF KEY PERSONNEL

1-65. The following paragraphs describe the duties and responsibilities of key members of the company team. The responsibilities can be adjusted by the commander as required.

COMMANDER

1-66. The commander is responsible for everything the company team does, or fails to do, in executing its assigned missions. The commander's responsibilities include leadership, training, tactical employment, administration, personnel management, supply, maintenance, sustainment activities, and more. These duties require the commander to understand the capabilities of the teams, Soldiers, and equipment and to understand how to employ them to the best tactical advantage. The commander must be able to visualize, describe, and direct subordinate leaders in clear, complete combat orders. At the same time, the commander must be well-versed in threat organizations, doctrine, and equipment. The commander's duties also include:

- Prepares and issues warning, operations, and fragmentary orders.
- Employs company as company team or integrates operations of decentralized platoons.
- Identifies and takes appropriate action in response to threats and opportunities.
- Understands and executes higher commander's intent.
- Confirms readiness for combat operations through confirmation and backbriefs, rehearsals, and precombat inspections (PCIs).
- Identifies and directs execution of appropriate battle drills prior to or when in contact.
- Provides operational assessments and recommendations to higher HQ.
- Integrates organic and attached assets into a combined arms team.
- Generally, positions self with the main effort and or at the decisive point.
- Establishes systems that ensure situational understanding of own unit and across the AO or area of interest.

1-67. Using this knowledge, commanders prepare their unit for combat operations. They lead by providing purpose and direction to accomplish the mission and by their presence and direction during operations. They increase effectiveness by delegating to subordinates the authority to accomplish their missions; holding subordinates responsible for their actions; and fostering a climate of mutual trust, cooperation, and teamwork. They organize their forces based on the mission of the higher HQ and a thorough understanding of METT-TC (I).

1-68. The commander uses the guiding principles of mission command to balance the art of command with the science of control. The seven principles of mission command are—

- Competence.

- Mutual trust.
- Shared understanding.
- Commander's intent.
- Mission orders.
- Disciplined initiative.
- Risk acceptance.

EXECUTIVE OFFICER

1-69. The XO is the company team's second in command, primary sustainment planner, and coordinator. (See chapter 6 for more information on the XO as a sustainment planner.) The XO, along with the vehicle crew, may serve as the team net control station for both radio and digital traffic. The XO's other duties include the following:

- Typically, responsible for routine situation reporting to higher HQ.
- Assumes command of the company team, as required.
- Responsible, in coordination with the first sergeant, for planning and execution of sustainment in support of company operations or decentralized platoon operations.
- Assists in preparation of the operation order (OPORD), specifically paragraph 4 (service support).
- Conducts tactical coordination with higher, adjacent, and supporting units.
- Assists the commander in issuing orders to the company team HQ and attachments, as required.
- On behalf of the commander, reports to higher HQ unit's situation report, slant report, and phase lines.
- Conducts additional missions as required, including serving as officer in charge for a quartering party, or as the leader of the detachment left in contact (DLIC) in a withdrawal.
- Assists the commander in preparations for follow-on missions, including rehearsal site preparation.
- Positions with supporting effort to provide control.
- Assists the commander in refining intelligence preparation of the battlefield (IPB) products during planning and portraying the enemy force during combined arms rehearsals.
- Manages the company timeline.
- Manages sustainment survivability assets (for example, dig assets/bulldozer during defensive operations).
- Facilitates the integration of attachments and enablers to the company team.
- Responsible for command post (CP) operations.
- Based on the commander's guidance, leads quartering parties.
- Coordinates for passage of lines.
- Coordinates for changes to task organization and ensures appropriate slices are detached with supported platoon.

FIRST SERGEANT

1-70. The first sergeant is the company's senior noncommissioned officer (NCO) and is its most experienced Soldier. The first sergeant is the commander's primary tactical advisor and an expert in individual and NCO skills. The first sergeant is also the company's primary sustainment operator and helps the commander and XO plan, coordinate, and supervise all logistics activities that support the company. The first sergeant operates where the commander directs or where the duties require. (See chapter 6 for more information on the first sergeant as a sustainment planner.)

1-71. The first sergeant's specific duties include the following:

- Executes and supervises routine operations. The first sergeant includes enforcing the tactical SOPs; planning and coordinating training; coordinating and reporting personnel and administrative actions; and supervising supply, maintenance, communications, and field hygiene operations.

- Supervises, inspects, or observes all matters designated by the commander. For example, the first sergeant may observe and report on a portion of the company team's AO, proof positions, or assist in proofing an EA.
- Plans, rehearses, and supervises key sustainment actions in support of the tactical mission. These activities include resupply of Classes I (rations and gratuitous issue of health, morale, and welfare items), III, and V products and materials; maintenance and recovery; medical support, casualty evacuation (CASEVAC); and processing.
- Assists and coordinates with the XO in all critical functions.
- Responsible, in coordination with the XO, for planning sustainment operations in support of company or decentralized platoon operations.
- Responsible for execution of sustainment during operations.
- Serves as quartering party noncommissioned officer in charge (NCOIC), as needed.
- Conducts training and ensures proficiency in individual and NCO skills and small-unit collective tasks. These duties support the company team's mission-essential task list.
- Establishes and maintains the foundation for company team discipline in conjunction with the commander.
- Integrates attachments.
- Assists the commander in maintaining 100-percent accountability.
- Ensures constant readiness of assigned, attached, or other designated medical evacuation (MEDEVAC), CASEVAC, or nonstandard evacuation vehicles.
- Conducts daily sustainment or logistics status reporting to higher HQ.
- Participates in logistics release point (known as LRP) meetings.
- Conducts company resupply operations.

PLATOON LEADER

1-72. The platoon leader (known as PL) is responsible to the company commander for leadership, discipline, training, and sustainment activities in the platoon. The PL is responsible for platoon equipment maintenance and for the platoon's success in combat. (See ATP 3-21.8 or ATP 3-20.15 for more information.)

1-73. The PL must be proficient in the tactical employment of the platoon in concert with the rest of the company team. PLs must have a solid understanding of troop leading procedures (TLP) and be able to apply them quickly and efficiently. They must know the capabilities and limitations of the platoon's personnel and equipment and be well-versed in enemy organizations, doctrine, and equipment.

PLATOON SERGEANT

1-74. The platoon sergeant (known as PSG) is second in the platoon's chain of command and is accountable to the PL for the leadership, discipline, training, and Soldiers' welfare in the platoon. The PSG coordinates the platoon's maintenance and logistical requirements and handles the personal needs of individual Soldiers. In the Armor platoon, the PSG fights the section in concert with the PL's section. As the PSG of the mechanized Infantry platoon, the PSG maneuvers the mounted element in support of the dismounted element in the absence of the PL. (See ATP 3-21.8 or ATP 3-20.15 for more information.)

FIRE SUPPORT OFFICER

1-75. The company fire support officer (FSO) coordinates all fires for the maneuver company. The FSO helps the commander plan, coordinate, and execute the team's fire support requirements and operations. The FSO integrates all fires to support the company commander's scheme of maneuver. During operational planning, the FSO develops and refines a fire support plan based on the commander's concept and guidance. (See ATP 3-09.30 for more information.) The duties include the following:

- Advises the commander on all fire support matters.

- Requests, adjusts, and directs all fire support.
- Trains the fire support team (FIST) in applicable fire support matters.
- Serves as the commander's primary advisor on the enemy's indirect fire capabilities.
- Assists the commander in developing the OPORD to ensure full integration of fires.
- Recommends targets and fire control measures (particularly fire support coordination measures) and determines methods of engagement and responsibility for firing the targets.
- Determines the specific tasks and instructions to plan and execute the fire support plan.
- Develops an observation plan with limited-visibility contingencies that supports the company team and CAB missions.
- Allocates forward observers and other observers to maintain surveillance of target and named areas of interest.
- Develops the fire support plan with the company commander and in coordination with the CAB's FSO. This includes locations of final protective fires (FPFs) and priority targets allocated to the team.
- Ensures that the fire support plan or fire support execution matrix (FSEM) is prepared and disseminated to key personnel.
- Assists the commander in briefing the fire support plan as part of the company team OPORD and coordinates with platoon forward observers to ensure understanding of the responsibilities.
- Refines and integrates the company team target worksheet; submits the completed worksheet to the CAB fires cell.
- Assists the commander in incorporating execution of the indirect fire plan into each company team rehearsal. This includes integrating indirect forward observers into the rehearsal plan.
- Alerts the company commander if a request for fires against a target has been denied.
- Monitors the location of friendly units and assists the commander in clearance of indirect fires.
- Requests counterbattery support in response to enemy artillery and mortar attacks.
- Provides emergency control of close air support (CAS) missions in the absence of qualified joint terminal attack controller.

COMPANY MASTER GUNNER

1-76. The master gunner is the company team's expert in vehicle gunnery. The master gunner also assists the commander in gunnery training and preparing for combat by ensuring that every crew and platoon can make effective use of firepower assets. These preparations include assisting tank and IFV crews by establishing or coordinating boresight lines, plumb and synchronize ramps (for M1A2 units), and use of live-fire screening and zero ranges.

1-77. The master gunner—

- Assists turret mechanics from the field maintenance team (FMT) in troubleshooting and repairing turret main armament and fire control systems.
- Assists in EA development and direct fire planning for both offensive and defensive operations, as the company teams direct fire weapons expert.
- Assists in sustainment coordination and execution.
- Serves as NCOIC of the CP.
- Assists the commander in designating/determining the location and emplacement of target reference points (TRPs) for both day and night visibility.
- Advises the commander on applicable battlesight ranges.
- Serves as the gunner on a command tank or IFV.

SUPPLY SERGEANT

1-78. The supply sergeant requests, receives, issues, stores, maintains, and turns in supplies and equipment for the company team. The supply sergeant coordinates all supply requirements and actions with the first sergeant and the CAB logistics staff officer. Usually, the supply sergeant's position is with the CAB field trains. The supply sergeant communicates with the company team using the task force administration/logistics radio net or digital systems. The supply sergeant's specific responsibilities are—

- Controls the company team cargo truck and water trailer and supervises the supply clerk/armorer.
- Monitors company team activities and the tactical situation.
- Anticipates and reports logistical requirements.
- Coordinates and monitors the status of the company team's logistics requests.
- Coordinates and supervises the organization of the company team LOGPAC in the field trains.

SIGNAL SUPPORT SYSTEMS SPECIALIST

1-79. The signal support systems specialist supervises the operation, maintenance, and installation of organic digital, wire, and frequency modulation (FM) communications. During tactical operations, the signal support systems specialist usually travels with the company FMT. In many situations, the signal support systems specialist is a Soldier with the rank of specialist or below that may or may not have the experience to take on additional duties such as NCOIC of the CP. The specific responsibilities include sending and receiving of routine traffic and making required communications checks. The signal support systems specialist—

- Performs limited troubleshooting of the company team's organic communications equipment and provides the link between the company team and the task force for maintenance of communications equipment.
- Supervises all activities for the company team's communications security equipment, which entails the requisition, receipting, training, maintenance, security, and employment of this equipment and related materials.
- Assists the commander in planning and employment of the team's communications systems. Using the commander's guidance, the signal support specialist may assist in preparation of paragraph 5 of the OPORD.
- Supervises or assists in company team CP operations. These include relaying information, monitoring the situation, establishing the CP security plan and radio watch schedule, and informing the commander and subordinate elements of significant events.

CHEMICAL, BIOLOGICAL, RADIOLOGICAL, AND NUCLEAR SPECIALISTS

1-80. Company-level CBRN specialists serve as the commander's primary technical experts for operations in CBRN environments. (See FM 3-11 for more information.) Primary roles and responsibilities include—

- Advising the commander on operations in CBRN environments.
- Advising the commander on CBRN readiness.
- Advising the commander on the integration of CBRN defense tasks into individual and collective training.
- Advising the commander on training-specific decontamination tasks.
- Maintaining the unit CBRN room.
- Training CBRN equipment operators.
- Maintaining appropriate and current publications associated with CBRN operations.
- Performing organizational-level maintenance and supervising operator-level maintenance for CBRN defense equipment.
- Coordinating unit supply activities associated with CBRN defense equipment.
- Maintaining the unit-level optical inserts program.
- Developing, in conjunction with the unit leaders, the unit-level administrative, deployment, and tactical SOPs, as appropriate.
- Managing unit reports related to CBRN operations, warning, and reporting system.

HABITUAL ATTACHMENTS

1-81. The key personnel listed in the following paragraphs are habitual attachments to the company team. Habitual attachments to the company team increases cohesion and understanding of SOPs in addition to building trust. The following paragraphs briefly describe the duties and responsibilities of each and provide references to where more information is located.

EMERGENCY CARE SERGEANT

1-82. The emergency care sergeant cares for sick, injured, or wounded company personnel. When the company is engaged, the emergency care sergeant remains with the first sergeant and provides medical advice, as necessary. As the tactical situation allows, the emergency care sergeant provides medical treatment and prepares patients for MEDEVAC. (See ATP 4-02.4 for more information.) The emergency care sergeant—

- Oversees and provides guidance to platoon medics, as required.
- Performs company-level triage and tactical combat casualty care for the sick and wounded.
- Oversees sick call screening for the company.
- Requests Class VIII (medical) supplies from the battalion aid station (known as BAS).
- Recommends locations for the company casualty collection point (CCP).
- Always maintains readiness of evacuation platforms to include load plans, maintenance, and communications.
- Provides training and guidance to the company's combat lifesavers (CLSs).

FIELD MAINTENANCE TEAM CHIEF

1-83. The FMT chief is the senior maintenance representative for the company team. Typically, all or part of an FMT travels with the company teams near the forward line of troops. The commander's operational plans must fully integrate FMTs into the operations. The FMT chief—

- Supervises the FMT.
- Decides whether damaged vehicles and equipment can be repaired in place or must be evacuated.
- Coordinates evacuation and repair operations.
- Manages requisition of Class IX supplies in conjunction with the task force maintenance officer.
- Manages the employment of the FMT mechanics and evacuation assets.
- Monitors the tactical situation.
- Directs maintenance team personnel during combat repair and recovery operations.
- If necessary, leads the company team combat trains in the first sergeant's absence.

Chapter 2

Offense

Offensive operations are aimed at destroying or defeating the enemy. Offensive operations impose the U.S.'s will on the enemy and achieve decisive victory. The Armor and mechanized Infantry company teams typically conduct offensive operations as part of a CAB or brigade combat team (BCT) to deprive the enemy of resources, seize decisive terrain, deceive, or divert the enemy, develop intelligence, or hold an enemy in position. Offensive operations enable the company team to create and maintain the initiative and choose the time and place that the enemy does not expect or in a manner that the enemy is unprepared for. The company teams can perform a variety of critical offensive actions because of their ability to move quickly and employ lethal firepower with a high level of protection. Company teams attack throughout the AO to defeat enemy forces. The offense ends when the company team achieves the purpose of its tasks, reaches a limit of advance (LOA), or reaches culmination. This chapter discusses basics of the offense, movement to contact (known as MTC), attack, exploitation, and pursuit.

SECTION I – BASICS OF THE OFFENSE

2-1. The basics of the offense establish a foundation for further discussion of how the Armor and mechanized Infantry company team conducts offensive operations. An offensive operation is an operation to defeat or destroy enemy forces and gain control of terrain, resources, and population centers. (See ADP 3-0 for more information.)

CHARACTERISTICS OF THE OFFENSE

2-2. Audacity, concentration, surprise, and tempo characterize the conduct of offensive operations. These characteristics are not listed in order of importance, as each receive equal consideration in the conduct of offensive operations. Company team commanders maneuver forces to advantageous positions before an operation. To shape their offensive operation, they initiate selective contact with enemy forces. The main effort capitalizes on the successful application of the characteristics of the offense. (See ADP 3-90 for more information.)

AUDACITY

2-3. Audacity is a simple plan of action, boldly executed. Commanders display audacity by developing bold, inventive plans that produce decisive results. Commanders demonstrate audacity by violently applying combat power. They understand when and where to take risks and do not hesitate as they execute their plan. Commanders dispel uncertainty through action; they compensate for lack of information by seizing the initiative and pressing the fight. Audacity inspires Soldiers to overcome adversity and danger. Audacity is not recklessness; commanders must balance tactical risks associated with audacious plans against the potential gains and take appropriate mitigation measures to minimize the chance of catastrophic failure. Audacity may manifest itself in terms of a bold scheme of maneuver, immediacy, the relentless application of combat power, or an attack in unexpected conditions (weather or visibility) or from an unexpected direction.

CONCENTRATION

2-4.   Concentration is the massing of overwhelming effects of combat power to achieve a single purpose. Advances in ground and air mobility, target acquisition, and long-rang precision fires enable attackers to concentrate effects rapidly. Command and control systems provide reliable, relevant information that assists commanders in determining when to concentrate forces to mass effects. Commanders balance the necessity for concentrating forces to mass effects with the need to disperse them to avoid creating lucrative targets. Commanders deliberately plan when to concentrate forces and when to disperse them.

2-5.   The Armor and mechanized Infantry company team achieves concentration through—

- Careful planning and coordination based on a thorough terrain and enemy analysis plus accurate reconnaissance.
- Designation of a main effort and allocation of resources to support it.
- Continuous information flow.
- Massing effects of direct and indirect fires through long-range precision fires, echelonment of fires, and maneuver.
- Conducting simultaneous operations rather than sequential operations.
- Ensuring sufficient terrain is available within which to disperse.

SURPRISE

2-6.   Commanders achieve surprise by striking the enemy at a time or place, or in a manner for which they are unprepared, by assessing the enemy commander's intent and denying that commander the ability to gain situational understanding. Estimating the enemy commander's intent and denying them the ability to gain thorough and timely situational understanding are necessary to achieve surprise. Unpredictability and boldness help gain surprise. The direction, timing, and force of the attack also help achieve surprise. Surprise delays enemy reactions, overloads and confuses command systems, induces psychological shock in enemy soldiers and leaders, and reduces the coherence of the defense. By diminishing enemy combat power, surprise enables the attackers to exposit enemy paralysis and hesitancy.

2-7.   The Armor and mechanized Infantry company team achieves surprise by—

- Gaining and maintaining information dominance by conducting thorough intelligence, surveillance and reconnaissance, and counterreconnaissance efforts.
- Striking the enemy from an unexpected direction at an unexpected time through the unique combination of rapid mounted movement and the ability of units to cross any type of terrain.
- Quickly changing the tempo of the operations.
- Being unpredictable.
- Maintaining operations security (OPSEC) through limiting electromagnetic, radio, thermal, visual, and audio signatures.
- Maintaining a dispersed and concealed unit footprint.

TEMPO

2-8.   Tempo is a combination of speed and mass that creates pressure on the enemy. Commanders build the appropriate tempo to provide the necessary momentum for attacks to achieve their objectives. Controlling or altering tempo between deliberate or rapid is necessary to retain the initiative. At the tactical level, company teams gradually increase the tempo of their operation. They focus on key pieces of information, terrain, and a small number of tasks. This focus allows them to approach their first objective at a deliberate pace ensuring that they initiate contact on favorable terms. Once they initiate their attack, they quickly penetrate barriers and defenses and destroy enemy forces in-depth before they can react. They hastily consolidate, reorganize, and continue to follow-on objectives based on combat information they gained from their attack. They can sustain a more rapid tempo to conduct follow-on operations due to their organization structure, command and control systems, and leadership. Tempo is not simply speed. Tempo is the constant application of maneuver elements against enemy combat power, balanced with tactical pauses to ensure appropriate conditions are set to enable continuous operations.

2-9. Commanders adjust the tempo to achieve synchronization. Speed is preferred to keep the enemy off balance by sustaining the attack and pursuing the enemy; however, speed is not always more valuable than is setting conditions. Establishing the conditions may require the tempo to be slowed as the pieces of the operation require synchronization. Once ready, the tempo is increased and the action resumes.

OFFENSIVE OPERATIONS

2-10. The four offensive operations are MTC, attack, exploitation, and pursuit. Company teams may conduct MTC and attack as an independent organization. However, company teams can only participate in the conduct of an exploitation or pursuit as part of a larger element of a higher HQ executing these operations. (See FM 3-90 for more information.)

MOVEMENT TO CONTACT

2-11. *Movement to contact* is a type of offensive operation designed to establish or regain contact to develop the situation (FM 3-90). It creates favorable conditions for subsequent tactical actions. The commander conducts an MTC when the enemy situation is vague or not specific enough to conduct an attack. An MTC may result in a meeting engagement.

2-12. A *meeting engagement* is a combat action that occurs when a moving force engages an enemy at an unexpected time and place (FM 3-90). The enemy force encountered may be either stationary or moving. A meeting engagement does not require both forces be surprised. The force making unexpected contact is the one conducting a meeting engagement. The force that reacts first to the unexpected contact generally gains an advantage over its enemy. MTCs include search and attack and cordon and search operations.

2-13. A meeting engagement may also occur when opponents are aware of each other, and both decide to attack to obtain a tactical advantage. Additionally, a meeting engagement may occur when one force attempts to deploy into a hasty defense while the other force attacks before its opponent can organize an effective defense. No matter how the force makes contact, seizing the initiative is the overriding imperative. Prompt execution of battle drills at platoon level and below, and standard actions on contact for larger units, can give that initiative to the friendly force.

2-14. Forces conducting an MTC seek to make contact with the smallest friendly force feasible. If friendly forces make contact with an enemy, the commander has five options:
- Attack.
- Defend.
- Bypass.
- Delay.
- Withdraw.

ATTACK

2-15. An *attack* is a type of offensive operation that defeats enemy forces, seizes terrain, or secures terrain (FM 3-90). Attacks incorporate coordinated movement support by direct and indirect fires. They may be either decisive or shaping operations. Attacks may be hasty or deliberate, depending on the time available for assessing the situation, planning, and preparing. However, based on mission variable analysis, the commander may decide to conduct an attack using only fires. An attack differs from an MTC because enemy main body dispositions are at least partially known, which allows the commander to achieve greater synchronization. This enables the massing of effects of the attacking force's combat power more effectively than in an MTC. Variations of the attack are ambush, counterattack, raid, and spoiling attack. The commander's intent and the mission variables guide which of these variations of attack to employ.

EXPLOITATION

2-16. An *exploitation* is a type of offensive operation following a successful attack to disorganize the enemy in depth (FM 3-90). Exploitations seek to disintegrate enemy forces to the point where they have no alternative but surrender or take flight. Exploitations take advantage of tactical opportunities, foreseen or unforeseen. While all units, regardless of their size, conduct exploitation, division and higher HQ normally plan exploitations as branches or sequels.

PURSUIT

2-17. A *pursuit* is a type of offensive operation to catch or cut off a disorganized hostile force attempting to escape, with the aim of destroying it (FM 3-90). A pursuit normally follows a successful exploitation. However, any offensive operation can transition into a pursuit if it is apparent that enemy resistance has broken down entirely and the enemy is fleeing the battlefield. Pursuits entail rapid movement and decentralized control.

OFFENSIVE PLANNING CONSIDERATIONS

2-18. The warfighting functions are critical tactical activities the commander can use to review, prepare, and execute planning. Synchronization and coordination between the warfighting functions are critical for success. Paragraphs 2-19 through 2-76 discuss selected warfighting functions and other additional planning considerations. The warfighting functions outline the planning considerations for offense.

COMMAND AND CONTROL

2-19. The commander's mission and intent determine the scheme of maneuver and the allocation of available resources. All planning for offensive operations addresses the mission variables of METT-TC (I). The command and control function of offensive operations for the company team include—

- Commander's intent.
- Mission objectives, including task and purpose, for each subordinate element.
- Scheme of maneuver.
- Location of key leaders.
- Suspected enemy locations, strengths, and capabilities.
- Courses of action (COAs).
- Required control measures and graphics.
- Priorities of fire.
- Bypass criteria.
- Reporting requirements.
- Primary, alternate, contingency, and emergency communications.

MOVEMENT AND MANEUVER

2-20. The commander directs the main effort against an objective, ideally maneuvering to avoid enemy strengths and create opportunities to increase the effects of friendly fires and ultimately lead to the collapse of the enemy's defenses. The commander secures surprise by making unexpected maneuvers, rapidly changing the tempo of ongoing operations, avoiding observation, and using deceptive techniques and procedures. The commander seeks to overwhelm the enemy with one or more unexpected blows before the enemy has time to react in an organized fashion. This occurs when the attacking force can engage the defending enemy force from positions that place the attacking force in a position of advantage, such as engaging the enemy from a flanking position.

Movement Formations

2-21. A *movement formation* is an ordered arrangement of forces for a specific purpose and describes the general configuration of a unit on the ground (ADP 3-90). A commander can use seven different combat formations depending on the mission variables: column, line, echelon (left or right), box, diamond, wedge, and vee. The enemy's anticipated disposition, combined with the effects of terrain, are the primary considerations in selecting a movement formation. The effects of micro-terrain and visibility determine the actual arrangement and location of the unit's personnel and vehicles within a given formation. The company's selected movement formation describes the relationship of subordinate platoons to each other on the ground.

Unless directed by the company commander, platoons will choose their own formations within the company formation (for example, company column, platoon wedge).

> *Note.* The formations shown in illustrations in this chapter are examples only; they generally are depicted without consideration of terrain and other METT-TC (I) factors that are always the most crucial element in the selection and execution of a formation. Leaders must be prepared to adapt their choice of formation to the specific situation. The box and diamond formation cannot be executed by the company team unless it is reinforced or as part of larger elements (see FM 3-90).

Column Formation

2-22. The *column formation* is a movement formation with elements arranged one behind another (FM 3-90). The column is used when speed is critical, when the company team is moving through restricted terrain on a specific route, and/or when enemy contact is not likely. Each platoon normally follows directly behind the platoon in front of it. If the situation dictates; however, vehicles can disperse laterally to enhance security. Figure 2-1 on page 2-6 illustrates this type of column movement. The column formation has the following characteristics, advantages, and limitations:

- It provides excellent control and fires to the flanks.
- It permits only limited fires to the front and rear.
- It is easy to control.
- It provides extremely limited overall security.
- It is normally used for traveling only.
- It exposes the company to the highest degree of risk.
- It requires time and distance to transition to other formations.

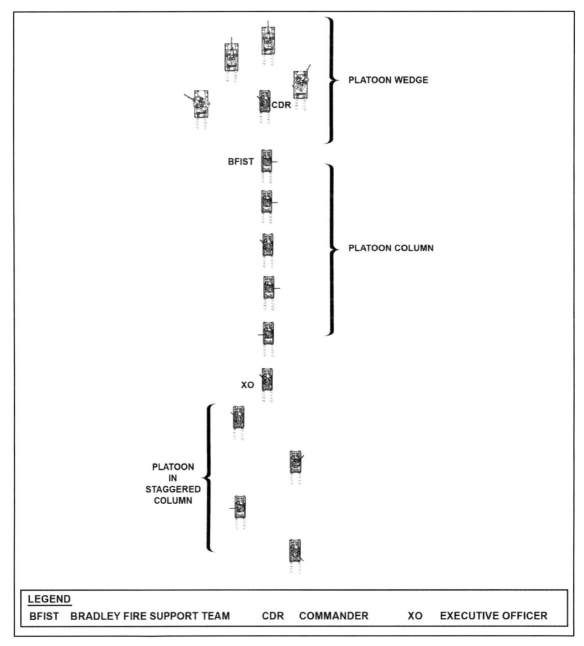

Figure 2-1. Company team column

Line Formation

2-23. A *line formation* is a movement formation in which elements move abreast of each other (FM 3-90). The line formation is primarily used when a unit or element is crossing a danger area or needs to maximize firepower to the front (see figure 2-2). In the company team line, platoons move abreast of one another and are dispersed laterally. The line formation has the following characteristics, advantages, and limitations:

- It permits maximum fires to the front or rear but minimum fires to the flanks.
- It is difficult to control.
- It is less secure than other formations because of the lack of depth.
- It may be used in the assault to maximize the firepower and or shock effect of the heavy company team. This is normally done when there is no more intervening terrain between the unit and the

enemy, when AT systems are suppressed, and or when the unit is exposed to artillery fire and must move rapidly.

- Because of associated risk, an element moving in line formation should be overwatched by a support force.

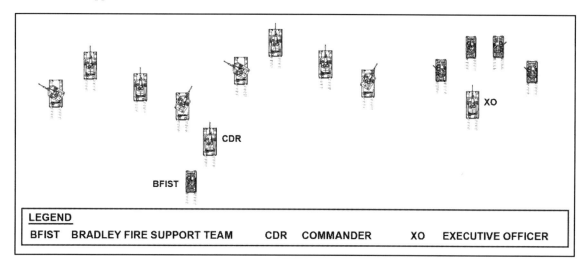

Figure 2-2. Company team in line

Echelon Formation

2-24. An *echelon formation* is a movement formation with elements arranged on an angle to the left or to the right of the direction of attack (echelon left, echelon right) (FM 3-90). The echelon formation is used when the task force wants to maintain security and/or observation of one flank and enemy contact is not likely (see figure 2-3 on page 2-8). The company team echelon formation (either echelon left or echelon right) has the lead platoon positioned farthest from the echeloned flank, with each subsequent platoon located to the rear of and outside the platoon in front of it. The echelon formation has the following characteristics, advantages, and limitations:

- It is difficult to control.
- It affords excellent security for the higher formation in the direction of the echelon.
- It facilitates deployment to the echeloned flank.
- It facilitates rapid deployment to the echeloned flank.
- Provides minimal security to the opposite flank.
- Typically used when the company team is moving on the flank of a higher echelon's formation.

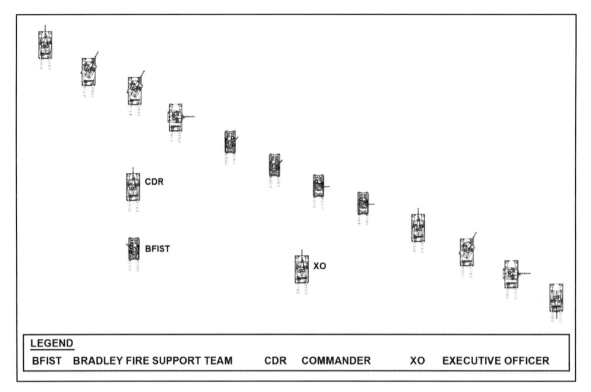

Figure 2-3. Company team in echelon

Wedge Formation

2-25. The *wedge formation* is a movement formation with one lead element and the trail elements are paired off abreast of each other on the flanks (FM 3-90). The wedge formation is often used when the enemy situation is unclear, or contact is possible. In the company team wedge, the lead platoon is in the center of the formation with the remaining platoons located to the rear of and outside the lead platoon (see figure 2-4). This formation is well-suited when the company team contains only a single tank platoon, which can occupy the least protected lead platoon position. The wedge has the following characteristics, advantages, and limitations:

- It permits excellent fires to the front and good fires to the flanks.
- It is easy to control.
- It provides good security to the flanks.
- It can be used with the traveling and traveling overwatch techniques.
- It allows rapid transition to bounding overwatch.
- Allows the company to make contact with the enemy with the smallest element, enabling maneuver by two platoons.
- Enables the company to break contact or avoid being fixed by enemy forces.

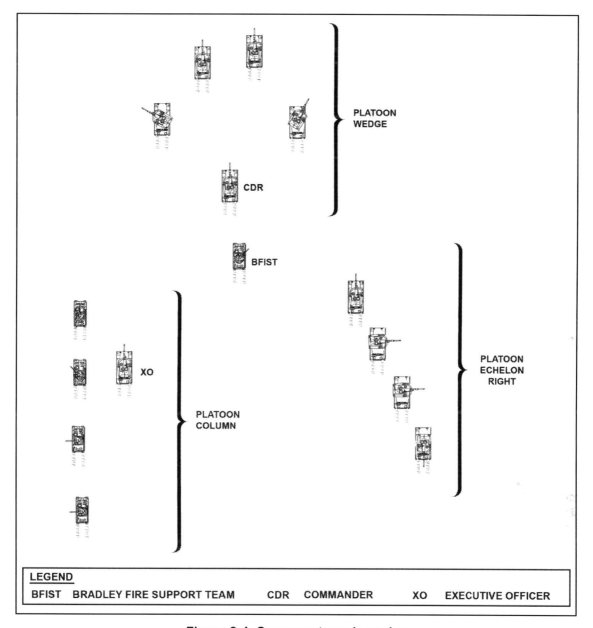

Figure 2-4. Company team in wedge

Vee Formation

2-26. A *vee formation* is a movement formation with two elements abreast and one or more elements trailing (FM 3-90). The vee formation is used when enemy contact is probable (see figure 2-5 on page 2-10). In the company team vee, the center platoon is in the rear of the formation, while the remaining platoons are to the front of and outside the center platoon. This formation is well-suited for relatively open terrain when the company has at least two tank platoons, where the Bradley platoon can occupy the more protected rear-platoon position. The vee has the following characteristics, advantages, and limitations:

- It permits more firepower to the front than the wedge and affords good fires to the flanks.
- It is more difficult to control than the wedge and makes it more difficult for vehicles to maintain proper orientation.
- It allows one platoon in the formation to maintain freedom of maneuver when contact occurs.

- It facilitates rapid deployment into any other formation.
- It can be used with the traveling and traveling overwatch techniques.
- It allows rapid transition to bounding overwatch.

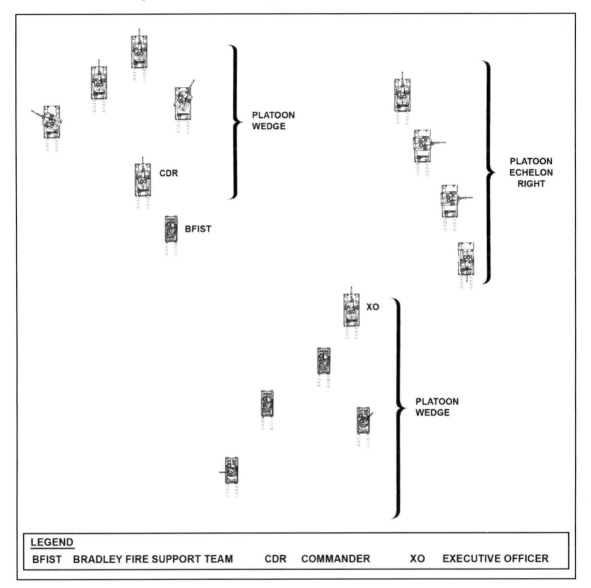

Figure 2-5. Company team in vee with platoons in different formations

Formation Selections

2-27. The company commander selects the formation that provides the proper security, direct fires, control, and speed for the operation. The commander's use of movement formations allows the unit to rapidly shift from one formation to another, giving additional flexibility when adjusting to changes in the mission variables of METT-TC (I). For this to be effective, commanders must require subordinates to rehearse so that they can change formations using standard responses to changing situations. By designating the movement formation planned for use, the commander—

- Establishes the geographic relationship between units.
- Indicates probable reactions once the enemy makes contact with the formation.
- Indicates the level of security desired.

- Establishes the preponderant orientation of subordinate weapon systems.
- Postures friendly forces for the attack.

2-28. Table 2-1 compares the five movement formations generally used by the company team.

Table 2-1. Comparison of movement formations

Formation	Security	Direct Fires	Control	Speed
Column	Good dispersion. Good all-around security.	Good to the front and rear. Excellent to the flanks.	Easy to control. Flexible formation.	Fast.
Line	Excellent to the front. Poor to the flank and rear.	Excellent to the front. Poor to the flank and rear.	Difficult to control. Inflexible formation.	Slow.
Echelon	Good to the echeloned flank and front.	Good to the echeloned flank and front.	Difficult to control.	Slow.
Wedge	Good all-around security.	Good to the front and flanks.	Less difficult to control than a line. Flexible formation.	Faster than the line.
Vee	Better to the front.	Very good to the front.	Very difficult to control.	Slow.

Movement Techniques

2-29. The company commander uses the movement formations described in table 2-1 in conjunction with three movement techniques: traveling, traveling overwatch, and bounding overwatch (see figure 2-6 on page 2-12). Movement techniques limit the unit's exposure to enemy fire and position it to react to enemy contact. The commander selects the appropriate movement technique based on the chance of enemy contact. While moving, use the terrain for protection when enemy contact is possible or expected. Use natural cover and concealment to avoid enemy fires. The following rules apply when using terrain for protection:

- Do not silhouette yourself against the skyline.
- Cross open areas quickly.
- Do not move directly forward from a concealed firing position.
- Avoid possible kill zones because it is easier to cross difficult terrain than fight the enemy on unfavorable terms.
- Avoid large, open areas, especially when they are dominated by high ground or by terrain that can cover and conceal the enemy.
- Take active countermeasures, such as using smoke and direct and indirect fire, to suppress or obscure suspected enemy positions.

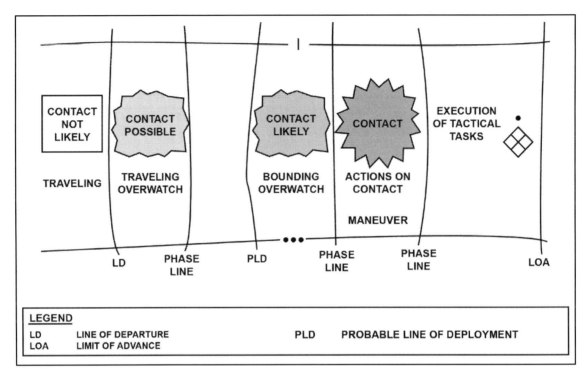

Figure 2-6. Transition from movement techniques to maneuver

2-30. The company team commander selects from the three movement techniques based on several factors:
- The likelihood of enemy contact.
- The type of contact expected.
- Availability of an overwatch element.
- The level of security required during movement.
- Timeline of higher HQ.

Traveling

2-31. *Traveling* is a movement technique used when speed is necessary and contact with enemy forces is not likely (FM 3-90). Traveling is characterized by continuous movement by all company team elements (see figure 2-7). It is best suited to situations in which enemy contact is unlikely and speed is important. Commanders and leaders locate where they can best control the situation.

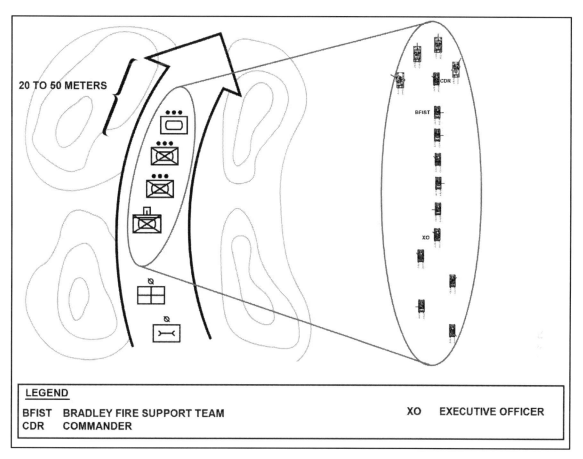

Figure 2-7. Traveling

Traveling Overwatch

2-32. *Traveling overwatch* is a movement technique used when contact with enemy forces is possible (FM 3-90). Traveling overwatch is an extended form of traveling that provides additional security when speed is desirable, but contact is possible. The lead element moves continuously. The trail element moves at various speeds and may halt periodically to overwatch movement of the lead element and scans possible enemy locations (see figure 2-8 on page 2-14). The company team's ability to engage accurately on the move with its main gun systems makes traveling overwatch the preferred movement technique across open terrain while mounted. Speed and dispersion are critical while moving across open areas to increase the difficulty for the enemy to acquire and engage friendly forces.

2-33. Dispersion between the two elements must be based on the trail element's ability to see well-beyond the lead element and to provide immediate suppressive fires in case the lead element is engaged. The intent is to maintain depth, provide flexibility, and maintain the ability to maneuver if any form of contact occurs. In the event of contact, a unit normally executes a contact or action drill and transitions to bounding overwatch.

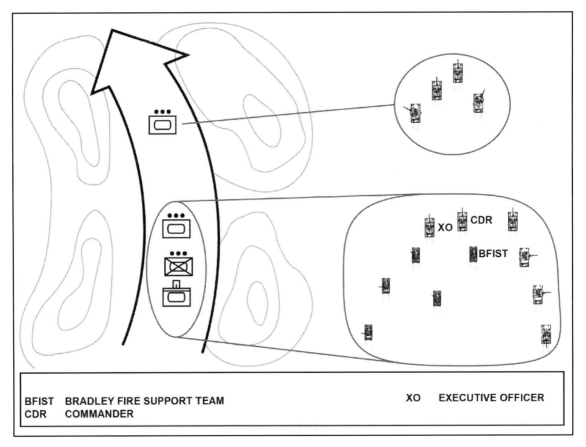

Figure 2-8. Traveling overwatch

Bounding Overwatch

2-34. *Bounding overwatch* is a movement technique used when contact with enemy forces is expected (FM 3-90). Bounding overwatch is used when physical contact is expected. It is the most secure, but slowest, movement technique. The purpose of bounding overwatch is to deploy before contact, giving the unit the ability to protect a bounding element by immediately suppressing an enemy force (see figure 2-9). The company team should not conduct bounding overwatch across open terrain with an absence of cover while mounted. Bounds should only ever be between covered positions which grant the stationary element a position of relative advantage. In the absence of covered positions, the company team should revert to traveling overwatch.

2-35. In all types of bounding, the overwatch element is assigned sectors to scan while the bounding element uses terrain to achieve cover and concealment. When practicable, the mechanized Infantry elements utilize dismounts to clear intervisibility lines and defiles prior to vehicles occupying their overwatch position. The commander may designate that the overwatch element conducts reconnaissance by fire to provide the bounding element increased security. The bounding element should avoid masking the fires of the overwatch element; it must never move beyond the range at which the overwatch element can effectively suppress likely or suspected enemy positions. The company team can employ either of two bounding methods, alternate and successive bounds; these are discussed in paragraphs 2-36 through 2-38.

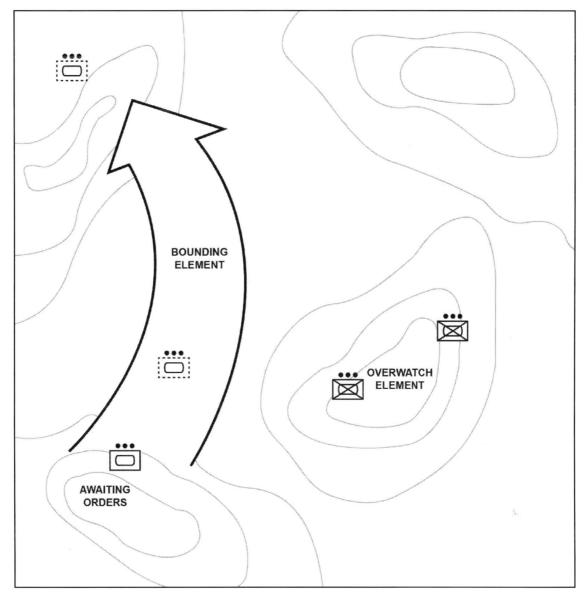

Figure 2-9. Bounding overwatch

Alternate Bounds

2-36. Covered by the rear element, the lead element moves forward, halts, and assumes overwatch positions. The rear element advances past the lead element and takes up overwatch positions. This sequence continues as necessary, with only one element moving at a time. This method is usually more rapid than successive bounds.

Successive Bounds

2-37. In the successive bounding method, the lead element, covered by the rear element, advances, and takes up overwatch positions. The rear element advances to an overwatch position roughly abreast of the lead element and halts. The lead element moves to the next position, and so on. Only one element moves at a time, and the rear element avoids advancing beyond the lead element. This method is easier to control and more secure than the alternate bounding method but is slower.

2-38. An example of successive bounds is using the dismounted Infantry from the IFVs to clear restrictive terrain as the tank and IFVs overwatch. The Infantry, as the lead element, clears the terrain (streets, buildings, or intervisibility lines) while the tanks and IFVs cover the movement. Once the lead element advances to an overwatch position, the trail element moves to a position online with the lead element and the lead element moves to the next position.

Clearing Defiles

2-39. Dismounting is an integral part of transition from movement to maneuver. While dismounting may slow down the tempo of the unit, it is necessary to survive first contact. Despite additional time requirements, when properly planned, integrated, and synchronized, the company team can use dismounts to maintain a steady tempo while presenting multiple dilemmas to the enemy along the entire friendly axis of advance. Critical to establishing tempo, commanders ensure the dismounted and mounted forces synchronize their movements to be mutually supported.

2-40. One technique for accomplishing the synchronization is for the company team to clear defiles. Clearing a defile can be understood as a deliberate and planning variation of the bounding overwatch (see paragraph 2-34) movement technique. When conducted correctly, the dismounted Infantry move ahead or to the flanks of the mounted elements and clear defile locations.

2-41. CABs and company teams must plan for and allow time and space for dismounted Infantry to approach and clear terrain, use obscuration fires or terrain to deny the enemy observation or other measures to dismount the Infantry closer to defiles. The commander may use UASs to conduct initial reconnaissance of known defiles. While the Infantry approaches the defile, CABs and companies must plan for their mounted elements to overwatch their movement and provide support. Company teams can provide direct-fire support from IFVs and main battle tanks. The CAB mortar platoon can also provide indirect-fire support.

2-42. Once a defile has been cleared or seized, the Infantry can secure that terrain and bound the mounted elements forward. Once the mounted elements are set, the Infantry can once again push forward to clear the next defile. As with the decision to dismount the Infantry, clearing a defile is slow and deliberate, sacrificing speed. However, it can maintain tempo with the goal of conserving enough combat power to get to the objective and achieve the mission.

Dismount Points for Infantry Squads

2-43. The PL, based off the company commander guidance, designates where the Infantry squads will dismount to begin execution of the fight. These dismount points can be short of the objective, on the objective, or beyond the objective.

Short of the Objective

2-44. The advantages of dismounting the squads before reaching the objective include protection of the Infantrymen during the dismount process, control at the dismount point, and the ability to continue suppression of the enemy by supporting indirect fires during the dismount.

2-45. The advantage of dismounting first is to use it to clear AT/ATGM positions to set conditions for the armored force to maneuver onto the objective. They can also conduct dismount breaches that enable dismounts to assault the objective under overwatch of the mounted elements. Disadvantages include exposure of the squads to indirect and small-arms fires as they maneuver to the objective area and the possibility that suitable dismount points will be targeted for enemy indirect fires.

On the Objective

2-46. The primary advantages of this option are greater speed and enhanced protection of the squads as the company team maneuvers to the objective area. There are several disadvantages in dismounting on the objective: difficulty in orienting the dismounted elements on specific locations and objectives while they are riding in the IFVs; problems that may arise in establishing control at dismount points; and vulnerability of IFVs and dismounts to short-range antiarmor weapons.

Beyond the Objective

2-47. This dismount option has several potential advantages—effective control at the dismount point; greater ease in orienting the dismounted elements to the terrain and the objectives of the assault; confusion or disorientation among enemy elements when they are forced to fight in an unexpected direction. At the same time, there are significant disadvantages, including vulnerability of the company team to attack from enemy positions in-depth or from enemy reserve forces; vulnerability of the IFVs to short-range antiarmor systems and increased risk of fratricide.

Forms of Maneuver

2-48. The commander conducts maneuver to avoid enemy strengths and to create opportunities to increase the effects of friendly fires. The commander achieves surprise by making unexpected maneuvers, rapidly changing the tempo of ongoing missions, avoiding observation, and using deceptive techniques and procedures.

2-49. Commanders select the form of maneuver based on analysis of METT-TC (I). Commanders synchronize the contributions of all warfighting functions to the selected form of maneuver. An operation may contain several forms of offensive maneuver. (See FM 3-90 for more information.) The forms of maneuver are as follows:

- Frontal attack.
- Penetration.
- Envelopment.
- Turning movement.
- Infiltration.

Frontal Attack

2-50. *Frontal attack* is a form of maneuver in which the attacking force seeks to destroy a weaker enemy force or fix a larger enemy force in place over a broad front (FM 3-90). The frontal attack is usually the least desirable form of maneuver because it exposes most of the offensive force to the concentrated fires of the defenders (see figure 2-10 on page 2-18). The company normally conducts a frontal attack as part of a lager operation against a stationary or moving enemy force.

2-51. Unless frontal attacks are executed with overwhelming and well-synchronized speed and strength against a weaker enemy, they are seldom decisive. The company assaults the enemy across a wide front and along the most direct approaches. It uses a frontal attack to overrun and destroy a weakened enemy force or to fix an enemy force. Frontal attacks are used when the commander possesses overwhelming combat power, and the enemy is at a clear disadvantage or when fixing the enemy over a wide front is the desired effect and a decisive defeat in that area is not expected.

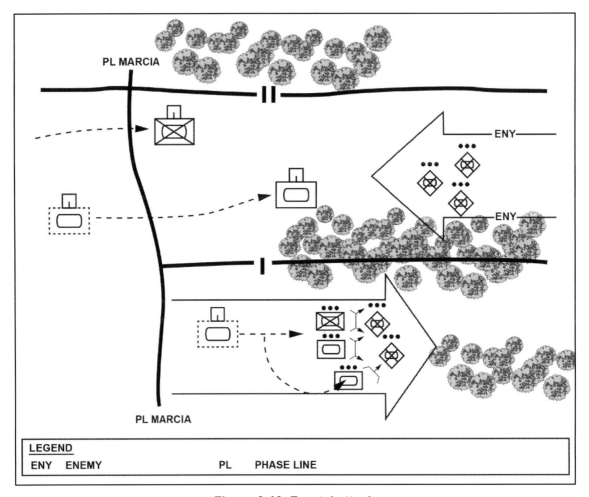

Figure 2-10. Frontal attack

Penetration

2-52. A *penetration* is a form of maneuver in which a force attacks on a narrow front (FM 3-90). The penetration extends from the enemy's main defensive positions through the security area into the enemy support area. Destroying the continuity of a defense enables the enemy force's subsequent isolation and defeat in detail by exploiting friendly forces. Commanders employ a penetration when enemy defenses are overextended or weak, or time pressures do not permit envelopment.

2-53. Successful penetration depends on the attacking force's ability to suppress enemy weapons systems, to concentrate forces to overwhelm the enemy defender at the point of attack, and to pass sufficient forces through the gap to defeat the enemy quickly. Critical tasks include allocating combat power to hold (or expand) the flanks and shoulders of the penetration and to prevent enemy forces from closing the penetration. If the attacker does not make the penetration sharply and secure objectives promptly, the penetration is likely to resemble a frontal attack. This may result in high casualties and permit the enemy to fall back intact, thus avoiding destruction. (See FM 3-90 for more information.)

Envelopment

2-54. *Envelopment* is a form of maneuver in which an attacking force avoids an enemy's principal defense by attacking along an assailable flank (FM 3-90). At the tactical level, envelopments focus on seizing terrain, destroying specific enemy forces, and interdicting enemy withdrawal routes, but are also prepared to engage enemy forces repositioning within the objective, or enemy reserves or counterattacking forces.

2-55. The company team focuses on attacking an assailable flank (see figure 2-11). It avoids the enemy's strength—their front—where the effects of fires and obstacles are the greatest. The commander conducts an envelopment instead of a penetration or a frontal attack to preserve the attacking force by potentially having fewer casualties while having the most opportunity to destroy the enemy.

2-56. The three variations of the envelopment are—

- *Single envelopment* is a variation of envelopment where a force attacks along one flank of an enemy force (FM 3-90).
- *Double envelopment* is a variation of envelopment where forces simultaneously attack along both flanks of an enemy force (FM 3-90).
- *Vertical envelopment* is a variation of envelopment where air-dropped or airlanded troops attack an enemy forces rear, flank, or both (FM 3-90).

2-57. The single and double envelopment force the enemy to fight in two or more directions simultaneously to meet the converging efforts of an attack. The Armor and mechanized Infantry company team, due to the amount of combat power that it has, can only conduct a single envelopment, but it can participate in a double envelopment as part of a larger organization. A double envelopment generally requires significant forces and can be difficult to control. (See FM 3-90 for more information.)

2-58. Commanders may have to create an assailable flank. To do so, they identify gaps or seams in the enemy's defensive positions and focus their attack at that location. They should use supporting direct and indirect fires, and battlefield obscurants, to isolate a portion of the defending enemy, and fix (or suppress) enemy forces in position to enable friendly forces to maneuver to a planned point of penetration from which to continue the envelopment.

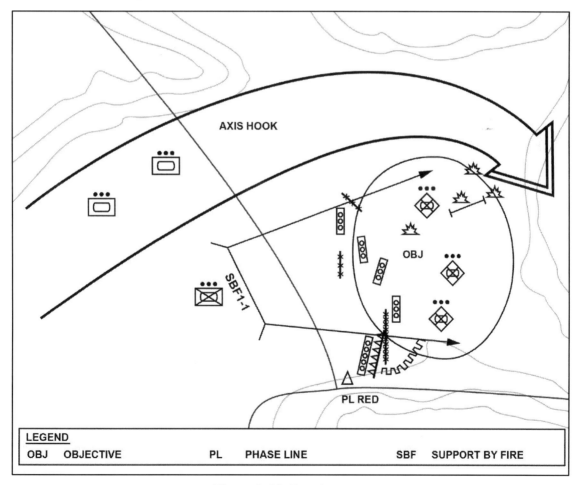

Figure 2-11. Envelopment

Turning Movement

2-59. A *turning movement* is a form of maneuver in which the attacking force seeks to avoid the enemy's principal defensive positions by attacking to the rear of their current positions forcing them to move or divert forces to meet the threat (FM 3-90). The objective of the turning movement is to make contact with the enemy, but at a location advantageous to the commander conducting the turning movement and out of the enemy's established EAs.

2-60. A turning movement differs from envelopment because the force conducting a turning movement seeks to make the enemy forces displace from their current locations, whereas an enveloping force seeks to engage the enemy forces in their current locations from an unexpected direction.

> *Note.* The company team conducts a turning movement as part of a larger force, most likely as a shaping operation or fixing force.

Infiltration

2-61. An *infiltration* is a form of maneuver in which an attacking force conducts undetected movement through or into an area occupied by enemy forces (FM 3-90). Infiltration occurs by land, water, air, or a combination of means. Moving and assembling forces covertly through enemy positions is time consuming. To infiltrate successfully, the force avoids detection and engagement. Since this requirement limits the size and strength of the infiltrating force, the company team commander is typically limited to use the dismounted Infantry within the IFV platoons to conduct this form of maneuver. Infiltrated forces alone can rarely defeat an enemy infiltration and is normally used in conjunction with other forms of maneuver.

2-62. The commander uses an infiltration to—
- Attack lightly defended positions or stronger positions from the flank or rear.
- Secure key terrain before mounted movement.
- Disrupt or harass enemy defensive preparations/operations.
- Relocate the company by moving to BPs around an EA.
- Reposition to attack vital facilities or enemy forces from the flank or rear.
- Conduct covert breaches.
- Destroy point targets (for example, AT systems) prior to movement of the main body.

INTELLIGENCE

2-63. The commander uses threat templates, the situation template, the most likely COA, the most dangerous COA, civil consideration products, terrain products, and other intelligence products to identify any aspect in the OE that affects the friendly force and enemy force. This information may come from the intelligence sections from within the CAB and brigade. (See ATP 2-01.3 for more information.) The commander uses the intelligence estimate to reflect analysis two echelons down.

2-64. The unit continuously conducts information collection during the mission because it is unlikely that the commander has complete knowledge of the enemy's intentions and actual actions. The commander receives constant updates from higher and adjacent units with the sharing of the common operational picture. The company team's organic small UAS can be used at specified points within the attack when feasible, to confirm or deny enemy BP locations or observing avenues of approach beyond the objective to identify incoming enemy reserves and reinforcements.

FIRES

2-65. Leaders' conduct fires planning concurrently with maneuver planning at all levels. BCTs and CABs typically use top-down fire support planning, with bottom-up refinement of the plans. As part of the top-down fire planning system, the CAB includes a fires annex with its OPORD. The company commander refines the fire plan from higher HQ to meet the mission requirements and ensures these refinements are incorporated into the higher HQ's plan.

2-66. A clearly defined concept of operations enables the company commander to articulate precisely how to use indirect fires to affect the enemy during the different phases of the operation. This allows the company team FSO to develop a fire support plan that supports the company's mission. The commander needs to understand the CAB's scheme of maneuver, but also understand the concept of fires and understand what, if any, resources that have been allocated. The company can possibly use CAB 120-millimeter (mm) mortars, fires from the field artillery (FA) battalion using 155-mm howitzers, and use of CAS. To develop an effective fires plan, the company FSO understands the commander's intent to conduct the fire planning process and address all the essential elements of a fire support plan.

2-67. Additional fire support considerations include the following:

- Use massed fires, especially time on target fires.
- Position fire support assets to support the reconnaissance effort.
- Plan suppressive and obscuration fires at the point of penetration.
- Plan fires on enemy positions supporting and overwatching the objective.
- Plan suppressive and obscuration fires to support breaching operations.
- Plan fires in support of the approach to the objective. These fires engage enemy security forces, destroy bypassed enemy forces, and screen friendly movement.
- Plan preparation fires on the objective to suppress, neutralize, or destroy critical enemy forces that can most affect the CAB's closure on the objective.
- Plan fires beyond the objective to support an attack or defense, or to isolate the objective to prevent the egress or ingress of threat forces.
- Use indirect fires and CAS to delay or neutralize repositioning enemy forces and reserves.
- Plan locations of critical friendly zones to protect critical actions such as support by fire (known as SBF) positions, breaching efforts, and mortar assets.
- Use risk estimate distances (known as REDs) to determine triggers to initiate, shift, and cease loading of rounds.
- Use echelon fires to maintain continuous suppression of enemy forces throughout the movement to and actions on the objective.
- Proper employment and positioning of attached FSOs where they can influence the fight.

SUSTAINMENT

2-68. The objective of sustainment in offensive operations is to ensure the tactical commander maintains the momentum. The commander wants to take advantage of windows of opportunity and launch offensive operations with minimum advance warning. Therefore, sustainment planners and operators anticipate these events and maintain the flexibility to support the offensive plan.

2-69. A key to successful offensive operations is the ability to anticipate the requirement to push support forward, specifically regarding ammunition, fuel, and water. The first sergeant requests supplies or supply packages based on the logistics status reports to consolidate sustainment requirements for the company. Future consumption planning factors, based on a change in mission, should be factored in for delivery up to 72 hours in advance when the company coordinates its logistical resupply for a specific time and location. (See chapter 6 for more information.)

- Logistics. Sustainment maintains momentum of the attack by delivering supplies as far forward as possible. The commander can use throughput distribution and preplanned and preconfigured packages of essential items to help maintain offensive momentum and tempo.
- Health service support. The burden on medical resources increases due to the intensity of offensive operations and the increased distances over which support is required as the force advances. The commander relocates medical resources as the tactical situation changes.

2-70. The company commander, with the first sergeant's and XO's assistance, plans for increased sustainment demands during the offense. Sustainment planners, at the CAB and ABCT level, synchronize and coordinate to determine the scope of the operation. Sustainment planners develop and continually refine the sustainment concept of support. Coordination between the CAB staff planners and subordinate company

XOs must be continuous to maintain momentum and freedom of action. The company commander anticipates where the greatest need may occur to develop a sustainment plan that meets the CAB commander's intent.

2-71. The primary sustainment units for the company team are elements from the FSC assigned in direct support to the CAB. The objective of sustainment during the offense is to assist the tactical commander to maintain momentum using the correct amount and type of sustainment support. The commander wants to be prepared for opportunities and be able to launch the offense with minimum advance warning time; therefore, operators, logistics, and personnel planners anticipate these events and maintain the flexibility to support the offensive plan accordingly. Sustainment commanders anticipate, rather than react, to support requirements. Habitual support relationships facilitate the ability to anticipate.

PROTECTION

2-72. The rapid tempo of offensive operations poses challenges in the protection of friendly assets. The forward movement of subordinate units is critical if the commander is to maintain the initiative necessary for successful offensive operations. Commanders maintain high operating tempo to deny the enemy a chance to plan, prepare, and execute an effective response to friendly offensive operations ultimately ensuring the survivability of the force. Using multiple routes, dispersion, highly-mobile forces, piecemeal destruction of isolated enemy forces, scheduled rotation, and relief of forces before they culminate, and wise use of terrain are techniques for maintaining a high tempo of offensive operations. The exact techniques employed in a specific situation must reflect the mission variables.

2-73. In the offense, survivability operations enhance the ability to avoid or withstand hostile actions by altering the physical environment. Camouflage and concealment typically play a greater role in survivability during offensive operations. Protective positions for indirect fire and logistics positions, however, still may be required in the offense. The use of terrain provides a measure of protection during halts in the advance, but the company team still should develop as many protective positions as necessary for key weapons systems, CPs, and critical supplies based on the threat level and unit vulnerabilities. During the early planning stages, geospatial engineer teams can provide information on soil conditions, vegetative concealment, and terrain masking along routes to facilitate the company's survivability.

2-74. Depending on the threat, primary protection concerns of the commander may be enemy artillery, air, and CBRN threats. If these threats exist, the commander prepares the unit and adjusts the scheme of maneuver accordingly. In the face of an enemy air threat, the company usually has only passive and active (with its organic weapons) air defenses. However, air defense assets may be located near the company and may provide coverage. If air defense elements are assigned, the commander, with the advisement of the air defense leader, determines likely enemy air avenues of approach and plans positions accordingly.

2-75. The commander integrates CBRN defense considerations into mission planning depending on the CBRN threat. This includes the CBRN core functions of assess, protect, and mitigate and the integrating activity of hazard awareness and understanding. Assessing the threats and hazards through integration with intelligence, targeting, and reconnaissance aid in implementation of the CBRN threat passive defense principles, such as contamination avoidance. CBRN protective measures reduce the risk to the force form CBRN hazards however, they may slow the tempo, degrade combat power, and increase logistics requirements. Personnel wearing individual protective equipment find it difficult to operate for an extended period. Mitigating hazards with a scaled response to CBRN incidents reduces the spread and impact on forces.

2-76. The commander protects subordinate forces to prevent the enemy from interfering in ongoing operations. That protection meets the commander's legal and moral obligations to the organization's Soldiers. To help protect the force, the commander ensures that all 16 protection tasks (see chapter 8) are addressed during the unit's planning, preparation, and execution while constantly assessing the effectiveness of those protection tasks. (See ADP 3-37 for more information.)

TACTICAL FRAMEWORK OF THE OFFENSE

2-77. The tactical framework helps visualize operations and to organize the force. The framework used to illustrate the execution of offensive operations tends to overlap each other during the conduct of offense. The execution of offensive operations for MTC and attack use the following framework to describe in detail actions that elements of the company take to:

- Find the enemy. Gain and maintain contact.
- Fix the enemy. Remove enemy options making them easier to destroy.
- Finish the enemy. Mass available combat power to accomplish the mission.
- Follow through. Defeat in detail, consolidate, reorganize, and transition.

FORMS OF CONTACT

2-78. In both offensive and defensive operations, contact occurs when a member of the company team encounters a situation that requires a lethal or nonlethal response to the enemy. These situations may entail one or more of the following nine forms of contact:

- Direct.
- Indirect.
- Nonhostile.
- Obstacles.
- CBRN.
- Aerial.
- Visual.
- Electromagnetic.
- Influence.

ACTIONS ON CONTACT

2-79. *Actions on contact* is a process to help leaders understand what is happening and to take action (FM 3-90). Commanders analyze the enemy throughout TLP to identify likely contact situations that might occur during an operation. Through planning and rehearsals conducted during TLP, they develop and refine COAs to deal with the probable enemy actions. The commander identifies and rehearses the appropriate battle drills to respond to contact.

FOUR STEPS OF ACTIONS ON CONTACT

2-80. The company team should execute actions on contact using a logical, well-organized process of decision making and action entailing these four steps:

- React.
- Develop the situation.
- Choose an action.
- Execute and report.

2-81. This four-step process is not intended to generate a rigid, lockstep response to the enemy. Rather, the goal is to provide an orderly framework that enables the company team and its platoons to survive the initial contact and apply sound decision making and timely actions to complete the operation. Ideally, the team acquires the enemy (visual contact) before being seen by the enemy; it then can initiate physical contact on its own terms by executing the designated action.

2-82. Once the lead elements react to the enemy, they conduct actions on contact. The unit treats obstacles like enemy contact, since it assumes that the obstacles are covered by fire. The unit's security force often gains a tactical advantage over an enemy force by using tempo and initiative to conduct these actions on contact, allowing it to gain and maintain contact without becoming decisively engaged. How quickly the unit develops the situation is directly related to its security. This tempo is directly related to the unit's use of well-rehearsed SOPs and drills.

2-83. Commanders must understand that properly executed actions on contact require time at both the company team and platoon levels. To develop the situation fully, a platoon or team may have to execute extensive lateral movement; dismount and remount Infantry squads; conduct reconnaissance by fire; or call for and adjust indirect fires. Each of these actions require time to execute. The commander must balance the time required for subordinate elements to conduct actions on contact with the need of the company team to maintain momentum. In terms of slowing the tempo of an operation, however, the loss of a platoon or team is usually more costly than the additional time required to allow the subordinate element to develop the situation properly.

React

2-84. If the commander expects contact (based on reports on the CAB command net, enemy symbols on digital systems, or through reconnaissance), the commander will already have deployed the company team by transitioning to the bounding overwatch movement technique. Contact, either visual or physical, usually is made by an overwatching or bounding platoon, which initiates the team's actions on contact. In some cases, the company team makes unexpected contact with the enemy while using traveling or traveling overwatch. The element in contact or, if necessary, the entire company team may have to deploy using battle drills to survive the initial contact. When making unexpected contact, the platoon in contact sends a contact report immediately to the commander. The company teams and platoons develop SOPs that harness the capabilities of the analog and digital systems while destroying the enemy force and protecting the company.

Develop the Situation

2-85. While the company team deploys, the commander evaluates the situation and continues to develop it. The commander quickly gathers as much information as possible, either visually or, more often, through reports of the platoon(s) in contact. The commander analyzes the information to determine critical operational considerations, including the following:

- Size of the enemy element.
- Location, composition, activity, and orientation of the enemy force.
- Impact of obstacles and terrain.
- Enemy capabilities (especially antiarmor capability).
- Probable enemy intentions.
- Location of enemy flanks and how to gain positional advantage over the enemy.
- The friendly situation (location, strength, and capabilities).
- Possible friendly COAs to achieve the specified end state.

2-86. Once the commander determines the size of the enemy force the company team has encountered, the commander sends a report to the CAB. However, after evaluating the situation, the commander may discover that there is not enough information to identify the necessary operational considerations. To make this determination, the commander further develops the situation according to the CAB commander's intent, using a combination of these techniques:

- Surveillance (using binoculars and other optical aids).
- Mounted or dismounted maneuver (includes lateral maneuver to gain additional information by viewing the enemy from another perspective).
- Indirect fire.
- Reconnaissance by fire.

2-87. The commander's development of the situation must lead to an understanding of whether the enemy force is able to be bypassed, or whether it is an inferior force (able to be defeated with organic forces) or a superior force (requiring additional assets to defeat). An accurate understanding of this is essential to inform the commander's next step.

Choose an Action

2-88. After the unit makes contact, the company commander determines if there is enough information to decide which action that both meets the requirements of the CAB commander's intent and is within the company team's capabilities.

2-89. The company commander has several options in selecting a COA. The following are procedures for selecting a COA:

- First, the action needs to be feasible. The action can accomplish the mission within the established time, space, and resource limitations. It must balance cost and risk with the advantage gained. The action must be suitable meaning that it can accomplish the mission within the commander's intent and planning guidance and distinguishable in that it differs significantly from the others (such as scheme of maneuver, lines of effort, phasing, use of the reserve, and task organization).

- If the development of the situation reveals no need for change, the company commander directs the company to execute the original plan.

- If the analysis shows that the original plan is still valid but that some refinement is necessary, the company commander informs the CAB commander (prior to execution, if possible) and issues a fragmentary order to refine the plan.

- If the analysis shows that the original plan needs to be changed but the selected action still complies with the CAB commander's intent, the company commander informs the CAB commander (prior to execution, if possible) and issues a fragmentary order to re-task subordinate elements.

- If the analysis shows that the original plan deviates from the CAB commander's intent and needs to be changed, the company commander must report the situation and based on known information in response to an unforeseen enemy or battlefield situation, recommends an alternative COA to the CAB commander.

- If the battlefield picture is still vague, the company commander must direct the company or a platoon to continue to develop the situation. This allows the commander to gather information needed to clarify a vague battlefield picture. The commander uses one of the first four options to report the situation, choose an action, and direct further action.

Note. The commander will not initiate an action that fundamentally changes the CAB or brigade's scheme of maneuver or commits high-value or limited resources (for example, breaching assets) without getting the higher commander's approval.

Execute and Report

2-90. In executing an action, the company continues to maneuver throughout execution (either as part of a tactical task or as an advance while in contact) to reach the point on the battlefield where it executes its tactical task. (See FM 3-90 for more information.) The company can employ several tactical tasks as actions, any of which might be preceded and followed by additional maneuver. As execution continues, more information becomes available to the company commander. Based on the emerging details of the enemy situation, the commander might have to alter the action during execution.

Limited-Visibility Operations

2-91. The capability to fight at night and under limited-visibility conditions is an important aspect of conducting maneuver. The commander conducts field training exercises under limited-visibility conditions to ensure that the unit has this capability. A commander plans offensive actions at night or under limited-visibility conditions. Offensive actions conducted in these conditions can achieve surprise, gain terrain required for further operations, and negate enemy visual target acquisition capabilities while taking advantage of the friendly force's night-fighting capabilities.

2-92. The mission variables normally require an operation conducted during limited visibility to be more deliberate than in daylight operations. Units planning night attacks consider how limited visibility complicates controlling units, Soldiers, and fires. Limited visibility also complicates identifying and engaging targets; navigating and moving without detection; locating, treating, and evacuating casualties; and locating, bypassing, or breaching obstacles. Examples of limited-visibility operations are nighttime, weather (blizzards, sandstorms, and heavy rain), and thick vegetation. When enemy forces have increased their limited-visibility capabilities, friendly forces must emphasize noise and light discipline during limited-visibility operations. For example, Soldiers who leave their laser sights on increase the likelihood of revealing their position and losing the element of surprise.

2-93. The organization of forces for a limited-visibility operation is the same during daylight operations. However, changing an existing task organization under limited-visibility conditions requires more time and effort than it does during daylight operations. Units plan for limited-visibility operations as they do for daylight operations while emphasizing—

- Keeping the plan simple.
- Taking additional time for reconnaissance.
- Taking advantage of easily identifiable terrain features, such as roads and railroad tracks, when establishing control measures.
- Using intermediate objectives as necessary to control and maintain the correct movement direction during the attack.
- Concealing preparations.
- Scheduling initial rehearsals during daylight, with the final rehearsal at night.

2-94. The company team establishes control measures to facilitate visualizing, describing, and directing subordinate and supporting forces during limited-visibility operations. Company teams also take advantage of the technical capabilities of advanced equipment as they become available.

SECTION II – MOVEMENT TO CONTACT

2-95. Movement to contact is a type of offensive operation designed to develop the situation and establish or regain contact. (See ADP 3-90 for more information.) Commanders conduct an MTC to create favorable conditions for subsequent tactical tasks. A commander conducts an MTC when the tactical situation is not clear or when the enemy has broken contact. A properly executed MTC develops the combat situation and maintains the commander's freedom of action after contact.

FUNDAMENTALS OF A MOVEMENT TO CONTACT

2-96. An MTC employs purposeful and aggressive movement, decentralized control, and the hasty deployment of combined arms formations from the march to conduct offensive and defensive operations or operations in support of stability operations. The fundamentals of an MTC are—

- Focus all efforts on finding the enemy.
- Make initial contact with the smallest force possible, consistent with protecting the force.
- Make initial contact with small, mobile, self-contained forces to avoid decisive engagement of the main body on ground chosen by the enemy. (This allows the commander maximum flexibility to develop the situation.)
- Task organize the force and use movement formations to deploy and attack rapidly in any direction.
- Keep subordinate forces within supporting distances to facilitate a flexible response.
- Maintain contact regardless of the COA adopted.

THE COMPANY TEAM AS PART OF A LARGER UNIT

2-97. The CAB commander determines whether the company team is part of the security force, such as the advance guard, or part of the main body. If time and conditions allow, the commander may consider infiltrating Infantry forces to positions of advantage to the suspected enemy's rear. The force may report and bypass enemy positions, such as roadblocks, to maintain its momentum. Army aviation, if available, can occupy attack by fire positions, conduct aerial insertion, MEDEVAC and Class VIII, and all other resupply operations.

2-98. An advance guard is a task-organized combined arms unit that precedes the main body to protect it from ground observation or surprise by the enemy. The CAB typically organizes an advance guard to lead the CAB with or without a covering force from a higher echelon. The advance guard composition is

METT-TC (I) dependent. Within the CAB however, only companies, or the scout platoon (with or without augmentation from one of the company's teams) have sufficient combat power to serve as an advance guard.

2-99. The main body consists of forces not detailed to security missions. The combat elements of the main body prepare to respond to enemy contact with the maneuver unit's security forces. FISTs may displace forward to be immediately responsive to calls for fire. The main body follows the advance guard and keeps enough distance between itself and the advance guard to maintain flexibility. The CAB commander may designate a portion of the main body as the reserve. The combat formation the CAB uses as part of the main body is METT-TC (I) dependent. The commander, however, must be responsive to the actions of the advance guard.

ORGANIZATION OF FORCES

2-100. An MTC organizes (at a minimum) with a forward security force, an advance guard, and a main body. Based on the mission variables of METT-TC (I), the commander may increase the unit's security by resourcing additional forward security forces and assets, as well as establishing flank and rear security (normally a screen or guard). The main body consist of forces not detailed to security duties and is normally the element that conducts the main effort within the conduct of the MTC. The main body may be composed with a portion of the commander's sustaining base. (See FM 3-90 for more information.) To meet the organization of forces, the company team can lead with a platoon moving in a vee formation, with the lead section assigned as the forward security element, and the trail section assigned as the advance guard.

FORWARD SECURITY FORCES

2-101. The composition depends on mission variables. The forward security force generally comprises an advance guard and flank and rear security. The forward security force moves as quickly and aggressively as possible but remains within supporting range of the main body's weapon systems. It is essential to provide early warning and reaction time for the main body. It destroys small enemy forces or causes the enemy to withdraw before they can disrupt the main body. Within a company team, a single platoon normally serves as the forward security force.

Advance Guard

2-102. The advance guard operates forward of the main body to provide security for the main body and ensure its uninterrupted advance. The advance guard protects the main body from surprise attacks and develops the situation to allow time and space for the deployment of the main body when it is committed to action. The advance guard accomplishes this by destroying or suppressing enemy reconnaissance or ambushes, delaying enemy forces, and marking bypasses for or reducing obstacles. When possible, commanders should refrain from placing IFVs within the advance guard due to their vulnerability and their inability to fire ATGMs while moving, and instead employ tank platoons in this role. An exception to this is when time and speed are not essential and the company team may employ dismounts supported by IFVs in the advance guard, or when terrain dictates. The commander must balance the risk of leading with tanks or IFVs based on terrain and the risk of ATGMs. The advance guard—

- Remains oriented on the main body.
- Reports enemy contact to the commander.
- Collects and reports all information about the enemy.
- Selects tentative fighting positions for following CAB units.
- Tries to penetrate enemy security elements and reach or identify the enemy main force.
- Destroys or repels enemy reconnaissance forces.
- Prevents enemy ground forces from engaging the main body with direct fires.
- Locates, bypasses, or breaches obstacles along the main body's axis of advance.
- Executes tactical tasks such as fix, contain, or block against enemy forces to develop the situation for the main body.
- May conduct a passage of lines with the main body.

Flank and Rear Guard

2-103.   Platoon-sized elements can serve as the flank guard for the CAB. This is done through formation selection. Normally, this element conducts a moving flank screen using alternating or successive bounds with squads or sections. These elements remain at a distance from the main body. Flank security elements operate far enough out to prevent the enemy from surprising the main body with direct fires.

2-104.   The company provides its own rear security, assisted by rapid forward movement, which gives the enemy less opportunity to react or reposition forces to attack the CAB. Units plan indirect fires on major flank and approaches, as well as active air defense measures against aerial threats to enhance security. Upon switching from an MTC to an attack, this platoon normally conducts follow and support of the main body.

Main Body

2-105.   The main body consists of forces not detailed to the security force and is normally the force that is the main effort within the conduct of the MTC. The main body contains most of the combat elements and is arrayed to achieve all-around security throughout the movement. Companies and platoons within the main body are prepared to deploy and attack, giving them the flexibility to maneuver to a decisive point on the battlefield to destroy the enemy. The commander and PLs anticipate changes within the plan to remain flexible and adaptive. The commander designates a portion of the main body for use as the reserve. The size of the reserve is based upon the mission variables of METT-TC (I) and the amount of uncertainty concerning the enemy.

2-106.   The main body's rate of movement is dictated by the advance guard. The main body maintains situational awareness (SA) of the advance guard's progress, the current enemy situation, and provides responsive support when the advance guard is committed. The use of standard formations and battle drills allows the commander, based on the information available, to shift combat power rapidly on the battlefield. During the movement, the company commander within the main body visualizes how the company will be employed into the larger fight and informs subordinate leaders of potential contingencies throughout.

COMPANY TEAM CONDUCTING A MOVEMENT TO CONTACT

2-107.   The company team normally conducts MTC as part of a CAB or larger element; however, based on the METT-TC (I) factors it can conduct the operation independently (see figure 2-12). Normally, a company conducts an MTC by advancing within an assigned zone toward a designated march objective. As an example, the company may conduct an MTC prior to occupation of a screen line. Because the enemy situation is not clear, the company moves in a way that provides security and supports a rapid buildup of combat power against enemy units once they are identified. Two additional techniques for conducting an MTC are the search and attack and cordon and search. If no contact occurs, the company might be directed to conduct consolidation on the objective. The company commander analyzes the situation and selects the proper tactics to conduct the mission. The commander reports all information rapidly and accurately and strives to gain and maintain contact with the enemy. The commander retains freedom of maneuver by moving the company in a manner that—

- Ensures adequate force protection measures are always in effect.
- Orients on planned march objectives.
- Makes enemy contact (ideally visual contact) with the smallest element possible. The commander plans for any forms of contact to identify enemy locations.
- Rapidly employs combat power upon enemy contact.
- Provides all round security for the unit.
- Supports the CAB commander's concept.

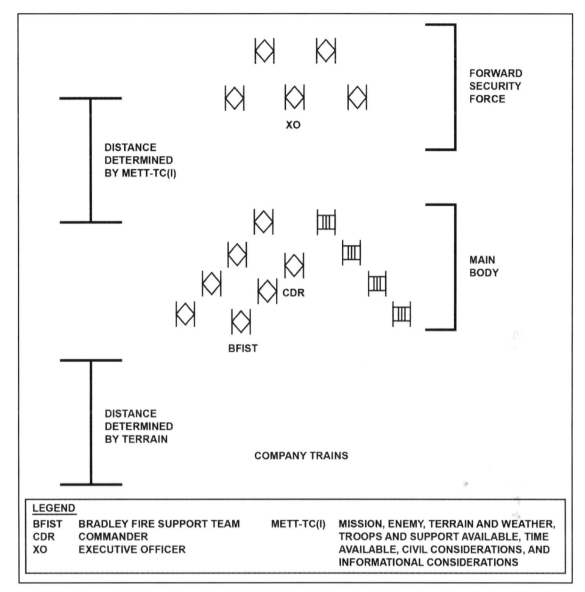

Figure 2-12. Company team conducting movement to contact

CONTROL MEASURES

2-108. The MTC usually starts from a line of departure (LD) at the time specified in the OPORD. The commander controls the MTC by using PLs, contact points, TRPs, and checkpoints, as required. Soldiers should be mindful of surface danger zones of their weapon systems to prevent friendly fire or collateral damage. The commander controls the depth of the MTC by using an LOA or a forward boundary. The commander could designate one or more objectives to limit the extent of the MTC and orient the force. However, these are often terrain-oriented and used only to guide movement. Although an MTC may result in taking a terrain objective, the primary focus should be on the enemy force. The commander should plan some other type of offensive action if there is enough intelligence to locate significant enemy forces.

2-109. Company commanders use positive control over maneuver units, coupled with battle drills and formation discipline. The commander can designate a series of PLs that can successively become the new rear boundary of the forward security elements as that force advances. Each rear boundary becomes the forward boundary of the main body and shifts as the security force moves forward. The rear boundary of the main body designates the rear security element's limit of responsibility. This line shifts as the main body moves forward.

PLANNING A MOVEMENT TO CONTACT

2-110. As in any type of operation, the commander plans to focus operations on finding the enemy and then delaying, disrupting, and destroying the enemy force as much as possible, utilizing direct and indirect fires. The commander analyzes the terrain to include enemy air avenues of approach and the enemy's most dangerous COA as determined in the war-gaming portion of the TLP. Due to the uncertainty of the enemy's precise location, the analysis during TLP may consist of multiple contingencies and branch plans. Because of the company's vulnerability, by the nature of an MTC, the enemy must not be underestimated.

2-111. An MTC is not a blind forward movement followed by a react to contact drill. The plan for the MTC addresses not only actions anticipated by the commander based on available information and intelligence, but also the conduct of meeting engagements at anticipated times and locations where they might occur. Company security is enhanced through a thorough analysis of the enemy by the company commander. The interpretation of the IPB products provided by the CAB, and ongoing understanding of the CAB commander's visualization of the enemy and indicating danger areas where platoons are most likely to make contact shapes the outcome of the enemy analysis. In analyzing the enemy, the company commander must understand the IPB. Although the commander does prepare IPB products for use in preparation of analysis, and orders, the commander does not prepare individual products for subordinates. The commander must be able to use the products of the CAB's IPB effectively, in the analysis and be able to inform subordinates based on the compilation of company and higher IPB products.

2-112. The commander reconnoiters visually to verify higher HQ's intelligence if time permits. The commander seeks to confirm priority intelligence requirements (PIRs) that support tentative plans. Usually, these PIRs consist of assumptions or critical facts about the enemy. This can include strength and location especially at template positions. In addition to the enemy, PIRs can include information about the terrain. If possible, the commander includes subordinate leaders in the reconnaissance efforts. The main body's planned movement formation should contribute to the goal of making initial contact with the smallest force possible. As information is collected, the company commander begins to complete the plan, including expanding selected or refined COAs into the OPORDs. The commander prepares overlays, refines the target list worksheet, completes sustainment and command and control requirements, and of course, updates the tentative plan based on the latest reconnaissance information.

2-113. The CAB's IPB products necessary to support company planning and operations include—

- Enemy situation overlays with associated COA statements and high-value target lists.
- Event templates and associated event matrices.
- Modified combined obstacle overlays, terrain effects matrices, and terrain assessments.
- Weather forecast charts, weather effects matrices, light and illumination tables, and weather estimates.
- Civil considerations, overlays, and assessments.

2-114. During the mission analysis, consideration of terrain and weather help to identify potential danger areas that are likely enemy defensive locations, EAs, observation posts (OPs), and obstacles. The utilization of military aspects of terrain; obstacles, avenues of approach, key terrain, observation and fields of fire, and cover and concealment (OAKOC), are used to analyze the ground. The leader determines the effects of each aspect of terrain on both friendly and enemy forces. These effects translate directly into conclusions that can apply to friendly or enemy COAs. Even if time is tight, the leader should allocate as much time as possible to these military aspects, starting at the objective area, and then analyzing other aspects of key terrain. Defining the most probable points of enemy contact within the AO and the probable line of contact and probable line of deployment (PLD) enable the company commander to reduce uncertainty and make contact with the enemy on their own terms. Detailed terrain and enemy analysis can enable the company team to plan hasty attacks against the most likely enemy locations, rather than stumbling into enemy contact. Conclusions include at least the following:

- Effective templating of enemy forces and key weapons systems.
- Effective positioning of own assets.

- Understanding of time and space relationships of events, leading to thorough contingency plans.
- Effective echeloning and identifying of enemy observation and indirect fires.
- Effective selecting of movement techniques and formations, to include when to transition to tactical maneuver.

2-115.   During an MTC, the commander seeks to gain contact with the enemy using the smallest elements possible. Units must begin rehearsals and preparation as soon as possible to ensure success. Leaders initiate necessary movement to continue mission preparations or to posture the unit for the start of the mission. Necessary movement can be executed at any time throughout the sequence of the TLP. It can include movement to an assembly area (AA), BP or new AO, or the movement of guides to quartering parties. As elements plan in parallel within the company, the company can continue preparations and rehearsals.

PREPARING TO CONDUCT A MOVEMENT TO CONTACT

2-116.   During preparation, the company commander and subordinate leaders must receive the most current information from organic and higher echelon information collection assets. The CAB staff must ensure that fragmentary orders are published and that plans are updated to reflect any changes to the company's mission. The company commander must ensure subordinates understand the CAB commander's intent and concept of operation and the company's concept of operation and commander's intent, in addition to their individual missions even as new information becomes available. The commander uses confirmation briefs, backbriefs, and rehearsals to ensure missions are understood and all actions are integrated and synchronized. Simple plans that are flexible and rehearsed repetitively against various enemy conditions and that rely on established tactical SOPs are essential to success.

2-117.   Subordinate unit preparations are reviewed to ensure they are consistent with the commander's intent and concept of operation. Subordinate rehearsals should emphasize movement through danger areas, actions on contact, passage of lines, and transitions. The commander and subordinate leaders ensure subordinate units (to include attachments) understand assigned missions during movement and maneuver options during execution. Plans are war-gamed and rehearsed against enemy COAs that would cause the company to execute various maneuver options at different times and locations. The goal is to rehearse subordinates on potential situations that may arise during execution to promote flexibility while reinforcing the commander's intent.

2-118.   The commander seeks to rehearse the operation from initiation to occupation of the final objective or LOA. Rehearsals include decision points and actions taken upon each decision. Often, the commander prioritizes maneuver options and enemy COAs to be rehearsed based on the time available. The rehearsal focuses on locating the enemy, developing the situation, executing a maneuver option, exercising indirect fire control measures and direct fire control measures (known as DFCMs), and exploiting success. The rehearsal must consider the potential of encountering stationary or moving enemy forces. Other actions to consider during rehearsals include—

- Actions to cross danger areas.
- Advance guard making contact with a small enemy force.
- Advance guard making contact with a large force beyond its capabilities to defeat.
- Advance guard making contact with an obstacle the reconnaissance force has not identified and reported.
- Flank/rear security force making contact with a small force.
- Flank/rear security force making contact with a large force beyond its capability to defeat.
- Actions to report and bypass of an enemy force (based on bypass criteria).
- Transitions and maneuver options.

EXECUTING A MOVEMENT TO CONTACT

2-119.   During execution, the company moves rapidly to maintain the advantage of a rapid tempo. However, the commander must balance the need for speed with the requirement for security. Because of this, the MTC will be executed as a series of movements from and to dominant terrain with elements in overwatch rather than rush to advance in zone. The commander bases the decision on the effectiveness of reconnaissance efforts, effects of terrain, and the enemy's capabilities. Each element of the force synchronizes its actions with adjacent and supporting units, maintaining contact and coordination as prescribed in orders and unit SOP.

FIND THE ENEMY, GAIN AND MAINTAIN CONTACT

2-120.   The commander uses all available sources of combat information to find the enemy's location and dispositions, which ensures that forces can be committed under optimal conditions. Sensors alone cannot confirm the exact disposition and location of all enemy forces. The optimal conditions could be making and maintaining contact with the smallest element possible. This allows the commander to develop the situation before committing the main body.

FIX THE ENEMY

2-121.   Once contact is made, the main body brings overwhelming fires onto the enemy to prevent them from conducting either a spoiling attack or organizing a coherent defense. The lead platoon maneuvers, as quickly as possible, to find gaps in the enemy's defenses. The commander gathers as much information as possible about the enemy's dispositions, strengths, capabilities, and intentions. While conducting a company team MTC, the lead platoon must assist the commander in making a rapid assessment of the situation, while the company FSO utilizes any available fires to disrupt the enemy's maneuver forces and decision-making capability.

2-122.   The commander initiates maneuver at a tempo the enemy cannot match, since success in a meeting engagement depends on effective actions on contact. The lead platoon does not allow the enemy to maneuver against the main body. The organization, size, and combat power of the lead platoon are the major factors that determine the size of the enemy force it can defeat without deploying the main body. The techniques a commander employs to fix the enemy when both forces are moving are different than those employed when the enemy force is stationary during the meeting engagement. In both situations, when the lead platoon cannot overrun the enemy by conducting a hasty frontal attack, the commander must deploy a portion of the main body. When this occurs, the unit is no longer conducting an MTC but an attack.

2-123.   The lead element in contact with the enemy may transition into a stationary SBF element, enabling the company team to maneuver. However, if there is no suitable cover for the lead element, it is imperative that the lead element continues to maneuver and increase speed and dispersion to maximize survivability. Obscuration with CAB mortars or FA smoke can assist in disrupting the enemy's ability to engage the lead elements in an absence of cover.

FINISH THE ENEMY

2-124.   If the lead platoon cannot overrun the enemy security forces with a frontal attack, the commander quickly maneuvers the main body to conduct a penetration, frontal attack, or envelopment. The commander does this to overwhelm the enemy before it can react effectively or reinforce. The commander attempts to defeat the enemy in detail while still maintaining the momentum of the advance. After a successful attack, the commander resumes the MTC. If the enemy was not defeated, or the commander assesses an attack will not be successful prior to committing the entire company team, the commander has three main options: bypass, transition to a more deliberate attack, or conduct a defense.

2-125.   Main body elements deploy rapidly to the vicinity of the contact if the commander initiates a frontal attack. The commander avoids piecemeal commitment except when rapidity of action is essential and combat superiority at the vital point is present and can be maintained throughout the attack, or when compartmentalized terrain forces a COA. When conducting an envelopment, the commander focuses on attacking the enemy's flanks and rear before countering these actions. The commander uses the security force to fix the enemy while the main body looks for an assailable flank or uses the main body to fix the enemy while the security force finds the assailable flank.

FOLLOW THROUGH

2-126.   If the enemy is defeated, the unit transitions back into an MTC and continues to advance. The MTC terminates when the unit reaches the final objective or LOA or it transitions to a more deliberate attack, a defense, or retrograde.

ASSESS A MOVEMENT TO CONTACT

2-127.   Assessments are a continuous process of examining inputs, activities, outputs, outcomes, and the impact on objectives. During the conduct of the operation, the commander should periodically compare the plan as to how the task is being executed. Lulls or tactical pauses after crossing PLs are normally the most advantageous times. The commander should notice differences and adjust the plan especially if contact is made in places unexpectedly. Once the tasks are complete, the commander should evaluate the original plan with what actions happened, annotate differences, and send to higher HQ for further analysis.

VARIATIONS OF A MOVEMENT TO CONTACT

2-128.   MTC has two variations: search and attack and cordon and search. The following paragraphs further discuss the two.

SEARCH AND ATTACK

2-129.   *Search and attack* is a variation of a movement to contact where a friendly force conducts coordinated attacks to defeat a distributed enemy force (FM 3-90). The commander employs the search and attack when the enemy is operating as a small, dispersed element, or when the task is to deny the enemy the ability to move within a given area. CABs and companies normally conduct search and attack operations. The commander conducts a search and attack for one or more of the following purposes:

- Protect the force. Prevent the enemy from massing to disrupt or destroy friendly military or civilian operations, equipment, property, and key facilities.
- Collect information. Gain information about the enemy and the terrain to confirm the enemy COA predicted by the IPB process. Help generate SA for the company and higher HQ.
- Destroy the enemy. Render enemy units in the AO combat ineffective.
- Deny the area. Prevent the enemy from operating unhindered in any area they are using for a base camp or for logistics support.

ORGANIZATION OF FORCES

2-130.   The commander task-organizes the unit into reconnaissance, fixing, and finishing forces, each with a specific purpose and task. The size of the reconnaissance force is based on the available intelligence about the size of enemy forces in the AO.

2-131.   The reconnaissance force conducts a zone reconnaissance to reconnoiter identified named area of interest. The reconnaissance force must be small enough to achieve stealth but large enough to provide adequate self-defense until fixing and finishing forces arrive.

2-132.   The fixing force can be a combination of mounted and dismounted company teams with enough combat power to isolate the enemy once the reconnaissance force finds them. The fixing force attacks if that action meets the commander's intent, and it can generate sufficient combat power against the detected enemy.

2-133.   The finishing force destroys the detected and fixed enemy. The commander may have the finishing force establish an area ambush and use reconnaissance and fixing forces to drive the enemy into ambushes. The finishing force must have enough combat power to destroy those enemy forces expected in the company team's AO.

CONTROL MEASURES FOR SEARCH AND ATTACK

2-134.   The commander establishes control measures that allow for decentralized actions and small-unit initiative to the greatest extent possible. The minimum control measures for a search and attack are an AO,

TRPs, objectives, checkpoints, and contact points (see figure 2-13). TRPs facilitate responsive fire support once the reconnaissance force makes contact with the enemy while boundaries and restrictive firing lines prevent direct fire fratricide. The commander uses objectives and checkpoints to guide the movement of subordinate elements. Coordination points indicate a specific location for the coordination of tactical actions between adjacent units (see FM 3-90). The commander uses other control measures, such as phase lines, as needed.

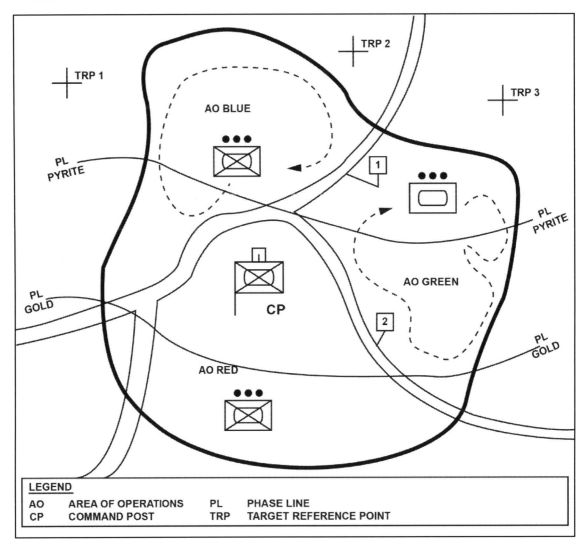

Figure 2-13. Control measures for search and attack

PLAN SEARCH AND ATTACK

2-135.   The search and attack plan places the finishing force as the main effort, where it can best maneuver to destroy enemy forces or essential facilities once located by reconnaissance assets. Typically, the finishing force occupies a central location in the AO. However, mission variables may allow the commander to position the finishing force outside the search and attack area. The commander weighs the main effort by using priority of fires and assigning priorities of support to available combat multipliers (such as engineer elements and rotary-wing lift support). The commander establishes control measures, as necessary, to consolidate units and concentrates the combat power of the force before the attack. Once the reconnaissance force locates the enemy, the fixing and finishing forces can fix and destroy the detected enemy force. The commander develops a contingency plan if the reconnaissance force is compromised.

2-136.   Each subordinate element operating in its own AO is tasked to destroy the enemy within its capability. The commander should establish graphics, DFCMs, and communications means between any closing elements to prevent fratricide. The reconnaissance force conducts a zone reconnaissance to reconnoiter identified named area of interest. The following paragraphs discuss executing a search and attack using the sequence of the offense.

2-137.   Once the reconnaissance force finds the enemy force, the fixing force develops the situation and executes one of two options based on the commander's guidance and mission variables. The first option is to block identified routes that the detected enemy can use to escape or for reinforcements. The fixing force maintains contact with the enemy and positions its forces to isolate and fix the enemy before the finishing force attacks. The second option is to conduct an attack to fix the enemy in their current positions until the finishing force arrives. Depending on the enemy's mobility and the likelihood of the reconnaissance force being compromised, the commander may need to position the fixing force before the reconnaissance force enters the AO.

2-138.   The commander uses the finishing force to conduct attacks, maneuvering to block enemy escape routes while another element conducts the attack or employs indirect fire and CAS to destroy the enemy. The finishing force must be responsive and require synchronization with all support forces to accomplish the desired end state.

2-139.   If conditions are not right to use the finishing force to attack the detected enemy, the reconnaissance or fixing force can continue to conduct reconnaissance and surveillance activities to further develop the situation. Whenever this occurs, the force maintaining surveillance must be careful to avoid detection and possible enemy ambushes.

2-140.   The finishing force may move behind the reconnaissance and fixing forces, or it may locate at a pickup zone and conduct an air movement into a landing zone near the enemy once they are located. The finishing force must be responsive enough to engage the enemy before they can break contact with the reconnaissance force or fixing force. The commander may have the finishing force establish an area ambush and use the reconnaissance and fixing forces to drive the enemy into ambushes.

2-141.   The commander uses the finishing force to destroy the enemy by conducting a hasty or deliberate attack, maneuvering to block enemy escape routes while another unit conducts the attack, or employing indirect fire or CAS to destroy the enemy.

2-142.   The commander may have part of the fixing force establish an area ambush and use the reconnaissance and remaining fixing forces to drive the enemy into the ambush, establish a reserve, and screen the objective area. After a search and attack, the commander transitions to the appropriate offensive or defensive operation for the existing tactical situation.

CORDON AND SEARCH

2-143.   *Cordon and search* is a variation of movement to contact where a friendly force isolates and searches a target area (FM 3-90). It is a common tactical mission during operations focused on stability. The purpose of cordon and search is to obtain weapon caches, materiel or information, a specific high-value target, or persons of interest.

2-144.   Searches are an important aspect of populace and resource control. The need to conduct search or to employ search procedures is a continuous requirement. A search can orient on people, materiel, buildings, or terrain. A search usually involves civilian police and Soldiers.

2-145.   It involves the emplacement of a cordon, or security perimeter, to prevent traffic in and out of the area. The cordon permits the search element to operate unimpeded within the secured area. Armored vehicles provide a means of establishing traffic control posts by using its size to block high-speed avenues of approach. When paired with another armored vehicle at a point, it can provide coverage on inner and outer cordon security.

TASK ORGANIZATION

2-146. The cordon and search force includes a command element, a security element, a search element, and a support element, each with a clear task and purpose. The security element sets up the cordon, which usually comprises an outer cordon "ring" and an inner cordon "ring." The search and assault element is the main effort and will clear and search suspected buildings to capture or destroy enemy or contraband. The support element may be the reserve, provide SBF, and be prepared to perform the other cordon and search tasks. The size and composition of the cordon and search force is based on the size of the area to be cordoned, the size of the area to be searched, and the suspected enemy situation.

2-147. The company often receives additional assets to assist in a cordon and search based on availability and the mission variables of METT-TC (I). Assets may be included as teams in the security element or the search element, or they may remain independent and on call. Assets may be internal or external to the CAB and company and can include military police, engineers, civil affairs, psychological operations, military intelligence, or artillery.

Command Element

2-148. The command element serves as the HQ of the cordon and search force. The commander applies the same planning (TLP) used in other operations. While sudden opportunities may arise with little planning time, the nature of a search and what it may uncover can result in significant amounts of time spent in the objective area. The commander must be prepared to execute cordon and searches with very little notice while simultaneously being prepared to spend many hours, even days, conducting the operation.

2-149. The command element considers numerous mission variables when planning and preparing for a cordon and search operation. The commander identifies elements and assigns units to them along with a clear task and purpose. Ideally, Infantry squads within the mechanized Infantry platoons are task organized into a search element with tanks and IFVs as security element and support elements for the cordon and search. These elements organize subelements as necessary to accomplish the mission. The command element (company primary CP and when established an alternate CP) normally nests within one of the other elements rather than travel as its own entity.

Security Element

2-150. The security element is responsible for sealing off the objective through emplacement of an outer and inner cordon. The security element limits or prevents enemy or civilian influence in the objective area and prevents targets from escaping the cordon. The security element may receive the bulk of the available combat power due to multiple avenues of approach and requirements to disperse widely across the objective area to accomplish its mission. It may have to establish multiple blocking positions, OPs, and conduct patrols to seal off the target area. It must have the inner and outer cordons in place, or nearly in place, prior to actions by other elements.

2-151. As security elements deploy to set up the outer and inner cordons, the actions of both reinforce each other, creating an environment in which unwanted influences and actions, from both outside the objective area and from within the target area, are prevented from interfering with the success of the mission. Cordon elements (outer and inner) focus both inward and outward for security purposes. As security elements deploy, actions are dictated by the requirements of the cordons, methods by which the security element moves into the objective area, and manner in which it chooses to occupy the positions that make up both cordons. The security element leader uses information collection assets internal and external to the company to observe the target area before the approach of security elements. The establishment of the cordon starts when the first security element reaches its release point position or similar control measure and ends as the security element has sealed off the objective area.

2-152. Establishment of the outer cordon, during the cordon phase requires detailed planning, coordination, and meticulous integration and synchronization to achieve the required effects. The outer cordon prevents anyone from entering the objective area and assists the inner cordon in preventing the enemy from escaping from the objective area. The element leader of the outer cordon maintains SA, and within the commander's abilities situational understanding to facilitate the progress of the operation, specifically the inner cordon and search efforts. Tactical tasks associated with the outer cordon security element include the following:

- *Block*—a tactical mission task that denies the enemy access to an area or an avenue of approach (FM 3-90).
- *Interdict*—a tactical mission task in which a unit prevents, disrupts, or delays the enemy's use of an area or route in any domain (FM 3-90).
- *Deny*—a task to hinder or prevent the enemy from using terrain, space, personnel, supplies, or facilities (ATP 3-21.20).

2-153.   Establishment of the inner cordon requires the same level of planning, coordination, and integration and synchronization to achieve desired effects as did the outer cordon. The inner cordon seals off the target area to protect the search element from enemy activity. It prevents enemy movement within the target area and prevents enemy entry or exit. The security element is properly armed and equipped to control the ground and mitigate the most likely issues it may to face as determined in the planning and reconnaissance phase. The cordon's primary orientation is inward toward the target area. However, the inner cordon performs a secondary function of controlling movement into the objective area as well. Tactical tasks associated with the inner cordon security element include—

- *Contain*—a tactical mission task in which a unit stops, holds, or surrounds an enemy force (FM 3-90).
- *Fix*—a tactical mission task in which a unit prevents the enemy from moving from a specific location for a specific period (FM 3-90).
- *Suppress*—a tactical mission task in which a unit temporarily degrades a force or weapon system from accomplishing its mission (FM 3-90).
- *Overwatch*—a task that positions an element to support the movement of another element with immediate fire (ATP 3-21.10).

2-154.   During the actions on the objective phase, the security element maintains the inner and outer cordons (see figure 2-14 on page 2-38). The inner cordon overwatches actions on the objective, prevents egress from the target area, and coordinates actions with the outer cordon. The outer cordon prevents external influences from entering the objective area, prevents or controls movement in and out of the objective area, and coordinates with the inner cordon.

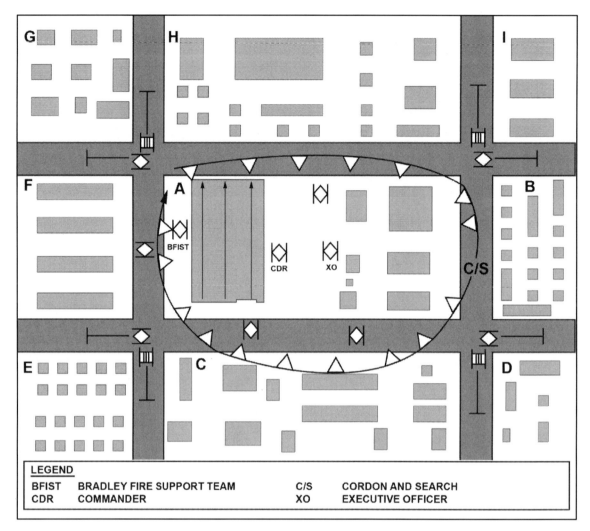

Figure 2-14. Inner and outer cordon

2-155. Whether the cordon and search force withdraws as a single force or moves in multiple elements on multiple routes, the security element normally is the last to depart. The inner and outer cordons provide overwatch for the search and support elements. Should the withdrawal be cancelled by design or by enemy action, the cordon remains in place. Once the other cordon and search force elements have committed to withdrawal, and are safely away from the target area, the security element first collapses the inner, then the outer cordon.

Search Element

2-156. The search element's mission is to clear, search, and conduct site exploitation on the objective to locate and seize contraband material; and identify, search, or detain suspected insurgents. The search element moves as either the second or the third element of movement, in the order of march. When resistance is not expected, or when speed and surprise are paramount, the commander places the search element as the second march element so it can move immediately and directly into the target area. When resistance is expected or when ensuring the target area is sealed off, the search element travels behind the security and support elements.

2-157. The search element can divide into three types of teams: search teams, security teams, and support teams. As these teams are most often in direct contact with the local populous and potential threats, these teams train and enable accordingly. Teams within the search element initiate actions once the outer and inner cordons are in place. Paragraphs 2-158 through 2-160 address the actions of each team.

Search Element Teams

2-158. Search teams focus on the actual conduct of the search and the processes of site exploitation. The search team is not normally part of the security of the target area, but can be, if required. The team relies on the support team for secondary tasks such as evidence and detainee processing.

2-159. Security teams are responsible for gaining access, clearing, and maintaining security of the immediate objective. Security functions include providing immediate security, protection, overwatch, and supervising movement in and out of the objective. The security team should not be tasked with actions that detract from security. In most cases, the existence of inner and outer cordons does not constitute local security for the search element.

2-160. Support teams are responsible for providing organized manpower to conduct continuing actions in the objective area and for providing direct assistance to the search team and security team, if required. Such actions might consist of, but are not limited to, detainee processing, evidence collection, and CASEVAC.

Support Element

2-161. Support elements are designed to act as a force multiplier during a cordon and search operation and should be positioned where they can best accomplish assigned tasks. Support elements may assist the cordon and search force by serving as a designated reserve, providing additional enabling teams to support all elements of the force, and conducting continuing actions such as establishing a temporary defensive position, conducting vehicle recovery, CASEVAC, and resupply.

2-162. The support element moves as either the second or the third element of movement in the order of march. When resistance is not expected, or when speed and surprise are paramount, the support element moves as the trail element, so it does not interfere with the security and search elements' movement, but is still positioned to support, begin, and continue actions in support of actions on the objective. When resistance is expected or when ensuring the target area is sealed off, the support element travels as the second element, allowing it to move into positions of support and security around the target area before the search element is committed.

2-163. As actions on the objective occur, the support element executes its assigned tasks for the cordon and search force. The support element establishes secure positions in or near the target area in which detainees, evidence, and casualties can be safely secured. These positions are established where they are readily assessable to cordon and search force, and if necessary defendable against attack. The support element may provide additional support to detainee processing and evidence collection teams to the search element, conduct CASEVAC, provide internal resupply, vehicle recovery, and hasty repair capabilities. Often the support element controls various enablers attached to the search element until they are needed. Tactical mission tasks associated with the support element include follow and assume and follow and support, which are defined in the following:
- *Follow and assume* is a tactical mission task in which a committed force follows and supports a lead force conducting an offensive operation and continues mission if lead force cannot continue (FM 3-90).
- *Follow and support* is a tactical mission task in which a committed force follows and supports a lead force conducting an offensive operation (FM 3-90).

2-164. The support element, normally with the command element nested, follows in trace of the search element and is the last of the cordon and search force to depart the target area while being overwatched by the security element. During the withdrawal, depending on tasking, the support element may transport multiple detainees or large amounts of captured material and tow downed vehicles.

SECTION III – ATTACK

2-165. An attack is a type of offensive operation that defeats enemy forces, seizes terrain, or secures terrain (see FM 3-90). When the commander decides to attack or the opportunity to attack occurs during combat operations, the execution of that attack must mass the effects of overwhelming combat power against selected portions of the enemy force with a tempo and intensity that cannot be matched by the enemy. An attack at the company team level is characterized by close combat, direct fire, maneuver, and support from indirect fires. When the company team commanders decide to attack, they must mass the effects of overwhelming combat power against the weak point of the enemy with a tempo and intensity that the enemy cannot match.

2-166. Attacks may be hasty or deliberate, depending on the time available for assessing the situation, planning, and preparing. The primary difference between a hasty and deliberate attack is the extent of planning and preparation that the attacking force conducts. At one end of the continuum, the company team launches hasty attacks as a continuation of a meeting engagement to exploit a combat power advantage and to preempt enemy actions. The other end of the continuum includes published, detailed orders with multiple branches and sequels, detailed knowledge of all aspects of enemy dispositions, a force that has been task organized specifically for the operation, and the conduct of extensive rehearsals. Most attacks fall between the ends of the continuum as opposed to either extreme.

2-167. An attack can be either a force-oriented objective or terrain-oriented objective. A force-oriented objective requires the attacker to focus its efforts on a designated enemy force. The enemy force may be stationary or moving. A terrain-oriented objective (at company level) requires the company to seize, secure, or retain a designated geographical area. All attacks depend on the synchronization and integration of combat power for success. They require planning, coordination, and time (although time may be limited) to prepare.

ORGANIZATION OF FORCES

2-168. Once the commander determines the scheme of maneuver for the attack, the commander task organizes the company to accomplish the mission. Normally, the attack is organized into a security force, main body, and a reserve, all of which are supported by a sustainment organization. The commander completes any changes in task organization in a timely manner so units can conduct rehearsals with their attached and supporting elements.

SECURITY FORCE

2-169. Security forces, under normal circumstances during an attack, are only resourced if the attack uncover one or more flanks or the rear of the attacking force as it advances. In this case, the commander designates a flank or rear security force and assigns it a screen or guard mission depending on the mission variables of METT-TC (I). Normally, an attacking unit does not need extensive forward security forces. An exception occurs when the attacking unit is transitioning from the defense to an attack and had previously established a security area as part of the defense.

MAIN BODY

2-170. The commander organizes the main body as the main effort and necessary shaping operations or supporting efforts. The commander aims the main body toward the respective decisive points. Decisive points can consist of the immediate and decisive destruction of selected enemy forces, the enemy force's capacity to resist, seizure of terrain objectives, or the defeat of the enemy force's plan. The maneuver scheme identifies the focus of the main effort. All the force's available resources operate in concert to assure the success of the main effort. The element designated to conduct the main effort can change during the attack. The commander must consider an assault, breach, and support force if the commander expects to conduct a breach operation during the attack.

RESERVE

2-171. The commander uses the reserve to exploit success, defeat enemy counterattacks, or restore momentum to a stalled attack. Once committed, the reserve's actions normally become or reinforce the echelon's main effort, and the commander makes every effort to reconstitute another reserve from units made available by the revised situation. Often the commander's most difficult and important decision concerns the time, place, and circumstances for committing the reserve. The reserve is not a committed force; it is not used as a follow and support force or a follow and assume force.

PLANNING AN ATTACK

2-172.   In an attack, the company team attempts to place the enemy in a position where the enemy can easily be defeated or destroyed. The commander seeks to keep the enemy off-balance while continually reducing the enemy's options. In an attack the commander focuses maneuver effects, supported by the other warfighting functions, on those enemy forces that seek to prevent the unit from accomplishing its mission and seizing its objective. Planning helps the commander synchronize the effects of combat power through TLP.

2-173.   The focus of planning is to develop a fully synchronized plan that masses all available effects of combat power against the enemy. (See appendix B for planning and TLP.) A critical aspect to the commander's plan is to generate and concentrate combat power. The commander avoids using resources and incurring needless casualties by attacking piecemeal. If an objective is small enough to be taken by a platoon attack, (dependent upon the overall mission) then the commander provides the necessary support to the attacking platoon. However, if the task requires it, the commander commits the entire company and all other available resources to destroy the enemy quickly and violently.

2-174.   The commander refines the plan based on continuous updates to the situation. While the CAB staff develops and updates the running estimates as information changes, the company commander is prepared to adjust the company plan as the situation changes throughout the operation. Subordinates conduct parallel planning as well as start their preparations for the attack immediately after the issuance of a warning order (WARNORD), OPORD, or fragmentary order. As the situation is updated, the commander revises orders and distributes order as quickly as possible to give subordinates more time to prepare for the attack. The commander's plan is as detailed as the time available allows. When planning time is constrained, commanders should place the most emphasis on understanding the terrain and enemy and their effects on potential friendly COAs. Sacrificing analysis of terrain and enemy to focus on other elements of TLP lead to a friendly plan not grounded and should be avoided in all instances.

2-175.   The commander uses the enemy situation template, probable COA, dangerous COA, and other products of the IPB process to identify aspects within the AO, area of interest, and area of influence that can affect how the friendly force accomplishes the mission. (See appendix B for more information.) An area of interest is that area of concern to the commander, including the area of influence, areas adjacent, and extending into enemy territory. This area also includes areas occupied by enemy forces who could jeopardize the accomplishment of the mission.

2-176.   By studying the terrain, the commander determines the principal mounted and dismounted avenues of approach to the objective. The commander determines the most advantageous area for the enemy's main defense to occupy, routes that the enemy may use to conduct counterattacks, and other factors, such as observation and fields of fire, avenues of approach, key terrain, obstacles, and cover and concealment. Information collection is continuously updated during planning to gain an increased understanding of the enemy's intentions, actions, and relative combat power. The outcome of this analysis should replicate how the commander would fight given the commander's own insight if the commander was in the enemy's position.

2-177.   When preparing for a deliberate operation, the company commander, in coordination with the CAB commander and staff, participates in the development of the information collection plan. A well-resourced and coordinated information collection effort paints a detailed picture of the enemy situation before an attack and provides the company commander and subordinate leaders a critical insight into how to prepare for the attack. The information collection effort includes redundant systems to ensure continuous flow of information to the CAB and correspondingly from the CAB to the companies. The commander uses this information to decide on a COA and make refinements to the plan. The information collection effort provides the commander with continuous updates during the attack to adjust execution of the operation based on the enemy's reactions.

Note. The commander rarely has complete information. The commander must balance the advantages of gathering more information with the advantages gained by an attack conducted with incomplete information but rapidly executed and with all available combat power. The commander that requires more complete information on the enemy may miss opportunities and allow the enemy to prepare their defenses more thoroughly.

2-178.   Utilizing information gained from the CAB or brigade intelligence staff officer (S-2), the company commander refines CAB S-2's intelligence products to focus on the AO/area of interest relevant to the pending company attack, and updates that analysis to develop an estimate of the enemy at the squad level within that reduced area. The company's information collection effort focuses on identifying indicators for confirming the enemy's actual COA within the company's AO. This information is vital in answering the commander's information and intelligence requirements and helps the commander in developing and refining plans. Ideally, the commander does not make final decisions on how to execute the attack until the current array of enemy forces is identified. Key areas to identify for a defending enemy force include—

* Composition, disposition, and strength of enemy forces along a flank or at an area selected for attack.
* Composition, strength, and disposition of security and disruption forces.
* Location, orientation, type, depth, and composition of obstacles.
* Locations of potential bypasses around obstacles.
* Composition, strength, and disposition of defending combat formations within the enemy's main battle area (MBA).
* Composition, strength, and location of reserves.
* Location of routes the enemy may use to counterattack or reinforce defenses.
* Type of enemy fortifications and survivability effort.

2-179.   The commander seeks to define the limits of the enemy EAs. This includes where the enemy can mass fires, weapon ranges, and direct fire integration with obstacles, ability to shift fires, and mutual support between positions. This analysis requires efficient, and effective terrain analysis, confirmed locations of enemy weapons systems, and a good understanding of the enemy's weapons capabilities and tactics. Reconnaissance forces and surveillance assets report locations, orientation, and composition of defending weapons systems and obstacles. The analysis of the enemy's direct and indirect fire plan assists the commander in developing the scheme of maneuver by—

* Determining the location of the probable line of contact.
* Identifying when the company must transition to maneuver.
* The targets and positioning of direct fire weapons.
* Identifying targets for indirect fires.

2-180.   Once the company commander has updated and refined the IPB products, based upon the CAB's intelligence, the commander is able to formulate and adjust the company's plan to fit within the anticipated enemy COAs. The company's plan that includes all changes to the initial plan, such as the scheme of maneuver and fires, must then be provided to the higher HQ normally in the form of a backbrief, or during the CAB combined arms rehearsal.

2-181.   The commander assigns sectors to subordinate forces and normally designates (as a minimum, regardless of whether the attack takes place in a contiguous or noncontiguous AO): a phase line as the LD (which may also be the line of contact) and point of departure; the time to initiate the operation; and the objective. The commander may designate checkpoints, additional phase lines, a PLD and final coordination line, assault positions, DFCMs, and fire support coordination measures; and can use either an axis of advance or a direction of attack to further control maneuver forces. Between the PLD and the objective, a commander can use a final coordination line, assault positions, SBF position, and attack by fire positions to control the final stage of the attack. Beyond the objective, the commander can designate hasty defensive positions or an LOA to control forward progress of the attack. When planning graphic control measures, the commander should ensure that the company team is enabled to not only execute the operation as planned, but also maintain enough flexibility to maneuver against unexpected contact as the situation develops. The commander may receive or be tasked with any number of those graphics and will also develop what is needed to complete the plan.

2-182.   The commander uses the reverse planning process to develop a timely and complete plan. By starting with actions on the objective and working back to the LD or point of departure, the company commander takes into consideration the most effective allocation of combat power, mobility assets, and indirect fires including suppression and obscuration based upon the higher HQ allocation to the company. The commander begins arraying combat power at the decisive point, ensuring the main effort has enough combat power to achieve the decisive point, and then moving backwards in the operation and through shaping operations to allocate combat power in descending order of importance. If a shortfall in combat power arises, the commander looks to reallocate combat power among shaping operations, alter the scheme of maneuver, request additional combat power from the CAB, or understand and accept risk somewhere in the operation. When possible, the commander plans avenues of approach that avoid strong enemy defensive positions, takes advantage of all available cover and concealment. Where cover and concealment are not available, the commander plans obscurants to conceal movement and maximizes speed, dispersion, and survivability drills.

2-183.   At the decisive point, the commander directs the main effort against an objective, ideally an identified enemy weakness, which will cause the collapse of the enemy defense. The commander seeks to attack the enemy's flanks, rear, or supporting formations. By so doing, the enemy loses control of its systems and the enemy commander's options are reduced. Concurrently, the company retains the initiative and reduces its own vulnerabilities. If the mission or purpose does not require it, the commander does not focus on the destruction of all enemy maneuver forces within the assigned AO or objective area if the company can defeat the enemy through other means. Rapid assaults which destroy command and logistics nodes or isolate the enemy from support can lead to a breakdown of enemy morale leading to capitulation or withdrawal.

2-184.   Commanders should coordinate during mission planning with the CAB operations officer for integration into the BCT's scheme of engineer operations. The BCT's brigade engineer battalion provides capabilities for bridging, breaching, route clearance, explosive hazards identification, and limited horizontal construction.

2-185.   The BCT and CAB will plan and manage most of the fires assets for the purpose of shaping the fight prior to the company arriving, but the company may be 1) allocated a target(s); or 2) tasked to execute/observe a brigade/CAB target. Then the CAB may allocate mortars to support the company operation. Over and above, the company commander should plan for/request/refine targets. Army attack helicopters and CAS may be available to destroy defensive positions and interdict enemy counterattack forces. During the attack, using preparation fires, counterfire, suppression fires, and electromagnetic warfare assets provide commanders with numerous options for gaining and maintaining fire superiority. Additional fire support considerations include should the following:

- Use massed fires, especially time on target fires.
- Position fire support assets to support the reconnaissance effort.
- Plan suppressive and obscuration fires at the point of penetration.
- Plan fires on enemy positions supporting and overwatching the objective.
- Plan suppressive and obscuration fires to support breaching operations.
- Plan fires in support of the approach to the objective.
- Plan preparation fires on the objective to suppress, neutralize, or destroy critical enemy forces.
- Plan fires beyond the objective to support an attack or defense, or to isolate the objective to prevent the egress or ingress of threat forces.
- Use indirect fires and CAS to delay or neutralize repositioning enemy forces and reserves.
- Plan locations of critical friendly zones to protect critical actions such as SBF positions, breaching efforts, and mortar assets.
- Use REDs to determine triggers to initiate, shift, and cease loading of rounds.
- Use echelon fires to maintain continuous suppression of enemy forces throughout the movement to and actions on the objective.
- Commanders develop appropriate technical and tactical triggers to ensure timely delivery of fires.

2-186. The considerations the commander needs to focus on are understanding planned targets, triggers, responsibilities with regards to those targets, the observer plan, and the company teams own FSO's positioning.

PREPARING THE ATTACK

2-187. The company utilizes the time available before the attack to conduct reconnaissance and rehearsals while concealing attack preparations from the enemy and making refinements to the plan (see paragraphs 2-68 through 2-82). The commander uses this preparation time to conduct confirmation briefs and backbriefs with subordinate PLs to ensure they understand their task and purpose, and plan and execute within the commander's intent. Usually during the preparation phase, reconnaissance forces conduct information collection to answer the commander's critical information requirements (CCIRs) and to confirm or deny the situation template. This allows the commander time to incorporate any changes to the original COA before executing it. Additional preparation activities, although not inclusive, include sustainment preparations, finalizing the task organization, and performing pre-operations checks and inspections.

2-188. The company usually conducts rehearsals, but the type and technique may vary based on time available and the security that is required. In addition to participating in the combined arms rehearsal when part of a CAB attack, the company internally conducts rehearsals to further emphasize (at the company level) enemy positioning and repositioning, employment of fires, and commitment of reserves. To preserve time, general rehearsals at crew, squad, and platoon (for example, platoon battle drills) should begin immediately upon receipt of a WARNORD. As with all rehearsals, the primary focus of the rehearsal is actions on the objective. Each subordinate leader addresses the conduct of the mission as the rehearsal progresses. The rehearsal places special emphasis on elements of the plan that require two or more units to coordinate in terms of sequencing, fires, maneuver (with associated triggers), or to conduct external coordination. All subordinate leaders must accurately understand how long it takes to complete assigned tasks and how much space is required by their force. Direct and indirect fire plans are covered in detail, to include the massing, distribution, shifting, and control of fires. The commander ensures subordinate plans are coordinated and consistent with the commander's intent. Additional areas to rehearse include—

- Plans to execute follow-on missions or exploit success.
- Likely times and locations where a reserve is needed and its commitment criteria.
- Execution of the fire support plan, to include shifting of fires, employment of combat air support and Army attack aviation, adjusting of fire support coordination measures, and positioning of observers.
- Breaching operations.
- Passage of lines.
- Contingency plans for actions against enemy counterattacks, repositioning, commitment of reserves, or use of CBRN capabilities.
- Consolidation and reorganization.
- Execution of branches or sequels.
- Execution of the sustainment plan.
- CASEVAC, location, and movement.
- Activities of echeloned trains, support area movement and activities, and resupply.
- Integration of key enablers.

EXECUTING THE ATTACK

2-189. A series of advances and assaults by attacking units until they secure the final objective characterizes the attack. Commanders at all levels use their initiative to shift their main effort rapidly between units to take advantage of opportunities and momentum that ensure the enemy's rapid destruction. Attacking units move as quickly as possible following reconnaissance elements or successful probes through gaps in the enemy's defenses. They shift their strength to reinforce success and carry the operation deep into the enemy's rear.

2-190. The commander does not delay the attack to preserve the alignment of subordinate units or to adhere closely to the preconceived plan of attack. The commander avoids becoming so committed to the initial plan that opportunities are neglected. The commander is mentally prepared to abandon failed attacks and to exploit any unanticipated successes or enemy errors by designating another unit to conduct the main effort in response to the changing situation. (See FM 3-90 for more information.)

2-191.   Gaining and maintaining contact with the enemy when they are determined to break that contact is vital to the success of offensive operations. A defending enemy establishes a security area around their forces to make early contact with the attacking forces to determine their capabilities, intent, chosen COA, and to delay their approach. The enemy commander wants to use this security area to strip away friendly reconnaissance forces and hide their dispositions, capabilities, and intent. The enemy commander's goal is to compel the attacking force to conduct an MTC against their forces to determine the exact location of the attacking forces.

2-192.   The company team gains and maintains contact through reconnaissance forward with sensors detecting the enemy and maneuvering to confirm or deny their presence. Information gained from reconnaissance is quickly shared through command and control systems laterally and vertically throughout the CAB to allow its company teams to maneuver and destroy the threat.

2-193.   Disrupting one or more parts of the enemy weakens their entire force and allows the friendly commander to attack the remaining enemy force in an asymmetrical manner. The commander integrates direct and indirect fires, terrain, and obstacles to upset an enemy's formation or tempo, interrupt the enemy's timetable, or cause enemy forces to commit prematurely or attack in a piecemeal fashion. The assessment and decisions regarding what to disrupt, when to disrupt, and to what end are critical.

2-194.   The unit attempting to disrupt must attack the defending enemy force with enough combat power to achieve the desired results with one mass attack or sustain the attack until it achieves the desired results. It may involve attacking the enemy force while it is still in its AAs or in an approach march before it can deploy into a movement formation.

2-195.   Once any form of contact is made with the enemy, the commander conducts shaping operations that strike at the enemy. The element of surprise disrupts the enemy's combined arms team and ability to plan and control their forces. Once this disruption process begins, it continues throughout the attack.

SET CONDITIONS

2-196.   The company commander employs fires to weaken the enemy's position and sets the conditions for success before closing within direct fire range of the enemy. Initially, preparation fire focuses on the destruction of key enemy forces that can most affect the scheme of maneuver. For example, during an attack to penetrate an enemy defense, the initial focus of preparation fire is to destroy the enemy positions at the selected point of penetration. Preparation fire may also—

- Suppress or neutralize enemy reserves. Emplace artillery delivered situational obstacles to block enemy reserve routes into the objective.
- Deceive the enemy as to the company's actual intentions.
- Destroy enemy security and disruption forces.
- Obscure friendly movements and deployment.
- Destroy or neutralize the enemy's local command and control system.

2-197.   The synchronization between indirect fires and maneuvering forces is critical. As maneuver forces approach the enemy defense, the commander uses triggers to shift fires and obscuration to maintain continuous suppression and obscuration of the enemy. Proper timing, adjustment of fires, and detailed triggers dictated by REDs enable a relatively secure closure by the maneuver force on the enemy's positions. The commander must monitor the success of the preparation fire to determine whether adequate conditions exist for commitment of the force. The commander may need to adjust the tempo of the company's approach to the objective based on the battle damage assessment. Before the assault, the company commander destroys the enemy or makes it ineffective through the employment of direct and indirect fires. The commander must understand what conditions to set in terms of maneuver element positioning and understand what effect on the enemy is sufficient to constitute "conditions are set." The commander must not be in a rush to move before setting those conditions.

2-198.   The attacking commander uses fires to fix enemy forces broadly on and in the vicinity of the objective to prevent enemy forces from reinforcing the objective. The commander limits the options available to the opponent. Fixing an enemy into a given position or a COA and controlling their movements limits their options and reduce risk to the mission within the AO.

2-199.   Fixing the enemy is done with the minimum amount of force. The commander allocates the bulk of the combat power to the force conducting the main effort, so fixing is, by necessity, shaping operations that illustrate economy of force as a principle of war. Therefore, the commander carefully considers which enemy elements to fix and targets only those that can significantly affect the outcome of the fight.

2-200.   One method of isolating the objective is to conduct a shaping operation using lethal and nonlethal effects. Lethal effects may range from sniper fire to a joint fire plan designed to destroy a selected portion of an enemy force. Nonlethal effects, such as deception (see FM 3-90 for more information), smoke, or illumination from the CAB can fix the enemy so they cannot respond to the decisive action.

2-201.   Obstacles are typically planned at the brigade level. Scatterable mine systems are vital components in supporting an envelopment (see ATP 3-34.22). Scatterable minefields can seal objectives from possible enemy reinforcement or counterattacks and block or disrupt enemy actions to the flanks.

2-202.   The commander maneuvers the forces to gain positional advantage to seize, retain, and exploit the initiative. The commander avoids the enemy's defensive strength and employs tactics that defeat the enemy by attacking through a point of relative weakness, such as a flank or the rear. The key to success is to strike hard and fast, overwhelm a portion of the enemy force, then quickly transition to the next objective or phase, thus maintaining the momentum of the attack without reducing the pressure. The commander considers the following to conduct maneuvers:

- Movement from AA to LD.
- Movement from the LD to the PLD.
- Actions at the PLD, assault position, or final coordination line.
- Breaching.
- Actions on the objective.
- Follow through.

Movement from the Assembly Area to Line of Departure

2-203.   The company team's movement from the AA to the LD is a deliberately planned element of the operation and may be the only portion of the operation that leaders are able to conduct reconnaissance on prior to the mission. Movement from dispersed positions in the AA, staging in march formations in the proper order of march, initiating movement, and crossing the route's start point at march speed and in march interval (often in limited visibility) requires substantial time and must reflect in the commander's planning timeline. Continued movement along a route may entail conducting a forward passage of lines through a friendly unit, for which additional time and coordination must be made. Once passage through friendly forward lines is complete, the unit next crosses the designated battle handover line (BHL) at which time the attacking commander assumes responsibility for direct and indirect fires to the unit's front.

Movement from Line of Departure to Probable Line of Deployment

2-204.   The company team usually transitions from movement to maneuver prior to crossing the LD arrayed in an appropriate movement formation. It moves as aggressively and quickly as terrain and the enemy situation allow. It uses appropriate movement techniques assisted by the fires of supporting units. Fire and movement are closely integrated and coordinated. Effective suppressive fires facilitate friendly movement, which facilitates more effective fires. Whenever possible, the attacking unit uses avenues of approach that avoid strong enemy defensive positions, takes advantage of available cover and concealment, and places the unit on the flanks and rear of the defending enemy. Where cover and concealment are not available, the unit uses obscurants to conceal its movement. During this phase of movement, the commander is judicious in where to use dismounted Infantry to clear the way prior to mounted movement as excessive use, too early, will exhaust the Infantry and delay movement.

Actions at the Probable Line of Deployment, Assault Position, or Final Coordination Line

2-205. The attacking unit maintains the pace of its advance as it approaches its PLD. The attacking unit splits into one or more assault and support forces once it reaches the PLD if not previously completed. At the PLD, the Infantry Soldiers dismount from their combat vehicles if required. All forces supporting the assault force should be set in their SFB positions before the assault force crosses the PLD. The commander synchronizes the occupation of these SBF positions with the maneuver of the supported attacking unit to limit the vulnerability of the forces occupying these positions. The commander uses unit tactical SOPs, battle drills, prearranged signals, EAs, and TRPs to control direct fires from these supporting positions. A commander normally designates restricted fire lines between converging forces.

2-206. The PLD can be collocated with the assault position. The commander ensures that the final preparations of the breach force in an assault position do not delay its maneuver to the point of breach (POB) as soon as the conditions are set. The final coordination line is a phase line close to the enemy position used to coordinate the lifting or shifting of supporting fires with the final deployment of maneuver elements. Final adjustments to supporting fires necessary to reflect the actual versus the planned tactical situation take place before crossing this line. It should be easily recognizable on the ground.

2-207. The assault force spends as little time as possible in the assault position, simply waiting for conditions to be set (for example, effective suppression of the objective, or, if necessary, a breach to be complete). The assault force may have to halt in the assault position while fires are lifted and shifted. In this case, if the enemy anticipates the assault, the assault force deploys into covered positions, screens its positions with smoke, and waits for the order to assault. If the assault force remains in the assault position, support forces continue their suppressive fires on the objective.

2-208. The support force employs direct and indirect fires against the selected enemy positions to destroy, suppress, obscure, or neutralize enemy weapons and cover the assault force's movement. The assault force must immediately assault to and through the objective, or to gain ground that offers continued positional advantage to take full advantage of the effects of those fires. This COA normally results in the fewest casualties.

Breaching Operations

2-209. If a breach is needed, once the support force sets the conditions, the breach force reduces, proofs, and marks the required number of lanes through the enemy's tactical obstacles to support the maneuver of the assault force. The commander must clearly identify the conditions that allow the breach force to proceed to avoid confusion. From the PLD, the assault force maneuvers against or around the enemy to take advantage of the support force's efforts to suppress the targeted enemy positions. (See appendix C for a more detailed explanation on breaching operations.)

Action on the Objective

2-210. The commander plans DFCMs to focus, distribute, and shift fires within the objective and enable the company's scheme of maneuver. The effects of the overwhelming and simultaneous application of fire, movement, and shock action characterize the final assault. This violent assault defeats, destroys, or drives the enemy from the objective area.

2-211. The support element must not reduce its suppressive fires as the assault element closes on the objective. These fires fix and isolate enemy forces on the objective, enabling the assault element to sequentially clear through the objective. Direct and indirect fires also prevent the enemy from repositioning within the objective or reinforcing or counterattacking from outside the objective. The commander employs all fire support means to suppress or destroy the enemy and sustain the momentum of the attack. By carefully synchronizing the effects of fires and available CAS, the commander improves the likelihood of success. Indirect fires are planned in series or groups to support maneuver against enemy forces on or near the geographical objective. As the assault element advances through the objective, the commander shifts direct and indirect fires and obscurants within the objective and then from the objective to other targets.

Actions Beyond the Objective

2-212. Actions beyond the objective are taken to secure the objective and defend against an enemy counterattack. The company commander uses TLP to plan and prepare for this phase of the operation and ensures the team is ready to conduct the following actions that usually are part of consolidation:

- Eliminate enemy resistance on the objective.
- Establish security beyond the objective by securing areas that may be the source of enemy direct fires or enemy artillery observation.
- Establish additional security measures such as OPs and patrols.
- Prepare for and assist the passage of follow-on forces (if required).
- Continue to improve security by conducting other necessary defensive actions, including EA development, direct fire planning, and BP preparation.
- Adjust FPFs and register targets along likely mounted and dismounted avenues of approach.
- Protect the obstacle reduction effort.
- Secure detainees.
- Prepare for the enemy counterattack.
- Continue improvement of BPs, as needed.

VARIATIONS OF ATTACK

2-213. Variations of attacks are ambush, counterattack, raid, and spoiling attack. (See FM 3-90 for more information.) The commander's intent and the mission variables of METT-TC (I) determine which variations of attack(s) to employ.

2-214. The commander's intent and METT-TC (I) mission variables and factors determine the specific attack variation. As subordinate attack tasks, they share many of the planning, preparation, and execution considerations of the attack.

Ambush

2-215. An *ambush* is a variation of attack from concealed positions against a moving or temporarily halted enemy (FM 3-90). An ambush stops, denies, or destroys enemy forces by maximizing the element of surprise. Ambushes can employ direct fire systems as well as other destructive means (such as command-detonated mines, indirect fires, and supporting nonlethal action). They may include an assault to close with and destroy enemy forces. In an ambush, ground objectives do not have to be seized and held.

2-216. The two methods of ambush are point and area. In a point ambush, a unit deploys to attack a single kill zone. The *kill zone* is the location where fires are concentrated in an ambush (FM 3-90). In an area ambush, a unit deploys into two or more related point ambushes. Units smaller than a platoon do not normally conduct an area ambush.

2-217. A specific type of a point ambush is an antiarmor ambush. The antiarmor ambush is significantly different from a typical point ambush in that it typically involves only crew-served weapons and antiarmor systems and can be conducted at longer ranges. Antiarmor ambushes focus on moving or temporarily halted enemy armored vehicles.

2-218. A typical ambush is organized into three elements: assault, support, and security. They are defined as follows:

- Assault. This element fires into the kill zone. Its goal is to destroy the enemy force. When used, the assault force may attack into and clear the kill zone and may be assigned additional tasks. These include searching for items of intelligence value, capturing prisoners, and completing the destruction of enemy equipment to preclude its immediate reuse.
- Support. This element supports the assault element by firing into and around the kill zone, and it provides the ambush's primary killing power. The support element attempts to destroy most of the enemy combat power before the assault element moves into the objective or kill zone.

- Security. This element isolates the kill zone, provides early warning of the arrival of any enemy relief force, and provides security for the assault and support elements. It secures the objective rally point and blocks enemy avenues of approach into and out of the ambush site, which prevents the enemy from entering or leaving.

Counterattack

2-219. A *counterattack* is a variation of attack by a defending force against an attacking enemy force (FM 3-90). The commander directs a counterattack normally conducted from a defensive posture to defeat or destroy enemy forces and exploit an enemy weakness (such as an exposed flank or to regain control of terrain and facilities after an enemy success). A unit conducts a counterattack to seize the initiative from the enemy through offensive action. A counterattacking force maneuvers to isolate and destroy a designated enemy force. It can attack by fire into an EA to defeat or destroy an enemy force, restore the original position, or block an enemy penetration. Once launched, the counterattack normally becomes a main effort for the commander conducting the counterattack.

2-220. To be decisive, the counterattack must occur when the enemy is overextended, dispersed, and disorganized during their attack. All counterattacks should be rehearsed in the same conditions that they would be conducted. Careful consideration must be given to planning for the event or conditions that trigger the counterattack and recognizing those conditions as they emerge on the battlefield.

Raid

2-221. A *raid* is a variation of attack to temporarily seize an objective with a planned withdrawal (FM 3-90). Raids are usually small scale, involving battalion size or smaller forces, and surprise attacks requiring detailed intelligence (planners require precise, time-sensitive, all-source intelligence), planning, and preparation. At the company level, a raid is a surprise attack against a position or installation for a specific purpose other than seizing and holding the terrain. A raid is conducted to destroy a position or installation and destroy or capture enemy Soldiers or equipment, or free prisoners. A raid patrol retains terrain just long enough to accomplish the intent of the raid. The raid ends with a planned exfiltration off the objective and a return to the main body.

2-222. The fundamentals of the raid include surprise and speed, coordinated fires, violence of action, and a planned exfiltration. Surprise and speed are accomplished through infiltration and moving to the objective undetected. Coordinated fires seal off the objective with well-synchronized direct and indirect fires. Violence of action overwhelms the enemy with fire and maneuver. The planned exfiltration allows friendly forces to move off the objective in a well-organized manner while maintaining security.

Spoiling Attack

2-223. A *spoiling attack* is a variation of an attack employed against an enemy preparing for an attack (FM 3-90). The objective of a spoiling attack is to disrupt the enemy's offensive capabilities and timelines while destroying targeted enemy personnel and equipment, not to seize terrain and other physical objectives. There are two conditions that must be met to conduct a successful and survivable spoiling attack. If a spoiling attack does not meet both conditions, it will likely fail, with grave consequences to the defense:

- The spoiling attack's objective must be obtainable before the enemy force can respond to the attack in a synchronized and coordinated manner.
- Commanders must prevent the over extension of forces conducting their spoiling attacks.

2-224. A commander conducts a spoiling attack whenever possible during the conduct of friendly defensive operations to strike an enemy force while it is in AAs or attack positions preparing for its own offensive operation or is stopped temporarily. The commander synchronizes the conduct of the spoiling attack with other defensive actions. A spoiling attack usually employs armored forces, attack helicopter, or fire support elements to attack enemy assembly positions in front of the friendly commander's main line of resistance or BPs. A commander conducts a spoiling attack to—

- Disrupt the enemy's offensive preparations.
- Destroy key assets that the enemy requires to attack, such as fire support systems, fuel and ammunition stocks, and bridging equipment.

- Gain additional time for the defending force to prepare its positions.
- Reduce the enemy's current advantage in the correlation of forces.

SECTION IV – EXPLOITATION AND PURSUIT

2-225. During the offense, combined arms maneuver involves taking the fight to the enemy and never allowing enemy forces to recover from the initial shock of the attack. *Exploitation*, which is a type of offensive operation that usually follows a successful attack to disorganize the enemy in-depth (FM 3-90) and *pursuit*, which is a type of offensive operation designed to catch or cut off a disorganized hostile force attempting to escape, with the aim of destroying it (FM 3-90). Commanders maintain momentum by anticipating and transitioning rapidly as the situation develops. Retaining the initiative pressures enemy commanders into abandoning their preferred COAs, accepting too much risk, or making costly mistakes. As these conditions occur, friendly forces seize opportunities and create new avenues for exploitation or pursuit to break the enemy's will through relentless and continuous pressure.

EXPLOITATION

2-226. Exploitation is the primary means of translating tactical success into operational advantage. Exploitation can occur regardless of the operational theme or point along the range of operations in which the exploitation occurs. Small tactical units also conduct exploitations but typically as part of large formations.

2-227. During the conduct of major operations, exploitation often follows a successful attack to take advantage of a weakened or collapsed enemy. The purpose of exploitation can vary, but it generally focuses on capitalizing on a temporary advantage or preventing the enemy from establishing an organized defense or conducting an orderly withdrawal. To accomplish this, the BCT or higher-level unit attacks rapidly over a broad front to prevent the enemy from establishing a defense, organizing an effective rear guard, withdrawing, or regaining balance. The CAB, as part of the ABCT, secures objectives, severs escape routes, and destroys enemy forces. Failure to exploit success aggressively gives the enemy time to reconstitute an effective defense or regain the initiative by a counterattack.

2-228. The conditions for exploitation develop quickly. Often the lead unit in contact identifies the collapse of the enemy's resistance. The higher-level commander must receive accurate assessments and reports of the enemy situation to capitalize on the opportunity for exploitation. Typical indications of good conditions for exploitation include—

- A significant increase in enemy prisoners of war.
- An increase in abandoned enemy equipment and material.
- The overrunning of enemy artillery, command and control facilities, and logistics sites.
- A significant decrease in enemy resistance or in organized fires and maneuver.
- A mixture of support and combat vehicles in formations and columns.
- An increase in enemy movement rearward, especially of reserves and fire support units.

2-229. Should the CAB conduct exploitation as part of a larger operation, it might receive the mission to seize a terrain-oriented objective. In this case, the CAB avoids decisive engagement and moves to the objective as quickly as possible. If assigned a force-oriented objective, the CAB seeks and destroys enemy forces anywhere within its AO. The exploitation ends when the enemy reestablishes its defense, all organized enemy resistance breaks down, or the friendly force culminates logistically or physically.

PURSUIT

2-230. A pursuit differs from the exploitation in that it always focuses on completing the destruction of fleeing enemy forces by destroying their ability and will to resist. Unlike an exploitation, which may focus on seizing key or decisive terrain instead of the enemy force, pursuit operations begin when an enemy force attempts to conduct retrograde operations. At that point, it becomes most vulnerable to the loss of internal cohesion and complete destruction. An aggressively executed pursuit leaves the enemy trapped, unprepared, and unable to defend, faced with the options of surrendering or complete destruction.

2-231. Pursuits include the rapid shifting of units, continuous day and night movements, hasty attacks, containment of bypassed enemy forces, large numbers of prisoners, and a willingness to forego some synchronization to maintain contact with and pressure on a fleeing enemy. Pursuits require swift maneuver and attacks by forces to strike the enemy's most vulnerable areas. A successful pursuit requires flexible forces, initiative by commanders at all echelons, and a high operations tempo during execution.

2-232. Two options exist when conducting a pursuit. Both pursuit options involve assigning a subordinate the mission of maintaining direct pressure on the rearward moving enemy force. The first option is a frontal pursuit that employs only direct pressure. The second is a combination that uses one subordinate element to maintain direct pressure and one or more other subordinate elements to encircle the retrograding enemy. The combination pursuit is more effective, generally. The subordinate applying direct pressure or the subordinate conducting the encirclement can conduct the operation in a combination pursuit.

2-233. During the pursuit, the commander exerts unrelenting pressure to keep the enemy force from reorganizing and preparing its defenses. The company team or CAB may be a part of a division or ABCT pursuit, either functioning as the direct pressure or encircling force. Although the CAB may pursue a physical objective, the mission is the destruction of the enemy's main force.

SECTION V – TRANSITIONS

2-234. A commander halts an offensive operation only when it results in complete victory and the end of hostilities, when it reaches a culminating point, or when the commander receives a change in mission from a higher commander. This change in mission results in a follow-on operation.

CONSOLIDATION

2-235. Consolidation is the process of organizing and strengthening in newly captured position so that it can be used against the enemy. Consolidation may vary from a rapid repositioning of forces and security elements on the objective to a reorganization of the attacking force and organization and detailed improvement of the position for defense (see paragraph 2-208).

2-236. Commanders continuously assess their combat power and determine if they are achieving their objectives. At times, they may need to consolidate after an attack. The company team maintains contact with those enemy forces that have abandoned their positions or objectives immediately after the friendly assaults conclude. The commander takes those actions necessary to regain contact with enemy forces if the attacking forces succeed in destroying all enemy forces or securing the objectives. The company team establishes security as soon as it occupies the objectives.

REORGANIZATION

2-237. *Reorganization* includes all measures taken by the commander to maintain unit combat effectiveness or return it to a specified level of combat capability (ATP 3-94.4). As with consolidation, the company commander plans and prepares for reorganization while conducting TLP. The commander ensures that the company team takes the following actions:

- Provides essential medical treatment and evacuates casualties as needed.
- Ensures that new leaders are designated as necessary.
- Treats and evacuates wounded detainees and processes the remainder of detainees.
- Cross-levels personnel and adjusts task organization as required to support the next phase or mission.
- Conducts resupply operations, including rearming and refueling.
- Redistributes ammunition.
- Conducts required maintenance.

TRANSITION TO STABILITY OPERATIONS

2-238. Upon order from higher HQ, the commander orders a transition to stability operations. These operations establish a safe, secure environment that facilitates reconciliation between local or regional threats. Stability operations aim to establish conditions that support the transition to legitimate host nation (HN) governance, a functioning civil society, and a viable market economy.

2-239. The company commander ensures that contingencies are planned for to transition quickly from offensive to stability operations and vice versa. For example, it may be wise for commanders to plan a defensive contingency with an on-order offensive mission for stability operations that could deteriorate.

2-240. Subordinate leaders need to be fully trained to recognize activities that would initiate this transition. Actions in one unit's AO can affect a change in whatever type task an adjacent unit is conducting. (For example, an offensive operation may cause noncombatants to be displaced to another section of the city, creating a need to support operation for the unit in that AO.)

CONTINUING OPERATIONS

2-241. For all offensive operations, the company team should plan to exploit success. However, at the conclusion of an offensive operation, the commander may be forced to defend. For short defensive operations, units make use of existing terrain to enhance their survivability. If a longer defense is envisioned, engineer assets immediately should refocus their efforts on providing survivability support (BPs and similar activities). Engineer assets should do this even as they sustain mobility and integrate countermobility into the planned defense. The company commander considers the higher commander's concept of operations, friendly capabilities, and the enemy situation when making the decision to defend or continue offensive operations.

Chapter 3
Defense

The company team conducts defensive operations to defeat an enemy attack, gain time, economize forces, and develop conditions favorable for offensive or stability operations. The defending commander's ability to select ground advantageous for defending force and disadvantageous for attacking forces is the defense's inherent strengths. The company team may occupy positions before the attack and use the available time to prepare the defenses and integrate combat multipliers. Defending forces seize opportunities afforded by lulls in the action to improve their positions and repair damage. The company team does not wait for an attack and aggressively seeks ways of attriting and weakening attacking enemy forces before close combat. This chapter discusses the basics of the defense, common defensive planning considerations, defensive techniques, EA development, and transitions.

SECTION I – BASICS OF THE DEFENSE

3-1.   Military forces conduct defensive operations only until they gain sufficient strength to attack. Though the outcome of decisive combat derives from offensive actions, commanders often find that it is necessary, even advisable, to defend. Once they make this choice, commanders must set the conditions for the defense in a way that allows friendly forces to withstand and hold the enemy while they prepare to seize the initiative and return to the offense.

CHARACTERISTICS OF THE DEFENSE

3-2.   Successful defenses employ the characteristics of disruption, flexibility, maneuver, mass and concentration, operations in-depth, preparation, and security. Defenders subvert an attacker's tempo, formations, and synchronization by countering their initiative and preventing them from massing overwhelming combat power. (See ADP 3-90 for more information.)

DISRUPTION

3-3.   The company team disrupts attackers' tempo and synchronization with actions designed to prevent the attackers from massing combat power. Disruptive actions attempt to unhinge the enemy's preparations and their attacks. Methods include deceiving or destroying enemy reconnaissance forces, breaking up combat formations, separating echelons, and impeding an enemy force's ability to synchronize its combined arms. Disruption attacks the enemy's will to fight and their means of effective command and control.

FLEXIBILITY

3-4.   Defensive operations require flexible plans. Planning focuses on preparation in-depth, use of reserves, and the ability to shift the main effort. Commanders add flexibility by designating supplementary positions, designing counterattack plans, and preparing to counterattack.

MANEUVER

3-5.   Maneuver allows the company team to achieve and exploit a position over an attacking force. Commanders can maneuver to take full advantage of the terrain within the AO.

MASS AND CONCENTRATION

3-6. The commander seeks to mass the effects of overwhelming combat power and shifts it to support the main effort. To obtain an advantage at decisive points, the commander economizes and accepts risk in some areas; retains and, when necessary, reconstitutes a reserve; and maneuvers to gain local superiority at the point of decision. The commander accepts risk in some areas to mass effects elsewhere. Obstacles, security forces, and fires can assist in reducing risk.

OPERATIONS IN-DEPTH

3-7. Simultaneous application of combat power throughout the AO improves the chances for success while minimizing friendly casualties. Quick, violent, and simultaneous action throughout the depth of the company team's AO can hurt, confuse, and even paralyze an enemy force when they are most exposed and vulnerable. Such actions weaken the enemy's will and do not allow any early successes to build the confidence. Operations in-depth prevent the enemy from gaining momentum in the attack. Synchronization of decisive, shaping, and sustaining operations facilitate mission success.

PREPARATION

3-8. Preparation, an inherent strength of the defense, provides the defender time to study the ground and select positions that allow the massing of fires on likely approaches. The company team uses available time to combine natural and man-made obstacles to canalize attacking forces into EAs, coordinate and rehearse actions on the ground, gaining intimate familiarity with the terrain, place security, intelligence, and reconnaissance forces throughout the AO, and continue defensive preparations in-depth, even as the close engagement begins.

3-9. During the preparation of the defense, time management is a critical task. There are three things the commander can do to make effective use of the time available:

- Occupy the defense as early as possible.
- Follow a methodical planning priority of work during concept development.
- Integrate the preparation priority of work in the time schedule.

3-10. The commander must define what tasks subordinate units must accomplish before they can occupy the defense. At the minimum, the unit should establish security and communications, reconnoiter the defensive sector or BP, and assign sectors of fire. The commander determines when units must occupy the defense to have enough time to complete the preparation priority of work before the defend time.

SECURITY

3-11. Security operations prevent enemy intelligence, surveillance, and reconnaissance assets from determining the company team locations, strengths, and weaknesses. These measures also provide early warning and continuously disrupt enemy attacks. Protection efforts preserve combat power. These measures all contribute to the defender's security. They inhibit or defeat enemy reconnaissance operations.

DEFENSIVE OPERATIONS

3-12. Defensive operations are used to defeat an enemy, gain time, economize forces, and develop conditions favorable for offensive operations (see ADP 3-0). There are three defensive operations—

- Area defense, which focuses on terrain. (See section III.)
- Mobile defense, which focuses on the movement of enemy forces.
- Retrograde, which focuses on the movement of friendly forces.

3-13. Each contains elements of the others, and usually contains both static and dynamic aspects. At the same time, each operation must be dealt with differently when planning and executing the defense. Company teams serve as the primary maneuver elements, or terrain controlling units, for the CAB in all defensive operations. They can defend AO or positions, or they can serve as security forces or reserves as part of the CAB's coordinated defense.

3-14. As part of defensive operations, the company team can defend, delay, withdraw, counterattack, and perform security tasks. The company team usually defends as part of the CAB's defense in the MBA.

MOBILE DEFENSE

3-15. *Mobile defense* is a type of defensive operation that concentrates on the destruction or defeat of the enemy through a decisive attack by a striking force (ADP 3-90). Mobile defense focuses on destroying the attacking force by allowing the enemy to advance into a position that exposes the enemy to counterattack and envelopment. The commander uses the fixing force to hold attacking enemy forces in position, help channel attacking enemy forces into ambush areas, and retain areas from which to launch the striking force. A mobile defense requires an AO of considerable depth. The commander must be able to shape the battlefield, causing an enemy force to overextend its lines of communication, expose its flanks, and dissipate its combat power. Likewise, the commander must be able to move friendly forces around and behind the enemy force targeted to be cut off and destroyed. Divisions and larger formations normally execute mobile defenses. However, the company team generally conducts an area defense or a delay as part of the fixing force as the commander shapes the enemy's penetration or it attacks as part of the striking force.

> *Note.* Units smaller than a division do not usually conduct a mobile defense because of their inability to fight multiple engagements throughout the width, depth, and height of their AO, while simultaneously resourcing the striking, fixing, and reserve forces.

3-16. The *striking force* is a dedicated counterattack force in a mobile defense constituted with the bulk of available combat power (ADP 3-90). A *fixing force* is a force designated to supplement the striking force by preventing the enemy from moving from a specific area for a specific time (ADP 3-90). The company team, as part of a larger organization, participates in a mobile defense as either part of the fixing force or part of the striking force, but not both. As part of the fixing force, the company team defends within its assigned AO, although the AO might be larger than usual.

3-17. As part of the striking force, the company team plans, rehearses, and executes offensive operations. The term "striking force" is used rather than the term "reserve" because reserve indicates an uncommitted force. The striking force is a committed force and has the resources to conduct a counterattack as part of the mobile defense. The striking force engages the enemy as they become exposed in their attempts to overcome the fixing force.

RETROGRADE

3-18. Company teams most often conduct retrogrades as part of a larger force but may conduct independent retrogrades as required. The CAB commander must approve the operation.

3-19. *Retrograde* is a type of defensive operation that involves organized movement away from the enemy (ADP 3-90). Such movements may be classified as delay, withdrawal, or retirement. It may be forced by the enemy or may be made voluntarily. In either case, the higher commander of the force executing the operation must approve the retrograde. A retrograde is conducted to improve a tactical situation or to prevent a worse situation from developing. Retrograde is a transitional operation; it is not considered in isolation.

3-20. The commander executes retrogrades to—
- Disengage from operations.
- Gain time without fighting a decisive engagement.
- Draw the enemy into an unfavorable situation or extend the enemy's line of communications.
- Preserve the force or avoid combat under undesirable conditions, such as continuing an operation that no longer promises success.
- Reposition forces to more favorable locations or conform to movements of other friendly troops.
- Position the force for use elsewhere in other missions.
- Simplify sustainment support of the force by shortening lines of communications.
- Position the force where it can safely conduct reconstitution.

- Adjust the defensive scheme, such as secure more favorable terrain.
- Deceive the enemy.

3-21. A *delay* is when a force under pressure trades space for time by slowing down the enemy's momentum and inflicting maximum damage on the enemy without becoming decisively engaged (ADP 3-90). Delays gain time to—

- Allow other friendly forces to establish a defense.
- Cover a withdrawing force.
- Protect a friendly force's flank.
- Allow other forces to counterattack.

3-22. *Withdraw* is to disengage from an enemy force and move in a direction away from the enemy (ADP 3-90). The commander's intent and mission variables determine which type of withdrawal the units use. Withdrawals may be assisted or unassisted and they may or may not take place under enemy pressure.

3-23. A *retirement* is when a force out of contact moves away from the enemy (ADP 3-90). A retiring unit organizes for combat but does not anticipate interference by enemy ground forces. Typically, another unit's security force covers the movement of one formation as the unit conducts a retirement. However, mobile enemy forces, unconventional forces, air strikes, air assaults, or long-range fires may attempt to interdict the retiring unit. The commander must plan for enemy actions and organize the unit to fight in self-defense. The commander usually conducts retirement operations to reposition forces for future operations or to accommodate the current concept of the operation. Units conduct retirements as tactical road marches where security and speed are the most important considerations of the warfighting functions.

PLANNING CONSIDERATIONS

3-24. Planning a defensive operation is a complex effort requiring detailed planning and extensive coordination. In the defense, synchronizing the effects of the company team's combat and supporting systems enable a commander to apply overwhelming combat power against selected advancing enemy forces. As an operation evolves, the commander knows there will probably be a need to shift decisive and shaping operations to press the fight and keep the enemy off balance.

3-25. The common defensive planning considerations apply to the conduct of all defensive operations. In the defense, synchronizing the effects of the warfighting functions with information and leadership allows commanders to apply overwhelming combat power against enemy forces to desynchronize an enemy commander's plan and destroy enemy combined arms teams. Defensive synchronization normally results from detailed planning and preparation. The defense is a mix of static and dynamic actions. As a defensive operation evolves, commanders shift decisive and shaping operations or main and supporting efforts to keep the enemy off balance. Synchronized prior planning and preparation bolster their combat power, increasing the effectiveness of the defense. The defensive plan addresses what happens when it succeeds and gains the opportunity to transition from defense to offense.

COMMAND AND CONTROL

3-26. A defensive mission generally imposes few restrictions on the commander. It allows freedom of maneuver within assigned boundaries but requires the commander to prevent enemy penetration of the rear boundary. The commander must ensure that subordinate unit defensive plans are compatible and that control measures, such as contact points and phase lines, are sufficient for flank coordination when assigning AO.

3-27. The commander's vision of anticipated enemy actions must be nested with the CAB's IPB. From that, the company commander refines the IPB to focus on the details of the operation in the company team's AO. The CAB commander usually defines where and how the CAB will defeat or destroy the enemy. The company commander envisions how the company team will execute its portion of the CAB fight.

MOVEMENT AND MANEUVER

3-28. Maneuver considerations employ direct fire weapons on the battlefield. In the defense, effective weapons positioning is critical to the company's success. Effective weapons positioning enables the company team to mass fires at critical points in the EA and shift fires as necessary. The company commander must exploit the strengths of the unit's weapons systems while minimizing the company's exposure to enemy observation and fires.

Depth and Dispersion

3-29. Dispersing positions laterally and in-depth helps to protect the force from enemy observation and fires. Company team and platoon positions are established in-depth, allowing sufficient maneuver space within each position to establish in-depth placement of vehicle weapon systems and dismounted Infantry elements. (See figure 3-1.)

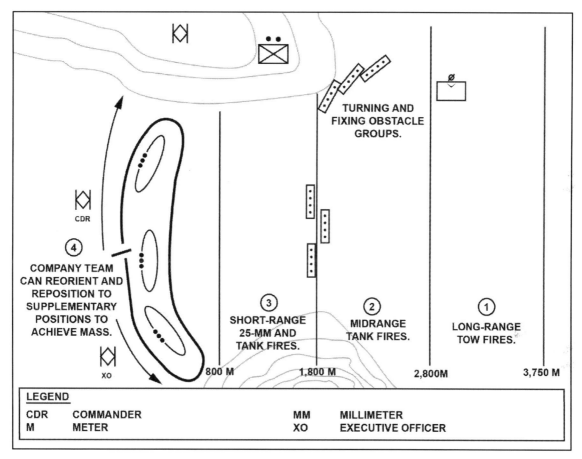

Figure 3-1. Company team achieving depth

3-30. Vehicle and Infantry fighting positions should be positioned to allow the massing of fires at critical points on the battlefield. Although METT-TC (I) factors ultimately determine the placement of weapon systems and unit positions, the following general guidelines apply:

- Tanks are best employed where they can engage targets with the main gun and with the coaxial machine gun.
- Tube launched, optically tracked, wire guided missiles are best employed at a range of 2,500 to 3,700 meters where targets can be tracked for at least 12 seconds.
- IFVs are best employed from flank positions and in positions from which they can destroy lightly armored vehicles and infantry or fix or severely limit the movement of tanks.
- Infantry squads should be positioned on reverse slopes or in restricted terrain where they cannot be engaged before they can take the enemy under fire.
- Infantry squads can supplement the antiarmor fires of the tanks and IFVs with Javelin missiles.

● Infantry squads can retain or deny key terrain if employed in strong points or well-covered positions and can protect obstacles or flank positions that are tied into severely restricted terrain.

Flank Positions

3-31. Flank positions enable a defending force to bring fires to bear on an attacking force from the side. An effective flank position provides the defender with a larger and more vulnerable target while leaving the attacker unsure of the location of the defense.

3-32. Major considerations for successful employment of a flank position are the defender's ability to secure the flank and the ability to achieve surprise by remaining undetected. Effective fire control and fratricide avoidance measures are critical considerations in the employment of flank positions. (See figure 3-2.)

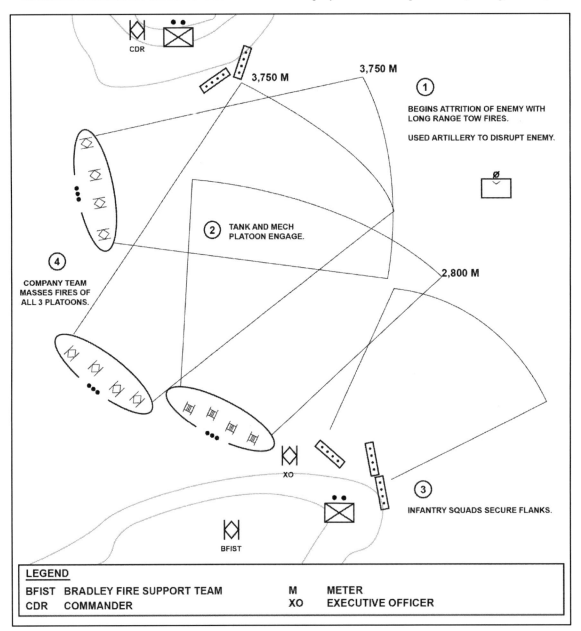

Figure 3-2. Company team depth and flank positions

Reserve

3-33. The commander must designate and position the reserve in a location where it can effectively react to several contingency plans. The commander must consider terrain, trafficability of roads, potential EAs, probable points of enemy penetrations, and commitment time. The CAB commander can have a single reserve under CAB control, or, if the terrain dictates, company teams can designate their own reserves. The reserve should be positioned in a covered and concealed position. Information concerning the reserve may be considered essential elements of friendly information and protected from enemy reconnaissance. The commander might choose to position the reserve forward initially to deceive the enemy or to move the reserve occasionally to prevent it from being targeted by enemy indirect fires.

INTELLIGENCE

3-34. The company commander never has all the information needed about the enemy. The commander receives and refines IPB products and integrates intelligence updates throughout the operation. To aid in the development of a flexible defensive plan, the IPB must present as many feasible enemy COAs as time permits. The essential areas of focus are—

- Analyze terrain and weather.
- Determine enemy force size and likely COAs with associated decision points.
- Determine enemy vulnerabilities and high-value targets.
- Impact of civilian population on the defensive operations.

3-35. The company commander analyzes the unit's role in the CAB fight and determines how to achieve success. The commander determines how and where to defeat the enemy based on available avenues of approach, terrain, and forces available. The CAB will define a defeat mechanism that includes single or multiple counterattacks to achieve success.

FIRES

3-36. For the fires plan to be effective in the defense, the company team plans and executes fires in a manner that achieves the intended task and purpose for each target. Fires serve a variety of purposes in the defense, including the following:

- Slow and disrupt enemy movement.
- Prevent the enemy from executing breaching operations.
- Destroy or delay enemy forces at obstacles using massed fires or pinpoint munitions.
- Disrupt enemy SBF elements.
- Defeat attacks along dismounted avenues of approach.
- Disrupt the enemy to enable friendly elements to disengage or conduct counterattacks.
- Obscure enemy observation friendly movement during disengagement and counterattacks.
- Provide smoke to separate enemy echelons or to silhouette enemy formations to facilitate direct fire engagement.
- Provide illumination as needed.
- Execute suppression of enemy air defense missions to support aviation operations.
- Provide FPFs.

3-37. In developing the fires plan, the company commander, along with FSO, evaluates fires systems available to provide support. Considerations when developing the plan include tactical capabilities, weapons ranges, and available munitions. These factors help the company commander and FSO determine the best method for achieving the task and purpose of each target in the fire plan. The company fire support personnel contribute significantly to the fight. Effective positioning is critical. The company commander and FSO must select positions that provide fire support personnel with unobstructed observation of the AO and ensure survivability.

3-38. Air and missile defense support to the company team may be limited. Units should expect to use their organic weapons systems for self-defense against enemy air threats.

SUSTAINMENT

3-39. In addition to sustainment functions required for all operations, the company commander's planning process includes pre-positioning of ammunition caches for platoons, positioning of company trains, and providing Class IV (construction materials)/V supply points.

3-40. The commander's mission analysis may reveal that the company's ammunition requirements during an upcoming operation will exceed its basic load. This requires the company to pre-position ammunition caches. The company usually positions ammunition caches at alternate or subsequent positions. The company may dig in and guard these caches to prevent their capture or destruction by the enemy.

3-41. The company train usually operates 500 to 1,000 meters or one terrain feature to the rear of the company to provide immediate recovery and medical support. The company trains conduct resupply and the evacuation of wounded and damaged equipment as required. The company trains are located in covered and concealed positions close enough to the company to provide responsive support, but out of enemy direct fire. The first sergeant or XO positions the trains and supervises sustainment operations. The company commander ensures all elements know the locations of the company CCP, the CAB combat and field trains, and the BAS. The company commander's analysis determines the most effective measures for every mission.

PROTECTION

3-42. Because the company defends to conserve combat power for future operations, therefore the commander must secure the force. The commander enables security, by employing reconnaissance forces and surveillance assets to identify enemy composition and disposition within the assigned AO.

3-43. Personnel and physical assets have inherent survivability, which can be enhanced through various means and methods. When existing terrain does not provide sufficient cover, the company can make physical improvements to ensure good fighting positions. Concealment may be improved using natural or artificial materials to camouflage fighting positions. Together, these are called *survivability operations*—those protection activities that alter the physical environment by providing or improving cover, camouflage, and concealment (ATP 3-37.34).

3-44. Survivability construction includes BPs, protective positions, and hardening. These are prepared to protect vehicles, personnel, and weapons systems. In coordination with the BCT, engineers play an essential role in countermobility, survivability, and EA development. Positions can be constructed and reinforced with overhead cover to increase the survivability of dismounts and crew-served weapons against shrapnel from airbursts. Vehicle positions can be constructed with both hull- and turret-defilade observation positions. The company team may use digging assets for ammunition caches at alternate, supplementary, or subsequent positions.

3-45. All leaders must understand the survivability plan and priorities. Typically, the engineer PL creates an information card, which enables the commander to track the survivability effort. One person in the company, usually the company XO or first sergeant, is designated to enforce the plan and priorities and ensures that the completion status is accurately reported and tracked.

3-46. Within the area defense, protective obstacles employed to protect people, equipment, supplies, and facilities against threats are key enablers to survivability operations. Protective obstacles provide local, close-in protection to prevent the enemy from delivering a surprise assault from areas close to defending positions. Protective obstacles protect the emplaced position by warning, mitigating, and preventing hostile actions and effects. The commander uses protective obstacle effects (warning, mitigation, and prevention) to convey intent and facilitate protective obstacle planning and design. Protective obstacles employed in support of the area defense must be capable of being rapidly emplaced and recovered or destroyed. FPFs are integrated within the protective obstacle plan to defeat the final assault of the enemy.

3-47. OPSEC in the defense relies on leaders managing information mediums of the Soldiers to preserve essential secrecy. The security plan should include means of redundant checks and indicators Soldiers should be informed to recognize and alert the formation of possible compromise. Procedures in case of compromise should be rehearsed and tested.

COMMON DEFENSIVE CONTROL MEASURES

3-48. The commander controls the defense by using control measures to provide the flexibility needed to respond to changes in the situation and allow the defending commander to concentrate combat power rapidly at the decisive point. Defensive control measures within a commander's AO include designating the security area, the BHL, the MBA with its associated forward edge of the battle area (FEBA), and echelon support.

3-49. The commander can use BPs and additional direct-fire support control measures to further synchronize the employment of combat power. The commander designates disengagement lines to trigger the displacement of subordinate forces.

BATTLE POSITIONS

3-50. A *battle position* is a defensive location oriented on a likely enemy avenue of approach (ADP 3-90). Units as large as CABs and as small as squads or sections use BPs. They may occupy the topographical crest of a hill, a forward slope, a reverse slope, or a combination of these areas. The commander selects positions based on terrain, enemy capabilities, and friendly capabilities (see figure 3-3 on page 3-10). A commander can assign all or some subordinates BPs within the AO.

3-51. There are five types of BPs—

- *Primary position* is the position that covers the enemy's most likely avenue of approach into the assigned area (FM 3-90).
- *Alternate position* is a is a defensive position that the commander assigns to a unit or weapon system for occupation when the primary position becomes untenable or unsuitable for carrying out the assigned task (FM 3-90). It allows the defender to carry out the original task. The following considerations apply for an alternate BP which:
  - Covers the same avenue of approach or sector of fire as the primary BP.
  - Is located slightly to the front, flank, or rear of the primary BP.
  - May be positioned forward of the primary BP during limited-visibility operations.
  - Is employed to supplement or support positions with weapons of limited range, such as dismounted positions.
- *Supplementary position* is a defensive position located within a unit's assigned area that provides the best sectors of fire and defensive terrain along an avenue of approach that is not the primary avenue where the enemy is expected to attack (FM 3-90). For example, an avenue of approach into a company's AO from one of its flanks could require the company to direct its platoons to establish supplementary positions to allow the platoons to engage enemy forces traveling along that avenue. The PL formally assigns supplementary positions when the platoon must cover more than one avenue of approach.
- *Subsequent position* is a position that a unit expects to move to during the course of battle (ADP 3-90). A defending unit may have a series of subsequent positions. Subsequent positions can have associated primary, alternate, and supplementary positions.
- *Strong point* is a heavily fortified battle position tied to a natural or reinforcing obstacle to create an anchor for the defense or to deny the enemy decisive or key terrain (ADP 3-90). The mission to create and defend a strong point implies retention of terrain to stop or redirect enemy formations. A strong point requires extensive time, engineer support, and Class IV resources to construct.

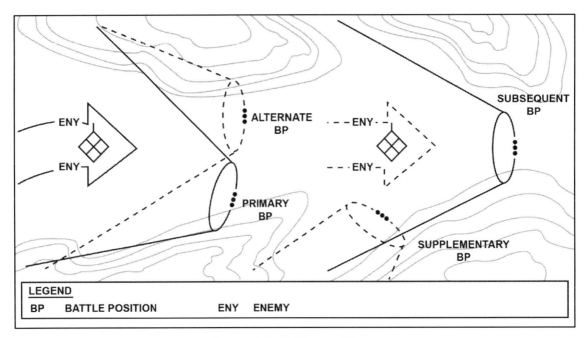

Figure 3-3. Battle positions

TACTICAL FRAMEWORK OF THE DEFENSE

3-52. Usually, as part of a larger element, the company team conducts defensive operations performing several integrated and overlapping activities. Sometimes a company team must defend against an enemy that does not have a conventional doctrine-based operational foundation. This enemy situation requires a more flexible plan that allows for more responsive and decentralized control of combat power rather than spreading it evenly throughout the company's AO. The company team may conduct perimeter defense operations along with offensive and patrolling operations.

FIND THE ENEMY

3-53. This typically occurs once friendly security forces make initial enemy contact. The security force takes an active role to find the enemy and report their location, disposition, strength, and likely COA. The commander uses the information available, in conjunction with military judgment, to determine the point at which the enemy commits to a COA.

3-54. Early detection of the enemy's COA provides the commander with reaction time to adjust the fixing force's positions and shapes the enemy's attack, which, in turn, provides the time necessary to commit the striking force or reserve force.

FIX THE ENEMY

3-55. The commander does everything possible to limit options available to the enemy when conducting an area defense. In addition to disrupting the enemy, the commander conducts shaping operations to constrain the enemy into a specific COA, control enemy movements, or fix the enemy in each location. These actions limit the enemy's options. While executing these operations, the commander continues to find and delay or attrit enemy follow-on and reserve forces to keep them from entering the MBA. The commander has several options to help fix an attacking enemy force. The commander can design shaping operations—such as securing the flanks and point of a penetration—to fix the enemy and allow friendly forces to execute decisive maneuver elsewhere.

3-56. The commander uses obstacles covered by fire to fix, turn, block, or disrupt to limit the enemy's available options. Properly executed obstacles are a result of the synthesis of top-down and bottom-up obstacle planning and emplacement. Blocking forces can affect enemy movement. A blocking force may achieve its mission from a variety of positions depending on the mission variables.

FINISH THE ENEMY

3-57. The main effort occurs in the MBA in an area defense. This is where the effects of supporting efforts, combine with the main effort of the main body forces to defeat enemy forces. Commanders' goals are to prevent enemy forces from further advances by using a combination of fires from prepared positions, obstacles, and mobile reserves.

3-58. Generating massed effects is especially critical when conducting the defense against enemy forces with significant advantages in combat power. An attacking enemy force can select the point and time of attack. Therefore, an attacking enemy force can mass forces at specific points, thus dramatically influencing the ratio of forces at these points of attack. The company team quickly determines their enemy force's intent and the effects of terrain. This allows the company team to concentrate the effects of combat power against enemy forces at those points and restore a more favorable force ratio.

3-59. The elements of the company team maneuver using massed direct and indirect fire and movement to gain positional advantage over assaulting enemy forces. Commanders also direct engineer obstacle and sustainment efforts by assigning priorities.

FOLLOW THROUGH

3-60. Defensive operations retain terrain and create conditions for a counteroffensive that regains the initiative. All defensive operations create the opportunity to transition to the offense. The area defense does this by causing the enemy to sustain unacceptable losses short of any decisive objectives. A successful area defense allows the commander to transition to an attack. An area defense could result in a stalemate with both forces left in contact with each other. Finally, it could result in the defender being overcome by the enemy attack and needing to transition to a retrograde operation. Any decision to withdraw must consider the current situation in adjacent defensive areas. Only the commander who ordered the defense can designate a new FEBA or authorize a retrograde operation.

SECTION II – ENGAGEMENT AREA DEVELOPMENT

3-61. The EA is where the commander intends to trap and destroy an enemy force using the massed fires of all available weapons. By studying the terrain, the commander tries to determine the principal enemy and friendly mounted, dismounted, and air avenues of approach. The commander determines the most advantageous area for the enemy's main attack, as well as the military aspects of terrain by OAKOC. (See ATP 3-34.80 for more information.)

3-62. The success of any defense depends on how effectively the commander can integrate the obstacle plan, indirect fire plan, and the direct fire plan within the EA to achieve the tactical purpose. EA development is a complex function, demanding parallel planning and preparation to accomplish the tasks for which it is responsible. Despite this complexity, EA development resembles a drill in that the commander and subordinate leaders use an orderly, standard set of procedures. The steps of EA development are not a rigid sequential process; steps with asterisks occur simultaneously to ensure the synchronization of combined arms. EA development steps begin with the evaluation of METT-TC (I) variables:

- Identify all likely enemy avenues of approach.
- Identify most likely enemy COA.
- Determine where to kill the enemy.
- Position subordinate forces and weapons systems. *
- Plan and integrate obstacles. *
- Plan and integrate indirect fires. *
- Rehearse the execution of operations in the EA.

IDENTIFY LIKELY ENEMY AVENUES OF APPROACH

3-63. The commander conducts initial reconnaissance of the terrain using OAKOC. If possible, the commander does this from the enemy's perspective along each avenue of approach into the sector of fire or EA. Command and control systems can graphically help the company commander by building a modified combined obstacle overlay. The following are techniques and considerations when identifying the enemy's likely avenues of approach (see figure 3-4):

- Identify key and decisive terrain. This includes locations that afford positions of advantage over the enemy, and natural obstacles and choke points that restrict forward movement.
- Determine which avenues provide cover and concealment for the enemy while allowing them to maintain their tempo. Command and control systems can graphically help the company commander by showing line of sight data which enables the commander to identify decision point positions.
- Determine which terrain the enemy is likely to use to support each avenue.
- Evaluate lateral routes adjoining each avenue of approach.

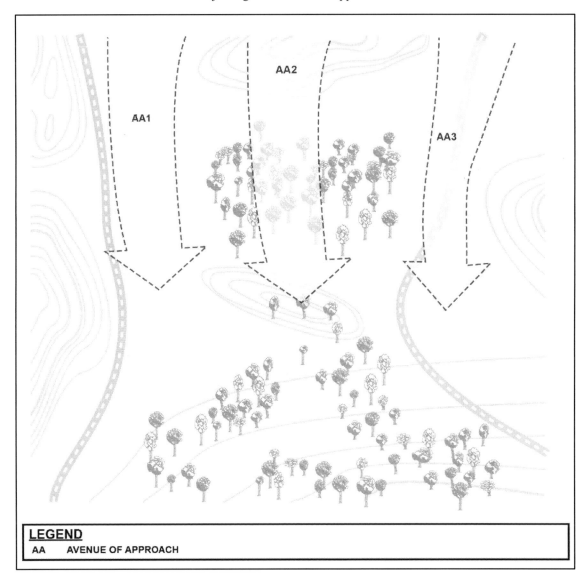

LEGEND

AA   AVENUE OF APPROACH

Figure 3-4. Likely enemy avenues of approach

IDENTIFY MOST LIKELY COURSE OF ACTION

3-64. After determining the likely enemy avenues of approach, the commander can use the following procedures to identify the enemy's likely COA. (See figure 3-5):

- Determine how the enemy will structure the attack.
- Determine how the enemy will use their reconnaissance assets. Will they attempt to infiltrate friendly positions?
- Determine where and when the enemy will change formations or establish SBF positions.
- Determine where, when, and how the enemy will conduct assault or breaching operations.
- Determine where and when they will commit follow-on forces.
- Determine the enemy's expected rates of movement.
- Assess the effects of combat multipliers, the anticipated locations, and areas of employment.
- Determine what reactions the enemy is likely to have in response to projected friendly actions.

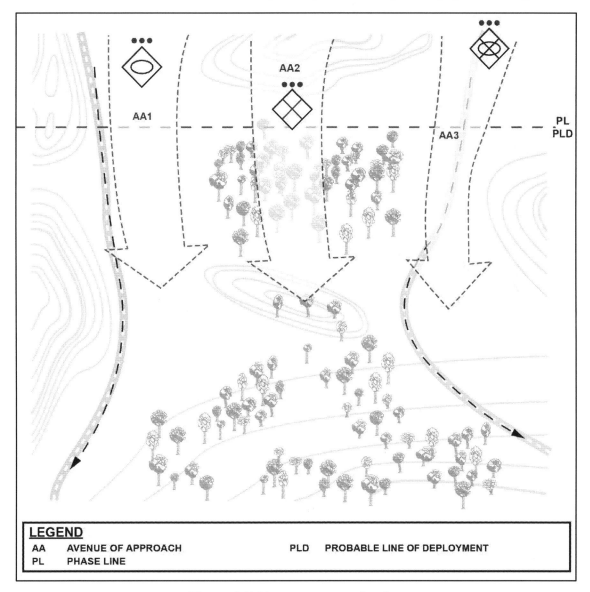

Figure 3-5. Enemy course of action

DETERMINE WHERE TO KILL THE ENEMY

3-65. Whether planning deliberately or rapidly when determining where to kill enemy, the CAB commander and subordinate commanders maintain a shared understanding of the steps within the IPB. The company commander focuses efforts to determine the effects of the terrain, weather, and civil considerations on the enemy avenues of approach identified. The following steps identify and mark where to kill the enemy (see figure 3-6):

- Identify TRPs that match the enemy's scheme of maneuver allowing the company to identify where it will engage enemy forces through the depth of the sector of fire.
- Identify and record the exact location, composition, and intent of each TRP. TRPs can be of different composition because of the use of different weapon systems to engage different types of targets.
- Determine how many weapons systems will engage fires on each TRP to achieve the desired end state.
- Determine engagement lines for all weapons systems.
- Determine which platoons will mass fires on each TRP.
- Establish EAs around TRPs.
- Develop the direct fire planning measures necessary to fire at each TRP.

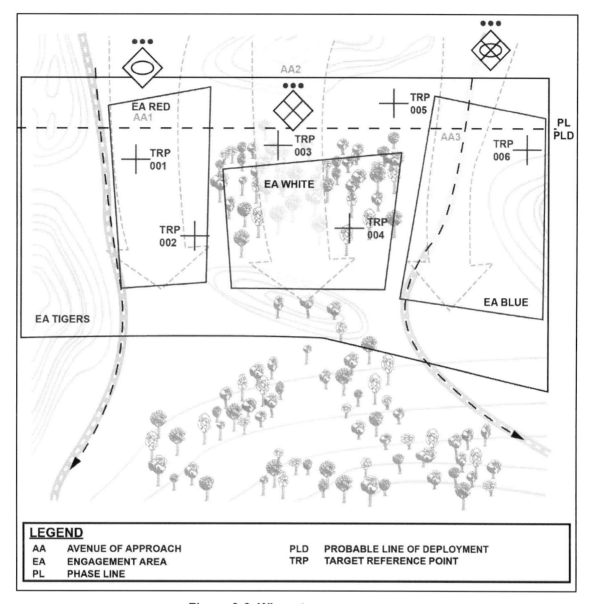

Figure 3-6. Where to engage enemy

POSITION SUBORDINATE FORCES AND WEAPONS SYSTEMS

3-66. The commander assigns subordinate platoons' BPs based on the mission variables of METT-TC (I). The commander can maximize decentralized execution empowering subordinate PLs to position BPs within their assigned AO, however it is necessary for the company commander to ensure the entire company is synchronized to support one another mutually. The commander addresses security requirements for the flanks of assigned AO by assigning responsibility to a subordinate element organizing a security element or directing emplacement of OPs to accomplish that mission. The following steps apply in selecting and improving BPs and emplacing the company vehicles, crew-served weapon systems, and Infantry positions. (See figure 3-7 on page 3-16.) The company commander—

- Selects tentative platoon BPs. When possible, these should be selected while moving in the EA, and examined from the enemy's perspective. Using the enemy's perspective enables the commander to assess survivability of the positions.
- Conducts a leader's reconnaissance of the tentative BPs.

- Drives the EA to confirm that selected positions are tactically advantageous.
- Confirms and marks selected BPs.
- Ensures that BPs do not conflict with those of adjacent units and that they are effectively tied in with adjacent positions.
- Selects primary, alternate, and supplementary positions to achieve the desired effect for each TRP.
- Ensures that PLs, PSGs, vehicle commanders, or Infantry squad leaders position direct fire weapon systems so that each TRP is effectively covered by the required number of weapons, vehicles, or platoons.
- Ensures that positions allow vehicle commanders, loaders, or gunners (as applicable for each vehicle) to observe the EA from the turret-down position and engages enemy forces from the hull down position.
- Stakes vehicle positions according to unit SOP so that engineers can dig in the positions while vehicle crews perform other tasks.
- Proofs all vehicle positions.

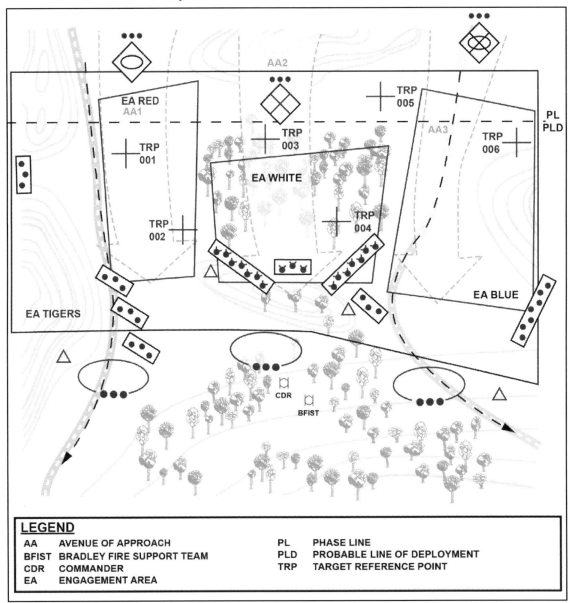

Figure 3-7. Position forces and weapons systems

PLAN AND INTEGRATE OBSTACLES

3-67. Countermobility planning addresses how security area and MBA forces reinforce the natural defensive characteristics of the terrain with the employment of obstacles. The company commander, with the assistance of the engineer leader (when attached), determines an obstacle group's intent relative to its location, and effect to block, disrupt, fix, and turn attacking enemy forces into planned EAs. Countermobility planning includes the positioning of protective obstacles to prevent the enemy from closing with defensive BPs, and integrating mines, wire, indirect fires, and direct fires in conjunction with placement. The commander sites each obstacle on the ground with the assistance of the available engineer leader. The commander, FSO, engineer, and PLs integrate obstacles within the company defense, and ensure the most effective coverage of direct and indirect fires are tied in. The following steps apply in planning and integrating obstacles in the company defense (see figure 3-8 on page 3-18):

- Determine the obstacle group's intent confirming the target, relative location, and effect. Ensure intent supports the task force scheme of maneuver.
- Identify, site, and mark the obstacles within the obstacle group.
- Integrate protective obstacle types and locations within company defense.
- Ensure coverage of all obstacles with direct fires.
- Assign responsibility for guides and lane closure, as required.
- Emplace obstacles based on analysis of the mission variables of METT-TC (I), secure Classes IV and V points, or secure obstacle work sites.
- Coordinate engineer disengagement criteria, actions on contact, and security requirements with the engineer PL at the obstacle work site if the company is supported by an engineer platoon.

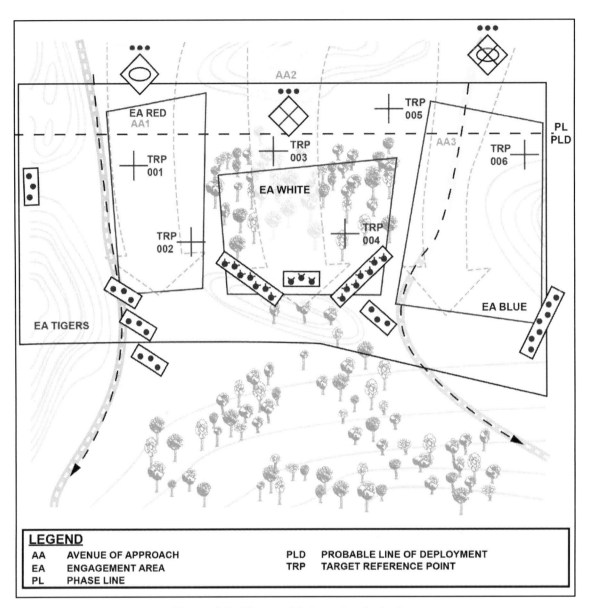

Figure 3-8. Plan and integrate obstacles

PLAN AND INTEGRATE FIRES

3-68. The commander, with the assistance of the FSO, determines the purpose of fires and where that purpose is best achieved. This plan provides the most effective fires resources and mitigates the risk of fratricide as the attacking enemy nears the designated EAs while supporting air assets conduct army aviation and CAS attacks. The establishment of an observation plan with redundancy is necessary for each target (observers could include members of the company FIST or maneuver elements with fire support execution responsibilities identified during planning). During EA development, DFCMs, and fire support coordination measures, such as TRPs, trigger lines (taking into consideration enemy movement rates), and FPFs enable observed fires and the obstacle plan to force the enemy to use avenues of approach covered by friendly EAs. These shaping operations typically focus on enemy high-payoff targets, such as command and control nodes, engineer, fire support, and air defense assets and follow-on forces for destruction or disruption. It is critical to identify friendly element locations (to include OPs) as no-fire area, to limit fratricide. The following steps apply in planning and integrating indirect fires (see figure 3-9):

- Determine the purpose of fires.
- Determine where that purpose will best be achieved.
- Establish the observation plan with redundancy for each target. Observers will include the FIST and members of maneuver elements with fire support responsibilities.
- Establish triggers based on enemy movement rates.
- Obtain accurate target locations using survey or navigational equipment.
- Refine target locations to ensure coverage of obstacles.
- Adjust artillery and mortar targets.
- Plan FPF.
- Request critical friendly zone for maneuver units and no fire areas for OPs and forward positions.

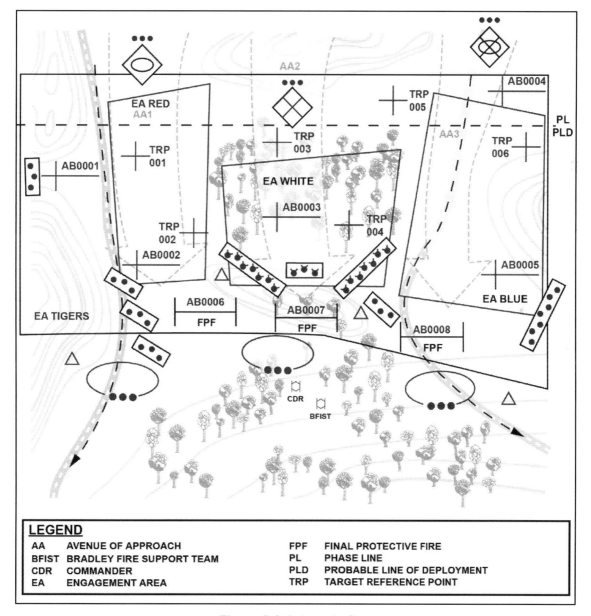

Figure 3-9. Integrate fires

ENGAGEMENT AREA REHEARSALS

3-69. The company coordinates and rehearses EA actions on the ground, gaining intimate familiarity with the terrain. The company commander, XO, engineer leader, FSO, and PLs, at a minimum, rehearse the sequence of events with subordinate leaders for each EA. The purpose of this rehearsal is to ensure that every leader and Soldier understands the plan and that elements are prepared to cover their assigned areas with direct and indirect fires. Although the company commander has several options, the most common and most effective type is the mounted rehearsal. One technique for the mounted rehearsal in the defense is to have the company trains, under the control of the company XO, move through the EA to depict the enemy force while the commander and subordinate platoons rehearse the operation from the company BP. The rehearsal should cover the following actions:

- Rearward passage of security forces (as required).
- Closure of passage lanes (as required).
- Movement from the hide position to the BP.
- Use of fire commands, triggers, or maximum engagement lines to initiate direct and indirect fires.
- Shifting of fires to concentrate and redistribute fire effects.
- Preparation and transmission of critical reports using FM and digital systems (as applicable).
- Assessment of enemy weapons systems effects.
- Displacement to alternate, supplementary, or subsequent BPs.
- Cross-leveling or resupply of Class V.
- Evacuation of casualties.

3-70. The company commander should coordinate the rehearsal with the CAB to ensure that there are no rehearsal conflicts with other units. Coordination leads to efficient use of planning and preparation time for all CAB units. It eliminates the danger of misidentification of friendly forces in the rehearsal area, which could result in fratricide.

SECTION III – AREA DEFENSE

3-71. The *area defense* is a type of defensive operation that concentrates on denying enemy forces access to designated terrain for a specific time rather than destroying the enemy outright (ADP 3-90). The company team's focus is on retaining terrain where the defending element positions itself in mutually supporting positions and controlling the terrain between positions.

3-72. The commander uses a reserve force to reinforce fires, add depth, block penetrations, restore positions, or counterattack to destroy enemy forces and seize the initiative. The company teams that support the MBA fight focus on retaining terrain, positioning platoons in mutually supporting BPs, and controlling the terrain between positions.

3-73. A company team in either the MBA fight or the reserve is always prepared to conduct local counterattacks or participate in major counterattacks either in an area to shore up the defense and prevent a penetration, or in reaction to a change in enemy situation where there is the opportunity to regain the initiative.

TWO METHODS OF AN AREA DEFENSE

3-74. The two methods in the area defense are defense in-depth and forward defense. While the company team commander usually selects a method of area defense to use, the higher commander often defines the general defensive scheme for the CAB. These two employment choices are not exclusionary. Part of a defending unit can conduct a forward defense, while the other part conducts a defense in-depth. The specific mission may also impose constraints such as time, security, and retention of certain areas, which are significant factors in determining how the unit will defend.

DEFENSE IN-DEPTH

3-75. A defense in-depth is normally the commander's preferred option. Forces defending in-depth absorb the momentum of the enemy's attack by forcing the enemy to attack repeatedly through mutually supporting positions in-depth. Depth provides more space and time to exploit information collection efforts and fire support to reduce the enemy's options, weaken the enemy force, and set the conditions for the enemy's destruction, disintegration, or dislocation. This provides more reaction time for the defending force to appropriately respond to the attack. The commander continues to gather additional information about the attacking enemy's intentions and capabilities between the time combat starts and the time the enemy commits to a COA. This reduces the risk of the enemy force quickly penetrating the main line of defense along an unexpected axis.

3-76. While defending in-depth, company teams plan and prepare primary, alternate, supplementary, and subsequent fighting positions (see figure 3-3 on page 3-10). As the attacking enemy force attempts to create a penetration, the company's platoons hold and or shift from one position to the next while coordinating the combined effects of direct and indirect. This enables the defenders to keep continuous pressure on the advancing enemy. The mobility, firepower, and protection of the tanks and fighting vehicles in the company teams' Armor and mechanized Infantry platoons enable the option of using a more dynamic rather than purely static defense. Commanders continuously look for the opportunity to conduct local counterattacks to destroy an enemy and seize the initiative.

3-77. The commander usually decides to conduct a defense in-depth when—
- The mission is not restrictive and allows the commander to fight throughout the depth of the battlefield.
- The terrain does not favor a defense well-forward, and there is better defensible terrain deeper within the AO.
- The AO is deep compared to its width, and there is significant depth available.
- The cover and concealment on or near the FEBA is limited.
- The enemy has several times the combat power of the defender.
- The enemy can employ large quantities of precision-guided munitions or weapons of mass destruction (WMD).

FORWARD DEFENSE

3-78. The intent of the forward defense is to prevent enemy penetration. Due to its lack of depth, a forward defense is the least preferred. The company team deploys most of its combat power into forward positions near the FEBA. The commander fights to retain its forward position and may conduct counterattacks against enemy penetrations or destroy enemy forces in forward EAs. Often, counterattacks are planned forward of the FEBA to defeat the enemy. While the CAB may lack depth, companies and platoons usually are able to array forces in-depth.

3-79. In general, the commander uses a forward defense when a higher commander directs the commander to retain forward terrain for political, military, economic, and other reasons. Alternatively, a commander may choose to conduct a forward defense when the terrain in that part of the AO—including natural obstacles—favors the defending force because—
- The best BPs are located along the FEBA.
- Strong, natural obstacles are located near the FEBA.
- Natural EAs occur near the FEBA.
- Cover and concealment in the rear portion of the AO is limited.

VARIATIONS OF THE AREA DEFENSE

3-80. There are three variations of the area defense (defense of a linear obstacle, perimeter defense, and reverse-slope defense) that have special purposes and unique considerations associated with each. When conducting a subordinate form of the area defense, proper evaluation, and organization of the company's AO are essential to maximize the effectiveness of the defending force. The commander exploits the advantages of occupying the terrain where the battle will occur and positions the company to engage the attacker from locations that give the defending force an advantage. In all three forms, the commander uses existing and reinforcing obstacles and other key terrain to impede the enemy's movement. The commander selects terrain that allows massing of friendly fires but forces the enemy to commit forces piecemeal into friendly EAs, exposing portions of the enemy force for destruction without giving up the advantages of fighting from protected positions. The three variations of the area defense provide distinct advantages to the defender and its subordinate units during an area defense and the operations of the fixing force during a mobile defense.

DEFENSE OF A LINEAR OBSTACLE

3-81. The defense of a linear obstacle is like a forward defense with the intent being to limit the terrain over which the enemy can gain influence or control. A linear obstacle adds to the strength of the defense and can be a river, a stream with steep embankments, or a man-made obstacle such as an embankment. The key to success in a defense of a linear obstacle is maintaining the integrity of the defense by preventing the enemy from securing a foothold on the friendly side of the obstacle. When the enemy can gain and maintain a foothold, the company must contain it and prevent its expansion. Defending units integrate additional obstacles to stop enemy forces, channel them into planned EAs, and to further enable the integrity of the linear obstacle. The defense of a linear obstacle usually forces the enemy to deploy, concentrate forces, and conduct breaching operations. (See figure 3-10.) When attacked, the defending force isolates the enemy, conducts counterattacks, and delivers fires onto the concentrated force to defeat attempts to breach the obstacle.

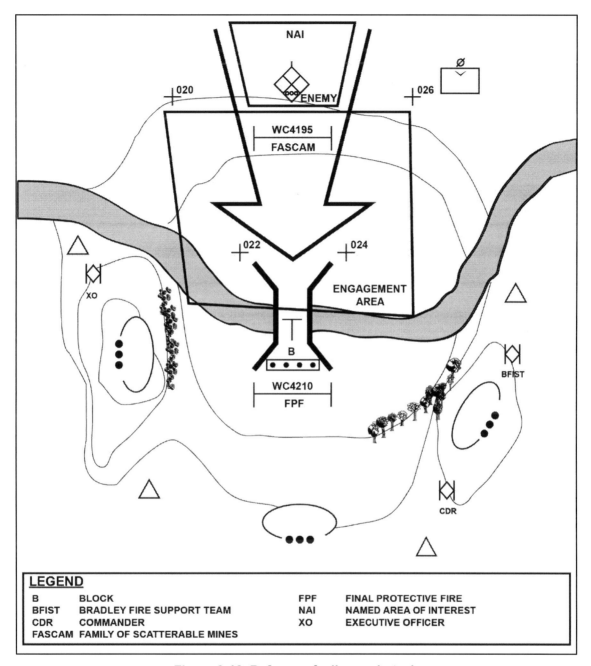

Figure 3-10. Defense of a linear obstacle

3-82. The main purpose of the defense of linear obstacle, as with any defense, is to force or deceive the enemy into attacking under unfavorable circumstances. The defending commander seeks to dictate where the fight will occur, preparing the terrain and other conditions to the defender's advantage while simultaneously denying the enemy adequate intelligence of friendly forces' defensive composition and disposition. During planning, the commander uses intelligence products to identify probable enemy objectives and approaches. From those probable objectives and approaches, named areas of interest and targeted areas of interest are developed. The commander considers the mission variables of METT-TC (I) to determine how best to concentrate efforts and economize forces. A detailed terrain analysis is likely the most important process that the commander completes. A successful defense relies on a complete understanding of terrain to determine likely enemy COAs and the best positioning of company assets to counter them.

PERIMETER DEFENSE

3-83. A perimeter defense is a defense oriented in all directions. A perimeter defense by design has a secure inner area with most of the combat power located on the perimeter. (See figure 3-11.) Perimeters vary in shape depending on the terrain and situation with the perimeter shape conforming to the terrain features that best use friendly observation and fields of fire. The commander in a perimeter defense designates the trace of the perimeter, BPs, contact points, and lateral and forward boundaries. When the commander determines the most probable direction of enemy attack, that part of the perimeter covering that approach may be reinforced with additional resources. The commander increases the effectiveness of the perimeter by tying it into a natural obstacle, such as a river, which allows the defending unit to concentrate its combat power in more threatened areas. Normally, if a reserve is identified by the company commander it is centrally located to react to any point of penetration along the company's perimeter.

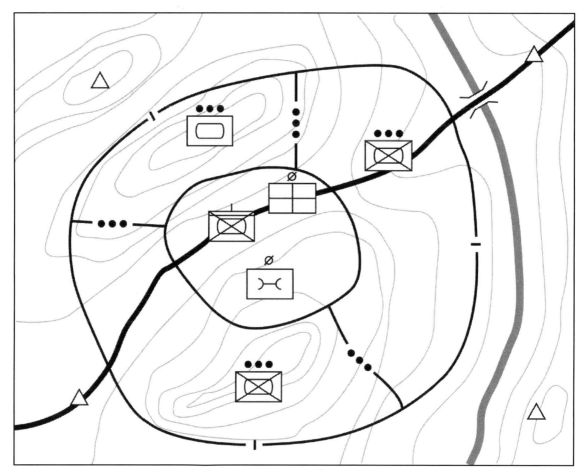

Figure 3-11. Perimeter defense

3-84. When conducting any of the perimeter defenses, the commander prevents gaps between defensive fighting positions when the unit is in restrictive terrain. At night or during periods of limited visibility, the commander may position tactical units closer together to retain the advantages of mutual support. Defending during periods of limited visibility or nighttime conditions, subordinate unit leaders must coordinate the nature and extent of their mutual support. The ability of the attacker to create conditions of smoke—including thermal neutralizing smoke—and the smoke and dust associated with a battle also means that the defending commander must be able to modify the defense rapidly to be effective during limited visibility.

3-85. The commander uses EAs, TRPs, FPFs, and principal direction of fire control measures. The commander designates EAs to cover each enemy avenue of approach into the perimeter. The commander determines the size and shape of the EA by the relatively unobstructed line of sight from the weapons systems' position and the maximum range of those weapons.

3-86. Once EAs are determined, the commander arrays available forces and weapon systems in positions to concentrate overwhelming effects into these areas. The commander routinely subdivides an EA into smaller EAs for subordinates using one or more TRPs or by prominent terrain features. The commander assigns a *sector of fire*, that area assigned to a unit or weapon system in which it will engage the enemy according to the established engagement priorities (FM 3-90), to subordinates within each EA. Indirect fires engage the enemy as far forward of the perimeter as possible and may support the company from within or outside the perimeter. Available fires from outside the perimeter are coordinated and integrated into the overall defensive plan. Using fire support from outside the perimeter conserves ammunition from within the perimeter.

REVERSE SLOPE DEFENSE

3-87. An alternative to defending on the forward slope of a hill or a ridge is to defend on a reverse slope. In such a defense, the company team is deployed on terrain that is masked from enemy direct fire and ground observation by the crest of a hill. Although some units and weapons might be positioned on the forward slope, the crest, or the counterslope (a forward slope of a hill to the rear of a reverse slope), most forces are on the reverse slope. (See FM 3-90 for more information.) The key to this defense is control of the crest by direct fire.

3-88. The commander can adopt a reverse-slope position when—
- Enemy fire makes the forward slope untenable.
- Lack of cover and concealment on the forward slope makes it untenable.
- The forward slope has been lost or has not yet been gained.
- The forward slope is exposed to enemy direct fire weapons fired from beyond the effective range of the defender's weapons. Moving to the reverse slope removes the attacker's standoff advantage.
- The terrain on the reverse slope provides better fields of fire than the forward slope.
- The defender must avoid creating a dangerous salient or reentrant in friendly lines.
- It is essential for the CAB to surprise and deceive the enemy as to the true location of the BPs.

3-89. When executing a reverse-slope defense, the company commander places special emphasis on the following:
- A fire support plan to prevent the enemy's occupation and use of the crest of the hill.
- The use of OPs or reconnaissance elements on the forward slope to provide observation across the entire front and security to the main BPs.
- A counterattack plan that specifies measures necessary to clear the crest or regain it from the enemy.
- Fire support to destroy, disrupt, and attrit enemy forces on the forward slope.

3-90. The forward edge of the position should be within small-arms range of the crest. It should be far enough from the crest that fields of fire allow the defender time to place well-aimed fire on the enemy before they reach friendly positions. The company establishes OPs on or forward of the topographical crest. This allows long-range observation over the entire front and indirect fire coverage of forward obstacles. OPs are usually provided by the unit that owns the terrain being observed and may vary in size from a few Soldiers to a reinforced squad. They should include forward observers. At night, their number should be increased to improve security. Considerations that commanders may apply when defending on a reverse slope are the following:
- Observation of the enemy is more difficult. Soldiers in this position see forward no farther than the crest. This makes it hard to determine exactly where the enemy is as they advance, especially when visibility is poor. OPs must be placed forward of the topographic crest for early warning and long-range observation.
- Egress from the position might be more difficult.
- Fields of fire are usually short.

- Obstacles on the forward slope can be covered only with indirect fire or by units on the flanks of the company unless some weapons systems are initially placed forward.
- If the enemy gains the crest, they can assault downhill, which may give them a psychological advantage.

TECHNIQUES OF CONDUCTING AN AREA DEFENSE

3-91. The company team can conduct an area defense using one of three basic techniques: defend a sector, defend a BP, and defend a strong point. Table 3-1 summarizes the factors a commander considers in selecting a BP versus a sector. Paragraphs 3-92 through 3-96 describe each technique.

DEFEND A SECTOR

3-92. A defensive sector is an area designated by boundaries that define where a unit operates and the terrain for which it is responsible. This technique allows the unit to maintain flank contact and security and ensures unity of effort within the scheme of maneuver. Sector boundaries never split an avenue of approach. Sectors are oriented on avenues of approach and are used when the commander wishes to allow maximum freedom of action.

DEFEND A BATTLE POSITION

3-93. A BP is a general location and orientation of forces on the ground which units defend from. The technique allows units to concentrate fires or place units in an advantageous position for a counterattack. The purpose of defend a BP includes:

- Destroy an enemy force in the EA.
- Block an enemy avenue of approach.
- Control key or decisive terrain.
- Fix the enemy force to allow another unit to maneuver.

3-94. The company team can maneuver in and outside of the BP as necessary to adjust fires or to seize opportunities for offensive operations within the commander's intent. When the commander maneuvers forces outside of the BP, the next higher commander must be notified.

Table 3-1. Defending from battle position versus a sector

FACTOR	BATTLE POSITION	SECTOR
Avenues of approach	Well-defined; enemy can be canalized	Multiple avenues prohibit concentration
Terrain	Dominates avenues of approach	Dominating terrain not available
Area of operations	Narrow	Wide
Mutual support between companies or platoons	Achievable	Cannot be achieved
Higher commander's ability to control	Good	Degraded

DEFEND A STRONG POINT

3-95. A strong point is a heavily fortified BP (see BPs in section I) tied to a natural or reinforcing obstacle to create an anchor for the defense or to deny the enemy decisive of key terrain. This technique implies retention of terrain with the purpose of stopping or redirecting enemy formations. Defense of a strong point is an uncommon mission for the company team. Strong points sacrifice the mobility of the unit's organic weapon systems.

3-96. Defending strong points require extensive engineer support to create obstacles and increase survivability efforts. This include providing all assets overhead protection, trenches, and other protective construction using both natural and man-made terrain. Commanders prepare a strong point for all-around defense. Commanders also establish a strong point when anticipating that enemy actions will isolate a defending force retaining terrain critical to the defense.

PLANNING

3-97. Planning an area defense is a complex effort requiring detailed planning and extensive coordination. In the defense, synchronizing the effects of warfighting functions allows the commander to apply overwhelming combat power against selected advancing enemy forces. An area defense is a mix of static and dynamic actions. As an operation evolves, the commander may shift decisive and shaping operations to disrupt and maintain pressure on the enemy. This denies the enemy initiative and constrains their freedom of maneuver. The commander's defensive plans must address how the preparations for, and the conduct of, the area defense impact the civilian population of the AO.

3-98. During planning, the following considerations are considered for planning and the TLP are applied as necessary. The six warfighting functions are the framework for discussing planning considerations that apply to all primary and subordinate operations. When the company commander conducts planning during TLP, the following areas (warfighting functions) are considered.

COMMAND AND CONTROL

3-99. Upon receipt of the CAB defensive WARNORD, the commander begins TLP (see appendix B for more information) and makes an estimate of the situation. The result of this estimate is a concept that includes control measures, the fires plan, the reconnaissance, surveillance, and security plans, logistics plan, and employment of the reserve if necessary.

3-100. The commander considers the mission variables of METT-TC (I) to determine how best to concentrate efforts and economize forces. A detailed terrain analysis might be the most important process that the commander completes. The commander conducts the mission analysis based on available products and information disseminated by the CAB commander and staff. A successful defense relies on a complete understanding of terrain to determine likely enemy COAs and the best positioning of the company's assets to counter them. Initially, integrated with the CAB staff's IPB, the company commander visualizes the enemy's anticipated actions. The company commander refines the CAB's IPB to focus on the details of the operation in the company's AO.

3-101. The company commander determines how and where to defeat the enemy, where it is believed the enemy will go, the terrain, the forces available, and the CAB commander's intent. The commander may define a defeat mechanism that includes the use of single or multiple counterattacks to achieve success. The commander analyzes the unit's role in the CAB fight and determines how to accomplish the CAB commander's intent. In an area defense, the company usually achieves success by massing the cumulative effects of obstacles and fires to defeat the enemy forward of a designated area, often in conjunction with a counterattack.

3-102. In planning, the commander develops a concept for each COA determined by the mission analysis. Each COA should be developed starting at a potential decisive point and determining the result that must be achieved at the decisive point to accomplish the mission. Determining the decisive point, times, and locations to project combat power allows the commander to anticipate the fight to come. The commander determines the purposes that must be achieved at the decisive point to accomplish the mission. Normally the purpose from the company mission statement clearly states task and purpose to subordinate units. In some instances, the commander must analyze the situation more closely to determine the desired result. The commander determines the purposes to be achieved by the main and supporting efforts (the two must be clearly linked). The main effort's purpose is often the purpose from the company's mission statement. At times the company purpose must be modified slightly to be appropriate for the main effort platoon. When modified, it must be clear that by achieving the main effort's purpose the company achieves its purpose. Supporting purposes are selected by determining what must be achieved to support the success of the main effort. The commander ensures that all essential tasks for subordinate units are identified, and that once accomplished, they achieve the desired end state.

MOVEMENT AND MANEUVER

3-103.   Maneuver allows the commander to take full advantage of the AO and to mass and concentrate when desirable. Maneuver, through movement in combination with fire, allows the company to achieve a position of advantage over the enemy to accomplish the mission. The commander studies the ground and selects positions that allow the massing of fires on likely approaches. The commander concentrates forces within the EA and positions security, intelligence, reconnaissance forces, and surveillance assets forward of defensive positions to gain early enemy forces approach of the EA.

3-104.   When conducting an area defense, the commander combines static and mobile actions to accomplish the mission. Static actions usually consist of fires from prepared positions. Mobile actions include using the fires provided by units in prepared positions as a base for counterattacks and repositioning units between defensive positions. The company commander can use the reserve and uncommitted forces to conduct counterattacks and spoiling attacks to desynchronize the enemy forces or prevent them from massing. The company may also be employed as a counterattack force in support of the CAB area defense.

Area of Operations

3-105.   An area defense in an AO provides the greatest degree of freedom of maneuver to achieve a position of advantage in respect to the enemy. The CAB most often selects this method, employing subordinate companies when it has an adequate amount of depth and width to the battlefield. For both the CAB and company defenses to be cohesive, phase lines, EAs, BPs, and obstacle belts help to coordinate subordinate maneuver forces and achieve synchronized action. Assignment of AO allow flexibility and prevents the enemy from concentrating overwhelming firepower on the bulk of the defending force. Forces defending against an enemy with superior mobility and firepower must use the depth of their positions to defeat the enemy. The depth of the defense must come from the initial positioning of units throughout the AO, not from maneuvering. A properly positioned, viable reserve and counterattack force enhances depth.

Engagement Area

3-106.   An *engagement area* is an area where the commander masses effects to contain and destroy an enemy force (FM 3-90). The success of any engagement depends on how effectively the commander integrates the direct fire plan, the indirect fire plan, the obstacle plan, Army aviation fires, CAS, and the terrain within the EA to achieve the tactical purpose. Within the defense, the company commander positions defending platoons (defense in-depth) in successive layers of BPs (primary, alternate, and strong point) along the enemy's most likely avenue of approach.

Engagement Area Development

3-107.   The commander develops EAs, to include engagement criteria and priority, to cover each enemy avenue of approach. Within the company MBA, the commander determines the size and shape of the EAs by the relatively unobstructed line of sight from the weapon systems firing positions and the maximum range of those weapon systems. Once the commander selects EAs, the commander arrays available forces and weapon systems in positions to concentrate overwhelming effects into these areas. The commander routinely divides the EAs into smaller EAs for subordinates using one or more TRPs or by terrain feature. The commander assigns sector of fires to subordinates to ensure complete coverage of EAs and prevent fratricide. Responsibility for an avenue of approach or key terrain is never split.

3-108.   *Engagement criteria* are protocols that specify those circumstances for initiating engagement with an enemy force (FM 3-90). Engagement criteria may be restrictive or permissive in nature. For example, the commander may instruct a subordinate PL not to engage an approaching enemy unit until the enemy commits to an avenue of approach. The commander establishes engagement criteria in the direct fire plan in conjunction with engagement priorities and other DFCMs to mass fires and control fire distribution.

3-109.   *Engagement priority* identifies the order in which the unit engages enemy systems or functions (FM 3-90). The commander assigns engagement priorities based on the type or level of threat at different ranges to match organic weapon systems capabilities against enemy vulnerabilities. Engagement priorities are situationally dependent and used to distribute fires rapidly and effectively. Subordinate elements can have different engagement priorities but will normally engage the most dangerous targets first, followed by targets in-depth or specialized systems, such as engineer vehicles.

3-110. A *target reference point* is a predetermined point of reference, normally a permanent structure or terrain feature that can be used when describing a target location (JP 3-09.3). The company and subordinate units may designate TRPs to define unit or individual sectors of fire and observation, usually within the EA. TRPs, along with trigger lines, designate the center of an area where the commander plans to distribute or converge the fires of all weapons rapidly to further delineate sectors of fire within an EA. Once designated, TRPs may also constitute indirect fire targets.

3-111. A *trigger line* is a phase line located on identifiable terrain used to initiate and mass fires into an engagement area at a predetermined range (FM 3-90). The commander can designate one trigger line for all weapon systems or separate trigger lines for each weapon or type of weapon system. The commander specifies the engagement criteria for a specific situation. The criteria may be either time- or event-driven, such as a certain number or certain types of vehicles to cross the trigger line before initiating engagement. The commander can use a time-based fires delivery methodology or a geography-based fires delivery.

Countermobility Operations

3-112. *Countermobility* is a set of combined arms activities that use or enhance the effects of natural and man-made obstacles to prevent the enemy freedom of movement and maneuver (ATP 3-90.8). Primary purposes of countermobility operations are to shape enemy movement and maneuver and to prevent the enemy from gaining a position of advantage. In support of the area defense, countermobility operations are conducted to disrupt enemy attack formations and assist in defeating the enemy in detail. Countermobility operations channel attacking enemy forces into EAs throughout the depth of the defense and protect the flanks of friendly counterattack forces. Countermobility operations shape engagements, maximize the effects of fires, and provide close-in protection around defensive positions to defeat the final assault of the enemy and to prevent and warn of intrusion into critical support area sites and fixed sites such as bases. (See ATP 3-90.8 for more information.)

Countermobility Planning

3-113. The company commander, using available CAB staff products, develops the countermobility plan concurrently with the fire support plan and defensive scheme of maneuver, guided by the CAB commander's intent. The conduct of countermobility operations typically involves engineers and includes proper obstacle integration with the maneuver plan, adherence to obstacle emplacement authority, and positive obstacle control. The engineer must advise the commander of the resource requirements based on its assigned tasks for countermobility and must coordinate through the appropriate channels to ensure that the unit is resourced accordingly.

3-114. Combined arms obstacle integration synchronizes countermobility operations into the concept of operations. Because most obstacles have the potential to deny the freedom of movement and maneuver to friendly forces and enemy forces, it is critical that the commander properly weighs the risk and evaluates the trade-off of employing various types of obstacles.

3-115. Obstacle control is essential in supporting the commander's plan. Responsibilities for executing tasks within countermobility operations can be broadly divided into two entities: emplacing unit and owning unit. This framework helps the commander plan for and assign responsibilities for obstacle execution to subordinate units. The responsibilities of each may vary based on the type of obstacle and the situation. The commander's concept of operations includes the following tasks:

- Site obstacles.
- Construct, emplace, or detonate obstacles.
- Mark, report, and record obstacles.
- Maintain obstacle integration.

3-116. Countermobility operations typically reinforce the terrain to block, fix, turn, or disrupt the enemy's ability to move or maneuver, giving the commander opportunities to exploit enemy vulnerabilities or react effectively to enemy actions. The commander reinforces the terrain to prevent the enemy from gaining a position of advantage by taking into account the natural restrictiveness of the existing terrain to minimize the time, effort, and materiel needed to achieve the desired obstacle effects. Reinforcing the terrain focuses on existing and reinforcing obstacles. Existing obstacles are inherent aspects of the terrain that impede movement and maneuver. Existing obstacles may be natural (rivers, mountains, wooded areas) or man-made (enemy explosive and nonexplosive obstacles and structures, including bridges, canals, railroads, and embankments associated with them).

3-117.   Reinforcing obstacles are those man-made obstacles that strengthen existing terrain to achieve a desired effect. Reinforcing obstacles must be planned and emplaced to support the maneuver commander's plan, while not hindering friendly-force mobility. Obstacle plans are developed based on a thorough understanding of the commander's intent and concept of operations, enemy mobility capabilities, and the effects of the natural terrain and existing obstacles. Only then can the true value of integrating obstacles, observation, fires, and maneuver be realized. The basic employment principles for reinforcing obstacles are—
- Support the maneuver commander's plan.
- Integrate with observation and fires.
- Integrate with other obstacles.
- Employ in-depth.
- Employ for surprise.

3-118.   Reinforcing obstacles are categorized as tactical and protective. Tactical obstacles help shape enemy maneuver and prevent the enemy from gaining a position of advantage, while protective obstacles protect people, equipment, supplies, and facilities against threats. The primary purposes of tactical obstacles are to shape enemy maneuver and to maximize the effects of fires. Tactical obstacles directly attack the ability of a force to move, mass, and reinforce; therefore, they affect the tempo of operations. Commanders integrate obstacles into the scheme of movement and maneuver to enhance the effects of fires. Preexisting obstacles that a unit reinforces and integrates with observation and fires may become tactical obstacles. The types of tactical obstacles are clearly distinguished by the differences in execution criteria. The three types are—
- *Directed obstacle*, an obstacle directed by a higher commander as a specified task to a subordinate unit (ATP 3-90.8).
- Situational obstacle, an obstacle that a unit plans and possibly prepares prior to starting an operation but does not execute unless specific criteria are met. The commander considers types of obstacles to employ, and the trigger.
- *Reserved obstacle*, obstacles of any type, for which the commander restricts execution authority (ATP 3-90.8).

Obstacle Intent

3-119.   An *obstacle* is any barrier designed or employed to disrupt, fix, turn, or block the movement and maneuver, and to impose additional losses in personnel, time, and equipment (JP 3-15). Obstacle intent describes how obstacles support the commander's concept of operations. Obstacle intent consists of the target, effect, and relative location. The target is the enemy force that the commander wants to affect with tactical obstacles. The commander usually identifies the target in terms of the enemy size and type, the echelon, the avenue of approach, or in combination. Tactical obstacles and fires—direct and indirect— manipulate the enemy in a way that supports the commander's intent and scheme of movement and maneuver.

3-120.   Obstacle effect describes the effect that the commander wants the obstacle(s), combined with fires, to have on the enemy. The obstacle effect drives integration, focuses subordinate fires, focuses obstacle effort, and multiplies firepower effects. It is important to remember, obstacle effects occur because of the combined effects of fires and obstacles, rather than from obstacles alone. Tactical obstacles produce one of the following effects: disrupt, turn, fix, or block. (See figure 3-12.) Obstacle effect symbols are used as control measures for obstacle groups and as elements of the control measures for obstacle zones and belts. During COA development, obstacle effect symbols are also used in developing and showing the initial obstacle plan that supports each COA.

OBSTACLE EFFECT	PURPOSE	FIRES AND OBSTACLES MUST:	OBSTACLE CHARACTERISTICS
DISRUPT	• BREAK UP ENEMY FORMATIONS. • INTERRUPT ENEMY'S TIMETABLE AND C2. • CAUSE PREMATURE COMMITMENT OF BREACH ASSETS. • CAUSE THE ENEMY TO PIECEMEAL HIS ATTACK.	• CAUSE THE ENEMY TO DEPLOY EARLY. • SLOW PART OF HIS FORMATION WHILE ALLOWING PART TO ADVANCE UNIMPEDED.	• DO NOT REQUIRE EXTENSIVE RESOURCES. • ENSURE OBSTACLES ARE DIFFICULT TO DETECT AT LONG RANGE.
FIX	• SLOW AN ATTACKER WITHIN AN AREA SO HE CAN BE DESTROYED. • GENERATE THE TIME NECESSARY FOR THE FRIENDLY FORCE TO DISENGAGE.	• CAUSE THE ENEMY TO DEPLOY INTO ATTACK FORMATION BEFORE ENCOUNTERING THE OBSTACLES. • ALLOW THE ENEMY TO ADVANCE SLOWLY IN AN EA OR AO. • MAKE THE ENEMY FIGHT IN MULTIPLE DIRECTIONS ONCE HE IS IN THE EA OR AO.	• ARRAY OBSTACLES IN DEPTH. • SPAN THE ENTIRE WIDTH OF THE AVENUES OF APPROACH. • AVOID MAKING THE TERRAIN APPEAR IMPENETRABLE.
TURN	• FORCE THE ENEMY TO MOVE IN THE DIRECTION DESIRED BY THE FRIENDLY COMMANDER.	• PREVENT THE ENEMY FROM BYPASSING OR BREACHING THE OBSTACLE BELT. • MAINTAIN PRESSURE ON THE ENEMY FORCE THROUGHOUT THE TURN. • MASS DIRECT AND INDIRECT FIRES AT THE ANCHOR POINT OF THE TURN.	• TIE INTO IMPASSABLE TERRAIN AT THE ANCHOR POINT. • USE OBSTACLES IN DEPTH. • PROVIDE A SUBTLE ORIENTATION RELATIVE TO THE ENEMY'S APPROACH.
BLOCK	• STOP AN ATTACKER ALONG A SPECIFIC AVENUE OF APPROACH. • PREVENT AN ATTACKER FROM PASSING THROUGH AN AO OR EA. • STOP THE ENEMY FROM USING AN AVENUE OF APPROACH AND FORCE HIM TO USE ANOTHER AVENUE OF APPROACH.	• PREVENT THE ENEMY FROM BY PASSING OR PENETRATING THROUGH THE BELT. • STOP THE ENEMY'S ADVANCE. • DESTROY ALL ENEMY BREACH EFFORTS.	• TIE INTO IMPASSABLE TERRAIN. • USE COMPLEX OBSTACLES. • DEFEAT THE ENEMY'S MOUNTED AND DISMOUNTED BREACHING EFFORT.

LEGEND
AO   AREA OF OPERATIONS   EA   ENGAGEMENT AREA
C2   COMMAND & CONTROL

Figure 3-12. Tactical obstacle effects

Mobility

3-121. When planning an area defense, the commander identifies the mobility requirements by analyzing the scheme of maneuver, counterattack options, reserve planning priorities, fire support, protection, and sustainment movement requirements. The commander also needs to take into account the adjacent and higher units' mission, movement, and maneuver. The commander, with the assistance of attached engineers (if available), integrates analysis into the obstacle plan while avoiding the impediment of friendly maneuver when possible. Because the bulk of the engineer force is committed to countermobility and survivability during preparation, the commander uses clear obstacle restrictions on specific areas within the AO to maintain mobility. Mobility support linkup and coordination is factored into the overall defensive preparation timeline.

3-122. When obstacles must be constructed along a mobility corridor that primarily supports friendly movement a lane or gap and associated closure procedures are planned and rehearsed. Lanes or gaps may be closed with situational or reserved obstacles. Beyond preparing and marking lanes and gaps through obstacles, engineers normally perform mobility tasks once defensive preparations are complete. Mobility assets may then be positioned to counter templated enemy situational obstacles, or be task organized to the reserve, counterattack force, or any other unit that must maneuver or move after the execution of the defense. To do this effectively, mobility assets and supported maneuver units integrate, prepare, and rehearse.

3-123. Although not specifically designed or intended as an obstacle, structures may pose as an obstacle based on existing characteristics or altered characteristics that result from combat operations or a catastrophic event. Structures such as bridges and overpasses present an inherent impediment to mobility based on weight and clearance restrictions.

INTELLIGENCE

3-124. IPB is a critical part of defensive planning. (See ATP 2-01.3 for more information.) IPB helps the commander determine where to concentrate combat power, where to accept risk, and where to plan the potential main effort. The CAB integrates intelligence from the higher echelon's collection efforts and from units operating forward of the CAB's AO and is then disseminated to subordinates to company commanders, who then conduct IPB at the company level. To aid in the development of a flexible defensive plan, the IPB presents all feasible enemy COAs that time allows. The essential areas of focus are terrain analysis, determination of enemy force size enemy vulnerabilities, and likely COAs with associated decision points.

3-125. In the defense, key terrain is usually within and behind the defensive area, such as terrain that gives good observation over avenues of approach to and through the defensive position; terrain that permits the defender to cover an obstacle by fire; or areas along lines of communications that affect the use of reserves or sustainment operations. Key terrain may include portions of the population, such as political, tribal, and religious groups or leaders; a localized population; infrastructure; or governmental organizations. Weather conditions can affect visibility as well. Temperature can affect the use of thermal sights. Cloud cover can negate illumination provided by the moon. Precipitation and other obscurants can have varying effects as well. Low visibility is beneficial to offensive and retrograde operations because it conceals concentration of maneuver forces, thus enhancing the possibility of surprise. Low visibility hinders the defense because cohesion and control become difficult to maintain, reconnaissance operations are impeded, and target acquisition is degraded.

FIRES

3-126. Supporting the commander's concept of operations during the defense involves attacking and engaging targets throughout the AO with massed or precision fires. The commander and available fire support planners (FSO, fire support NCO, and FIST teams) make maximum use of any preparation time available to plan and coordinate supporting fires. Planners ensure fires complement and support all security forces forward of the MBA as these fires play a key role in disrupting the attacker's tempo and synchronization. Fire support planning and execution must address flexibility through operations in-depth and support to defensive maneuver. The commander promotes freedom of action within the MBA by using the least restrictive control measures necessary to implement the scheme of maneuver. The commander ensures all key avenues of approach, and obstacles are considered when employing indirect fires, incorporating all available firepower where the enemy will likely attack.

3-127. The company may utilize UASs, remote sensors, and reconnaissance and security forces to call for fire on the enemy throughout the AO. Quick, violent, and simultaneous action throughout the depth of the defender's AO can degrade, confuse, and paralyze an enemy force when they are most exposed and vulnerable. Though the company may receive priority of fires for a specific mission or phase of the defense, the commander must not overly rely on indirect fire assets available from the higher HQ. Additional fire support considerations for supporting the commander's concept of operations include—

- Allocating initial priority of fires to security forces forward.
- Developing observation plans.
- Planning targets along enemy reconnaissance mounted and dismounted avenues of approach.
- Engagement of approaching enemy formations at vulnerable points along their route of march.
- Planning the transition of fires from the security area through the MBA fight.
- Planning the echelonment of fires. (See appendix D for more information.)
- Developing clear triggers to initiate fires and adjust priority of fires.
- Ensuring integration of fires in support of obstacle effects.
- Ensuring integration of fires with the counterattack plan and repositioning contingency plans.
- Identifying and targeting high priority targets.
- Deconflicting airspace.

- Integration and positioning of organic mortars.
- Planning FPFs.

SUSTAINMENT

3-128.   Sustainment considerations in the defense require the preplanned coordination for the effective forecasting and delivery of preconfigured Class IV barrier and construction packages at least 72 hours in advance of a projected change in mission due to the limited organic assets to move them. Advanced planning for sustainment operations throughout the security area is critical to reduce the signature of sustaining reconnaissance and security operations. Forces operating within the security area should maximize the stockage of Classes I, IX, and V. Preconfigured combat loads are positioned in the combat trains to expedite resupply operations. (See chapter 6 for more information.)

3-129.   Medical operations are complicated by enemy actions, the maneuver of combat forces, and depth and dispersion of the defense. Army Health System support should be planned and synchronized as medical personnel will have less time to reach a patient, complete emergency medical treatment, and evacuate the patient from the point of injury. During the enemy's initial attack and the CAB's counterattack are also the most likely times for the enemy's use of artillery and CBRN weapons which may produce the heaviest patient workload. These enemy attacks may disrupt ground and air evacuation routes which may delay evacuation of patients to and from treatment elements.

PROTECTION

3-130.   Because the company defends to conserve combat power for use elsewhere or later, the commander must secure the force. The commander enables security, by means of providing information about the activities and resources of the enemy, through the employment of reconnaissance forces and surveillance assets within the assigned AO.

3-131.   One way the CAB can enhance survivability when existing terrain features offer insufficient cover, protection from the effects of fires, concealment, or protection from observation or surveillance, is by altering the physical environment to provide or improve cover and concealment. This consideration also includes attempts to reduce thermal and electronic signatures, as well as conceal information within the cyberspace domain. Similarly, natural or artificial materials may be used as camouflage to confuse, mislead, or evade the enemy. Although survivability encompasses capabilities of military forces while on the move and when stationary, survivability operations focus more on stationary capabilities such as constructing fighting and protective positions and hardening facilities. (See ATP 3-37.34 for more information.)

3-132.   Within the area defense, protective obstacles employed to protect people, equipment, supplies, and facilities against threats are key enablers to survivability operations. Protective obstacles provide local, close-in protection to prevent the enemy from delivering a surprise assault from areas close to defending positions. Protective obstacles protect the emplaced position by warning, mitigating, and preventing hostile actions and effects. (See ATP 3-90.8 for more information.) The commander uses protective obstacle effects (warning, mitigation, and prevention) to convey intent and facilitate protective obstacle planning and design. Protective obstacles employed to support the area defense must be capable of being rapidly emplaced, recovered, or destroyed. FPFs are integrated within the protective obstacle plan to defeat the final assault of the enemy.

3-133.   As the company conducts survivability operations within its limits, engineer and CBRN assets provide additional capabilities to support the company. Engineer support is essential to the integration of survivability priorities for units within and supporting the CAB. (See FM 3-34 for more information.) CBRN assets support survivability through contamination avoidance and mitigation measures. Units have the capability to conduct immediate and operational decontamination with organic equipment to continue operations in contaminated environments. CBRN reconnaissance assets determine likely locations for enemy employment of CBRN weapons. CBRN contamination mitigation includes measures to minimize the vulnerabilities to CBRN effects.

ORGANIZATION OF FORCES

3-134. The commander must have a clear understanding of what the task and purpose is. This understanding assists in the organization of the units. The commander has the option of defending forward or defending in-depth. When the commander defends forward within an AO, the force is organized so that most of the available combat power is committed early in the defensive effort. To accomplish this, the commander may deploy forces forward or plan counterattacks well-forward in the MBA or even beyond. If the commander has the option of conducting a defense in-depth, security forces and forward MBA elements are used to identify, define, and control the depth of the enemy's main effort while holding off secondary attacks. This allows the commander to conserve combat power, strengthen the reserve, and better resource the counterattack.

INFORMATION COLLECTION

3-135. Commanders use information collection assets to determine the locations, strengths, and probable intentions of attacking enemy forces before and throughout their defense. They prioritize early identification of the enemy's main effort within their AO. Fighting for information can have two benefits: it can make enemy forces reveal their intentions and their preparations. In the defense, information collection tasks overlap unit planning and preparing phases.

SECURITY

3-136. The commander balances the need to create a strong security force to shape the battle with the resulting diversion of combat power from the main body. The commander can allocate security forces to provide early warning and protect those forces, systems, and locations necessary from unexpected enemy contact.

3-137. A company team assigned a security mission within the CAB's security area is primarily tasked with the following:
- Provide early warning and disrupt enemy attacks early and continuously.
- Protect the main body of the CAB to preserve combat power for the main defense.
- Deceive the enemy as to friendly locations, strengths, and weaknesses.
- Inhibit or destroy enemy reconnaissance forces.

MAIN BATTLE AREA

3-138. The company team commanders position their subordinate forces in mutually supporting positions in-depth to absorb enemy penetrations or canalize them into prepared EAs. This is done in accordance with the CAB's defensive plan to defeat enemy attacks through concentration of effects and combat power. The MBA includes the area where the defending force creates an opportunity to deliver a decisive counterattack to defeat or destroy the enemy.

3-139. The commander builds the defense around identified decisive points, such as key terrain or high-payoff targets. The commander normally positions the main body into prepared positions within the MBA where the commander wants to conduct operations.

RESERVE

3-140. A company team task organized as the reserve typically locates in an AA or a concealed location until committed to the fight. The CAB commander determines the size and task organization of the reserve based on METT-TC (I) analysis. Typically, the reserve will have few if any other mission tasks during preparation and execution of the defense other than rehearsing to respond to possible contingencies and the movement routes and techniques to move anywhere in the unit's AO once committed. The reserve is not a committed force. In certain situations, it may become necessary to commit the reserve to restore the integrity of the defense by blocking an enemy penetration or reinforcing fires into an EA.

SUSTAINMENT

3-141.   The sustainment plan should include prepositioning Classes III, IV, and V supply stock forward to support defending units. This reduces the need for logistics trains to be exposed to enemy fires and enables the defending forces to resupply rapidly during an enemy advance.

3-142.   Company trains are located between 500 and 1,000 meters, or one major terrain feature, away from the company's main defensive position. By placing at least one terrain feature between it and the enemy, the company trains will be out of the enemy's direct fire weapons. In some circumstances, it may be necessary to emplace caches forward of the company trains, and to the rear of the CP in a defilade position with cover, when possible, for easier access throughout the duration. During the area defense it is important for the company commander, with the assistance of the first sergeant, to locate the company trains where it is easily defended, and within reasonable proximity to the logistics resupply point. In some instances, the company trains will collocate within the CAB combat trains with caches of supply placed in proximity of the forward defending elements.

PREPARATION

3-143.   Preparation activities help the commander and subordinate units of the company team (including attachments) understand the situation and their roles in the overall operation. The commander takes every opportunity to improve situational understanding before execution through the integration of intelligence and operations. The commander continuously plans, tasks, and employs aggressive information collection assets and forces throughout the preparation of the defense.

3-144.   The company commander may need to adjust the plan or be forced to adjust the plan due to changes in the CAB's security plan or because of intelligence updates (from higher or within the company). These adjustments might put the company in a role to screen, guard, or secure to support the CAB concept.

SECURITY

3-145.   Just as the company ensures it can support the CAB's security plan, the commander also ensures the company security plan is in place to keep the enemy from observing or surprising the company. Security is established and sustained throughout the defensive. The commander bases this plan on tasks received from the CAB, on the enemy situation, the terrain, and on visibility conditions. The commander should ensure the usage of active measures, passive measures, and counterreconnaissance. Active control measures include OPs, reconnaissance, patrolling, and 100-percent security. Passive measures consist of camouflage, movement control, light and noise discipline, proper radio etiquette, and unmanned ground sensors. Counterreconnaissance includes denying the enemy information and deceiving the enemy into motivating them to do what the defender wants them to do.

REHEARSALS

3-146.   Rehearsals allow the commander to assess subordinate preparations and identify areas that may require more supervision. The commander considers time, preparation activities, and OPSEC when selecting a rehearsal type. (See appendix B for more information.) Rarely will the company have enough time to conduct a full-force rehearsal given the tempo of operations and the potentially large size of the AO. When possible, the commander considers conducting key leader map and terrain board rehearsals at night. This allows them to focus on supervising defensive position preparations with subordinate leaders during daylight. Rehearsals should cover—

- Security operations.
- Battle handover and passage of lines.
- Security area and MBA engagement rehearsals.
- Closure of lanes (as required).
- Movement from hide positions to BPs.
- Usage of fire commands, triggers, and maximum engagement lines for both direct and indirect systems.

- Shifting of fires to refocus and redistribute effects.
- Displacement to BPs (subsequent, supplementary, and alternate BPs).
- Engagement, disengagement, reposition, and withdrawal criteria.
- Cross leveling and resupply of critical classes of supply (Class V).
- Actions to deal with enemy penetrations, major enemy efforts along areas of risk or flank avenues of approach, and enemy actions in the rear area.
- Sustainment, particularly CASEVAC, emergency resupply operations, and reorganization.
- Execution of routes for repositioning, movement of the reserve, withdrawal, and movement to CCPs, and higher echelon exchange points.
- Execution of follow-on missions to exploit defensive success.

SURVIVABILITY AND COUNTERMOBILITY

3-147. Much of the strength of a defense rests on the integration and construction of reinforcing obstacles, exploitation of existing obstacles, and actions to enhance the survivability of the force through construction of fighting positions and fortifications. The commander's intent focuses survivability and countermobility preparation through the articulation of obstacle intent (target, effect, and relative location) and establishment of priorities for survivability and countermobility.

3-148. Although engineers prioritize the engineer effort within the commander's guidance and construct fighting positions to standard, the maneuver unit sites each position and develops the BP. The maneuver unit should designate a representative as the onsite point of contact to guide the execution of the required engineer support. (See ATP 3-37.34 for more information.)

3-149. With the assistance of available engineer support, the company commander establishes coordinated priorities of work. The priority of work tasks established by the commander outline survivability and countermobility instructions for attached and subordinate units. The commander should instruct subordinates to augment and assist engineering attachments and assets to expedite improvement of the defense. If little to no engineer support is available, the company commander must establish these same priorities early for subordinate platoons to begin as soon as possible due to the lack of engineer assets. In some instances, this may require that obstacles intended to limit mobility, and survivability locations are fully prepared by organic company elements.

TIME MANAGEMENT

3-150. A critical aspect of defensive planning is managing available time. The commander decides what must be accomplished during daylight to enable platoons and Infantry squads to continue defensive preparations into darkness. Because there is never enough time to prepare the defense, the commander must make use of all time.

3-151. Platoon positions identified and prepared during hours of limited visibility may not be completely effective during daylight. The commander's initial estimate of the time available includes how much daylight is needed for subordinate leaders to identify primary positions. Additionally, using engineer digging assets during hours of limited visibility is often very difficult and can be dangerous. Safety precautions need to be taken if daylight hours run short and digging assets are still being employed.

3-152. The commander may establish a detailed time schedule for completing key actions and events in the priority of work. This ensures that all units are generally at the same point in the priority of work. This also allows rehearsals to be scheduled effectively for the entire unit. An example of this time schedule might be—

- 1000–Primary BPs dug and camouflaged.
- 1500–Company rehearsal for the counterattack.
- 1600–Leader's sand-table rehearsal of the indirect fire plan.
- 1900–Primary positions complete, platoons rehearse disengagement, and movement to supplementary positions.
- 2200–Limited-visibility rehearsal for the counterattack.

MONITORING PREPARATIONS

3-153. The commander assisted by the XO and first sergeant directly monitors preparatory actions. The command team also tracks higher and adjacent unit status, as well as the current enemy situation. The commander establishes priorities of work that may include but are not limited to establishing security a plan, preparing BPs, conducting EA rehearsals, obstacle employment (mines or wire), and marking TRPs.

3-154. Establishing priority of work is a method of controlling the preparation of a defense. The SOP's description of "priority of work" should include individual duties. The company team commander changes priorities based on the situation. All leaders in the company team should have a specific priority of work for their duty position. Although listed in sequence, several tasks are performed at the same time. An example priority of work sequence is as follows:

- Post local security.
- Establish company reconnaissance and surveillance operation.
- Position vehicles, AT weapons, machine guns, and assign sectors of fire.
- Position other assets (for example, company CP and company trains).
- Designate final protective lines and FPFs.
- Clear fields of fire and prepare range cards and sector sketches.
- Adjust indirect fire FPFs. The firing unit fire direction center (FDC) should provide a safety box that is clear of all friendly units before firing any adjusting rounds.
- Prepare fighting positions.
- Install wire communications, if applicable.
- Emplace obstacles and mines.
- Mark (or improve marking for) TRPs and DFCMs (day/night).
- Improve primary fighting positions.
- Prepare alternate and supplementary positions.
- Establish a sleep and rest plan.
- Reconnoiter movements.
- Rehearse engagements and disengagements or displacements (day/night).
- Adjust positions and control measures as required.
- Stockpile ammunition, food, and water.
- Dig trenches between positions.
- Reconnoiter routes.
- Continue to improve positions.

3-155. As subordinate units position elements and execute defensive preparations, the commander coordinates their activities within the overall situation. The commander monitors the enemy situation through information collection efforts at the company and CAB level. The commander continually analyzes information on the enemy situation to determine the effects on preparation time available and any changes to the COA. Company information collection reporting thresholds are updated as the situation changes and as the information collection effort answers information requirements.

3-156. The commander monitors the status of subordinate rehearsals and conducts company rehearsals and updates the plan as needed based on continuously updated intelligence and the status of preparations. The XO analyzes the status of logistics and maintenance of equipment within the company to determine any required adjustments to the plan or task organization. The commander and attached engineer assets monitor the progress of all engineer efforts within the AO. The commander continually adjusts the projected completion of engineer tasks based on current and anticipated work rates. The commander, assisted by recommendations from available engineer support, identifies potential shortfalls early and determines how to shift assets to make up for them or where to accept risk.

EXECUTION

3-157. Throughout the area defense, the commander conducts shaping operations designed to regain the initiative by limiting the attacker's options and disrupting the enemy's plan. Shaping operations prevent enemy forces from massing, creating windows of opportunity for the conduct of decisive maneuver, and allowing the defending force to defeat the attacking enemy in detail. The mission variables of METT-TC (I) determine how closely the commander synchronizes supporting efforts with the main effort.

FIND THE ENEMY

3-158. The security force predominantly focuses on reconnaissance, counterreconnaissance, target acquisition, reporting, destruction, delay of the enemy main body, and battle handover. Security forces integrate these actions with friendly forces forward of them, maintaining information flow. Security forces may execute battle handover with forward elements and then assist them in executing a rearward passage. Throughout security area operations, security forces coordinate and crosstalk with units to their rear. When security forces execute rearward passage of lines and battle handover, they may then move to the flanks of the MBA or occupy an AA to the rear to plan for future operations. On approaches that the enemy does not use, the commander may desire to leave elements of the security force forward to preserve observation and access to enemy flanks.

3-159. Information collection within the security force provides the commander with information to support decision making, to provide early warning and reaction time, and to support targeting. Guided by the CCIRs, the four primary tasks conducted as part of information collection (reconnaissance, security operations, surveillance, and intelligence operations) help provide the following information—

- Location, movement, and destruction of enemy reconnaissance and security forces and surveillance assets.
- Speed, direction, composition, and strength of enemy formations.
- Locations of high-payoff targets (for example, indirect fire, bridging, and command and control assets).
- Enemy actions at decision points.
- Enemy flanking actions, breaching operations, and force concentrations.
- Battle damage assessment.
- Movement of follow-on forces.

FIX THE ENEMY

3-160. The commander has several options to help fix an attacking enemy force. The commander can design shaping operations—such as securing the flanks and point of a penetration—to fix the enemy and allow friendly forces to execute decisive maneuver elsewhere. Combat outposts and strong points can also deny enemy movement to or through a given location. The commander uses obstacles covered by fire to fix, turn, block, or disrupt to limit the enemy's available options. Properly executed obstacles (situational and reserved) are a result of the synthesis of top-down and bottom-up obstacle planning and emplacement. Blocking forces can also affect enemy movement. A blocking force may achieve its mission from a variety of positions depending on the mission variables of METT-TC (I).

3-161. The commander shapes and decides the engagement by massing the effects of combat power. Effects are synchronized in time and space and should be rapid and unexpected so that they break the enemy's offensive tempo and disrupt the enemy's attack. Synchronized prior planning and preparation bolster the effects of combat power, increasing the effectiveness of the defense.

3-162. Depending on the defensive scheme of maneuver, the defender may fight primarily from a single series of positions, or it may conduct delay operations, capitalizing on movement and repeated attacks to defeat the enemy in-depth. Forward positioned forces, obstacles, and fires are used to break the enemy's momentum, force the enemy to deploy earlier than desired, reduce the enemy's numerical advantage, disrupt enemy formations and tempo, and force the enemy into positions of vulnerability.

3-163.   As the operation evolves, the commander knows that there will probably be a requirement to shift the main effort and supporting effort(s) to press the engagement and keep the enemy off balance. The commander integrates information collection tasks to shift the effects of fires and maneuver forces so that they are repeatedly focused, and refocused to achieve decisive, destructive, and disruptive effects upon the enemy's attack. IPB enables information collection to determine likely enemy actions, while security forces and MBA forces confirm or deny those actions.

FOLLOW THROUGH

3-164.   The company team, as part of the CAB, may conduct local counterattacks to restore or preserve defensive integrity. If the CAB can organize a counterattack force, this force must have mobility or be pre-positioned in a position of advantage to attack the enemy from an unexpected flank. Within the context of the ABCT's operations, a defending CAB and its company teams may execute a counterattack in support of the ABCT's defensive posture, as part of a larger force seeking to complete the destruction of the enemy's attack, or as part of a transition to offensive operations.

SECTION IV – MOBILE DEFENSE

3-165.   While the Armor and mechanized Infantry company team or the CAB do not have resources or the capability in combat power conduct a mobile defense, both can participate in one as a member of a striking force or a fixing force. The following paragraphs describe the mobile defense and the role that the company team can conduct in support of a mobile defense operation.

> *Note.* A division is the smallest unit that can conduct a mobile defense. This is because of its ability to fight multiple engagements throughout the width, depth, and height of the division AO while simultaneously resourcing fixing, striking, and reserve forces.

MOBILE DEFENSE

3-166.   The mobile defense is a type of defensive operation that concentrates on the destruction or defeat of the enemy through a decisive attack by a striking force. (See ADP 3-90 for more information.) Mobile defense focuses on destroying the attacking force by allowing enemy to advance into a position that exposes the enemy to counterattack and envelopment. Division commanders use the fixing force to hold attacking enemy forces in position, help channel attacking enemy forces into ambush areas, and retain areas from which to launch the striking force. A mobile defense requires an AO of considerable depth. The division commander must be able to shape the battlefield, causing an enemy force to overextend its lines of communication, expose its flanks, and dissipate its combat power. Likewise, the commander must be able to move friendly forces around and behind the enemy force targeted to be cut off and destroyed. (See FM 3-90 for more information.)

STRIKING FORCE

3-167.   The striking force is a dedicated counterattack force in a mobile defense constituted with the bulk of available combat power. (See ADP 3-90 for more information.) The attack by the striking force in the EA isolates the targeted penetrating enemy force and defeats or destroys that enemy force, if possible. The striking force must execute the counterattack rapidly and violently, employing all combat power necessary to ensure success. The striking force may be committed at a different time than anticipated and in an entirely different area than planned. Thus, it must be able to respond to unexpected developments rapidly and decisively.

FIXING FORCE

3-168.   A fixing force is a force designed to supplement the striking force by preventing the enemy from moving from a specific area for a specific time. (See ADP 3-90 for more information.) In a mobile defense, an ABCT attached to the division is normally part of the fixing force. The fixing force conducts either an area defense or a delay structured to establish the conditions necessary for the successful conduct of the striking force's attack. Within the mobile defense, fixing forces reposition as necessary and conduct local counterattacks to control the depth and breadth of an enemy penetration and ensure the retention of ground from which the striking force can launch the decisive counterattack. When facing large enemy penetrating forces, division shaping operations or supporting efforts repeatedly isolate portions of the enemy force that are then attacked by the striking force, which defeats the enemy in detail. (See sections III and V of this chapter for additional information on the conduct of an area defense or delay, respectively.)

SECTION V – RETROGRADE

3-169.   A *retrograde movement* is any movement to the rear or away from the enemy (FM 3-90). The enemy may force these operations, or a commander may execute them voluntarily. In either case, the higher commander of the force executing the operation must approve the retrograde. Retrograde operations are transitional operations; they are not considered in isolation. In a retrograde, the CAB and subordinate companies are usually part of a larger scheme of maneuver designed to regain the initiative and defeat the enemy. (See FM 3-90 for more information.)

GENERAL CONSIDERATIONS FOR RETROGRADE

3-170.   Retrograde movements may be classified as delaying, withdrawal, or retirement actions. In each action, a force moves to the rear, using combinations of combat formations and marches. The commander may use all three actions singularly or in combination with other offensive or defensive operations. The commander may use all three actions singularly or in combination with other offensive or defensive operations. The commander executes retrogrades to—

- Disengage from operations.
- Gain time without fighting a decisive engagement.
- Resist, exhaust, and damage an enemy in situations that do not favor a defense.
- Draw the enemy into an unfavorable situation or extend the enemy's lines of communications.
- Preserve the force or avoid combat under undesirable conditions, such as continuing an operation that no longer promises success.
- Reposition forces to locations that are more favorable or conform to movements of other friendly troops.
- Position the force for use elsewhere in other missions.
- Simplify sustainment of the force by shortening lines of communications.
- Position the force where it can safely conduct reconstitution.
- Adjust the defensive scheme to secure terrain that is more favorable.
- Deceive the enemy.

DELAY

3-171.   A *delay* is when a force under pressure trades space for time by slowing down the enemy's momentum and inflicting maximum damage on enemy forces without becoming decisively engaged (ADP 3-90). When conducting a delay, the company team yields ground to gain time while retaining flexibility and freedom of action. The company team may execute a delay when it has insufficient combat power to attack, defend, or when the higher unit's plan calls for drawing the enemy into an area for a counterattack.

3-172.   The delay is one of the most demanding of all ground combat operations. A delay wears down the enemy so that friendly forces can regain the initiative through offensive action, buys time to establish an effective defense, or determines enemy intentions as part of a security operation. The purpose of the delay is to control the enemy's tempo by forcing the enemy to deploy multiple times and repeatedly concentrate its combat power to defeat the delaying force. Although the company must establish and maintain contact, it should avoid becoming decisively engaged, except when directed to prevent enemy penetration of a phase line for a specific duration. It is critical that the commander's intent defines what is more important to the mission: gaining time, inflicting casualties on the enemy, or protecting the force. Normally in a delay, inflicting casualties on the enemy is secondary to gaining time. The commander establishes risks for each delay but ordinarily maintaining freedom of action and avoiding decisive engagement is of ultimate importance.

PLANNING

3-173. Conducting a delay requires the close coordination of forces and a clear understanding by subordinates of the commander's intent, the scheme of maneuver, and detailed mission graphics. The potential for the loss of control is high in delay operations, making cross talk and coordination between commanders and subordinate leaders extremely important. Subordinate initiative is critical, but it must be in the context of close coordination with others. Plans must be flexible, with control measures throughout the AO allowing forces to maneuver to address all possible enemy options.

Parameters of the Delay

3-174. The commander clearly articulates the parameters of the delay in the order. Specifically, subordinate missions in terms of space, time, and friendly strength. Through these parameters, normally stated in paragraph 3 of the delay order tasks to subordinate units, the commander provides direction for actions during the delaying operation as planned, and when a subordinate is unable to meet the initial terms of the delay mission.

3-175. First within these parameters, the company commander is directed to conduct one of two directed approaches to conduct the delay: delay within the AO or delay forward of a specified line or terrain feature for a specified time. Time during the conduct of a delay is usually based on another unit completing its activities, such as establishing rearward defensive positions. A mission of delay within an AO implies that force integrity is a prime consideration. In this case, the company delays the enemy as long as possible while avoiding decisive engagement. Generally, this force displaces once predetermined criteria have been met, such as when the enemy force reaches a *disengagement line*—a phase line located on identifiable terrain that, when crossed by the enemy, signals to defending elements that it is time to displace to their next position (ADP 3-90).

3-176. The second parameter the order must specify is what is considered acceptable risk. Acceptable risk ranges from accepting decisive engagement by holding terrain for a given period, to avoiding decisive engagement to maintain the delaying force's integrity. The depth available for the delay, the time needed by the higher HQ, and subsequent missions for the delaying force determine how much acceptable risk.

3-177. Third, the order must specify whether the delaying force may use the entire AO or whether it must delay from specific BPs. A delay using the entire AO is preferable, but a delay from specific positions may be required to coordinate two or more units in the delay. The CAB commander normally assigns the company an AO when—

- There is no dominating terrain on the enemy avenues of approach.
- The AO is extremely wide.

3-178. The company commander then may assign AO or initial and subsequent delay positions for subordinate platoons. The commander defends and withdraws by platoons bounding them to the rear. The CAB commander normally assigns the company a series of BPs if—

- The CAB is delaying in restrictive terrain where the enemy can be canalized into selected areas.
- There is terrain that dominates the avenues of approach.
- The AO covers a narrow frontage.

3-179. When the CAB commander has assigned the company a series of BPs from which to delay, the company moves from one BP to another, as directed by the CAB commander. If it coincides with the CAB's plan, the company commander may choose platoon BPs and fight a delay action between assigned companies BPs. The company commander must decide which positions require preparation and allocate time and resources to them.

3-180. The CAB commander has greater control of the delay when delaying from BPs. However, the company commander has more control when delaying in an AO. The CAB commander can impose more control of the company's rearward movement by assigning PLs and times for these lines to be crossed, in conjunction with the CAB's scheme of maneuver. The company has the same control by assigning its own triggers for platoons crossing PLs as well. If the delay is conducted over a long distance, either method may be used. No matter which is used, the company commander chooses the platoon positions and the routes to them. If there is terrain that is defendable forward of a CAB-established phase line, the commander may consider defending there for the required amount of stated time for that particular phase line.

Organization of Forces

3-181.   The CAB's organization of forces depends on how the ABCT has structured its forces unless the CAB operates independently. The ABCT normally organizes into a security force, main body, and reserve, though operations extended across large areas may preclude the use of an ABCT-controlled security force and reserve. In some cases, the ABCT may direct the CAB to organize its own security, main body, and reserve forces; the same as if the CAB was operating independently.

3-182.   When the CAB operates independently or establishes its own security force, the CAB normally uses the scout platoon and the sniper squad as a screening force. These elements position to observe the most likely enemy avenues of approach and can initiate fires to slow and weaken the enemy. These elements may be reinforced with other elements of the CAB, for example, platoon from a company team, forward observers, and FISTs executing direct and indirect fire targets on a primary enemy avenue of approach.

3-183.   When conducting a delay, the company team does not typically fight on its own, but as part of the CAB. The company team can delay and draw the enemy into vulnerable positions. The company tries to cause the enemy casualties to stop them when possible. The company team is expected to aggressively fight, without becoming decisively engaged. This is done by defending, disengaging, moving, and defending again. This will also include counterattacks, and spoiling attacks when possible. The company commander must ensure that the company plan fits into the framework of the higher echelon commander to afford forces maximum efforts in moving during the delay. This means that the company commander will assign AO, or BPs to platoons to best coordinate the company tasks within the delay operations.

Delay Techniques

3-184.   When conducting a delay, the both the CAB and company, commanders normally assign subordinate units contiguous AO that are deeper than they are wide. The commanders synchronize the employment of these combined arms teams throughout the depth of each assigned AO for the delay. When commanders expect to delay for only a short time or the AO lacks depth, the delaying unit may be forced to fight from a single set of positions. When commanders expect the delay to last for a longer period, or if sufficient depth is available, the delaying unit may delay from either alternate or subsequent positions. In both techniques, delaying units normally reconnoiter delay positions before occupying them and, if possible, post guides on one or two positions. The company commander typically sends a quartering party to conduct the reconnaissance of routes, and positions to employ weapons systems effectively. Sending a quartering party to the delay location may also guide arriving units into their positions and preposition ammunition, and other supplies at each position. The quartering party is also able to coordinate with any units to the rear of the company when a passage of lines is required. If the company has thoroughly reconnoitered and rehearsed the delay, the quartering party may not be required.

3-185.   In executing both methods of delay, it is critical that the delaying units maintain contact with the enemy between delay positions. Table 3-2 summarizes the comparison of two delay techniques.

Table 3-2. Delay techniques comparison

Method of Delay	Use When	Advantage	Disadvantage
Delay from alternate positions	Area of operation is narrow. Forces are adequate to split between different positions (in-depth).	Allows positioning in-depth. Harder for enemy to isolate units. Increases flexibility. Allows more time for maintenance.	Requires continuous coordination. Requires passage of line, increasing vulnerability and fratricide potential. Engages only part of the force at one time.
Delay from subsequent positions	Area of operation is wide. Forces available are not adequate to position in-depth.	Reduced fratricide risk. Ease of command and control. Repeated rearward passages not required.	Limited depth to the delay positions. Easier to penetrate or isolate units. Less time is available to prepare each position. Less flexibility.

3-186. In a delay from alternate positions (see figure 3-13 on page 3-44), two or more units in a single AO occupy delaying positions in-depth. As the first unit engages the enemy, the second occupies the next position in-depth and prepares to assume responsibility for the operation. The first force disengages and passes around (preferred method) or through the second force. The force then moves to the next position and prepares to reengage the enemy while the second force takes up the fight. If the AO is narrow, the company employs platoons in-depth occupying alternate positions. This enables a strong delay, with forces available to counterattack or assist in the disengagement of the forces in contact. Using alternate positions helps maintain pressure on the enemy and helps prevent the company and subordinate platoons from being decisively engaged. A delay from alternate positions is particularly useful on the most dangerous avenues of approach because it offers greater security and depth than a delay from subsequent positions. However, it also poses the highest potential for fratricide and vulnerability as units pass near or through each other.

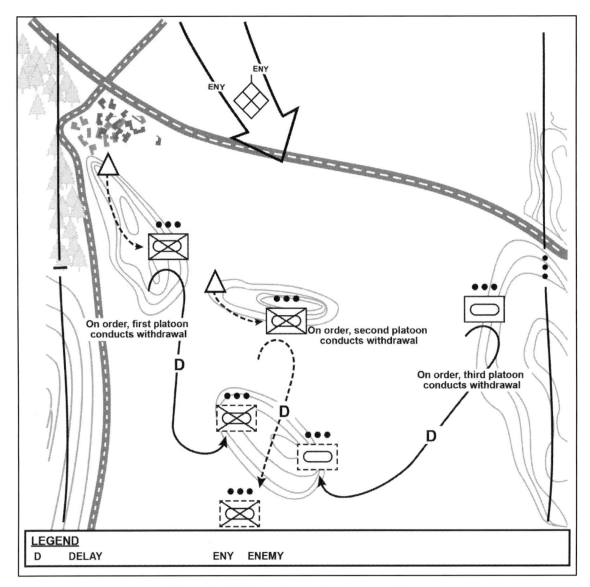

Figure 3-13. Delay from alternate position

3-187.   A delay from subsequent positions is used when the assigned AO is so wide that available forces cannot occupy more than a single layer of positions. (See figure 3-14.) In a delay from subsequent positions, most forces are arrayed along the same phase line or series of BPs. The forward forces delay the enemy from one phase line to the next within their assigned AO. This is the least preferred method of delaying since there is a much higher probability of forces becoming isolated or decisively engaged, particularly if the delay must be maintained over more than one or two subsequent positions. The delay force also has limited ability to maintain pressure on the enemy as it disengages and moves to subsequent positions unless it has been allocated additional and adequate indirect-fire support.

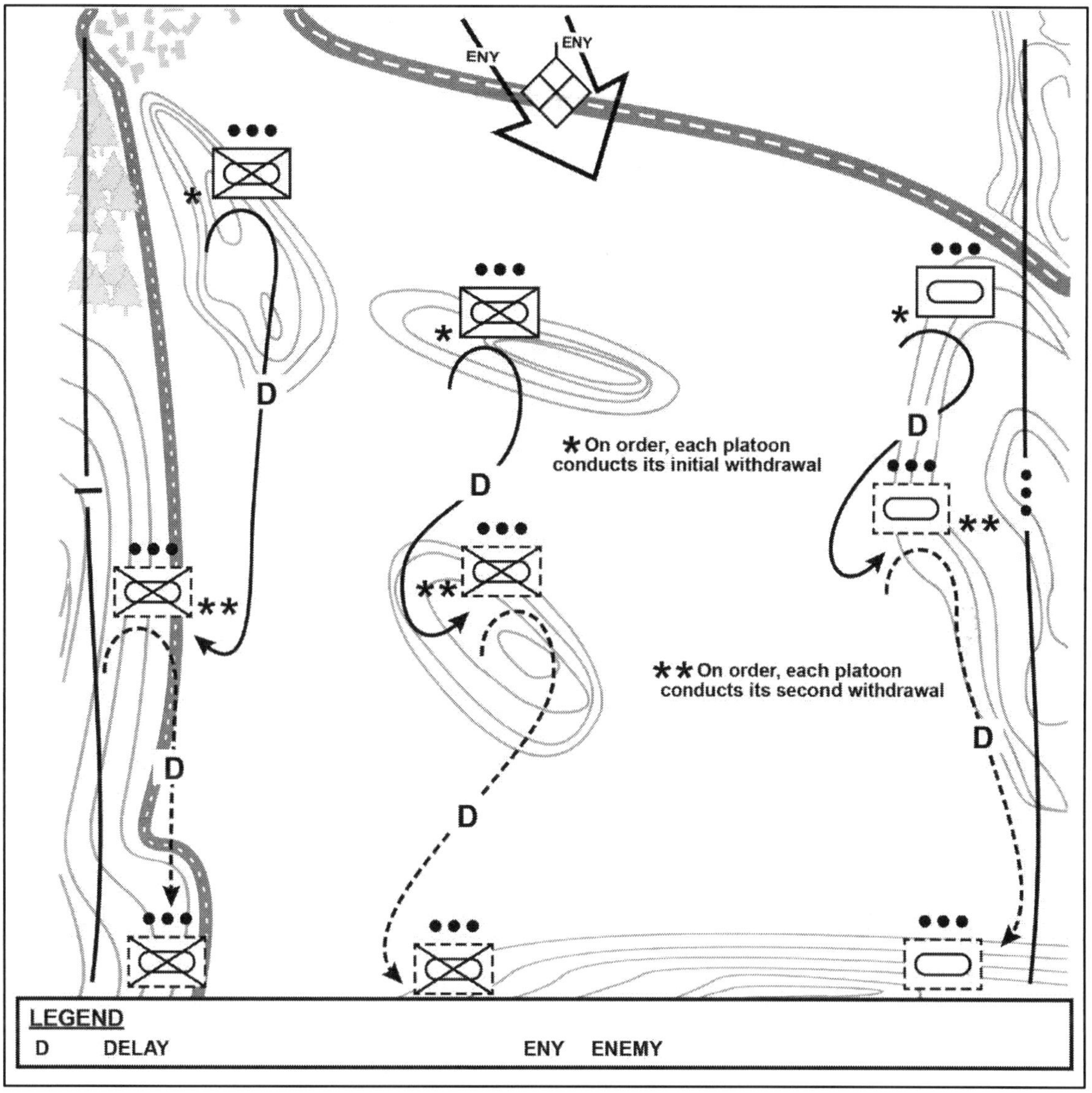

*On order, each platoon conducts its initial withdrawal

**On order, each platoon conducts its second withdrawal

LEGEND
D   DELAY   ENY   ENEMY

Figure 3-14. Delay from subsequent position

PREPARATION

3-188.   Defensive preparations for the conduct of an area defense discussed in section II of this chapter also apply during the conduct of a delay. Resources, including the time available to prepare, determine the extent of preparations. Throughout preparation, the commander assigns a high priority to security operations. Additionally, the preparation of alternate, supplementary, and subsequent positions receives a higher priority than in either a mobile or an area defense. Understanding that it is not always possible to complete all preparations before starting the delaying operation, delaying units continue to prepare and adapt plans as the situation develops.

Rehearsal

3-189.   When conducting a rehearsal, key leaders, as a minimum rehearse the operation against all feasible enemy COAs to promote flexibility during decision making. The commander examines each subordinate unit's plan as they fight the delay during the rehearsal, paying close attention to the following:

- Direct and indirect fire instructions.

- Timing of movements (to include in limited visibility).
- Delaying actions from one position to the next, to include disengagement criteria and triggers.
- Means and methods of disengaging from the enemy.
- Maintaining contact with the enemy as the force moves to alternate and subsequent positions.
- Execution of situational and reserved obstacles to include closure of lanes.
- Movement times, routes, and positioning of fire support, engineer, protection, and sustainment assets.

3-190.   The commander also rehearses contingencies to deal with enemy penetrations and decisive engagement and the opportunity to resume the offense. Rehearsals serve to synchronize the movement of maneuver forces, fire support, protection, and sustainment units. During rehearsal, it is especially important to portray movement times and required routes realistically to identify potential conflicts.

Precombat Checks and Inspections

3-191.   Preparations include precombat checks (PCCs) and inspections of subordinates. The commander and subordinate leaders check and inspect subordinate units to ensure—

- Subordinate units, Soldiers, and systems are as fully capable and ready to execute the mission as time and resources permit.
- Delaying forces have the resources necessary to accomplish the mission.
- Movement, maneuver, fire support, and obstacle plans are consistent with the commander's intent and concept of operations.
- Delaying units coordinate to maintain cohesion and mutual support during the delay.
- Subordinate unit EAs enable the company and higher echelon scheme of maneuver.
- EA development includes disengagement criteria, routes, and triggers that support the maneuver plan within its AO.

EXECUTION

3-192.   When the company is part of a larger scheme of maneuver designed to regain the initiative and defeat the enemy, the complex nature of a delay requires maneuver elements within the delaying operation to execute different, complementary, actions. In a single delaying operation, attacks, area defenses, mobile defenses, and other actions may occur in any sequence or simultaneously. When conducting a delay, as in an area defense, the company defends using a variety of tactics, techniques, and procedures to accomplish the mission. Security forces are deployed well-forward of the initial delay positions of the main body to buy time, to establish an effective delay, and to give early warning of any enemy approach. Forward security forces detect and report as enemy forces approach to confirm the enemy's probable COA. The company commander should receive the following:

- The initial delay positions.
- The CAB's plan for controlling engagements, disengagements, and movement.
- AO and BPs.
- The location of AAs (if necessary).
- General routes.
- Quartering party instructions (if used).
- Special instructions concerning attachments.
- Priorities and efforts of supporting engineers.

3-193.   As with the area defense, the commander ensures security plans are in place to employ security and OPs to identify enemy advances. Once the most forward company force (or forward positioned force) makes contact with the enemy, it maintains contact. Security forces use covered, concealed, and coordinated routes to avoid enemy and friendly fires.

3-194.   Security forces fix, defeat, and destroy the enemy's reconnaissance and security elements without risking decisive engagement. These forces direct fires at the approaching enemy force as far forward of the delay positions as possible to disrupt and fix the enemy. Engaging a moving enemy at long ranges tends to inflict far more casualties on an attacking enemy than the enemy can inflict on the delaying force; it also slows the enemy force's tempo of operations. The more a delaying force can blind an enemy force through the elimination of that force's reconnaissance assets, the more likely the enemy force is to hesitate and move with caution.

3-195.   As the enemy closes with security forces, company forces move back through or around the initial positions of the main body to subsequent positions that allow them to observe the main body area and assist in the disengagement and movement of forces to their next positions. This also prevents the enemy from finding gaps between delaying units and attacking the exposed flanks of delaying units. When the company occupies the forward line of own troops, engagements forward of the company's initial delaying positions are normally limited to observed fires to continue the disruption and attrition of the attacking enemy.

3-196.   The company maneuvers to force the enemy to deploy multiple times and repeatedly concentrate its combat power to defeat the delaying forces of the company. The commander makes decisions about disposition, displacement, timing, and engagement in the context of the higher commander's intent and priority for the delay. For example, when time is more important than force preservation, or vice versa. In many instances, the delaying force elements must accept decisive engagement to execute the mission in conjunction with the actions of another force.

3-197.   As delaying forces displace, they move to the flanks of delay positions and do not move through friendly EAs or TRPs, unless the tactical situation makes such movement necessary. Delaying forces ensure their routes do not reveal the locations of other friendly elements to include stay-behind forces and forward observers. Delaying forces may move by bounds within the platoon, and company to maintain direct fires on the enemy and cover movement. Short, intense engagements at near maximum range with sustained fires and covering obscurants, are key to forcing the enemy into deploying early and often for a decisive engagement. Observers position to the flanks in-depth to observe and shift fires as forces delay to alternate and subsequent positions.

3-198.   Once a delay starts, subordinate units displace rapidly between positions using obstacles and defensive positions in-depth to slow and canalize the enemy. The commander exploits the mobility of the company to confuse and defeat the enemy. Whenever possible, the commander grasps any fleeting opportunity to seize the initiative, even if only temporarily. By aggressively contesting the enemy's initiative through offensive action, the delaying force avoids passive patterns that favor the attacking enemy.

WITHDRAWAL

3-199.   A withdraw is to disengage from an enemy force and move in a direction away from the enemy. (See ADP 3-90 for more information.) Withdrawing units, whether all or part of a committed force, voluntarily disengage from the enemy to preserve the force or release it for a new mission. Based on the higher HQ's order and the enemy situation, the company team's withdrawal may be assisted or unassisted and may occur with or without enemy pressure.

3-200.   Withdrawals are inherently dangerous because they involve moving units to the rear and away from what is usually a stronger enemy force. The heavier the previous fighting and the closer the contact with the enemy, the more difficult the withdrawal. Ideally, the commander avoids withdrawing from action under enemy pressure, though this is not always possible.

PLANNING

3-201.   The commander plans and coordinates a withdrawal in the same manner as a delay though some mission variables of METT-TC (I) apply differently because of the differences between a delay and a withdrawal. A withdrawal may precede a retirement operation or follow a delaying operation. Control measures used in the withdrawal are the same as those in a delay or an area defense.

3-202.   Because a withdrawing force is most vulnerable if the enemy attacks, the commander normally plans for a withdrawal under enemy pressure. The commander then develops contingencies for a withdrawal without pressure. The commander's main considerations include—
 ● Plan for the next mission following the withdrawal.
 ● Disengagement criteria (time, friendly situation, enemy situation).

- Plan for a deliberate break in contact from the enemy.
- Plan for deception to conceal the withdrawal for as long as possible.
- Rapid displacement of the main body, safeguarded from enemy interference.
- Selection and protection of primary withdrawal routes and alternate withdrawal routes.
- Sitting of obstacles behind the DLIC to complicate the enemy's pursuit.
- Ensure fire support and sustainment assets remain within distance to support withdrawing units, security forces, and DLICs.

3-203. Planning for a withdrawal normally begins with the preparation of the plan for the next mission. Initial planning includes the development of disengagement criteria, route selection, and displacement timing based on the friendly and enemy situation. The follow-on mission for the company drives the end state of the withdrawal to best position units to accomplish the next mission. The desired end state can include withdrawing to an AA for follow-on missions or the establishment of a new defensive position. Alternatively, subordinate units of the company can withdraw indirectly to either area through one or more intermediate positions. When preparing the new defensive position, the commander balances the need for security with the need to get an early start on the defensive effort.

3-204. The commander's plan for the withdrawal clearly defines how to deceive the enemy as to the execution of the withdrawal; how to disengage from the enemy; and the end state of the operation in terms of time, location, and disposition of friendly and enemy forces. The commander usually confines rearward movement to times and conditions when the advancing enemy force cannot observe the activity and easily detect the withdrawal operation. To help preserve secrecy and freedom of action, for example, the commander considers visibility conditions and times when the enemy's reconnaissance efforts can observe friendly movements.

3-205. When planning for the deliberate break from the enemy, the commander has essentially two options: break contact using deception and stealth or break contact quickly and violently under the cover of supporting fires reinforced by obstacles to delay enemy's pursuit. In either option, the commander may employ obscuration to assist with breaking contact with the enemy or to deceive the enemy of the company's actual intentions. Terrain that hinders the mobility and surveillance capabilities of enemy combat systems and supporting tactical vehicles can offer concealment and cover for the movement of friendly forces.

Assisted and Unassisted Withdrawal

3-206. When the withdrawal is assisted, the assisting force(s) occupies positions to the rear of withdrawing forces and prepares to accept control of the situation. The assisting force can also assist withdrawing forces with route reconnaissance, route maintenance, fire support, protection, and sustainment. Both forces closely coordinate the withdrawal. After coordination, the withdrawing force delays to a BHL, conducts a passage of lines, and moves to its destination. Generally, in an assisted withdrawal, the withdrawing force coordinates the following with the assisting force:

- Rearward passage of lines.
- Reconnaissance of withdrawal routes.
- Forces to secure choke points or key terrain along the withdrawal routes.
- Forces to assist in movement control such as traffic control.
- Required combat, fire support, protection, and sustainment to assist the withdrawing CAB in disengaging from the enemy.

3-207. In an unassisted withdrawal, the withdrawing force establishes its own security and disengagement from the enemy. Subordinate units reconnoiter and secure routes used in its rearward movement while fire support and sustainment unit support the withdrawal. The commander establishes a security force as the rear guard while the main body withdraws. The commander, if possible, designates a flank security, or a screen as the situation requires. Sustainment and other support forces normally withdraw first, followed by combat forces not tasked with the security or reserve mission. However, sustainment and other support forces as they move to the rear must continue to maintain the ability to support the withdrawing force. To deceive the enemy as to friendly movement and if withdrawing under enemy pressure, the commander establishes a DLIC. As subordinates withdraw, the DLIC disengages from the enemy and follows the main body to its final destination.

Withdrawal Under and Without Enemy Pressure

3-208. When withdrawing under enemy pressure, all subordinate units withdraw simultaneously when available routes allow, using delaying tactics to fight their way to the rear. In the usual case, when simultaneous withdrawal of all forces is not practical, the commander decides the order of withdrawal. The commander then makes three interrelated key decisions: when to start the movement of selected sustainment and main body elements, when forward elements should start thinning out, and when the security force should start its disengagement operations. The commander avoids premature actions that lead the enemy to believe a withdrawal is being contemplated. The commander anticipates the enemy's means of interference and plans the employment of security forces, FA, and Army and Air Force aviation assets to counter this interference. Additional factors influencing this decision may include—

- Subsequent missions.
- Availability of transportation assets and routes.
- Disposition of friendly and enemy forces.
- Level and nature of enemy pressure.
- Degree of urgency associated with the withdrawal.

3-209. When withdrawing without enemy pressure the commander plans when to begin the withdrawal and has the option of taking prudent risks to increase the displacement capabilities of the withdrawing force. For example, the main body may be ordered to conduct a tactical road march instead of moving in tactical formations. The commander can plan for stay-behind forces as part of the operation.

Detachment Left in Contact

3-210. When the company is part of the CAB's scheme of maneuver, a DLIC is generally a company-size element that remains behind to deceive the enemy into believing the CAB is still in position while most of the unit withdraws. The detachment simulates—as nearly as possible—the continued presence of the main body until it is too late for the enemy to react to the main body's withdrawal. The CAB commander develops specific instructions about what the detachment is to do when the enemy attacks and when and under what circumstances the detachment continues to delay or conduct withdrawal. When the DLIC disengages from the enemy, the detachment uses the same techniques as in the delay. When required, and if available, the CAB commander provides the detachment with additional recovery, evacuation, and transportation assets to use after disengagement to speed its rearward movement.

3-211. The commander uses two methods to resource the DLIC. The first is for each forward subordinate maneuver element (generally the company) of the CAB to leave a subelement in place. For example, each forward company leaves a task-organized platoon or detachment in contact. This is the least desirable option since it complicates command and control and task organization. The CAB commonly uses this option when the subordinate companies have lost significant portions of their command and control systems. Typically, these elements fall under a detachment commander designated by the CAB commander.

3-212. The second method involves one forward subordinate maneuver element (generally a subordinate company) of the CAB staying behind as the DLIC. For example, a CAB with three or two maneuver companies positioned forward leaves one of the forward positioned companies as the DLIC. The DLIC normally repositions its forces (expanding its security responsibilities) to cover the width of the CAB's AO.

3-213. When the company is selected as the CAB's DLIC, the commander repositions platoons and weapons to cover the CAB's withdrawal. This normally includes repositioning a platoon in each of the other company positions (relief in place) to cover the most dangerous avenues of approach into those positions, and repositioning systems to cover the most dangerous avenues of approach into the CAB's AO. Normally, the DLIC company is task organized and reinforced by the CAB, for example, attached mortar section or another external enabler (if available).

PREPARATION

3-214.   Preparation for a withdrawal is conducted in the same manner as a delay. Preparation activities ensure subordinate units and Soldiers have a clear understanding of the withdrawal plan and the current enemy situation. To the extent possible, subordinate leaders conduct inspections and rehearse key portions of the plan to ensure maneuver units and Soldiers understand their portion of the plan or role and that supporting elements and equipment are positioned and ready to execute the withdrawal.

3-215.   When preparing for an assisted withdrawal, the commander ensures adequate coordination for battle handover and passage of lines. The focus of the rehearsal for the withdrawal is on actions to maintain security, disengagement from the enemy (when under enemy pressure), and the movement of forces. When possible, key leaders or liaisons from the assisting force attend rehearsals. During rehearsals, control measures are confirmed to include fire support coordination measures. Leaders rehearse the plan against the full range of possible enemy actions. The commander rehearses contingencies for reverting to a delay, commitment of the reserve, and enemy interdiction of movement routes.

3-216.   In an unassisted withdrawal, the unit establishes its own security force and reserve and coordinates those actions with the unit's main body. The unit reconnoiters and secures routes to the rear and the support areas it will use during movement to the rear. In both unassisted and assisted withdrawals, the unit rehearses the plan to disengage from the enemy. Because the force is most vulnerable if the enemy attacks, the commander always plans for a withdrawal under pressure, then develops contingencies for a withdrawal without pressure.

3-217.   Prior to the withdrawal subordinate leaders must has a clear understanding of the mission. During backbriefs, the commander reinforces the following points:
- When the withdrawal will start.
- Location of company AA (if used), and what each platoon is to do upon its arrival.
- Identification of routes to take from the company AAs to the CAB's AA or their next position.
- Determination of the size, composition, and mission of the DLIC, and who the commander will be.
- Identification of upcoming company mission(s).
- Movement of company vehicles to the rear (including times and sequencing).
- Special instructions on the control of attachments.
- Deception plan.

EXECUTION

3-218.   As the company executes the withdrawal, the designated security force counters the enemy's attempt to disrupt the withdrawal or pursue. If the security force and the reserve cannot prevent the enemy from closing on the main body, the commander commits some or all of the main body to prevent the enemy from interfering further with the withdrawal.

3-219.   The main body delays, attacks, or defends as the situation requires. In this event, the withdrawal resumes at the earliest possible time. If the enemy blocks movement to the rear, the CAB must adjust its order of withdrawal march to ensure sustainment and supporting elements are not the primary fighting force to eliminate the threat. Friendly forces shift to alternate routes and bypass the interdicted area. Alternatively, they may attack through the enemy.

3-220.   With the most probable threat to a withdrawing force being a pursuing enemy, the commander organizes the majority of available combat power to the security force as a rear guard or a DLIC. When an enemy security zone exists between friendly and enemy forces, the existing security force can transition on order to a rear-guard mission. When the withdrawing force is in close contact with the enemy, this security zone does not normally exist. Withdrawal, under these conditions, requires that security forces, performing a rear-guard mission, adopt different techniques. A DLIC provides a way to sequentially break contact with the enemy.

3-221.   Once the company successfully disengage from the enemy, the commander has two options. The company team can rejoin the overall defense under more favorable conditions or transition into a retirement and continue to move away from the enemy and towards its next mission. Once out of contact with the enemy, the company, when required, may reconstitute and/or conduct a task organization change.

RETIREMENT

3-222. A retirement is when a force out of contact moves away from the enemy. (See ADP 3-90 for more information.) Retirements are conducted to reposition forces for future operations or to accommodate the current concept of operation. The CAB or individual companies normally conduct retirement as a tactical road march where security and speed are the most important considerations. When moving to an AA, the retiring force's ability to defend from the AA and protect itself during movement are major factors in positioning the AAs and identifying the retirement route(s). Though interference from enemy ground forces is not anticipated, mobile enemy forces, unconventional forces, air strikes, air assault operations, or long-range fires may attempt to interdict the retiring force. Typically, within this type of retrograde another unit's security force covers the movement of the retiring force.

SECTION VI – TRANSITION

3-223. During the planning for any operation, the commander must consider the follow-on missions from the higher HQs' OPORD and begins to plan how to achieve them. The company commander and leaders began to plan to conduct consolidation and reorganization before the next operation.

CONSOLIDATION, REORGANIZATION, AND CONTINUING OPERATIONS

3-224. The company commander plans and prepares for this phase of the operation as part of TLP for the entire mission, ensuring that the company is ready to conduct the following actions that usually are part of consolidation:

- Eliminate enemy resistance on the objective.
- Establish security beyond the objective by securing areas that may be the source of enemy direct fires or artillery observation.
- Establish additional security measures such as OPs and patrols.
- Prepare for and assist the passage of follow-on forces (if required).
- Continue to improve security by conducting other necessary defensive actions. These defensive actions include EA development, direct fire planning, and BP preparation.
- Adjust FPFs and register targets along likely mounted and dismounted avenues of approach.
- Protect the obstacle reduction effort.
- Secure detainees.
- Prepare for the enemy counterattack.

3-225. Reorganization is usually conducted concurrently with consolidation. It includes actions taken to prepare the company for follow-on operations. As with consolidation, the company commander plans and prepares for reorganization while conducting TLP and ensures the company takes the following actions:

- Provides essential medical treatment by applying tactical casualty combat care.
- Treats and evacuates wounded detainees and processes the remainder of detainees.
- Cross-levels personnel and adjusts task organization, when necessary, to support the next phase or mission.
- Conducts resupply operations, to include rearming and refueling.
- Redistributes ammunition and other supplies.
- Conducts required maintenance.
- Continues improvement of defensive positions, as needed.

3-226. The company may continue the defense, or if ordered, transition to focus on the conduct of offensive or stability operations at the conclusion of an engagement. The commander must assess the status of the forces before continuing operations. Once assessed, the commander considers the higher commander's concept of operations, friendly capabilities, and the enemy situation when making any decision. All missions should include plans for exploiting success or assuming a defense.

TRANSITION TO OPERATION FOCUSED ON STABILITY TASKS

3-227. The company commander should plan a defensive contingency with on-order offensive missions in an operation focused on stability tasks that could deteriorate. Subordinate leaders need to be fully trained to recognize activities that would initiate this transition, such as the disbandment of government or conventional security forces.

3-228. Company commanders and Soldiers need to be aware that elements of the BCT could be conducting offensive, defensive, and stability operations simultaneously within a small radius of each other. Rules of engagement (ROE) are assessed, updated, disseminated, and trained on while this transition occurs. Establishing security within the AO for the civilian population may call for a rapid response and initiative. The company team rapidly makes these transitions through dissemination of information with command and control systems, leadership that takes the initiative, and active reconnaissance.

TRANSITIONING TO RETROGRADE OR OFFENSE

3-229. A defending commander may transition from participating in a higher echelon's area or mobile defense to the retrograde as a part of continuing operations. A retrograde usually involves a combination of delay, withdrawal, and retirement operations. These operations may occur simultaneously or sequentially. As in other operations, the commander's concept of operations and intent drive the planning for retrograde operations. Each form of retrograde operation has its specific planning considerations, but considerations common to all retrograde operations are risk, the need for synchronization, and rear operations.

3-230. Higher HQ may order the company team to conduct an attack, MTC, or participate in exploitation. In some cases, the defensive operations might immediately transition into a pursuit.

3-231. The company may execute a counterattack, to destroy exposed enemy elements and free decisively engaged friendly elements. A base of fire element suppresses or fixes the enemy force while the counterattack (maneuver) element moves on a concealed route to a subsequent BP to engage the enemy in the flank or rear. The counterattack element maneuvers rapidly to its firing position, often fighting through enemy flank security elements to complete the counterattack before the enemy can bring follow-on forces forward to influence the fight.

3-232. Execution of the counterattack is like that for an attack by fire. Planning and preparation considerations for the counterattack vary depending on the purpose and location of the operation. For example, the counterattack may be conducted forward of friendly positions, requiring the reserve force to move around friendly elements and through the protective and tactical obstacles. In other situations, the commander may use a counterattack by fire to block, fix, or contain a penetration. In any case, the reserve force conducts the counterattack as an enemy-oriented operation.

Chapter 4

Stability

Operations focused on stability ultimately aim to establish conditions the local populace regards as legitimate, acceptable, and predictable. Stability operations focus on identifying and targeting the root causes of instability and building the capacity of local institutions. Sources of instability are actors, actions, or conditions that exceed the legitimate authority's capacity to exercise effective governance, maintain civil control, and ensure economic development. This chapter discusses the company's planning and operations considerations and transitions.

SECTION I – OVERVIEW

4-1.   Stabilization is a process in which personnel identify and mitigate underlying sources of instability to establish the conditions for long-term stability. Sources of instability manifest themselves locally. Instability may be caused by a catastrophic event, humanitarian crisis, foreign power-instigated violence, insurgency, or domestic rebellion and civil war. First, instability stems from decreased support for the government based on what locals expect from their government. Second, instability grows from increased support for antigovernment elements, which usually occurs when locals see spoilers as helping to solve the priority grievance. Third, instability stems from the undermining of the normal functioning of society where the emphasis must be on a return to the established norms. (See ADP 3-07 for more information.)

FUNDAMENTALS OF STABILIZATION

4-2.   Based on the four fundamentals (conflict transformation, unity of effort, building HN capacity and capabilities, and HN ownership and legitimacy) that lay the foundation for long-term stability. Army units conduct operations focused on stabilizing the environment and transforming conditions of the environment and the state toward normalization. Units at different echelons balance these principles to mitigate fragile state characteristics prevalent at the national, regional, and local levels. Long-term stabilization efforts within an OE transform the drivers of conflict while maintaining *unity of effort*, which is coordination and cooperation toward common objectives, even if the participants are not necessarily part of the same command or organization that is the product of successful unified action (JP 1, Vol 2), among diverse actors. Building partner capacity addresses potentially the most important effort to support and enable partners so they can perform their roles effectively. Fundamental to long-term stability and critical to the HN's ownership and legitimacy is to build trust and confidence among the states populace and is its involvement.

STABILITY FRAMEWORK

4-3.   The fragile state's framework forms the basis for the stabilization framework, which is a tool for understanding and prioritizing the broad range of activities that embody unity of effort in an OE characterized by a fragile state. These activities occur within distinct categories—initial response, transformation, and fostering sustainability—that collectively represent the tasks of area security and stability for consolidation of gains necessary to achieve security and reestablish stable, lasting peace.

4-4.   Actions of the initial response generally reflect activity executed to stabilize a crisis state in the AO. Army conventional force units typically perform initial response actions during, or directly after, a conflict or disaster in which the security situation prohibits the introduction of civilian personnel. Initial response actions aim to provide a secure environment that allows relief forces to attend to the immediate humanitarian needs of the local population. They reduce the level of violence and human suffering while creating conditions that enable other actors to participate safely in relief efforts.

4-5.   Stabilization, reconstruction, and capacity-building are transformation actions that are performed in a relatively secure environment. Transformation is essentially a consolidation of gains. Transformation actions occur in crisis or vulnerable states. There is the presence of a legitimate authority either interim or established, as well as indigenous HN security forces. These actions aim to build HN capacity across multiple sectors. Transformation actions are essential to the continuing stability of the environment. These actions are essential for fostering stability within the area.

4-6.   Fostering sustainability actions encompass long-term efforts, which capitalize on capacity building and reconstruction activities. Successful accomplishment of these actions establishes conditions that enable sustainable development. Usually, military forces perform fostering sustainability actions only when the security environment is stable enough to support efforts to implement the long-term programs that commit to the viability of the institutions and economy of the HN. Often, military forces conduct these long-term efforts to support broader, civilian-led efforts.

UNDERSTANDING THE OPERATIONAL ENVIRONMENT

4-7.   Operations focused on stability require the company commander to demonstrate cultural understanding and a clear appreciation of the myriad stability operations to determine which are fundamentally essential to mission success. The commander and subordinate leaders must understand the potential for conflicts among individuals and agencies with differing cultural backgrounds. For example, interagency conflict may arise because of perceived differences in organizational goals or attitudes about the appropriateness of military involvement. Anticipating counterproductive confrontations and taking steps to resolve individual and organizational conflicts constructively is paramount to successful collaboration. Additional preemptive strategies for managing conflict include ensuring all stakeholders are identified and included in making decisions.

INTER-ORGANIZATIONAL COLLABORATION

4-8.   During stability, the commander ensures the key players support interagency partnership, established ground rules, and collaborative interagency strategies to accomplish the mission. The commander must understand the importance of ensuring that interagency partners explore various alternatives and that all partners participate. The commander adopts consensus-building leadership behavior, to include open discourse, friendly debate, and discussion with opinion sharing and feedback from participants.

4-9.   One information related capability to conduct information operations that is available to every unit down to the squad/team/crew is Soldier and leader engagement. Soldier and leader engagement can build relationships, solve conflicts, convey information, calm fears, and refute rumors, lies, or misinformation or disinformation. Soldier and leader engagement can occur as a random face-to-face encounter or be a planned meeting. The medium for conducting Soldier and leader engagement is any communications method, such as telephone calls or texts, video teleconferences, or other audiovisual mediums, including social media. Commanders consider and choose the best candidate to conduct deliberate engagements or negotiations. (See ATP 3-13.5 for more information.)

4-10.   Understanding an OE includes understanding organizational goals or attitudes for all stability partners. Within operations focused on stability, the commander must act cooperatively rather than competitively, building relationships to achieve coordinated goals. Organizations can increase collaboration by providing their representatives with a clear understanding of their organization's functions and authority within the larger civil-military partnership. Regular interaction with interagency partners also contributes to an increased understanding of roles and mission requirements. Success in operations focused on stability requires an awareness of trends that influence views of the actors and an understanding of factors that shape or constrain options and capabilities for partner organizations.

4-11.   During operations focused on stability, military forces provide support to facilitate the execution of operations for which the HN is normally responsible. Typically, these tasks have a security component ideally performed by military forces. However, military forces sometimes provide logistic, medical, or administrative support to enable the success of civilian agencies and organizations. Operations that the company performs to support stability generally falls into one of three categories. The following represents the collective effort associated with a stability mission:

- Operations for which military forces retain primary responsibility.
- Operations for which civilian agencies or organizations likely retain responsibility, but military forces are prepared to execute.
- Operations for which civilian agencies or organizations retain primary responsibility.

MILITARY AND CIVILIAN ORGANIZATIONAL CULTURES

4-12. Military and civilian organizational cultures differ in significant ways comprising factors such as shared values, norms, expectations, and practices. An organizational culture influences how individuals approach work and what they regard as mission accomplishment. When team members with different organizational cultures interact with one another, differences become evident and can create tension in the group. The commander and subordinate leaders can minimize difficulties by educating themselves on these organizational differences—in mission objectives, size, and resource capabilities, and neutrality among others—and challenges in information-sharing and improving their understanding of and attitudes toward partners. The commander develops the information needed to understand partner organizations, their component teams, and their place in the stability activities and goals to achieve the desired end state conditions. This understanding forms the backdrop for assessing the effect of military actions, plans, and decisions on partner organizations. A poor understanding of the partners must be avoided because it can hamper trust and impair integration of military team members in interagency decision-making.

4-13. Operations focused on stability, range across all military operations and offer perhaps the most diverse set of circumstances the company team faces. The objective of operations focused on stability is to create conditions that the local populace regards as acceptable in terms of violence; the functioning of governmental, economic, and societal institutions; and that adhere to local laws, rules, and norms of behavior. During decisive action, the company commander seeks to create and maintain the conditions necessary to seize, retain, and exploit the initiative; and to consolidate gains, which is the activities to make enduring any temporary operational success and set the conditions for a stable environment allowing for a transition of control to legitimate authorities. The company, in coordination with the CAB and partner organizations, provides the means to secure and stabilize the OE and to conduct operations to establish and maintain stability or to reestablish stability. The commander keeps in mind how these operations transition in a comprehensive approach to avoid considering them in isolation. (See FM 3-07 for more information.)

SECTION II – STABILITY OPERATIONS

4-14. A stability operation is an operation conducted outside the United States in coordination with other instruments of national power to establish or maintain a secure environment and provide essential governmental services, emergency infrastructure reconstruction, and humanitarian relief. (See ADP 3-0 for more information.) Army forces conduct the following six primary stability operations: establish civil security, establish civil control, restore essential services, support to governance, support to economic and infrastructure development, and security cooperation. (See ATP 3-07.5 for more information.)

4-15. At the company team level and below, the primary stability operations are too broad to direct efforts to execute independently. They require partnership with outside organizations because they ultimately invoke political objectives executed in partnership with civic, security, humanitarian, and military organizations. At lower tactical echelons, efforts require understanding of specific aspects of the local situation to identify and mitigate sources of instability. The company team commander uses sewage, water, electricity, academics, trash, medical, security, other considerations (SWEAT-MSO), and PMESII-PT to address the need to bring about stability in the AO. (See ATP 3-07.5 for more information.)

4-16. The company makes the greatest contribution in establishing civil security, civil control, and security cooperation during the initial response and transformation phases of stability operations. Restore essential services, support to governance, support to economic infrastructure and development are tasks that the company utilizes partnership with unified action partners to improve the local situation. Unity of command and an understanding with all unified action partners to include civil affairs units, HN security forces, HN government forces, international aid organizations, and others for a single focused direction of progress in these efforts.

ESTABLISH CIVIL SECURITY

4-17. Establishing civil security involves providing for the safety of the HN and its population, to include security from internal and external threats. It is essential to provide a safe and secure environment. Civil security includes a diverse set of activities. These range from enforcing peace agreements to conducting disarmament, demobilization, reintegration, and includes biometric identity data collection to identify or nominate to the biometric-enabled watch list persons of interest, criminal elements, known and suspected terrorists, and other irregular forces. (See ATP 3-07.5 for more information.)

4-18. Until a legitimate civil government can assume responsibility for security, military forces perform the tasks associated with civil security. At the same time, they help develop HN security and police forces. Normally, the responsibility for establishing and maintaining civil security belongs to military forces from the onset of operations through transition when HN security and police forces assume this role.

4-19. Security force assistance (SFA) is the unified action to generate, employ, and sustain local, HN, or regional security forces in support of a legitimate authority. It is integral to successful operations focused on stability operations and extends to all security forces. Forces are developed to operate across the range of military operations—combating internal threats (such as, insurgency, subversion, and lawlessness; defending against external threats; or serving as coalition partners in other areas). SFA at the company team level requires the unit to conduct these actions: advise, teach, mentor, and augment.

ESTABLISH CIVIL CONTROL

4-20. Establishing civil control is an initial step toward instituting stable, effective governance. Although establishing civil security may be the primary responsibility of military forces in a stability mission, this can only be accomplished by restoring civil control. Internal threats may manifest themselves as an insurgency, subversive elements within the population, organized crime, or general lawlessness.

4-21. Civil control regulates selected behavior and activities of individuals and groups. This control reduces risk to individuals or groups and promotes security. Curfews and traffic checkpoints, together with biometric identity data collection, are examples of actions the company team conduct to support civil control. (See ATP 3-07.5 for more information.)

RESTORE ESSENTIAL SERVICES

4-22. The company team can provide only the most essential services. Normally, the company team supports civil affairs personnel and other government, intergovernmental, and HN agencies. Essential services include the following:

- Ensuring emergency medical care and rescue.
- Providing food and drinking water.
- Providing emergency shelter.

SUPPORT TO GOVERNANCE

4-23. Operations focused on stability operations establish conditions that enable interagency and HN actions to succeed. Support to governance focuses on restoring public administration and resuming public services. The CAB commander focuses on transferring control to a legitimate civil authority according to the desired end state which is to establish a functional, effective system of political governance. The company team, as part of larger unit, can provide support to governance that could include the following:

- Checkpoints to regulate traffic and searches for smuggled contraband.
- Properly detaining suspected criminals and properly holding criminal evidence for the HN's civil administration of justice.
- Training HN security forces and police.
- Security at election sites and ballot transfers.

SUPPORT TO ECONOMIC AND INFRASTRUCTURE DEVELOPMENT

4-24. Support to economic and infrastructure development helps a HN develop capability and capacity in these areas. It may involve direct and indirect military assistance to local, regional, and national entities. Company teams are capable of coordinating with local officials/leaders to fund limited projects using a commander's emergency response program. These limited projects can support the local economy and assist with rebuilding the local infrastructure.

4-25. As conflict, disaster, and internal strife overwhelm the government, the economic viability of a state is one of the first elements to exhibits stress and ultimately fracture. This stress includes rapid increases in unemployment, inflation, uncontrolled escalation of debt, and decline in the ability to support the well-being of people. Infrastructure development complements and reinforces efforts to stabilize a HN's economy.

CONDUCT SECURITY COOPERATION

4-26. Establishing or reestablishing competent HN security forces is fundamental to providing lasting safety and security for the HN and its population. These forces also assist in other key missions including disaster relief, humanitarian assistance, and some other internal military threats. *Security cooperation* is all Department of Defense interactions with foreign security establishments to build security relationships that promote specific U.S. security interests, develop allied and partner military and security capabilities for self-defense and multinational operations, and provide U.S. forces with peacetime and contingency access to allies and partners (JP 3-20). Security cooperation is often coordinated by the U.S. military's security cooperation organization in a country.

4-27. Security cooperation aims to promote stability, develop alliances, and gain and maintain access through security relationships that build partner capacities and capabilities. The capacities and capabilities of partners directly correlate to the type of activities undertaken. Goals range from creating a positive relationship that allows freedom of movement to creating global security interoperability with core partners to addressing regional security organizations and alliance organizations. A broad range of interconnected and integrated security cooperation activities accomplishes security cooperation.

4-28. Security cooperation contributes to the security by building security relationships, alliances, partner capability and capacity, and access through a broad range of interconnected and integrated security cooperation activities that include security assistance, SFA, internal defense and development, and security sector reform.

SECTION III – OPERATIONS CONDUCTED DURING STABILITY

4-29. The company team conducts an area security operation to perform various actions that simultaneously support numerous stability operations. Area security missions are numerous, complex, and generally never ending. For this reason, the commander synchronizes and integrates security efforts, focusing on protected forces, installations, routes, and actions within the company's assigned AO. Protected forces within the company, range from subordinate units and elements, echeloned CPs, and sustainment (external support elements and company trains when established). Protected installations can be part of the sustainment base, or they can constitute part of the area's civilian infrastructure. Protected ground lines of communication include the route network to support the numbers, sizes, and weights of tactical and sustainment area movement within the company's AO. Actions range from securing key points (bridges and defiles) and terrain features (ridgelines and hills) to large civilian population centers and their adjacent areas.

4-30. During the conduct of stability-focused tasks, area security missions are a mixture of offensive and defensive activities involving not only subordinate companies and platoons, but also those HN security forces over which the company or CAB has a command relationship such as operational control or can otherwise influence. Offensive area security activities include subordinate tasks of MTC (search and attack or cordon and search missions) and combat patrols, when required, designed to ambush detected enemy forces and/or to conduct raids within the company's AO. Defensive area security activities include the establishment of a perimeter defense base perimeter security, combat outposts, OPs, surveillance, moving and stationary screens, and guard missions.

AREA SECURITY

4-31. Area security preserves the commander's ability to help establish political, legal, social, and economic institutions while supporting the transition to legitimate HN governance. When conducting an area security mission, the company team prevents threat elements from supporting instability in otherwise safe and secure environments.

4-32. The commander may direct subordinate platoons to employ a variety of techniques such as OPs, traffic control posts, sniper team employment, BPs, ambushes, mounted and dismounted (or a combination of both) patrols, searches, and combat outposts to accomplish this security mission. A reserve or quick reaction force enables the commander to react to unforeseen contingencies. Using the assigned UAS and the information collection capability available to the CAB, the company team can execute missions proactively with greater precision.

4-33. Due to the possibility of tying forces to fixed installations or sites, security missions may become defensive in nature. When this occurs the company commander carefully balances with the need for offensive action. Early warning of enemy activity through information collection is paramount in the conduct of area security missions to provide the commander with time to react to any threat or other type change identified within the stability environment. The IPB identifies the factors effecting security missions within the assigned AO. Factors, although not inclusive, include—

- The natural defensive characteristics of the terrain.
- The existing roads and waterways for military lines of communication and civilian commerce.
- The control of land and water areas and avenues of approach surrounding the area security.
- The control of airspace.
- The proximity to critical sites such as airfields, power generation plants, and civic buildings.

4-34. During area security operations, forces must retain readiness over longer periods without contact with the enemy. This occurs most often when the enemy commander knows that enemy forces or insurgents are seriously overmatched in available combat power. In this situation, the enemy commander normally tries to avoid engaging friendly forces, unless it is on terms favorable to the enemy. Favorable terms include the use of mines and booby traps. Area security forces must not develop a false sense of security, even if the enemy appears to have ceased operations in the secured area. The commander must assume that the enemy is observing friendly operations and is seeking routines, weak points, and lax security for the opportunity to strike with minimum risk. This requires the commander to influence subordinate small-unit leaders to maintain the vigilance and discipline of their Soldiers to preclude this opportunity from developing.

SECURITY FORCE ASSISTANCE

4-35. SFA contributes to unified action by the U. S. Government to support the development of the capacity and capability of foreign security forces (FSF) and their supporting institutions, whether of a partner nation or an intergovernmental organization (regional security organization). The development of capacity and capability is integral to successful stability missions and extends to all organizations and personnel under partner nation control that have a mission of securing its population and protecting its sovereignty from internal and external threats. FSF are duly constituted foreign military, paramilitary, police, and constabulary forces such as border police, coast guard, and customs organizations, as well as prison guards and correctional personnel, and their supporting institutions.

4-36. SFA activities are conducted to organize, train, equip, rebuild (or build), and advise FSF forces from the ministerial/department level down through the tactical units. The DOD maintains capabilities for SFA through conventional forces, special operations forces, the civilian expeditionary workforce, and when necessary, contractor personnel in both joint operational area and a nonjoint operational area environments. SFA activities require carefully selected and properly trained and experienced personnel (as trainers or advisors) who are not only subject matter experts, but also have the sociocultural understanding, language skills, and seasoned maturity to relate to more effectively and train FSF. Ideally, SFA activities help build the FSF capacity to train their own forces independent of sustained U.S. Government efforts.

SECURITY FORCE ASSISTANCE TASKS

4-37. SFA activities normally use the following general developmental tasks of organize, train, equip, rebuild and build, advise and assist, and assess (known as OTERA-A). These functional tasks, serving as SFA capability areas, are used to develop the capabilities required by the FSF. OTERA-A tasks are a tool to develop, change, or improve the capability and capacity of FSF. Through a baseline assessment of the FSF, and considering U.S. interests and objectives, the commander and staff planners can determine which OTERA-A tasks will be required to build the proper capability and capacity levels within the various units of the FSF. Assessments of the FSF against a desired set of capabilities will assist in developing an OTERA-A based plan to improve FSF. (See FM 3-22 for more information.) The following are basic descriptions of the OTERA-A tasks:

- Organize. All activities taken to create, improve, and integrate doctrinal principles, organizational structures, capability constructs, and personnel management. This may include doctrine development, unit or organization design, command and staff processes, and recruiting and manning functions.
- Train. All activities taken to create, improve, and integrate training, leader development, and education at the individual, leader, collective, and staff levels. This may include task analysis, the development and execution of programs of instruction, implementation of training events, and leader development activities.
- Equip. All activities to design, improve, and integrate materiel and equipment, procurement, fielding, accountability, and maintenance through life cycle management. This may also include fielding of new equipment, operational readiness processes, repair, and recapitalization.
- Rebuild or build. All activities to create, improve, and integrate facilities. This may include physical infrastructures such as bases and stations, lines of communication, ranges and training complexes, and administrative structures.
- Advise/Assist. All activities to provide subject matter expertise, guidance, advice, and counsel to FSF while carrying out the missions assigned to the unit or organization. Advising may occur under combat or administrative conditions, at tactical through strategic levels, and in support of individuals or groups.
- Assess. All activities for determining progress toward accomplishing a task, creating an effect, or achieving an objective using measure of effectiveness and measure of performance to evaluate foreign security force capability. Once an objective is achieved, the focus shifts to sustaining it.

SECTION IV – TRANSITIONS

4-38. Transitions mark a change between phases or between the ongoing set of tasks and execution of a branch or sequel. Shifting priorities between the elements of decisive action—such as from the offense to operations focused on stability operations—involves a transition.

4-39. Transitions require planning and preparation well before their execution to maintain the momentum and tempo. The force can be vulnerable during transitions, so commanders establish clear conditions for their execution. Transitions may create unexpected opportunities and may make forces vulnerable to enemy threats.

TRANSITION TO OFFENSE OR DEFENSE

4-40. During an operation focused on stability operations there may be instances where units quickly transition back to operations focused on offensive operations against irregular forces or defensive operations to defeat counterattacks. To facilitate the transition, commanders consider an offensive contingency while conducting operations focused on stability operations. They consider how to generate combat power quickly to take the initiative. It can come from organic, partnered, joint, and HN forces depending on the situation.

4-41. Commanders ensure that transitions from defensive operations to stability operations and vice versa are planned. For example, it may be tactically wise for commanders to plan a defensive contingency if there is a significant global, national, or regional event that negatively affects the AO. Transitioning to a defense should not negate the progress made during stability operations. It should be a temporary change made until the initiative can be regained or until the partnered nation can assume responsibility.

4-42. The conditions for transitioning from stability to a retrograde normally occur during transformation or fostering stability phases. The company will probably support a withdrawal or a retirement as part of a larger force. Most likely, it provides security as personnel, equipment, and property and moved out of the HN.

TRANSFER OF AUTHORITY

4-43. Stability operations include transitions of authority and control between military forces, civilian agencies and organizations, and the partner nation. Each transition involves inherent risk. Transitions are identified as decisive points on lines of effort. They typically mark a significant shift in effort and signify the gradual return to civilian oversight and control of the partner nation.

4-44. Often during stability missions' release in place or transfer of authority (TOA) occurs. Besides the normal responsibilities of a relief, commanders deal with civilians or multinational partners. During stability operations, units generally know whether they will be relieved at the end of their tour. Planning for the TOA begins as soon as the unit occupies the AO.

4-45. Before the TOA, the departing unit develops a continuity book with the necessary information on the AO. The book should include lessons learned; details about the populace, village, and patrol reports; updated maps and photographs; and anything that helps arriving unit the company OE. CAB units should be familiar with their incoming counterparts particularly if it is a different organization that could include motorize or light Infantry or other foreign or North Atlantic Treaty Organization units. Clear articulation of unit organization skills and the OE helps the incoming unit identify needs and gaps distinguishing between the different units. Commanders should ensure that these continuity books are updated during the unit's tour of duty. This extensive effort reduces casualties and increases the established and succeeding units' efficiency and knowledge of operations.

4-46. A consistent theme from recent operations is the importance of the transition training (right seat/left seat rides) with incoming Soldiers during TOA. A detailed and programmed TOA allows Soldiers to learn the culture and effectively work with partner nation personnel during the deployment. Typical training during the relief includes the following:

- Use of the AO specific equipment not available before TOA.
- Enemy tactics, techniques, and procedures for obstacles.
- Personal meetings with nongovernmental organizations, contractors, interpreters, informants, and local police that operate in the unit's AO.
- Negotiation techniques with local tribal, religious, and government officials.
- Operations and intelligence handover of databases, plans, products, and briefings.
- Information collection procedures, processes, and policies.

TRANSITION TO CIVILIAN OR PARTNER NATION SECURITY FORCE CONTROL

4-47. During long-term SFA, conditions on the ground, not time, determine the TOA from U.S. forces control or partnership to partner-nation control. The overall authority for the handover and the subsequent TOA lies with the commander ordering the change. The authority for determining the handover process lies with the incoming commander assuming responsibility for the mission. This changeover process may affect conditions under which the mission continues. (See FM 3-07, ATP 3-07.10, and FM 3-22 for more information.)

4-48. Changes in the OE such as increased attacks, significant destabilization with the infrastructure or people, culturally impacting events inside or outside the OE, or development of security forces may require reshaping force packages as situations change. Internal administrative concerns might prompt or support the commander's decision to rotate units. Mission handover is necessary and defined as the process of passing an ongoing mission from one unit to another with no discernible loss of continuity.

4-49. Commanders make specific considerations along with METT-TC (I) when making a handover to a multinational force. For units relieved of a function by a government agency, procedures typically entail longer handover times and more complex coordination. Outgoing units that have past, present, or future projects planned with agencies prepare to transfer these projects to responsible agents in the incoming unit.

This page intentionally left blank.

Chapter 5

Direct Fire Planning and Control

Suppressing or destroying the enemy with direct fires is fundamental to success in close combat. Commanders plan to employ fires through DFCMs. These DFCMs allow commanders to focus, distribute, control, and, when necessary, shift their fires to achieve mass throughout the width and depth of planned or unplanned EAs. Commanders plan for DFCMs in both the offense and defense to rapidly orient their forces and maximize the effectiveness of their direct fire systems. The direct fire plan should be integrated with the indirect fire plan to maximize effects on the enemy. Because fire and movement are complementary components of maneuver, the commander must be able to mass the fires of all available resources at critical points and times to be successful on the battlefield. This chapter discusses principles of direct fire control, the fire control process, direct fire planning, and direct fire control.

SECTION I – FIRE CONTROL TECHNIQUES

5-1. To bring direct fires against an enemy force successfully, commanders and leaders must continuously apply the steps of the fire control process. At the heart of this process are two critical actions: rapid, accurate target acquisition and the massing of fire to achieve decisive effects on the target.

5-2. *Target acquisition* is the detection, identification, and location of a target in sufficient detail to permit the effective employment of capabilities that create the required effects (JP 3-60). Target acquisition is further described as the discovery of any object in the OE such as personnel, vehicles, equipment, or objects of potential military significance. Target acquisition occurs during target search as a direct result of observation and the detection process.

5-3. Massing of fires is not simply the number of systems or rounds fired but entails focusing fires at critical points and distributing the fires for optimum effect in terms of both destructive and psychological impacts on the enemy. The ideal mass for a company team would be three platoons, each firing a volley, resulting in the simultaneous destruction of 12 enemy vehicles, including the highest value, while avoiding any overkill.

- Focus: Direct attention on targets, TRPs, man-made or natural objects, or terrain features.
- Distribute: Establishing different priorities for similar friendly systems simultaneously among multiple, similar targets.
- Control: To direct and coordinate the actions of subordinate forces to meet their intent.
- Shift: Given when friendly forces are moving toward the target area and is used as a control measure to protect friendly forces.

FIRE CONTROL PROCESS

5-4. The following discussion examines target acquisition and massing of fires using these basic steps of the fire control process:

- Identify probable enemy locations and determine the enemy scheme of maneuver.
- Determine where and how to mass fires.
- Orient forces to speed target acquisition.
- Shift fires to refocus or redistribute.

IDENTIFY PROBABLE ENEMY LOCATIONS AND DETERMINE ENEMY SCHEME OF MANEUVER

5-5. The commander and subordinate leaders plan and execute direct fires based on their estimate of the situation. An essential part of this estimate is analyzing the terrain and the enemy force, which aids the commander in visualizing how the enemy will attack or defend a particular piece of terrain. A defending enemy's defensive positions or an attacking enemy's support positions are normally driven by terrain. Typically, there are limited points on a piece of terrain that provide both good fields of fire and adequate cover for a defender. Similarly, an attacking enemy has only a limited selection of avenues of approach that provide adequate cover and concealment.

5-6. Coupled with available intelligence, an understanding of the effects of a specific piece of terrain on maneuver assists the commander in identifying probable enemy locations and likely avenues of approach both before and during the fight. (See figure 5-1.) The commander may use any or all the following products or techniques in developing and updating the analysis.

5-7. Situation template based on the analysis of terrain and enemy:
- Spot report (SPOTREP) or contact report on enemy locations and activities.
- Reconnaissance of the AO.

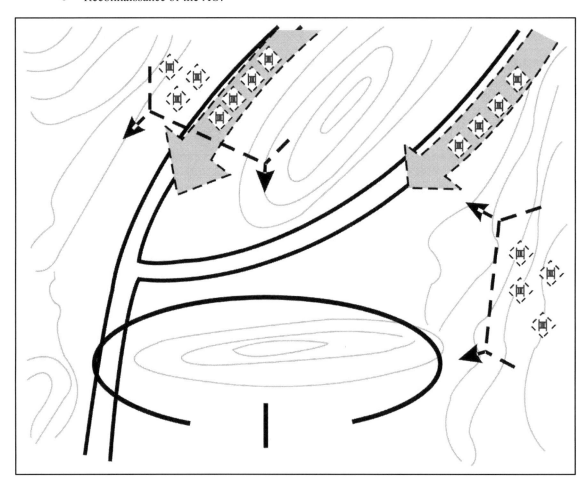

Figure 5-1. Identifying probable enemy locations and determining enemy scheme of maneuver, example

DETERMINE WHERE AND HOW TO MASS FIRES

5-8. To achieve decisive effects, friendly forces must mass their fires. Effective massing requires the commander both to focus the fires of subordinate elements and to distribute the effects of the fires. Based on the estimate of the situation and the commander's concept of the operation, the commander identifies the best points to focus the unit's fires. In the defense, these may be choke points, obstacle belts, or firing lines. In the offense, such as possible enemy positions throughout the depth of sector, terrain which allows for cover and concealed routes and choke points within the sector. These are areas in which the enemy is most likely to pause, change directions, slow down, or otherwise provide opportunities to mass fires. Commanders should designate DFCMs in planning to address these opportunities. Commanders may also designate basic fire commands in conjunction with planned DFCMs. However, because platoons may not make contact in the vicinity of planned DFCMs, the commander should be prepared to respond to contact at any point by designating hasty DFCMs and issuing an appropriate fire command. At the same time, the commander must use DFCMs to distribute the fires of the combat elements effectively, which are now focused on the same point. (See figure 5-2.)

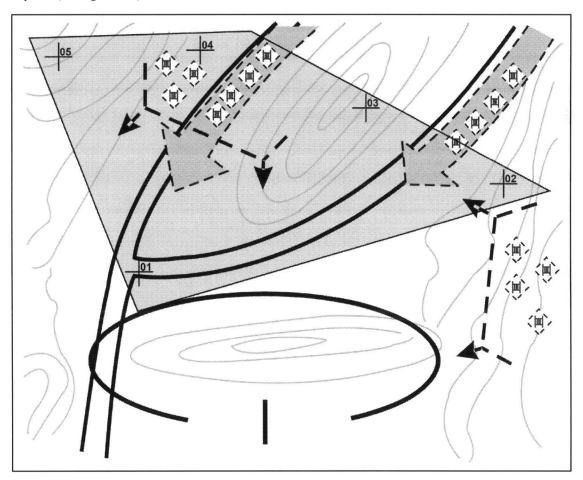

Figure 5-2. Determining where and how to mass fires, example

ORIENT FORCES TO SPEED TARGET ACQUISITION

5-9. To engage the enemy with direct fires effectively, friendly forces must rapidly and accurately acquire enemy elements. Orienting friendly forces on probable enemy locations and likely avenues of approach speeds target acquisition. Conversely, failure to orient subordinate elements results in slower acquisition; this greatly increases the likelihood that enemy forces will be able to engage first. The clock direction orientation method, which is prescribed in most unit SOPs, is good for achieving all-around security; however, it does not ensure that friendly forces are most effectively oriented to detect the enemy. To achieve this critical orientation, the commander typically designates TRPs on or near probable enemy locations and avenues of approach. This allows commanders to orient subordinate elements quickly by referring to specific TRPs and then taking them on from there (for example, "to the left of TRP 103"). (See figure 5-3.)

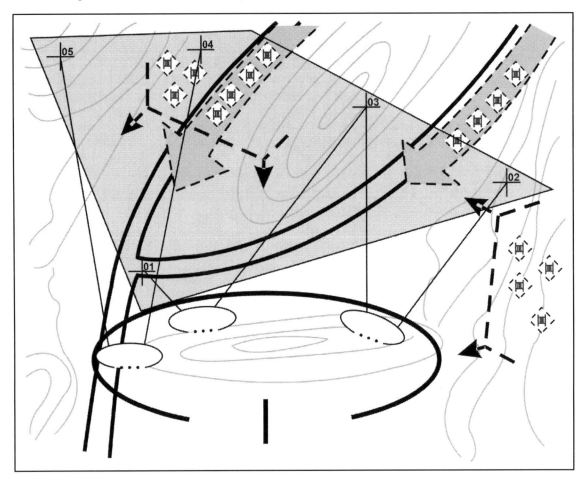

Figure 5-3. Orienting forces to speed target acquisition, example

SHIFT FIRES TO REFOCUS AND REDISTRIBUTE

5-10. As the engagement proceeds, the commander must shift fires to refocus and redistribute the effects based on the evolving estimate of the situation. SA becomes an essential part of the fire control process at this point. The commander and subordinate leaders apply the same techniques and considerations, including fire control measures used earlier to focus and distribute fires. A variety of situations dictate shifting of fires, including the following:

- Appearance of an enemy force posing a greater threat than the one currently being engaged.
- Extensive attrition of the enemy force being engaged, creating the possibility of target overkill.
- Attrition of friendly elements that engage the enemy force.
- Change in the ammunition status of the friendly elements that engage the enemy force.
- Increased fratricide risk as a maneuvering friendly element closes with the enemy force being engaged.

PRINCIPLES OF DIRECT FIRE CONTROL

5-11. Effective fire control requires a unit to acquire the enemy and mass the effects of fires rapidly to achieve decisive results in the close fight. When planning and executing direct fires, the commander and subordinate leaders must know how to apply several fundamental principles. The purpose of direct fire is not to restrict the actions of subordinates. Applied correctly, direct fire helps the company team accomplish its primary goal in any direct fire engagement; that is, to acquire first and shoot first. These principles give subordinates the freedom to act quickly upon acquisition of the enemy. (See TC 3-20.31-4 for more information.) This discussion focuses on the following principles:

- Mass the effects of fire.
- Destroy the greatest threat first.
- Avoid target overkill.
- Employ the best weapon for specific target.
- Minimize exposure.
- Plan and implement fratricide avoidance measures.
- Plan for limited-visibility conditions.
- Plan for degraded capabilities.

MASS EFFECTS OF FIRE

5-12. The company team must mass its fires to achieve decisive results. Massing entails focusing fires at critical points and distributing the effects. Random application of fires is unlikely to have a decisive effect. For example, concentrating the company team's fires at a single target may ensure its destruction or suppression; however, that fire control technique will probably not achieve a decisive effect on the enemy formation or position.

DESTROY GREATEST THREAT FIRST

5-13. The order in which the company team engages enemy forces is in direct relation to the danger they present. The threat posed by the enemy depends on their weapons, range, and positioning. Presented with multiple targets, usually a unit initially concentrates fires to destroy the greatest threat and then distributes fires over the remainder of the enemy force. Units must be able to identify an enemy force that is posing a greater threat.

AVOID TARGET OVERKILL

5-14. A company team should use only the amount of fire required to achieve necessary effects. Target overkill wastes ammunition and ties up weapons that are better employed acquiring and engaging other targets. The idea of having every weapon engage a different target, however, must be tempered by the requirement to destroy the greatest threats first.

EMPLOY BEST WEAPON FOR SPECIFIC TARGET

5-15. Using the appropriate weapon for the target increases the probability of rapid enemy destruction or suppression; at the same time, it saves ammunition. The company team has many weapons with which to engage the enemy. Target type, range, and exposure are key factors in determining the weapon and ammunition that should be employed, as are weapons and ammunition availability and desired targets effects. Additionally, commanders should consider individual crew capabilities and proficiency when deciding on the employment of weapons systems. The commander task-organizes and arrays forces based on the terrain, enemy, and desired effects of fires. For example, if an enemy dismounted assault is expected in restricted terrain, the commander would employ Infantry squads, taking advantage of their ability to best engage numerous targets.

MINIMIZE EXPOSURE

5-16. Units increase their survivability by exposing themselves to the enemy only to the extent necessary to engage them effectively. Natural or artificial defilade provides the best cover from lethal direct fire munitions. Crews and squads minimize their exposure by constantly seeking effective available cover, attempting to engage the enemy from the flank, remaining dispersed, firing from multiple positions, and limiting engagement times.

PLAN AND IMPLEMENT FRATRICIDE AVOIDANCE MEASURES

5-17. The commander must be proactive in reducing the risk of fratricide/friendly fire and noncombatant casualties. Identification training for combat vehicles and aircraft, the unit's weapons safety status, the weapons control status (WCS), recognition markings, crosstalk, information dissemination to ensure SA, the use of combat identification panels, and a common operational picture are all tools to assist the commander in this effort.

> *Note.* Because it is difficult to distinguish between friendly and enemy Soldiers, the commander must constantly monitor the position of friendly Soldiers.

PLAN FOR LIMITED-VISIBILITY CONDITIONS

5-18. At night, limited-visibility fire control equipment enables the company team to engage enemy forces at nearly the same ranges that are applicable during the day. Obscurants such as dense fog, heavy smoke, and blowing sand; however, can reduce the capabilities of thermal and infrared (IR) equipment. The commander should, therefore, develop contingency plans for such extreme limited-visibility conditions. Visibility is also reduced in rolling and urban terrain. Although decreased acquisition capabilities have minimal effect on area fire, point target engagements will likely occur at decreased ranges. Typically, BPs, whether offensive or defensive, must be adjusted closer to the area or point where the commander intends to focus fires. Another alternative is using visual or IR illumination when there is insufficient ambient light for passive light intensification devices.

> *Note.* Vehicles equipped with thermal sights can assist squads in detecting and engaging enemy forces in conditions such as heavy smoke and low illumination.

PLAN FOR DEGRADED CAPABILITIES

5-19. Leaders initially develop plans based on their units' maximum capabilities. They make backup plans for implementation if casualties or weapons are damaged or fail. While leaders cannot anticipate or plan for every situation, they should develop plans for what they view as the most probable occurrences. Building redundancy into these plans, such as having two systems observe the same sector, is an invaluable asset when the situation (and the number of available systems) permits. Designating alternate sectors of fire provides a means of shifting fires if adjacent elements are out of action.

SECTION II – DIRECT FIRE PLANNING

5-20. This section discusses direct fire planning that includes an overview and SOPs. Direct fire planning is fundamentally the same for both offensive and defensive operations. The challenge for the commanders in the offense is to control the focus and distribution of fires on the move against a generally static enemy. While in the defense, the goal is to build an EA where the leaders can mass fires by properly focusing and distributing the company's firepower.

OVERVIEW

5-21. Commanders plan direct fires to distribute and control their fire in both offensive and defensive operations. Determining where and how the company team can mass fires is an essential step in this process.

5-22. Based on where and how they want to focus and distribute fires, leaders can establish weapons-ready postures for their elements as well as triggers for initiating fires. During mission preparation, leaders plan and conduct rehearsals of direct fires (and of the fire control process) based on the estimate of the situation.

5-23. The commander plans direct fires in conjunction with development of the situation and completion of the plan. When planning direct fire, the commander must plan within the CAB commander's intent.

Determining where and how the company team can and will mass fires are essential steps as the commander develops the concept of the operation.

5-24. After identifying probable enemy locations, the commander determines points or areas where to focus combat power. Visualization of where and how the enemy will attack or defend assists the commander in determining the volume of fires that must be focus on points to have a decisive effect. If massing the fires of more than one subordinate element, the commander must establish the means for distributing fires effectively.

5-25. Based on where and how they want to focus and distribute fires, the commander and subordinate leaders can establish weapons-ready postures for company team elements as well as triggers for initiating fires. Additionally, the commander must evaluate the risk of fratricide and establish controls to prevent it; these measures include the designation of recognition markings, WCS, and weapons-safety status.

5-26. After determining where and how they will mass and distribute fires, the commander and subordinate leaders must orient elements so they can rapidly and accurately acquire the enemy using the fire control measure (see section III). They can war-game the concept of the operation to determine probable requirements for refocusing and redistributing fires and to establish other required controls. During mission preparation, the commander plans and conducts rehearsals of direct fires (and of the fire control process) based on the estimate of the situation.

5-27. The commander and subordinate leaders must continue to apply planning procedures and considerations throughout execution. They must be able to shift direct fires based on a continuously updated estimate of the situation, combining SA with the latest available intelligence. When necessary, they must apply effective direct fire SOPs, which are covered in the following discussion.

STANDARD OPERATING PROCEDURES

5-28. A well-rehearsed direct fire SOP ensures quick, predictable actions by all members of the company team. The fires SOP can be standardized to include TRP numbering conventions, labeling of quadrants or target arrays, establishing 'floating' TRPs (identified during offensive operations), sectors of fire or gun-tube orientation, planned WCS (anticipated threat), or battle sight ranges (anticipated engagement ranges). The commander bases the various elements of the SOP on the capabilities of available forces and on anticipated conditions and situations. The commander should adjust the direct fire SOP whenever changes to anticipated and actual mission variables become apparent.

5-29. If the commander does not issue any other instructions, the company team begins the engagement using the SOP. The commander can subsequently use a fire command to refocus or redistribute fires. The following paragraphs discuss specific elements for focusing fires, distributing fires, orienting forces, and preventing fratricide that should be included in the SOP.

FOCUSING FIRES

5-30. TRPs are a common means of focusing fires in both offensive and defensive operations. One technique is to establish a standard respective position for TRPs in relation to friendly elements and then to consistently number the TRPs, such as from left to right. This allows leaders to determine and communicate the location of the TRPs quickly.

DISTRIBUTING FIRES

5-31. Two useful means of distributing the company team's fires are engagement priorities and target array. One technique is to assign an engagement priority, by type of enemy vehicle or weapon, for each type of friendly weapons system. The target array technique can assist in distribution by assigning specific friendly elements to engage enemy elements of approximately similar capabilities. The following are examples for distributing the fires of a company team (one tank platoon, two mechanized Infantry platoons) moving in a wedge or line formation with the tank platoon in the center:

- Tanks engage tanks first, then personnel carriers (known as PCs).
- IFVs engage PCs first, then other AT weapons.

- If the company team masses fires at the same target, the tank platoon engages tanks; the left flank platoon engages the left half of the enemy formation; and the right flank platoon engages the right half of the enemy formation.

ORIENTING FORCES

5-32. A standard means of orienting friendly forces is to assign a primary direction of fire, using TRPs, to orient each element on a probable enemy position or likely avenue of approach. To provide all-around security, the SOP can supplement the primary direction of fire with sectors using a friendly-based quadrant. The following example SOP elements illustrate these techniques:

- The center (front) platoon's primary direction of fire is TRP 2 (center) until otherwise specified; the platoon is responsible for the front two quadrants.
- The left flank platoon's primary direction of fire is TRP 1 (left) until otherwise specified; the platoon is responsible for the left two friendly quadrants (overlapping with the center platoon).
- The right flank platoon's primary direction of fire is TRP 3 (right) until otherwise specified; the platoon is responsible for the right two friendly quadrants (overlapping with the center platoon).

AVOIDING FRATRICIDE

5-33. Finally, the SOP must address the most critical requirement of fratricide prevention—maintaining SA. It must direct subordinate leaders to inform the commander, adjacent elements, and subordinates whenever a friendly force is moving or preparing to move.

5-34. A primary means of avoiding fratricide is to establish a standing WCS of, WEAPONS TIGHT, which requires positive enemy identification before engagement. The SOP must dictate ways of identifying friendly mechanized Infantry squads and other dismounted elements. Techniques include using armbands, heating pads, or an IR light source or detonating a smoke grenade of a designated color at the appropriate time (see paragraph 5-17). Minimizing the risk of fratricide in the company team can be accomplished through a digital command and control system (if equipped); however, this does not replace the company commander's responsibility to plan for fratricide avoidance.

SECTION III – DIRECT FIRE CONTROL

5-35. The company commander communicates to subordinates the manner, method, and time to initiate, shift, and mass fires, and when to disengage by using DFCMs. Commanders should control their unit's fires so they can direct the engagement of enemy systems to gain the greatest effect. The commander uses IPB and reconnaissance to determine the most advantageous way to use DFCMs to mass the effects on the enemy and reduce fratricide from direct fire systems.

FIRE CONTROL MEASURES

5-36. Fire control measures are how the commander or subordinate leaders control fires. Application of these concepts, procedures, and techniques assists the unit in acquiring the enemy, focusing fires on them, distributing the effects of the fires, and preventing fratricide. At the same time, no single measure is sufficient to control fires effectively. At the company team level, fire control measures are effective only if the entire unit has a shared understanding of what they mean and how to employ them. The following discussion focuses on the various fire control measures employed by the company team. (See table 5-1.)

Table 5-1. Common fire control measures

Terrain-Based Fire Control Measures	Threat-Based Fire Control Measures
Target Reference Point	Rules of Engagement
Engagement Area	Weapons Ready Posture
Sector of Fire	Weapons Safety Posture
Direction of Fire	Weapons Control Status
Terrain-Based Quadrant	Engagement Priorities
Friendly-Based Quadrant	Trigger
Maximum Engagement Line	Engagement Techniques
Final Protective Line	Target Array
Restrictive Fire Line	Fire Patterns

TERRAIN-BASED FIRE CONTROL MEASURES

5-37. The company commander uses terrain-based fire control measures to focus and control fires on a particular point, line, or area rather than on a specific enemy element. The following paragraphs describe the tactics, techniques, and procedures associated with this control measure.

Target Reference Point

5-38. A TRP is an easily recognizable point on the ground (either natural or man-made) used to initiate, distribute, and controls fires. (See JP 3-09.3 for more information.) In addition, when leaders designate TRPs as indirect fire targets, they can use the TRPs when calling for and adjusting indirect fires. Leaders designate TRPs at probable enemy locations and along likely avenues of approach. These points can be natural or artificial. A TRP can be an established site (for example, a hill or a building), or an impromptu feature designated as a TRP on the spot (for example, a burning enemy vehicle or smoke generated by an artillery round). Friendly units can construct markers to serve as TRPs. Ideally, TRPs should be visible in three observation modes (unaided, light intensifying, and thermal) so that all forces can see them. (See figure 5-4 on page 5-10.) Examples of TRPs include the following features and objects:
- Prominent hill mass.
- Distinctive building.
- Observable enemy position.
- Destroyed vehicle.
- Ground-burst illumination.
- Smoke round for immediate engagements only; this is the least preferred method.

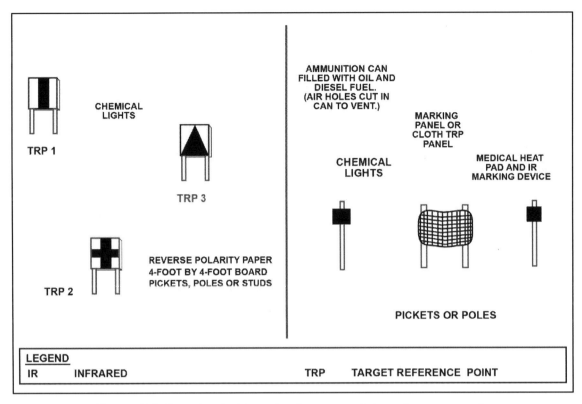

Figure 5-4. Constructed target reference point markers, example

Engagement Area

5-39. An EA is where the commander intends to contain and destroy an enemy force. (See ADP 3-90 for more information.) The size and shape of the EA is determined by the degree of relatively unobstructed intervisibility available to the unit's weapons systems in the BPs and by the maximum range of those weapons. Typically, commanders delineate responsibility within the EA by assigning each platoon both primary and alternate sectors of fire. They may further refine the EA with additional measures such as a quadrant or a target array.

Sector of Fire

5-40. A sector of fire is that area assigned to a unit or weapon system in which it will engage the enemy according to the established engagement priorities. (See FM 3-90 for more information.) Commanders assign sectors of fire to subordinate elements, leaders refine this and assign sectors of fire, crew served weapons and individual Soldiers to ensure coverage. They may limit the sector of fire of an element or weapon to prevent accidental engagement of an adjacent unit. In assigning sectors of fire, commanders and subordinate leaders consider the number and types of weapons available. They consider acquisition system type and field of view in determining the width of a sector of fire. For example, while unaided vision has a wide field of view, its ability to detect and identify targets at range and in limited-visibility conditions is restricted. Conversely, most fire control acquisitions systems have greater detection and identification ranges than the unaided eye, but their field of view is narrow. Means of designating sectors of fire include the following:

- TRPs.
- Clock direction.
- Fire patterns.
- Terrain-based quadrants.
- Friendly-based quadrants.

Direction of Fire

5-41. A direction of fire is an orientation or point used to assign responsibility for a particular area on the battlefield that must be covered by direct fire. Leaders designate directions of fire for the purpose of acquisition or engagement by subordinate elements, crew-served weapons, or individual Soldiers. Direction of fire is most employed when assigning sectors of fire would be difficult or impossible because of limited time or insufficient reference points. A primary direction of fire may also serve as the left or right limit to a sector of fire. Means of designating a direction of fire include the following:

- Closest TRP.
- Clock direction.
- Cardinal direction.
- Tracer on target.
- IR laser pointer.

Quadrants

5-42. Quadrants are subdivisions of an area created by superimposing an imaginary pair of perpendicular axes over the terrain to create four separate areas or sectors. Quadrants can be based on the terrain, on friendly forces, or on the enemy formation.

> *Note.* The technique in which quadrants are based on the enemy formation is usually referred to as the target array; it is covered in the discussion of threat-based fire control measures.

5-43. The method of quadrant numbering is established in the unit SOP; however, care must be taken to avoid confusion when quadrants based on terrain, friendly forces, and the enemy formations are used simultaneously.

Terrain-Based Quadrant

5-44. A terrain-based quadrant uses a TRP, either existing or constructed, to designate the center point of the axes that divide the area into four quadrants. This technique can be employed in both offensive and defensive operations. In the offense, the commander designates the center of the quadrant using an existing feature or by creating a reference point (for example, using a ground-burst illumination round, a smoke-marking round, or a fire ignited by incendiary or tracer rounds). The axes delineating the quadrants run parallel and perpendicular to the direction of movement. In the defense, the commander designates the center of the quadrant using an existing or constructed TRP.

5-45. In the examples shown in figure 5-5 on page 5-12, quadrants are marked using the letter "Q" and a number (Q1 to Q4); quadrant numbers are in the same relative positions as on military map sheets (from Q1 as the upper left-hand quadrant clockwise to Q4 as the lower left-hand quadrant).

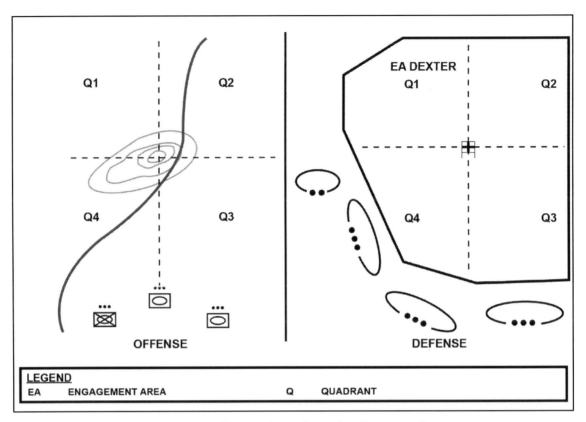

Figure 5-5. Terrain-based quadrants, example

Friendly-Based Quadrant

5-46. The friendly-based quadrant technique entails superimposing quadrants over the unit's formation. The center point is based on the center of the formation, and the axes run parallel and perpendicular to the general direction of travel. For rapid orientation, the friendly quadrant technique may be better than the clock direction method; this is because different elements of a large formation are rarely oriented in the same exact direction and because the relative dispersion of friendly forces causes parallax to the target. (See figure 5-6.)

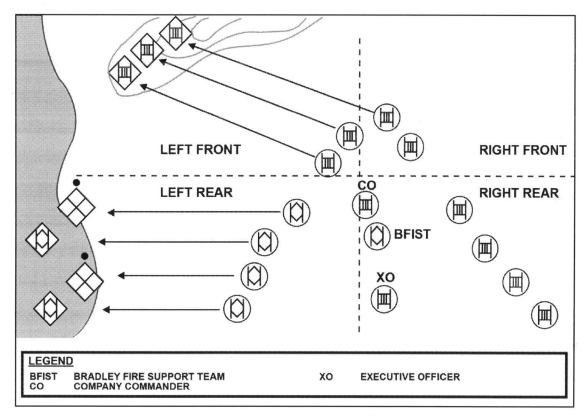

Figure 5-6. Friendly-based quadrants, example

Maximum Engagement Line

5-47. A maximum engagement line is the linear depiction of the farthest limit of effective fire for a weapon or unit. This line is determined by either the weapon's or unit's maximum effective range and by the effects of terrain. For example, slope, vegetation, structures, and other features provide cover and concealment that may prevent the weapon from engaging to the maximum effective range. A maximum engagement line serves several purposes. The commander can use it to prevent crews from engaging beyond the maximum effective range, to define criteria for the establishment of triggers, and to delineate the maximum extent of AO on the sector sketch.

Restrictive Fire Line

5-48. A *restrictive fire line* is a specific boundary established between converging, friendly surface forces that prohibits fires or their effects from crossing (JP 3-09). In the offense, the commander can designate a restrictive fire line (RFL) to prevent a base of fire element from firing into the area where an assaulting element is maneuvering. This technique is particularly important when armored vehicles support the maneuver of Infantry squads. In the defense, the commander may establish an RFL to prevent the unit from engaging a friendly mechanized Infantry squad positioned in restricted terrain on the flank of an avenue of approach.

Final Protective Line

5-49. The *final protective line* is a selected line of fire where an enemy assault is to be checked by interlocking fire from all available weapons and obstacles (FM 3-90). The unit reinforces this line with protective obstacles and with FPF whenever possible. Initiation of the FPF is the signal for elements, crews, and individual Soldiers to shift fires to their assigned portion of the final protective line. They spare no ammunition in repelling the enemy assault, a particular concern for machine guns and other automatic weapons.

THREAT-BASED FIRE CONTROL MEASURES

5-50. The company commander uses threat-based fire control measures to focus and control fires by directing the unit to engage a specific enemy element rather than to fire on a point or area. The following paragraphs describe the tactics, techniques, and procedures associated with this control measure.

Rules of Engagement

5-51. ROE specify the circumstances and limitations under which forces may engage; they include definitions of combatant and noncombatant elements and prescribe the treatment of noncombatants. Factors influencing ROE are national command policy, the mission and commander's intent, the OE, and the law of war. ROE always recognize a Soldier's right of self-defense and clearly define other circumstances where force is authorized.

Weapons Ready Posture

5-52. The weapons ready posture is a means by which leaders use their estimate of the situation to specify the ammunition and range for the most probable anticipated engagement. The ammunition selection is dependent on the target type, but the leader may adjust it based on engagement priorities, desired effects, and effective range. Range selection is dependent on the anticipated engagement range; it is affected by terrain intervisibility, weather, and light conditions. Within the company team, weapons ready posture affects the types and quantities of ammunition loaded in ready boxes, stowed in ready racks, and carried by rifle squads. The following considerations apply:

- For tanks, weapons ready posture is defined as the battle carry.
- For IFVs, weapons ready posture covers the selected ammunition and the indexed range.
- For Infantry squads, weapons ready posture is the selected ammunition and indexed range for individual and crew served weapons. For example, an M320 grenadier whose most likely engagement is to cover dead space at 200 meters from the position might load high-explosive dual purpose and set 200 meters on the quadrant sight. To prepare for an engagement in a wooded area where engagement ranges are extremely short, an antiarmor specialist might dismount with an AT4 instead of a Javelin.

Weapons Safety Status

5-53. Weapons safety status is an ammunition-handling instruction that enables the commander to control the safety of owned unit's weapons precisely. Leaders' supervision of the weapons safety status, as well as Soldiers' adherence to it, minimizes the risk of accidental discharge and fratricide. (See table 5-2.) The statuses are:

- Green, fully safe.
- Amber, substantially safe.
- Red, marginally safe.
- Black, not safe.

5-54. When setting and adjusting the weapons safety status, the commander must weigh the desire to prevent accidental discharges against the requirement for immediate action based on the enemy threat. If the threat of direct contact is high, for example, the commander could establish the weapons safety status as, Black. If the requirement for action is less immediate, the decision to lower the status to Red or Green might be given. Additionally, the commander can designate different weapons safety status for different elements of the unit. For example, in the attack position, tanks and IFVs could switch to Black, while mechanized Infantry squads riding in IFVs remain at Red.

Table 5-2. Weapons safety status levels

Weapons Safety Status	Tank Weapons and Ammunition	Bradley Fighting Vehicle Weapons and Ammunition	Infantry Squad Weapons and Ammunition
Green	All weapons cleared of ammunition. Coaxial: chamber empty, bolt assembly forward, mechanical safe on fire, electrical safe. 50-caliber: chamber empty, bolt forward, mechanical safe. Main gun: breech open, mechanical and electrical safe. Smoke grenade: discharger tubes empty.	All weapons cleared of ammunition. Coaxial: chamber cleared, bolt assembly forward, mechanical safe on fire, electrical safe. 25-mm: feeder cleared of ammunition, mechanical and electrical safe. TOW: TML cleared, electrical safe, TOW mode unselected. Smoke: cleared of grenades, unselected.	All weapons cleared of ammunition. Rifle and carbine: chamber cleared, magazine well empty, on safe. Machine gun: chamber cleared, bolt forward on fire. Grenade launcher: weapon is clear, cocking lever to the rear, firing assembly on fire.
Amber	Coaxial: Ammunition on feed tray, bolt assembly locked to rear, mechanical and electrical safe. 50 caliber: ammunition on feed tray, bolt forward with chamber empty, mechanical safe. Main gun: ammunition loaded with breech closed, mechanical and electrical safe. Smoke grenade: discharger tubes loaded.	Coaxial: ammunition on feed tray, bolt assembly locked to rear, mechanical and electrical safe. 25-mm: ammunition in feeder assembly, mechanical arm, electrical safe, ammunition unselected. TOW: TML loaded, electrical safe, TOW mode unselected. Smoke grenades: loaded, unselected.	Rifle and carbine: chamber is empty, bolt forward, magazine locked in the magazine well, on safe. Machine gun: M249 and M240 series machine gun does not have Amber status. Grenade launcher: Does not have an Amber status.
Red	Coaxial: Ammunition on feed tray, bolt open and locked to the rear, mechanical safe. 50 caliber: ammunition on feed tray, bolt forward with a round in the chamber, mechanical safe. Main gun: ammunition loaded with breech closed, mechanical safe on safe. Smoke grenades: discharger tubes loaded. Appropriate weapons electrical safe is armed.	Coaxial: ammunition on feed tray bolt assembly locked to rear position, mechanical fire, electrical arm. 25-mm: ammunition in feeder assembly, mechanical arm, electrical arm, ammunition selected. TOW: TML loaded, TML raised, electrical arm, TOW mode and missile selected. Smoke: grenades loaded, selected.	Rifle and carbine: round is in chambered, magazine locked in the magazine well, on safe. Machine gun: ammunition is on the feed tray, bolt locked to the rear, on safe. Grenade launcher: weapon is loaded, cocking lever is cocked, safety catch on the firing mechanism is on safe.
Black	Vehicle commander issues command of execution in fire command to initiate Black status. Appropriate weapon system mechanical and electrical safe is armed, firer's finger is on the trigger in position to fire the weapon. Once firing is complete, applicable weapon is returned to Red status.	Vehicle commander issues command of execution in fire command to initiate Black status. Appropriate weapon system mechanical and electrical safe is armed, firer's finger is on the trigger in position to fire the weapon. Once firing is complete, applicable weapon is returned to Red status.	Leader issues command of execution in fire command to initiate Black status. Rifle and carbine: firer's finger is on the trigger, weapon of fire. Machine gun: firer's finger is on the trigger, weapon of fire. Grenade launcher: firer's finger is on the trigger, firing mechanism on fire. Once firing is complete, applicable weapon is returned to Red status.

Legend: mm – millimeter; TML – TOW missile launcher; TOW – tube launched, optically tracked, wire guided

Weapons Control Status

5-55. The three levels of WCS outline the conditions, based on target identification criteria, under which friendly elements can engage. The commander sets and adjusts the WCS based on friendly and enemy disposition, and the clarity of the situation. The higher the probability of fratricide, the more restrictive the WCS. The three levels, in descending order of restrictiveness, are—

- WEAPONS HOLD. Engage only if engaged or ordered to engage.
- WEAPONS TIGHT. Engage only targets that are positively identified as enemy.
- WEAPONS FREE. Engage any targets that are not positively identified as friendly (subject to the ROE and law of armed conflict).

5-56. As an example, the commander may establish the WCS as, WEAPONS HOLD, when friendly forces are conducting a passage of lines. By maintaining situational understanding of owned elements and adjacent friendly forces, however, the WCS may be lowered. In such a case, WEAPONS FREE status may be set when the commander knows there are no friendly elements in the vicinity of the engagement. This permits elements to engage targets at extended ranges even though it is difficult to distinguish targets accurately at ranges beyond 2,000 meters under battlefield conditions.

Engagement Priorities

5-57. Engagement priorities, which entail the sequential ordering of targets to be engaged, can serve one or more of the following critical fire control functions:

- Prioritize high-priority targets. In conjunction with the planned concept of the operation, the commander determines which target types provide the greatest payoff; the commander then can set these as a unit engagement priority. For example, the commander may decide that destroying enemy engineer assets is the best way to prevent the enemy from breaching an obstacle.
- Employ the best weapons for the target. Establishing engagement priorities for specific friendly systems increases the effectiveness with which the unit employs its weapons. As an example, the engagement priority for the company team's tanks could be enemy tanks first, then enemy PCs; this would decrease the chance that the team's lighter systems will have to engage enemy armored vehicles.
- Distribute the unit's fires. Establishing different priorities for similar friendly systems helps to prevent overkill and achieve effective distribution of fires. For example, the commander may designate the enemy's tanks as the initial priority for one IFV platoon, while making the enemy's PCs the priority for another platoon. This would decrease the chances of units launching multiple tube launched, optically tracked, wire guided (TOW) missiles against two enemy tanks, while ignoring the dangers posed by the PCs.

Triggers

5-58. A trigger is a specific set of conditions that dictates initiation of fires. Often referred to as engagement criteria, a trigger specifies the circumstances in which subordinate elements should engage. The circumstances can be based on a friendly or enemy event. For example, the trigger for a friendly platoon to initiate engagement could be three or more enemy combat vehicles passing or crossing a given point or line. This line can be any natural or artificial linear feature, such as a road, ridgeline, or stream. It may be a line perpendicular to the unit's orientation, delineated by one or more reference points.

Engagement Techniques

5-59. Engagement techniques are effects-oriented fire distribution measures. The following engagement techniques, the most common in company team operations, are covered in this discussion:

- Point fire.
- Area fire.
- Simultaneous (volley) fire.
- Alternating fire.
- Observed fire.

- Sequential fire.
- Time of suppression.
- Reconnaissance by fire.

Point Fire

5-60. Point fire entails concentrating the effects of a unit's fire against a specific, identified target such as a vehicle, machine gun bunker, or ATGM position. When leaders direct point fire, all the unit's weapons engage the target, firing until it is destroyed, or the required time of suppression has expired. Employing converging fires from dispersed positions makes point fire more effective because the target is engaged from multiple directions. The unit may initiate an engagement using point fire against the most dangerous threat, and then revert to area fire against other, less threatening point targets.

Area Fire

5-61. Area fire involves distributing the effects of a unit's fire over an area in which enemy positions are numerous or are not obvious. If the area is large, leaders assign sectors of fire to subordinate elements using a terrain-based distribution method such as the quadrant technique. Typically, the primary purpose of the area fire is suppression; however, sustaining effective suppression requires judicious control of the rate of fire.

Simultaneous (Volley) Fire

5-62. Units employ simultaneous fire to rapidly mass the effects of their fires or to gain fire superiority. For example, a unit may initiate an SBF operation with simultaneous fire, then revert to alternating or sequential fire to maintain suppression. Simultaneous fire is employed to negate the low probability of the hit and kill of certain antiarmor weapons. As an example, a mechanized Infantry platoon may employ simultaneous fire with its weapons systems to ensure rapid destruction of the enemy section that is engaging a friendly position. Simultaneous fire should be employed with a designated fire pattern to reduce the likelihood of overkill.

Alternating Fire

5-63. In alternating fire, pairs of elements continuously engage the same point or area target one at a time. For example, a company team may alternate the fires of two platoons; a tank or mechanized platoon may alternate the fires of its sections; or a mechanized Infantry platoon may alternate the fires of a pair of machine guns. Alternating fire permits the unit to maintain suppression for a longer duration than does volley fire; it forces the enemy to acquire and engage alternating points of fire. It also allows the nonfiring element to reposition to an alternate firing position while overwatched by the firing element.

Observed Fire

5-64. Observed fire is usually used when the company team is in protected positions with engagement ranges more than 2,500 meters. Observed fires can be employed by using vehicles with laser range finders to establish range for systems without (as in crew served weapons AT4) or for vehicles with inoperable laser range finders that are firing in degraded mode. The commander or PL directs one element or section to engage. The remaining elements or sections observe fires and prepare to engage on order in case the engaging element consistently misses its targets, experiences a malfunction, or runs low on ammunition. Observed fire allows for mutual observation and assistance while protecting the location of the observing elements.

Sequential Fire

5-65. Sequential fire entails the subordinate elements of a unit engaging the same point or area target one after another in an arranged sequence. For example, a mechanized Infantry platoon may sequence the fires of its four IFVs to gain maximum time of suppression. Sequential fire can help to prevent the waste of ammunition, as when a rifle platoon waits to see the effects of the first Javelin before firing another.

Time of Suppression

5-66. Time of suppression is the period, specified by the commander, during which an enemy position or force is required to be suppressed. Suppression time is typically dependent on the time it will take a supported element to maneuver. Normally, a unit suppresses an enemy position using the sustained rate of fire of its automatic weapons. In planning for sustained suppression, leaders must consider several factors: the estimated time of suppression, the size of the area being suppressed, the type of enemy force to be suppressed, range to the target, rates of fire, and available ammunition quantities. The following example lists steps that a unit might take in calculating time of suppression capabilities:

- The IFVs in a mechanized Infantry platoon are given the task of suppressing an area to support the assault of another element.
- One IFV, firing 25-mm high-explosive incendiary tracer ammunition at a sustained rate of 60 rounds per minute, expends 180 rounds (capacity of the large ready box, minus sufficient rounds for easy reloading) in 3 minutes.
- Given an adjusted basic load of 720 rounds of high explosive, a single IFV can sustain fire for four periods of 3 minutes, requiring three reloads of 180 rounds into the large ready box.
- An IFV crew, using a loader in the troop compartment, can reload the large ready box with 180 rounds in about 3 minutes if the ammunition is already prepared for loading.
- Using an individual IFV's sustained rate of fire of 60 rounds per minute and alternating the fire of sections to permit reloading (one section fires for 3minutes while the other reloads), the platoon can sustain 120 rounds per minute for 24 minutes.

Reconnaissance by Fire

5-67. *Reconnaissance by fire* is a technique in which a unit fires on a suspected enemy position (FM 3-90). This response permits the commander and subordinate leaders to make target acquisition and then to mass fires against the enemy element. Typically, the commander directs a subordinate element to conduct the reconnaissance by fire. For example, an order may be giving to direct an overwatching platoon to conduct the reconnaissance by fire against a probable enemy position before initiating movement by a bounding element.

Fire Patterns

5-68. Fire patterns are a threat-based measure designed to distribute the fires of a unit simultaneously among multiple, similar targets. They are most often used by platoons to distribute fires across an enemy formation. Commanders designate and adjust fire patterns based on terrain and the anticipated enemy formation. (See figure 5-7.) The fire patterns are as follows:

- Frontal.
- Cross.
- Depth.

Frontal Fire

5-69. Leaders may initiate frontal fire when targets are arrayed in front of the unit in a lateral configuration. Weapons systems engage targets to their respective fronts. For example, the left flank weapon engages the left-most target; the right flank weapon engages the right-most target. As weapons systems destroy targets, weapons shift fires toward the center of the enemy formation from near to far or far to near as appropriate.

Cross Fire

5-70. Leaders initiate crossfire when targets are arrayed laterally across the unit's front in a manner that permits diagonal fires at the enemy's flank, or when obstructions prevent unit weapons from firing frontally. Right flank weapons engage the left-most targets; left flank weapons engage the right-most targets. Firing diagonally across an EA provides more flank shots, thus increasing the chance of kills; it reduces the possibility of the enemy detecting friendly elements should the enemy continue to move forward. As friendly elements destroy targets, weapons shift fires toward the center of the enemy formation.

Depth Fire

5-71. Leaders initiate depth fire when enemy targets disperse in-depth, perpendicular to the unit. Center weapons engage the closest targets; flank weapons engage deeper targets. As the unit destroys targets, weapons shift fires toward the center of the enemy formation.

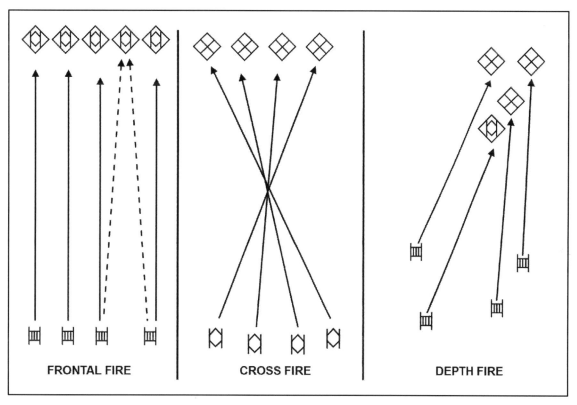

Figure 5-7. Fire patterns, example

Target Array

5-72. Target array enables the commander to distribute fires when the enemy force is concentrated, and terrain-based controls are inadequate. Target arrays are useful in both the offense and defense. Commanders can plan them in advance or designate hasty target arrays with an associated fire command. Target arrays can be centered on a TRP (terrain feature, tracer or laser marker, ground burst illumination), or simply based on the perceived center of the visible enemy formation. Commanders can designate subsections of a target array in a variety of ways, typically including near/far, left/right, near/far left/far right, or a quadrant. This fire control measure is effective against an enemy with a well-structured organization and standardized doctrine. However, it may prove less effective against an enemy that presents few organized formations or does not follow strict prescribed tactics. Depending on the lateral distance between friendly forces, subordinate elements may perceive relative locations within the target array differently. (See figure 5-8 on page 5-20.)

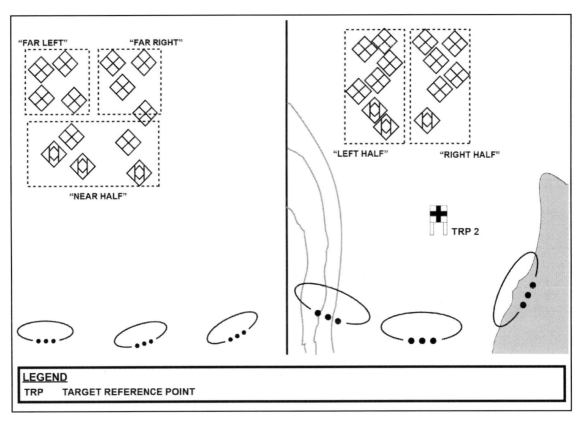

Figure 5-8. Target array, example

FIRE COMMANDS

5-73. Fire commands are oral orders issued by commanders and leaders to focus and distribute fires as required to achieve decisive effects against the enemy. They allow leaders to articulate their firing instructions using a standard format rapidly and concisely. Unit fire commands include these elements, which are discussed in the following paragraphs:

- Alert.
- Weapons or ammunition (optional).
- Target description.
- Orientation.
- Range (optional).
- Method.
- Controls (optional).
- Execution.
- Termination.

ALERT

5-74. The alert specifies the elements that are directed to fire. It does not require the leader initiating the command to identify themselves. The alert performs two functions: it notifies (alerts) the small unit of a pending engagement, and it can identify who fires within the unit. Although a contact report can be considered an alert, only the leader can issue the alert element for the collective fire command. Examples of the alert element (call signs and code words based on unit SOP) include the following:

- GUIDONS (could indicate all subordinate elements).
- RED (could indicate first platoon only).
- CONTACT.

WEAPONS OR AMMUNITION (OPTIONAL)

5-75. Target description designates which enemy elements are to be engaged. This identifies to the small unit which weapon or ammunition type is fired during the engagement. This element may be omitted when the leader intends to utilize the entire unit's combat power. Leaders may use the description to focus fires or achieve distribution. Examples of target description include the following:

- TOW.
- TWO ROUNDS SABOT.

TARGET DESCRIPTION

5-76. The third element of the fire command is target description. More appropriately, it is the description of the threat or threats that the crew will be engaging. All types of fire commands must have a target description. The target description may contain up to three components to enable leaders to identify the threat clearly. The three components are:

- Description. The leader identifies in the clearest manner what the enemy threat is in relation to the friendly force. This component is mandatory. (Tanks, troops, PC.)
- Quantity. This is an optional component. It provides the actual or estimated size of the enemy threat to be engaged. This allows subordinate leaders to assign rates of fire, engagement techniques (methods), and manage their unit's ammunition. (Three PCs, troops in open.)
- Action. This is an optional component. This is used to distinguish one enemy threat from another when target description is identical.

ORIENTATION (DIRECTION OR ELEVATION)

5-77. This element identifies the location of the target. The leader may use direction or elevation terms to assist the firer acquiring the correct target. This element may include elevation to better direct the firer onto the desired target. There are numerous ways to designate the location of target, including the following:

- Closest TRP. Example: TRP 13.
- Clock direction. Example: ONE O'CLOCK.
- Terrain quadrant. Example: QUADRANT ONE.
- Friendly quadrant. Example: LEFT FRONT.
- Target array. Example: FRONT HALF.
- Tracer on target. Example: ON MY TRACER.
- Laser pointer. Example: ON MY POINTER.

RANGE (OPTIONAL)

5-78. The range element identifies the distance to the target. Announcing range is not necessary for systems that are range finder-equipped or that employ command-guided or self-guided munitions. For systems that require manual range settings, leaders have a variety of means for determining range, including the following:

- Predetermined ranges to TRPs or PLs.
- An M1 tank crew announcing the range for an M2A2-equipped platoon.
- Handheld range finders.
- Range stadia.
- Milliradian reticle.

METHOD

5-79. The sixth element of the fire command defines the method the small unit will use to engage the threat. When there are multiple targets, the leader is required to better identify the targets and accurately describe which target to engage first. The leader may use multiple methods when necessary. For collective fire commands, this can also indicate the fire pattern used to engage the threats. Multiple methods may be used in one fire command. (See paragraphs 5-68 through 5-72.)

CONTROLS (OPTIONAL)

5-80. The controls element provides the leader the ability to control the fires of the small unit. The commander or PL may use this element to direct desired target effects, distribution methods, or engagement techniques. The leader may include the control element to support the commander's instructions and achieve effective distribution. The leader has several methods to control the fires of the unit to best manage ammunition, follow the commands of the next higher element, or to allow for synchronization of other direct or indirect fires. These methods include delay, engagement criteria, WCS, and the ROE.

Delay

5-81. The leader can use AT MY COMMAND to delay the firing of the engagement. This command implies that the command of execution follows shortly and to remain prepared to engage. AT MY COMMAND is used when the issuing leader maintains the timing of the engagement, not a senior leader. The leader can announce, STAND BY to delay for longer periods of time, specifically when the timing of the engagement is controlled by an external senior leader for synchronization of an action or event.

Engagement Criteria

5-82. Engagement criteria are a specific set of conditions that dictate initiation of fires. By specifying the engagement criteria, the leader provides the firing element the circumstances where subordinate elements are authorized to engage. These circumstances may be based on a friendly or enemy's action, event, or a point in time.

Weapons Control Status

5-83. When applicable, the PL or commander may impose a WCS in addition to the internal weapons safety status induced by leaders for all weapons systems. A WCS outlines the conditions, based on target identification criteria, under which friendly elements may engage. This status is adjustable as necessary. Typically, changes to the WCS occur and correspond with the phases of an operation. (See paragraph 5-55.)

Rules of Engagement

5-84. ROE specify the circumstances and limitations under which forces may engage; they include definitions of combatant and noncombatant elements and prescribe the treatment of noncombatants. Factors influencing ROE are national command policy, the mission and commander's intent, the OE, and the law of armed conflict.

EXECUTION

5-85. All fire commands (initial, subsequent, or supplemental) are executed for the firer to commence the engagement. The vehicle commander is the only crewmember authorized to announce a command of execution after the control element conditions to engage are met. Fire is the standard and most common command of execution for all weapons systems.

TERMINATION

5-86. Termination is the last element of the fire command. It informs the Soldiers to stop firing all weapons and systems in their control. All fire commands are terminated. This command may be given by any Soldier or crewmember for any reason, typically safety. The leader that issued the fire command is required to terminate the fire command at the completion of every engagement, regardless of if another Soldier or crewmember announced it. All fire commands, regardless of type or who issued them, are terminated by the announcement of, CEASE FIRE.

This page intentionally left blank.

Chapter 6

Sustainment

Sustainment is the provision of the logistics, financial management, personnel services, and health service support necessary to maintain operations until successful mission completion (ADP 4-0). In the company team, the commander has the ultimate responsibility for sustainment. The XO and the first sergeant are the team's primary sustainment coordinators and executors; they work closely with the CAB staff to ensure they receive the required support for the team's assigned operations. This chapter discusses sustainment planning, personnel services, maintenance, health service support, and unit loads needed to support operations.

SECTION I – SUSTAINMENT PLANNING

6-1. This section discusses sustainment planning including development of the company sustainment plan, company trains operations, emergency resupply, pre-positioned supplies, transportation, maintenance, human resources support, and medical support.

CONCEPT OF SUPPORT

6-2. The company teams are dependent on the CAB's FSC for resupply and most sustainment operations. The company XO, first sergeant, and supply sergeant are the key personnel in the company for coordinating and executing company-level sustainment.

6-3. The two methods of resupply operations are planned and emergency resupply. The company team SOP specifies cues and procedures for each method, which the company team rehearses during team training exercises. The actual method selected for resupply depends on the mission variables.

6-4. The company team must plan, prepare, and execute its portion of the CAB sustainment plan. Concurrent with other operational planning, the team develops its sustainment plan during mission analysis and refines it in the war-gaming portion of the TLP. Rehearsals normally conducted at both the CAB and company team levels ensure the company receives a smooth, continuous flow of materiel, supplies, and services.

DEVELOPMENT OF COMPANY SUSTAINMENT PLAN

6-5. The commander develops the company sustainment plan by determining exactly which supplies that are on hand and then estimating the support requirements as determined by LOGPAC cycles. If equipped with a digital command and control system, the commander reviews the tracked item list and verifies the supply status at any time. The commander uses available information from the mission analysis and war-gaming to aid in the development of the sustainment plan.

6-6. The commander formulates a logistics execution plan and submits support requests based on the results of the COA analysis and the war-gaming and refinement of the maneuver plan. The sustainment plan should answer a variety of operational questions, such as—

- Based on the nature of the operation and specific tactical factors, what support will the company team need?
  - Are we required to provide support to any external elements? (For example, scouts on screenline or reserve element.)

- What is our task organization? Mechanized heavy or armor heavy? Attachments? What are the command and support relationships? Do they bring their own sustainment capabilities? When does task org take effect? (Impacts: LOGPAC, meals, and so forth.)
- In which quantities will this support be required? These questions should be answered:
  - Will emergency resupply be required during the battle? If so, who is the likely priority for support?
  - Does this operation require prestock supplies?
- What is the composition, disposition, and capabilities of the expected enemy threat and how will these factors affect logistics operations during the battle? These questions should be answered:
  - Where and when will the expected contact occur?
  - Based on the nature and location of expected contact, what are the company team's expected casualties and vehicle losses?
  - Is the company's ambulance expected to conduct evacuation from point of injury to company CCP, CCP to BAS, or both legs of evacuation?
  - What ambulance exchange points are active during the battle? And when?
  - What impact will the enemy's special weapons capabilities (such as CBRN) have on the battle and expected sustainment requirements?
  - How many detainees are expected and where?
- How will terrain and weather affect sustainment operations during the battle? These questions should be answered:
  - What ground will provide optimum security for the trains?
  - What ground will provide optimum security for maintenance and CCPs?
  - What are the company team's vehicle and CASEVAC routes?
  - What are the team's "dirty" routes for evacuation of contaminated personnel, vehicles, and equipment?
- When and where will the company team need sustainment? These questions should be answered:
  - When must we receive our next LOGPAC resupply and what must we have delivered? (Class III bulk fuel resupply is normally every 6 to 8 hours for tanks.)
  - Based on the nature and location of expected contact, which sites are best for the maintenance collection points (known as MCPs)?
  - Where are we most likely to require recovery assets?
  - Based on the nature and location of expected contact, which sites are the best for the CCPs? Where will the detainee collection points be located?
  - Can the company's attached medics handle the anticipated load of casualties? Do we need to request additional medical treatment support?
  - Can the company's attached MEDEVAC platforms handle the anticipated load of casualties? Do we need to identify dedicated CASEVAC assets and be prepared to execute CASEVAC with platforms of opportunity?
  - Which LRP will be active during the battle? When will they be active?
- What are the criteria and triggers for the movement of the company combat trains?
- Who is the designated main effort by phase? Who is likely to be tasked with a contingency mission (branch or sequel)? These questions should be answered:
  - Which platoon has priority for emergency Class III resupply?
  - Which platoon has priority for emergency Class V resupply?
- Will there be lulls in the battle that will permit support elements to conduct resupply operations in relative safety? If no lulls are expected, how can the company team best minimize the danger to the sustainment vehicles?
- Based on information developed during the sustainment planning process, which resupply technique should be used?

6-7. Thorough briefings and comprehensive rehearsals are important keys to effective sustainment planning. These activities play a critical role to ensure that the company team executes its sustainment plans efficiently. They allow the commander, subordinate leaders, and each crewman to discover potential problem areas and to develop contingency plans to preclude unforeseen difficulties.

6-8. The commander has several options for conducting sustainment rehearsals. One is to integrate the sustainment rehearsal into the unit's larger maneuver rehearsals. Another is for the unit's sustainment operators to conduct a separate rehearsal with the maneuver elements they are supporting. The company commander directs the XO and first sergeant to rehearse sustainment operations with the team's PSG, maintenance team chief, and emergency care sergeant. Explosive ordnance disposal personnel are included as required by the mission.

COMPANY SUSTAINMENT PERSONNEL AND ORGANIZATION

6-9. The company team's basic sustainment responsibilities are to report and request support requirements through the correct channels and to ensure that it efficiently coordinates, deconflicts, and executes sustainment resupply in accordance with the maneuver plan once support elements arrive in the team area. The XO and first sergeant typically control these functions with guidance and oversight provided by the commander. They must submit accurate personnel and logistical reports, along with other necessary information and requests.

EXECUTIVE OFFICER

6-10. The XO is the company team's primary sustainment planner and coordinator, reporting directly to the commander. During preparations for the operation, the XO works closely with the first sergeant to determine specific support requirements of the tactical plan. Proper arrangements to provide those support requirements are also made. The XO performs these logistical functions:

- Determines the location of the team's resupply point based on data developed during operational planning.
- Compiles DA Form 5988-E (*Equipment Maintenance and Inspection Worksheet*), which is available through the Global Combat Support System-Army, from the PLs, PSGs, first sergeant, and maintenance team chief, and provides updates to the commander as required.
- Along with the first sergeant, ensures that the company team executes sustainment operations according to the CAB's plan.
- Leads the company team sustainment rehearsal in cooperation with the company first sergeant.
- Assists the commander in developing sustainment priorities and guidance according to the CAB concept of support and enforces those priorities.
- Conducts close coordination with the CAB logistics staff officer and CAB operations staff officer for planning and to resource company missions.

FIRST SERGEANT

6-11. The first sergeant is the company team's primary sustainment operator that executes the team's logistical plan, relying heavily on team and CAB's SOPs. The first sergeant directly supervises, controls the company trains, and performs these sustainment functions:

- Leads sustainment rehearsals with the XO and integrates sustainment into the team's maneuver rehearsals.
- Collects logistics requirements from platoons and all attachments and submits to the CAB following their logistics status reporting standards.
- Monitors the company team net and operates on the CAB administration/logistical net.
- Coordinates and synchronizes human resources support with the CAB personnel staff officer (S-1). This includes personnel accountability reports, casualty reports, replacement operations, personnel readiness management, mail operations, essential personnel services, and other administrative or personnel requirements.

- Ensures medical assets remain flexible and responsive to tactical operations by directing and supervising evacuation tasks.
- Establishes and organizes the company team resupply point.
- Meets the LOGPAC at the LRP; guides it to the company team resupply point; supervises resupply operations there; and, if necessary, guides the LOGPAC to its subsequent destination.
- Monitors LOGPAC throughput to ensure 100-percent participation.
- Provides a company team orientation for new personnel and in consultation with the commander, assigns replacements to the team's subordinate elements.
- Supervises evacuation of casualties, detainees, and damaged equipment.
- Directs and supervises the collection, initial identification, and evacuation of human remains to the mortuary affairs collection point.
- Maintains the company team battle roster, including any changes to task organization.
- Coordinates for field services/religious support.

SUPPLY SERGEANT

6-12. The supply sergeant is the company team's representative in the CAB's field trains. The supply sergeant performs these logistical functions:

- Coordinates with the FSC based off the logistical status and plan for resupply of Classes I, III, V, and IX.
- Maintains individual supply and clothing records, and requisitions Class II (clothing, individual equipment, tentage, tool sets, and administrative and housekeeping supplies and equipment) resupply as needed.
- Requisitions Class IV and Class VII (major end items, including tanks, helicopters, and radios) equipment and supplies.
- Picks up replacement personnel and, as needed, delivers them to the first sergeant.
- Receives and evacuates human remains to the mortuary affairs collection point in the brigade support area.
- Transports detainees as required.
- Guides the LOGPAC, along with detainees and damaged vehicles (if applicable), back to the brigade support area.
- Coordinates with the CAB's S-1 section to turn in or pick up mail and personnel action documents.
- Collects waste designated for retrograde, including hazardous waste and bagged contaminated soil, and transports it to collection points in accordance with LOGPAC procedures.
- Maintains and provides supplies for team field sanitation activities.
- Manages commander's property book and prepares financial liability investigations of property loss.

COMPANY TRAINS OPERATIONS

6-13. Company trains provide sustainment for a company during combat operations. Company trains include the first sergeant, company medical asset teams, supply sergeant, and the armorer. The FSC provides an FMT, with capabilities for maintenance, recovery, and limited combat spare parts. The supply sergeant can collocate in the combat trains if it facilitates LOGPAC operations. The first sergeant directs movement and employment of the company trains although the company commander may assign the responsibility to the company XO. Generally, company trains are located between 500 and 1,000 meters away from the company's combat operations. By placing at least one terrain feature between them and the enemy, the company trains will be out of the enemy's direct fire weapons.

Note. Mission variables ultimately dictate the actual distance at which the trains operate.

6-14. Configuring the company trains with the personnel described in paragraph 6-13 and gives the team almost immediate access to essential logistical functions while allowing the trains to remain in a covered and concealed position out of enemy contact. The company trains usually include the following vehicles, with corresponding crews:

- Recovery vehicle.
- Maintenance vehicle.
- First sergeant's armored vehicle.
- Armored ambulance vehicle.
- Command wheeled vehicles.

6-15. Because the security of sustainment elements is critical to the success of the company team missions, the company trains develop plans for continuous security operations. Where feasible, they plan and execute a perimeter defense. The trains, however, can lack the personnel and combat power to conduct a major security effort.

SUPPLY OPERATIONS

6-16. There are two methods of resupply operations, planned and emergency. Normally planned resupply operations that are rehearsed and synchronized with the maneuver plan are essential to conducting operations. Emergency resupply should only be used in critical situations where the supply is essential to mission success. The company team SOP specifies cues and procedures for each method, The actual method used for resupply in the field depends on mission variables.

PLANNED RESUPPLY

6-17. Planned resupply operations cover items in Classes I, III, V, and IX as well as mail and any other items the company team requests. Whenever possible, the company team should conduct planned resupply daily, ideally during periods of limited visibility. Because tanks and other major combat vehicles consume large amounts of fuel (for example, M1-series tanks generally require refueling every 6 to 8 hours), the company team should consider resupply LOGPACs of Class III at every opportunity and include any other classes of supply.

6-18. The commander, first sergeant, and XO must be alert to opportunities to deconflict sustainment operations with the scheme of maneuver to ensure the company and platoons are able to refuel/rearm before they commit to the fight, as opposed to afterwards. Before requesting emergency resupply, the first step is to cross-level supplies as much as possible on systems (for example, cross-leveling ammunition from semi-ready to ready racks/from under floor in the Bradley to upload/ready boxes) and then cross-leveling within sections and platoons.

6-19. There are multiple techniques for the resupply of supplies, personnel, and equipment. The following are examples of techniques for planned resupply:

- LOGPAC.
- Pre-positioned supplies.
- Cache.
- Modular system exchange.

LOGISTICS STATUS REPORT

6-20. The logistics status is an internal status report that identifies logistics requirements, provides visibility on critical shortages, and allows commanders to project mission capability. Accurate reporting of the logistics and Army Health System support status is essential for keeping units combat ready. The company first sergeant or XO compiles reports from all platoons, to include attachments, and completes the unit's logistics status report. Once completed, reports are forwarded from a unit to its higher HQ and its supporting logistics HQ. Logistics status reports should be completed at least daily (based off unit SOP) but may be required more frequently during periods of increased intensity or high operating tempo. (See ATP 3-90.5 and FM 4-0 for more information.)

6-21. The first sergeant must control redistribution of supplies when fuel and ammunition cannot be delivered or when only limited supplies are available. The PSG continually monitors the platoon's supply status through logistical reports and automated situation reports. The PSG notifies the first sergeant before a specific vehicle or the platoon is critically short of these major classes of supply.

6-22. In planning for refueling operations, the first sergeant and XO should balance the range and fuel capacity of the unit vehicles against the requirements of future operations. The company must top off vehicles (to include attachments) whenever the tactical situation permits. When time is limited, however, the first sergeant must choose between topping off vehicles that need the most fuel first or give limited amounts to each. The PSG must ensure each vehicle crew maintains a stock of oil, grease, and hydraulic fluid, replenishing these petroleum, oils, and lubricants products every time refueling takes place.

LOGISTICS PACKAGE OPERATIONS

6-23. The LOGPAC technique is a simple, efficient way to accomplish routine resupply operations. The key feature is a centrally organized resupply convoy originating at the CAB trains. It carries all items needed to sustain the company team for a specific period (normally 6 to 8 hours based on fuel) or until the next scheduled LOGPAC. Company team and CAB's SOPs specify the exact composition and march order of the LOGPAC. (See ATP 3-90.5 for more information.)

Preparation

6-24. After the first sergeant collects all platoon supply requests, the company team supply sergeant compiles and organizes the company's supply requests. Based on the requests, the supply sergeant then assembles the LOGPAC under the supervision of the FSC personnel or the HQ and HQ company/FSC commander. Items to be obtained include the following:

- Class I, Class III (bulk and packaged products), and Class V supplies from the FSC. This usually entails employment of one or two fuel trucks and one or two cargo trucks.
- Class II, Class IV (basic load resupply only), Class VI (personal demand items), and Class VII supplies from CAB logistics staff personnel in the field trains.
- Routine Class IX supplies and maintenance documents (as required) from the prescribed load list/shop stock section in the field trains.
- Replacement personnel and Soldiers returning from a medical treatment facility (MTF).
- Vehicles returning to the company team area from maintenance.
- Mail and personnel action documents (including awards and finance and legal documents) from the FSC S-1 section.

6-25. When LOGPAC preparations are completed, the supply sergeant conducts tactical movement to the LRP under the supervision of the distribution PL or senior NCO. The supply sergeant and LOGPAC linkup with the first sergeant at the LRP.

Actions at Logistics Release Point

6-26. The first sergeant arrives at the active LRP at a designated time, typically 30 or 60 minutes prior to the designated LRP time. Upon arrival, the first sergeant parks in a dispersed and covered/concealed position and participates in the LRP meeting with first sergeants and the CAB's sustainment leaders. Activities focused on the next 72 to 96 hours occur, including submitting all personnel, maintenance and logistical reports, task organization changes and their effective times, and an update on the tactical situation, currently active LRPs, and any other relevant sustainment considerations. Shortly before the arrival of the LOGPAC, the first sergeant prepares to pick up the dedicated portion of the LOGPAC and lead it to the planned resupply location.

Note. In some circumstances, units may conduct twice daily, but the LRP meeting will typically only happen once.

RESUPPLY PROCEDURES

6-27. The time required for resupply is an important planning factor. Units must conduct resupply as quickly and efficiently as possible to ensure operational effectiveness and to allow the company team LOGPAC to return to the LRP on time to allow the CAB's LOGPAC convoy to return to the field trains as a complete unit. Units must also consider security while conducting LOGPAC operations. This can be using one platoon to secure the LOGPAC area, while the remaining company executes resupply. METT-TC (I) determines the security requirements. The company team should establish unit SOP and rehearse it to ensure all elements, to include attachments, understand resupply procedures.

RETURN TO THE LOGISTICS RELEASE POINT

6-28. Once the unit completes resupply operations, the unit prepares LOGPAC vehicles for the return trip. Company team vehicles requiring recovery for maintenance or salvage are lined up and prepared for towing. Damaged or inoperable weapons and Class IX parts are also prepared to be backhauled. Cargo trucks, fuel trucks, or damaged vehicles transport those killed in action. Detainees ride in the cargo trucks and are guarded by walking wounded or other company team personnel. All supply requests, human resources actions, and outgoing mail are consolidated for forwarding to the field trains, where the appropriate staff section processes them for the next LOGPAC.

Note. Wounded and dead are not to be carried on any vehicles that carry Class I.

6-29. The first sergeant or the supply sergeant leads the LOGPAC back to the LRP, and linkup is conducted with the distribution PL. Whenever possible, the reunited task force LOGPAC convoy returns to the field trains together. When mission variables dictate or when the LOGPAC arrives too late to rejoin the larger convoy, company team vehicles must return to the field trains on their own. Because only minimal security assets are available, this situation should be avoided.

RESUPPLY METHODS

6-30. As directed by the commander or XO, the first sergeant establishes the company team resupply point using the service station method, the tailgate method, or a combination of both. The first sergeant briefs each LOGPAC driver on which method or methods to use. When the resupply point is ready, the first sergeant informs the commander, who in turn directs each platoon or element to conduct resupply based on the tactical situation.

Service Station Resupply

6-31. With the service station method, vehicles move individually or in small groups to a centrally located resupply point. Depending on the tactical situation, one vehicle or section or even an entire platoon moves out of its position, conducts resupply operations, and then moves back into position. This process continues until the entire company team has been resupplied.

6-32. When using this method, vehicles enter the resupply point following a one-way traffic flow. Only vehicles requiring immediate maintenance stop at the maintenance holding area. Vehicles move through each supply location, with crews rotating individually to eat, pick up mail and sundries, and refill or exchange water cans. Any detainees are centralized and guarded. Soldiers killed in action and their personal effects are brought to the holding area, where the first sergeant takes charge of them. When all platoon vehicles and crews have completed resupply, they move to a holding area, where, time permitting, the PL and PSG conduct a PCI. The company command group (company commander, XO, and first sergeant) can take this opportunity to conduct focused PCIs of each platoon as they pass through the resupply point (see figure 6-1 on page 6-8).

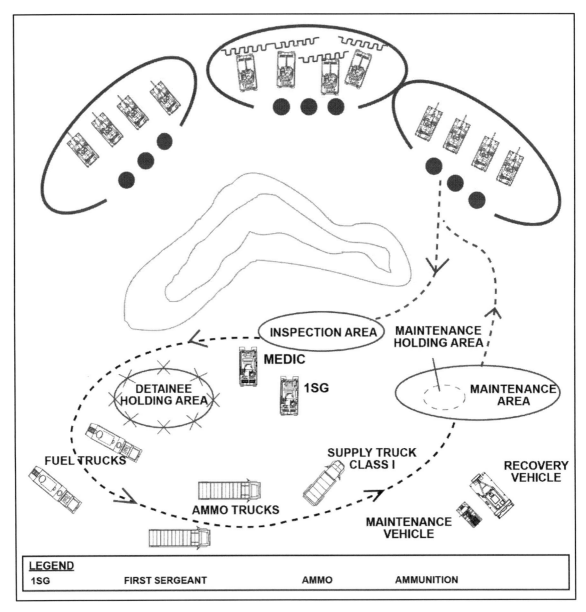

Figure 6-1. Service station method

Tailgate Resupply

6-33. Tailgate resupply usually requires significantly more time than service station operations. Usually, the company only uses the tailgate method when the tactical situation necessitates it; for example, during an ongoing security/counterreconnaissance operation or when defensive operations are imminent. Combat vehicles remain in their vehicle positions or back out a short distance to allow trucks carrying Class III and Class V supplies to reach them. Individual crewmen rotate through the feeding area, pick up mail and sundries, and fill or exchange water cans. (See figure 6-2.)

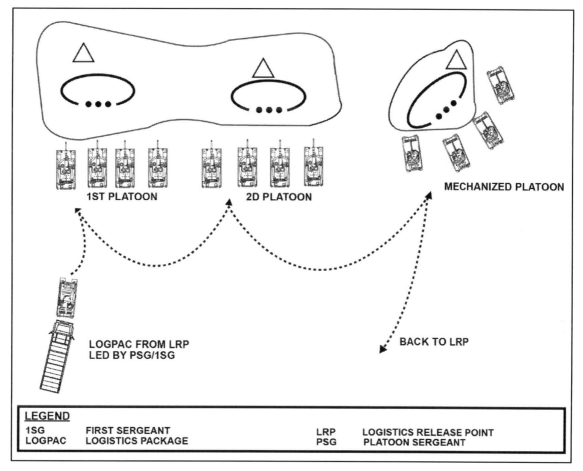

Figure 6-2. Tailgate resupply method

Combination of Service Station and Tailgate Resupply

6-34. The company team may select to employ the tailgate resupply method, but selected platoons may have to use the service station resupply method. Selected platoons may use the service station method while some of the sections may have to use the tailgate method. This may happen when the company is supporting a platoon attached to the CAB and operating in area coverage, such as air defense, engineers, and so forth, or in the case of support to the CAB's scout platoon.

PRE-POSITIONED SUPPLIES

6-35. Pre-positioning of supplies is most often required in defensive, or operations focused on stability operations. Usually, only Class V items are pre-positioned. Class III supplies can be pre-positioned. However, this requires company team vehicles to refuel before moving into positions during initial occupation of the BP or to move out of their positions to conduct refueling operations at the rear of the BP.

6-36. Leaders at every level carefully plan and execute pre-positioning supplies. All leaders, down to vehicle commander and squad leader, know the exact locations of prestock sites, which they verify during reconnaissance or rehearsals. The company team takes steps to ensure survivability of prestock supplies. These measures include digging in prestock positions and selecting covered and concealed positions. The commander develops a plan to remove or destroy pre-positioned supplies to prevent the enemy from capturing them. (See figure 6-3 on page 6-10, which shows prestock resupply operations, Method 1. See figure 6-4 on page 6-11, which shows prestock resupply operations, Method 2.)

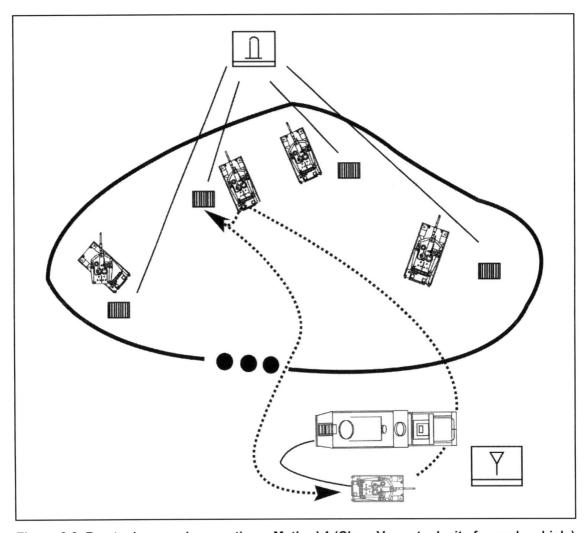

Figure 6-3. Prestock resupply operations: Method 1 (Class V prestock site for each vehicle)

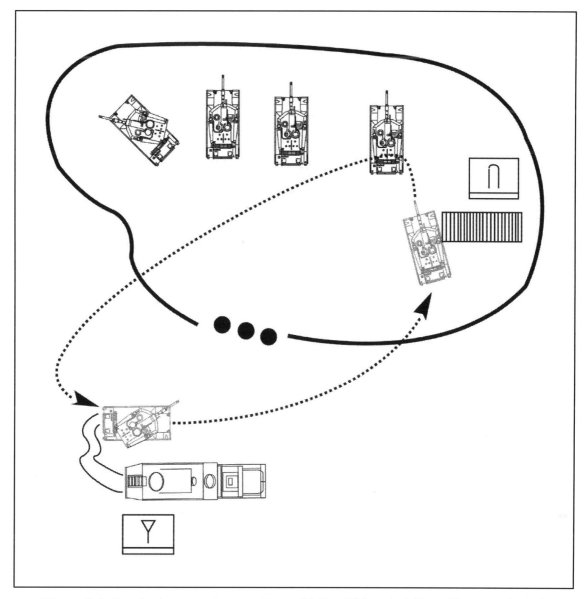

Figure 6-4. Prestock resupply operations: Method 2 (central Class V prestock site)

6-37. During offensive operations, pre-positioning of supplies in the offense is normally limited to refueling. The refuel on the move technique is planned and organized at CAB or higher level to sustain vehicles during long movements. Although restriction of movement can be tailored to other tactical situations, its two primary purposes are to: provide a timed allotment or specific quantity of fuel for operational formations or convoy movements to extend maneuverability to reach the intended destination when complete refueling operations are either not practical or unnecessary; or provide fuel between engagements to extend the time. (See ATP 4-43 for more information.)

CACHE

6-38. A cache is a pre-positioned and concealed supply point. Caches are different from standard pre-positioned supplies because the supported or supporting units conceal the supplies from the enemy whereas units might not conceal other pre-positioned supplies. Caches can reduce Soldiers' loads, and units can establish caches for a specific mission or as a contingency measure. Units may conceal cache sites above or below ground. Above ground caches are easier to access but are more vulnerable to discovery by the enemy, civilians, or animals.

EMERGENCY RESUPPLY

6-39. Occasionally (usually during combat operations), the company team has such an urgent need for resupply that it cannot wait for a routine LOGPAC. Emergency resupply may involve Classes III, V, VIII, and IX as well as CBRN equipment and, on rare occasions, Class I. The CAB usually uses the FSC's supply and transportation platoon, and medical assets located in the CAB combat trains to conduct emergency resupply of the company team.

6-40. Emergency resupply can be conducted using either the service station or tailgate method, although procedures may have to be adjusted when the company team is in contact with the enemy. In the service station method, individual vehicles pull back during a lull in combat on order of the commander or PL; they conduct resupply and then return to the fight. With tailgate resupply, the company team brings limited supplies forward to the closest concealed position behind each vehicle or element.

SECTION II – PERSONNEL SERVICES

6-41. Human resources support all functions that affect the Soldier's status, readiness, and welfare. It includes essential personnel services such as evaluations, leaves and passes, awards and decorations, rest and recuperation, postal, personnel accountability, casualty operations, strength reporting, retention operations, and personnel information management.

POSTAL SERVICES

6-42. The CAB mail clerk receives and distributes Soldier mail to the company mail clerk, usually the supply sergeant, who delivers it to the first sergeant, PSG, or to the Soldier in conjunction with LOGPAC. All outgoing and returned mail is given to the supply sergeant or first sergeant during resupply and is turned over to the S-1 section when the LOGPAC returns to the field trains.

PERSONNEL MANAGEMENT AND STRENGTH REPORTING

6-43. Personnel accounting is the process of recording by-name data on Soldiers when they arrive, depart, change duty location, or change duty status. Strength reporting is the numerical product of the by-name accounting process. First sergeants are critical participants in this process. They must be very sensitive to the accuracy and timeliness of all personnel accounting reports. They should pay special attention to Soldiers who have changed status in the medical treatment process and task organization changes when they submit their reports. Accuracy in strength reporting, and clarity in the time that task organization is effective, are essential to building an accurate company team LOGPAC.

CASUALTY OPERATIONS

6-44. Casualty operations include production, dissemination, coordination, validation, and synchronization of information regarding each casualty. This information includes casualty reporting, casualty notification, casualty assistance, line-of-duty determination, disposition of remains, disposition of personal effects, military burial honors, and casualty mail coordination.

UNIT REPORTING

6-45. As casualties occur, the nearest observer informs the company first sergeant via the most expedient method available (for example, utilizing a digital command and control system or FM voice). The first sergeant submits a personnel status report to the S-1 section. This report documents duty status changes on all casualties. Casualties are taken to CCP for classification of injury type (routine, urgent, return to duty), evacuation, and integration into the medical treatment system. The first sergeant ensures all completed DA Form 1156 (*Casualty Feeder Card*) are forwarded to the S-1, who then enters the data into the defense casualty information processing system.

6-46. Commanders and their first sergeants must establish procedures to ensure that official HQ DA notification procedures are not disregarded or circumvented. The potential for unofficial communications that exist, that is, the use of cell phones and computers in proximity to the AO enables many Soldiers to contact their home station regarding the casualty. Such communication is unofficial and unacceptable. The next of kin for Soldiers wounded or killed in action should not receive notification through unofficial means. There usually is a communication blackout until the next of kin is notified. No internet or phone calls home are permitted.

MEDICAL AND PERSONNEL ACCOUNTING

6-47. When a Soldier becomes a casualty, the platoon combat medic or senior combat medic records the medical treatment the Soldier receives on the Soldier's DD Form 1380 (*Tactical Combat Casualty Care [TCCC] Card*). The BAS and brigade support medical company read the Soldier's DD Form 1380 when they treat the Soldier. The S-1 should receive a notification to update the Soldier's patient tracking status. In turn, this notification should be forwarded to the company. In this manner, a casualty's location can be determined, and the Soldier is properly accounted for by the company.

SECTION III – MAINTENANCE

6-48. The Army has two levels of maintenance: field and sustainment. Field maintenance consists primarily of troubleshooting, repairing, or replacing parts and assemblies on the user's system or platform. Sustainment maintenance is performed by U.S. Army Materiel Command elements normally comprised of civilians and contractors who return equipment to a national standard, after which the equipment is placed back into the Army's overall supply system.

6-49. The link between the using organization and maintenance support is a trained operator/crew who can properly use and maintain the equipment. The continued demand for equipment requires that the operator and/or crew perform preventive maintenance checks and services. Maintainers usually diagnose down to the major component failure. They then replace that component and return the system to operational condition. Based on METT-TC (I), the Soldier can diagnose and replace subcomponent items depending on the availability of tools, parts, and time.

6-50. Replace forward means a Soldier performs "on-system" maintenance. "On-system" refers to replacing components or subcomponents at the point of repair, the breakdown site, or the MCP. Repair rear means that Soldiers perform "off-system" maintenance. "Off-system" refers to those actions taken to return components and subcomponents of weapons systems to serviceable condition. These repairs are performed at designated places throughout the battlefield.

FIELD MAINTENANCE

6-51. Field maintenance is on-system maintenance and mainly involves preventive maintenance and replacement of defective parts. The goal of field maintenance is to repair and return equipment to the Soldier. It includes some "off-system" maintenance critical to mission readiness.

6-52. Company commanders ensure that vehicle crews and equipment operators perform preventive maintenance checks and services. To provide quick turnaround of maintenance problems, each maneuver company has an FMT from the supporting FSC dedicated to support them. These FMTs have forward repair systems and mechanics trained in the company's equipment. The company first sergeant usually positions the FMT in the company trains.

SUSTAINMENT MAINTENANCE

6-53. Sustainment maintenance consists of repairing components off the user's platform. Those repaired components then go back into the supply system. Echelons above BCT perform this level of maintenance. To maximize unit combat readiness, maintenance personnel must repair and return the equipment to the user as quickly as possible.

LOCATION OF THE FIELD MAINTENANCE TEAM

6-54. During offensive operations, the FMT usually follows one terrain feature behind the company team. In the defense, it is usually located in a static location one terrain feature behind the company team. This positioning enhances security and enables the FMT to react quickly when platoons request support. In some situations, METT-TC (I) factors dictate that the FMT be positioned at the MCP to further enhance security and survivability.

BATTLE DAMAGE ASSESSMENT AND REPAIR

6-55. Commanders should address using battle damage assessment and repair in the logistics section of their OPORD. This provides the crews and maintainers with a clear understanding of when and at what risk level they can perform battle damage assessment and repair which uses emergency expedient repairs to return the system to fully or partially mission-capable status. Under combat conditions, personnel can perform battle damage assessment and repair on fueled or armed systems. The commander may also waive other precautions. All operations must be conducted as safely as possible. (See ATP 4-31 for more details about battle damage assessment and repair procedures.)

MAINTENANCE COLLECTION POINT OPERATIONS

6-56. When a vehicle or piece of equipment cannot be fixed quickly on site, it is moved to the CAB's MCP, where it is repaired by the FSC. When not involved in onsite actions, the FMT can assist with operations in the MCP.

SECTION IV – HEALTH SERVICE SUPPORT

6-57. *Health service support* is support and services performed, provided, and arranged by the Army Medicine to promote, improve, conserve, or restore the behavioral and physical well-being of personnel by providing direct patient care that include medical treatment (organic and area support) and hospitalization, medical evacuation to include medical regulating, and medical logistics to include blood management (FM 4-02).

BATTALION MEDICAL PLATOON

6-58. A medical platoon is organic to each combat battalion HQ and HQ company. The platoon is organized with an HQ section, a treatment squad (two treatment teams), an ambulance squad, and a combat medic section (see ATP 4-02.4 for more information).

6-59. In the Armor company team, the normal flow of care for combat casualties is self-aid/buddy-aid then to enhance first aid provided by the CLS (at the point of injury); to emergency medical treatment provided by combat medic (at the company CCP); to advanced trauma management provided by the physician or the physician assistant (at the BAS).

6-60. In the mechanized Infantry company, there is only one difference in the flow of care. Since there are platoon combat medics in the mechanized Infantry company, casualty flow goes from the CLS to the emergency medical treatment provided by the platoon medic (at the point of injury or at a platoon CCP) then to the senior company team combat medic).

CASUALTY COLLECTION POINT

6-61. Company leaders play an important role in recovery of combat casualties and coordinating for medical treatment and their expedient evacuation to a CCP where medical treatment is available. Selecting a site for the CCP should be addressed during the COA development step of TLP. The unit first sergeant and the company senior medic designates the location for the company team's CCP and ensures the location are on appropriate overlays. All platoons and attachments must be informed and provided locations of the company CCP. However, METT-TC (I) will become a factor as operations commence. Listed in the following bullets are some factors to consider a tactical location for a CCP:

- Proximity to the fight.
- Near templated areas of expected high casualties.
- Cover and concealment.
- Access to evacuation routes (foot, vehicle, and aircraft).
- Avoid natural or enemy choke points.
- Area allowing passive security (inside the perimeter).
- Good drainage.
- Trafficable to evacuation assets.
- Expandable if casualty load increases.

6-62. At the collection point, the senior combat medic conducts triage of all casualties, takes the necessary steps to stabilize their condition, and initiates the process of moving them to the rear for further treatment. CASEVAC or MEDEVAC requests are initiated on following the established communications plan with a follow-up digital report if possible.

CASUALTY CARE

6-63. Effective casualty care has a positive impact on the morale of a unit. Casualties are cared for at the point of injury (or under nearby cover and concealment) and receive self-aid or buddy aid, enhanced first aid from the CLS, or emergency medical treatment from the platoon or company combat medic.

6-64. Unit SOPs and OPORDs address casualty treatment and evacuation in detail. They cover the duties and responsibilities of key personnel, the evacuation of chemically contaminated casualties (on separate routes from noncontaminated casualties), and the priority for operating key weapons and positions. They specify the primary and the preferred methods of evacuation and make provisions for retrieving and safeguarding the weapons, ammunition, and equipment of the casualties. Slightly wounded personnel are treated and returned to duty by the lowest echelon possible. Company combat medics evaluate sick Soldiers and either treat or evacuate them as necessary.

6-65. Role 1 medical treatment is the first medical treatment a Soldier may receive. Role 1 medical treatment is provided at the CCP by the combat medics, and the patient may receive further treatment at the Role 1 BAS by the physician or physician assistant.

6-66. During the fight, casualties should remain under cover where they received initial treatment (self-aid or buddy aid). As soon as the situation allows, casualties are moved to the platoon or company CCP. From the platoon or company CCP and then back to the BAS or other facility in the CAB or brigade support area. Unit SOPs addresses these activities, to include the marking of casualties in limited-visibility operations. Small, standard, or IR chemical lights work well for this purpose. Once the casualties are collected, evaluated, and treated, they are prioritized for evacuation back to the company CCP. Once they arrive at the company CCP, the process is repeated while awaiting their evacuation back to the support area(s).

6-67. At the CCP, the senior combat medic conducts triage of all casualties, takes the necessary steps to stabilize their condition, and initiates the process of evacuating them to the rear for further treatment. The senior combat medic helps the first sergeant arrange evacuation via ground or air ambulance, or by nonstandard means. Company elements that conduct MEDEVAC and CASEVAC must know the location of the BAS and the route to and from the BAS must be rehearsed in both day and hours of limited visibility.

6-68. An effective technique, particularly during an attack, is to task-organize a logistics team under the first sergeant. These Soldiers carry additional ammunition forward to the platoons and evacuate casualties to either the company or the CAB's CCP. The commander determines the size of the team during mission analysis.

6-69. Each individual Soldier is trained in a variety of specific first-aid procedures. These procedures include aid for chemical casualties with particular emphasis on lifesaving tasks. This training enables the Soldier or a buddy to apply tactical combat casualty care. Each Soldier is issued an individual first-aid kit to accomplish first-aid tasks. First aid (self-aid/buddy aid) refers to urgent and immediate lifesaving and other measures which can be performed for casualties (or performed by the victims themselves) by nonmedical personnel when medical personnel are not immediately available.

6-70. Nonmedical personnel performing first-aid procedures assist the combat medics in their duties. First aid is administered by an individual (self-aid or buddy aid) and enhanced first aid is provided by the CLSs.

6-71. A *combat lifesaver* is a nonmedical Soldier of a unit trained to provide enhanced first aid as a secondary mission (FM 4-02). The CLS may need to support the combat medic prior to or after the combat medics arrival. For example, at a company CCP, the combat medic may be conducting triage and directing multiple CLS to execute the treatment interventions while the combat medic continues to move between casualties. Although not a health care provider, this Soldier is a recipient or consumer of medical materiel.

6-72. The Class VIII resupply of individual first aid kits, and CLS bags during operations may be challenging. It is important that commanders and first sergeants account for medical supply expenditures based off of the casualty estimate during planning and coordinate with their supporting medical organization to have Class VIII resupply packets, also known as push-package, prepositioned in the company trains. Units with organic medical support receives normal Class VIII resupply through the medical platoon. Units without organic medical support should be resupplied with Class VIII by the medical element providing area support coordinated through the battalion logistics officer. Class VIII resupply should flow through the normal sustainment channels outlined in the organizations SOP.

6-73. The combat medic medical equipment set is not designed to resupply the individual first aid kit or the CLS bag. This type of Class VIII resupply should not be practiced on a routine basis as it presents logistics problems for the combat medic. The organic medical platoon can expedite Class VIII resupply through the use of emergency push-packages, as discussed in paragraph 6-72, delivered to the company senior combat medic through ambulance backhaul and then distributed by the first sergeant.

EVACUATION

6-74. When possible, the battalion medical platoon ambulances provide evacuation and en route care from the company's CCP to the BAS. The ambulance team supporting the company works in coordination with the senior combat medic supporting the rifle platoons. In mass casualty situations, nonmedical vehicles can be used to assist in CASEVAC as directed by the commander. Plans for the use of nonmedical vehicles to perform CASEVAC should be included in the unit SOP. Ground ambulances from the brigade support medical company or other supporting ambulances evacuate patients from the BAS back to the brigade support medical company MTF located in the brigade support area.

6-75. Leaders minimize the number of Soldiers required to evacuate casualties. Casualties with minor wounds can walk or even assist with carrying the more seriously wounded. Soldiers can make field-expedient litters by cutting small trees and putting the poles through the sleeves of buttoned uniform blouses. A travois, or skid, might be used for CASEVAC. Wounded are strapped on this type of litter, then one person can pull it. It can be made locally from durable, rollable plastic. Tie-down straps are fastened to it. In rough terrain, or on patrols, litter teams can evacuate casualties to the BAS. If casualties cannot be evacuated to the BAS, they are carried with the unit either until transportation can reach them or until they are left at a position for later pickup.

6-76. When the company is widely dispersed, the casualties might be evacuated directly from the platoon CCP by vehicle or air ambulance. Enemy air defenses must be considered because when enemy air defense capabilities preclude using air ambulances in forward areas, air ambulances may be used to evacuate patients from Role 1 ambulance exchange points to Role 2 MTFs. In most cases, the casualties should be moved to the company CCP before evacuation. If the capacity of the CAB's organic ambulances is exceeded, unit leaders may re-role supply or other vehicles to backhaul or otherwise transport nonurgent casualties to the BAS. In other cases, the PSG may direct platoon litter teams to carry the casualties to the rear.

6-77. Before casualties are evacuated to the CCP or beyond, leaders should remove all key operational or sensitive items and equipment, including communications security devices or signal operating instructions, maps, position location devices. Every unit should establish an SOP for handling the weapons and ammunition of its wounded or killed in action. Protective masks must stay with the individual.

MEDICAL EVACUATION VERSUS CASUALTY EVACUATION

6-78. *Medical evacuation* is the timely and effective movement of the wounded, injured, or ill to and between medical treatment facilities on dedicated and properly marked medical platforms with en route care provided by medical personnel (ATP 4-02.2). MEDEVAC is the key factor to ensuring the continuity of care provided to our Soldiers by providing en route medical care during evacuation, facilitating the transfer of patients between medical treatment facilities to receive the appropriate specialty care. This ensures that scarce medical resources (personnel, equipment, and supplies [to include blood]) can be rapidly transported to areas of critical need on the battlefield. The primary means for maneuver forces to execute MEDEVAC is by ground ambulances with the preferred method of evacuation air ambulances.

6-79. MEDEVAC is not the same as CASEVAC. *Casualty evacuation* is the movement of casualties aboard nonmedical vehicles or aircraft without en route medical care (FM 4-02). CASEVAC typically relies on organic nonmedical assets (often called nonstandard assets) without specialized trauma care. CASEVAC may occur at any point in the scheme of evacuation, whether from the point of injury to a platoon or company CCP, or from either the point of injury or a CCP directly to the BAS. The company should designate some vehicles as nonstandard evacuation assets prior to any operation and ensure they are fitted with litters, litter straps, and any other key equipment.

6-80. Vehicle commanders arrange for transport of the casualty to the platoon CCP, or the casualty is evacuated to the CCP. From the platoon's CCP, the casualty may be transported via CASEVAC or by supporting ground ambulances to the company's CCP. Depending on METT-TC (I) the casualty may be medically evacuated from the point of injury directly to the supporting Role 2 or Role 3 MTF by air ambulance.

Note. Company team members and attached company combat medics should rehearse crew evacuation by position to improve the ability to remove casualties from combat vehicles safely.

6-81. When air ambulance evacuation is not necessary or when these assets are not available, the team has these options for transporting those wounded in action:

- The primary method is the medical platoon's ambulance section should evacuate casualties from the company CCP to the Role 1. Ambulances can be task organized as needed. In many cases, they are habitually associated with the company team. The team's assigned ambulance evacuates wounded in action to the BAS, and then returns to the team location.
- In the alternate method, the senior combat medic can transport casualties to the BAS personally. Wounded in action are turned over to the medical team at the BAS on arrival. The senior combat medic also obtains any needed medical supplies and then returns to the company team location.

6-82. The first sergeant must understand the linkage between the company's CCP, the BAS, and the location of the company medics based off the unit's MEDEVAC plan. Under some operational scenarios, when a treatment team is positioned with a company team's CCP, the attached ambulance may evacuate back to the ambulance exchange point. From the ambulance exchange point, patients are evacuated to the Role 2 MTF. Soldiers evacuated to the Role 2 MTF receive medical treatment are evacuated for further treatment or are returned to duty. Responsibility for further evacuation from the BAS is the mission of the brigade support medical company ground ambulances or supporting air ambulance.

SECTION V – UNIT COMBAT AND BASIC LOAD

6-83. There are few, if any, contingencies in which U.S. military forces have all the supplies they need for an operation. Because of this, every unit's daily logistical reports must accurately reflect not only its operational needs but what supplies and equipment are on hand.

6-84. As much as possible, logistics planners try to standardize "push" packages, providing all units with enough of each supply item in anticipation of their requirements. Together with the commander's guidance for issuance of scarce, but heavily requested, supply items, accurate reporting allows planners to forecast supply constraints quickly and submit requisitions to alleviate projected shortages. Inaccurate or incomplete reporting can severely handicap efforts to balance unit requirements and available supplies. As a result, some units may go into combat without enough supplies to accomplish their mission while others may have an excess of certain items.

6-85. The *combat load* is the minimum mission-essential equipment and supplies as determined by the commander responsible for carrying out the mission, required for Soldiers to fight and survive immediate combat operations (FM 4-40). The makeup of combat loads is not standard, and they do not have defined quantities established. The types and quantities of supplies vary depending on the current mission. The combat load is replenished by the next higher source of supply. The company team's combat load includes supplies that it carries into the fight. The CAB commander dictates minimum requirements; however, the company commander or the unit SOP specifies most items. Specific combat loads vary by mission. (See Platform-10 manuals for information on ammunition specific to each platform in support of mission and logistical planning.)

6-86. The *basic load* is the quantity of supplies required to be on hand within, and moved by a unit or formation, expressed according to the wartime organization of the unit or formation and maintained at the prescribed levels (JP 4-09). The quantity of most supply items in the basic load is related to the number of days in combat the team may be required to sustain itself without resupply. For Class V, the basic load is a quantity of ammunition, specified by the higher command or by SOP that the team is required to have on hand to meet combat needs until resupply can be accomplished. The higher command or the SOP specifies the Class V basic load. (See ADP 3-90 and ATP 4-35 for more information.)

6-87. Combat-configured loads are packages of potable and nonpotable water, CBRN defense supplies, barrier materials, ammunition, petroleum, oils, lubricants, medical supplies, and repair parts tailored to a unit. Regularly scheduled combat-configured loads enable offensive momentum and freedom of action. If communications are degraded, the FSC automatically pushes critical supplies to units in the offense.

6-88. A mission-configured load is an ammunition load configured to support specific mission requirements. Mission-configured loads are delivered as far forward as possible.

Chapter 7

Enabling Operations and Activities

Enabling tasks are specialized missions that units plan and conduct to seize or retain a tactical advantage. Units execute these operations as part of the offense, defense, or operations focused on stability operations. The fluid nature of the modern battlefield increases the frequency with which the company team conducts these enabling operations. This chapter establishes techniques and procedures that the company team can apply to these specialized missions. This chapter discusses reconnaissance, security, relief in place, passage of lines, tactical deception, linkup operations, patrols, troop movement, AA procedures, and gap crossings.

SECTION I – RECONNAISSANCE

7-1. *Reconnaissance* is a mission undertaken to obtain information about the activities and resources of an enemy or adversary, or to secure data concerning the meteorological, hydrographic, geographic or other characteristics of a particular area, by visual observation or other detection methods (JP 2-0). Reconnaissance primarily relies on the human dynamic rather than technical means. (See FM 3-90 for more information.)

7-2. Reconnaissance identifies terrain characteristics, enemy and friendly obstacles to movement, and the disposition of enemy forces and civilian population so the commander can maneuver forces freely and rapidly. Reconnaissance also answers the CCIRs. *Commander's critical information requirement* is specific information identified by the commander as being essential to facilitate timely decision making (JP 3-0). (See ADP 5-0 for more information.) Reconnaissance before unit movements and occupation of AAs is critical to protecting the force and preserving combat power. It keeps the force free from contact if possible so that it can concentrate on its mission.

7-3. Reconnaissance can be passive or active. Passive reconnaissance includes such techniques as map and photographic reconnaissance and surveillance. Active methods available to the company team include mounted and dismounted ground reconnaissance and reconnaissance by fire. Active reconnaissance operations are classified as stealthy or aggressive.

RECONNAISSANCE FUNDAMENTALS

7-4. The seven fundamentals of successful reconnaissance operations are as follows:
- Ensure continuous reconnaissance.
- Do not keep reconnaissance assets in reserve.
- Orient on the reconnaissance objective.
- Report all required information rapidly and accurately.
- Retain freedom of maneuver.
- Gain and maintain enemy contact.
- Develop the situation rapidly.

7-5. Effective reconnaissance is continuous. The company team conducts reconnaissance before, during, and after all operations. Before an operation, reconnaissance focuses on filling gaps in information about the enemy and terrain. During an operation, reconnaissance focuses on providing the commander with updated information that verifies the enemy's composition, dispositions, and intentions as the battle progresses. After an operation, reconnaissance focuses on maintaining contact with the enemy to determine their next move and collecting information necessary for planning subsequent operations.

7-6. Reconnaissance assets are never kept in reserve. When committed, reconnaissance assets use all resources to accomplish the mission. This does not mean that all assets are committed all the time. The commander uses reconnaissance assets based on the capabilities and mission variables to achieve the maximum coverage needed to answer the CCIR.

7-7. Commanders use the reconnaissance objective to focus their unit's reconnaissance efforts. The reconnaissance objective is a terrain feature, geographic area, or an enemy about which the commander wants to obtain additional information.

7-8. Reconnaissance assets must acquire and report accurate and timely information about the enemy, civil considerations, and the terrain over which operations are to be conducted. Information may quickly lose its value. Reconnaissance assets must report exactly what they see and, if appropriate, what they do not see.

7-9. Reconnaissance assets must retain battlefield mobility to complete the missions successfully. If these assets are decisively engaged, reconnaissance stops and a battle for survival begins. Reconnaissance assets must have clear engagement criteria that support the commander's intent. They must employ proper movement and reconnaissance techniques, use overwatching fires, and SOPs.

7-10. Once a unit conducting reconnaissance gains contact with the enemy, it maintains that contact unless the commander directing the reconnaissance orders otherwise or the survival of the unit is at risk. This does not mean that individual scout and reconnaissance teams cannot break contact with the enemy. The commander of the unit conducting reconnaissance is responsible for maintaining contact using all available resources.

7-11. When a reconnaissance asset encounters an enemy force or an obstacle, it must quickly determine the threat it faces. For an enemy force, it must determine the enemy's composition, dispositions, activities, and movements and assess the implications of that information. For an obstacle, it must determine the type and extent of the obstacle and whether it is covered by fire. Obstacles can provide the attacker with information concerning the location of enemy forces, weapon capabilities, and organization of fires. In most cases, the reconnaissance unit developing the situation uses actions on contact.

FORMS OF RECONNAISSANCE

7-12. The four forms of reconnaissance that apply to the company team are—
- Route.
- Zone.
- Area.
- Reconnaissance in force.

ROUTE RECONNAISSANCE

7-13. Route reconnaissance focuses on a specific line of communication, such as a road, railway, or cross-country mobility corridor. A *route reconnaissance* is a form of reconnaissance operation to obtain detailed information of a specified route and all terrain from which the enemy could influence movement along that route (FM 3-90). It is oriented on a specific area of movement, such as a road or trail, or on a more general area, like an axis of advance. A route reconnaissance is usually conducted when the commander wants to use the route in question.

7-14. Route reconnaissance tasks are the following:
- Find, report, and clear all enemy forces that can influence movement along the route in accordance with engagement criteria.
- Determine the trafficability of the route; can it support friendly force?
- Reconnoiter all terrain that the enemy can use to dominate movement along the route, such as choke points, ambush sites, pickup zones, landing zones, and drop zones.
- Reconnoiter all built-up areas, contaminated areas, and lateral routes along the route.
- Evaluate and classify all bridges, defiles, overpasses and underpasses, and culverts along the route.

- Locate any fords, crossing sites, or bypasses for existing and reinforcing obstacles (including built-up areas) along the route.
- Locate all obstacles and create lanes as specified in execution orders.
- Report the route information to the HQ initiating the route reconnaissance mission, to include providing a sketch map or a route overlay.
- Answer CCIRs.

ZONE RECONNAISSANCE

7-15. *Zone reconnaissance* is a form of reconnaissance operation that involves a directed effort to obtain detailed information on all routes, obstacles, terrain, and enemy forces within a zone defined by boundaries (FM 3-90). Teams usually conduct zone reconnaissance when the enemy situation is vague or when information concerning cross-country trafficability is required. Like route reconnaissance, mission variables and the commander's intent dictate the company team's actions during a zone reconnaissance.

7-16. Zone reconnaissance tasks are the following:
- Find and report all enemy forces within the zone.
- Clear all enemy forces, based on engagement criteria, in the designated AO within the capability of the unit conducting reconnaissance.
- Determine the trafficability of all terrain within the zone, including built-up areas.
- Locate and determine the extent of all contaminated areas in the zone.
- Evaluate and classify all bridges, defiles, overpasses, underpasses, and culverts in the zone.
- Locate any fords, crossing sites, or bypasses for existing and reinforcing obstacles (including built-up areas) in the zone.
- Locate all obstacles and create lanes as specified in execution orders.
- Report information to the commander directing the zone reconnaissance, to include providing a sketch map or overlay.
- Answer CCIRs.

AREA RECONNAISSANCE

7-17. *Area reconnaissance* is a form of reconnaissance operation that focuses on obtaining detailed information about the terrain or enemy activity within a prescribed area (FM 3-90). The area can be any location that is critical to the unit's operations. Examples include easily identifiable areas covering a large space (such as towns or military installations), terrain features (ridgelines, wood lines, choke points), or a single point (like a bridge or building). The tasks of an area reconnaissance are the same as those for a zone reconnaissance. Area reconnaissance differs from zone reconnaissance in that the unit moves to the assigned area by the most direct route. Once in the area, the tasked unit reconnoiters in detail using zone reconnaissance techniques.

RECONNAISSANCE IN FORCE

7-18. *Reconnaissance in force* is a form of reconnaissance operation designed to discover or test the enemy's strength, dispositions, and reactions or to obtain other information (FM 3-90). CABs or larger organizations usually conduct a reconnaissance in force mission. A company team will not conduct a reconnaissance in force independently but may participate as part of a larger force.

TASK ORGANIZATION

7-19. Although not optimally organized for reconnaissance, the company can conduct route, zone, or area reconnaissance. The company may conduct a reconnaissance operation during preparation for another operation of its own (for example, performing zone reconnaissance before initiating a stationary guard operation); or it can conduct the reconnaissance to gain information for a higher HQ. Usually, the company is task-organized with additional combat or sustainment assets as needed to meet the requirements of the reconnaissance operation.

PLANNING CONSIDERATIONS

7-20. Commanders provide clear reconnaissance guidance that offers freedom of action to develop the situation and adequate direction. Reconnaissance planning starts with the commander identifying the CCIR. This process may be conducted while the unit is planning or preparing for an operation; in many cases, it continues throughout the operation. (See FM 3-98 for more information.) The commander's guidance consists of four elements:

- Reconnaissance focus.
- Reconnaissance tempo.
- Engagement criteria both lethal and nonlethal.
- Disengagement criteria.

7-21. The commander considers mission variables when planning for mounted, dismounted, aerial, or reconnaissance by fire. Conditions that lead to a decision about the type of reconnaissance include—

- Time constraints.
- Required detail level of reconnaissance.
- Availability of air units to perform coordinated reconnaissance with ground assets.
- IPB information.
- Avenues of approach that support friendly movement and exploit enemy weaknesses.
- Key positions, especially flanks that can be exploited.
- Information from OPs.
- Type of terrain.
- Environmental conditions, such as deep snow and muddy terrain that greatly hinder mounted reconnaissance.

7-22. The commander considers employing UAS for reconnaissance. UAS platforms provide the commander with flexible options to conduct reconnaissance options to determine essential terrain and enemy information. Most UASs can operate in daylight or limited visibility but may be vulnerable to enemy air defense if present.

7-23. Leaders at all echelons coordinate and synchronize reconnaissance efforts. The key point is to use reconnaissance assets based on their capabilities and use their complementary capabilities to verify and expand on available information.

7-24. Sustainment planning is indispensable throughout the planning process. The commander assesses all constraints and considers the following:

- Resupply procedures for mounted and dismounted reconnaissance missions.
- Predetermined locations and times for resupply.
- Tactics, techniques, and procedures for CASEVAC and MEDEVAC.
- Pickup points and times for pickup and aerial extraction of casualties.
- Resupply procedures for Class VIII by Army Health System support elements.

SECTION II – SECURITY

7-25. *Security operations* are those operations performed by commanders to provide early and accurate warning of enemy operations, to provide the force being protected with time and maneuver space within which to react to the enemy, and to develop the situation to allow commanders to effectively use their protected forces (ADP 3-90). Security operations are operations to provide early and accurate warning of enemy operations, to provide the force being protected with time and maneuver space within which to react to the enemy, and to develop the situation to allow commanders to effectively use their force. Security operations include reconnaissance aimed at reducing terrain and enemy unknowns; gaining and maintaining contact with the enemy to ensure continuous information; and providing early and accurate reporting of combat information to the protected force. Security forces orient in any direction from a stationary or moving force. (See ADP 3-90 for more information.)

SECURITY OPERATIONS

7-26. Security operations encompass four tasks—screen, guard, cover, and area security.

- *Screen* is a type of security operation that primarily provides early warning to the protected force (ADP 3-90).
- *Guard* is a type of security operation done to protect the main body by fighting to gain time while preventing enemy ground observation of and direct fire against the main body (ADP 3-90). Units performing a guard cannot operate independently. They rely upon fires, functional support, and multifunctional support assets of the main body.
- *Cover* is a type of security operation done independent of the main body to protect them by fighting to gain time while preventing enemy ground observation of and direct fire against the main body (ADP 3-90).
- *Area security* is a type of security operation conducted to protect friendly forces, lines of communications, installation routes and actions within a specific area (FM 3-90).

7-27. Screen, guard, and cover, respectively, contain increasing levels of combat power and provide increasing levels of security for the main body. However, more combat power in the security force means less for the main body. Area security preserves the commander's freedom to move unit reserves, position fire support means, provide for command and control, and conduct sustaining operations. Local security provides immediate protection for the forces.

7-28. The company team can conduct screen or guard operations without external augmentation. The company team can only participate in covering force operations as part of a larger element. It can conduct area security operations on its own but will usually participate as part of a CAB area security force. All forces, including the company team, must provide their own local security. Local security includes OPs, security patrols, perimeter security, and other close-in measures.

FUNDAMENTALS OF SECURITY OPERATIONS

7-29. The five fundamentals of security operations are—

- Provide early and accurate warning.
- Provide reaction time and maneuver space.
- Orient on the protected force, area, or facility to be secured.
- Perform continuous reconnaissance.
- Maintain enemy contact.

PROVIDE EARLY AND ACCURATE WARNING

7-30. The security force provides early, accurate warning by detecting the threat force quickly and reporting information accurately to the commander. Early warning of threat activity provides the commander with the time, space, and information needed to retain the tactical initiative and to choose the time and place to concentrate against the threat. At a minimum, the security force should operate far enough from the main body to prevent enemy ground forces from observing or engaging the main body with direct fire. Position maneuver forces, sensors, and tactical UAS to provide long-range observation of expected threat avenues of approach.

7-31. In operations focused on stability operations, providing early and accurate warning is much harder to achieve. In many cases, threat personnel in the AO are indistinguishable from civilian noncombatants; they might elude positive identification as a threat until their actions reveal them as such. This fundamental may be expressed in the environment in the following ways:

- Identification of and regular communication with key civil and religious leaders.
- Continuous surveillance of known or suspected terrorist meeting locations.
- Proactive, friendly engagement with the indigenous population to ascertain threat developments in their community that may otherwise be transparent to the unit.

PROVIDE REACTION TIME AND MANEUVER SPACE

7-32. The security force operates as far from the protected force as possible within supporting range of the protected force, consistent with the factors of METT-TC (I). More distance usually yields greater reaction time and maneuver space for the protected force commander if communications are maintained. The security force fights as necessary to gain and retain adequate time and space for the protected force commander, allowing the commander to maneuver and concentrate forces to counter the threat.

ORIENT ON THE PROTECTED FORCE, AREA, OR FACILITY TO BE SECURED

7-33. The security force focuses all actions to protect the secured force, area, or facility and provide maximum early warning of threat activity. It operates between the main body and known or suspected enemy units. The security force must move as the main body moves and orient on its movement. The security commander must know the main body's scheme of maneuver in order to maneuver forces so it remains between the main body and the enemy. The value of terrain occupied by the security force depends on the protection it provides to the main body commander.

7-34. In operations focused on stability operations, the security force should orient on the routes or areas where ambushes, snipers, and mortar attacks have frequently occurred. They could focus on locations where explosive hazards, to include improvised explosive devices have been repeatedly used. Another example is the security force that orients surveillance on the offices occupied by a newly seated foreign government whose legitimacy may be contested and targeted for violence by threat factions.

PERFORM CONTINUOUS RECONNAISSANCE

7-35. Security comes in large part from knowing as much as possible about the threat and terrain within the assigned AO. This detailed knowledge results from ongoing, focused reconnaissance that aggressively and continuously reconnoiters key terrain; seeks the location, composition, and disposition of the threat; and determines the threat's COA early so that the company team can counter it. Stationary security forces use combinations of OPs, UAS, patrols, and other information collection assets to perform continuous reconnaissance. Moving security forces accomplish this fundamental by performing area, zone, or route reconnaissance in conjunction with temporary OPs and BPs.

7-36. In operations focused on stability operations, units conduct continuous reconnaissance with patrols, UAS, and urban OPs that keep a specific location under observation for extended periods. Additionally, reconnaissance may be linked to specific route clearance operations.

MAINTAIN ENEMY CONTACT

7-37. Unless otherwise directed, contact, once gained, is not broken. The individual or sensor that first makes contact does not have to maintain it; however, the security force, collectively, must maintain contact. The security force must continuously gather information on the threat's activities and prevent the threat from surprising the main body or endangering adjacent friendly forces.

7-38. The fundamentals of maintaining enemy contact require—

- Continuous contact (visual, electronic, sensor, or a combination).
- Capability to use direct and indirect fires.
- Freedom to maneuver.
- Depth (of observers in time and space).

SCREEN

7-39. A screen primarily provides early warning by observing, identifying, and reporting enemy actions. Generally, a screening force engages and destroys enemy reconnaissance elements within its capabilities, but otherwise fights only in self-defense. (See FM 3-98 for more information.)

7-40. A screen is appropriate to cover gaps between forces, the exposed flanks or rear of stationary and moving forces, or the front of a stationary formation. Units use screens when the likelihood of enemy contact is remote, the expected enemy force is small, or the friendly main body needs only a minimum amount of time, once it is warned to react effectively. Units usually accomplish screening by establishing a series of OPs and conducting patrols to ensure adequate surveillance of the assigned sector.

7-41. The following are screen tasks:

- Allow no enemy ground element to pass through the screen undetected and unreported.
- Maintain continuous surveillance of all avenues of approach larger than a designated size into the area under all visibility conditions.
- Destroy or repel all enemy reconnaissance patrols within its capabilities.
- Locate the lead elements of each enemy advance guard and determine its direction of movement in a defensive screen.
- Maintain contact with enemy forces and report any activity in the AO.
- Maintain contact with the main body and any security forces operating on its flanks.
- Impede and harass the enemy within its capabilities while displacing.

GUARD

7-42. A guard differs from a screen in that a guard force contains sufficient combat power to defeat, cause the withdrawal of, or fix the lead elements of an enemy ground force before it can engage the main body with direct fire. A guard force routinely engages enemy forces with direct and indirect fires. A screening force, however, primarily uses indirect fires or CAS to destroy enemy reconnaissance elements and slow the movement of other enemy forces. A guard force uses all means at its disposal, including decisive engagement, to prevent the enemy from penetrating to a position where it could observe and engage the main body. It operates within the range of the main body's fire support weapons, deploying over a narrower front than a comparable-size screening force to permit concentrating combat power. (See FM 3-98 for more information.)

7-43. The three types of guard operations are advance, flank, and rear (see figure 7-1 on page 7-8). A commander can assign a guard mission to protect either a stationary or a moving force.

7-44. The advance guard is responsible for clearing the axis of advance or designated portions of the AO of enemy elements. This allows the main body to move unimpeded, prevents the unnecessary delay of the main body, and defers the deployment of the main body for as long as possible. An advance guard for a stationary force is defensive in nature. It defends or delays according to the main body commander's intent. An advance guard for a moving force is offensive in nature and normally conducts an MTC.

7-45. The flank guard protects against an exposed flank of the main body. The commander of the main body designates the general location of the flank guard's positions. AO assigned to the flank guard should be sufficiently deep to provide early warning and reaction time. However, flank guards must remain within supporting range of the main body.

7-46. The rear guard protects the exposed rear of the main body. This occurs during offensive operations when the main body breaks contact with flanking forces or during a retrograde. The commander may deploy a rear guard behind moving and stationary main bodies. The rear guard for a moving force displaces to successive BPs along PLs or delay lines in-depth as the main body moves. The nature of enemy contact determines the exact movement method or combination of methods used in the displacement (successive bounds, alternate bounds, and continuous marching).

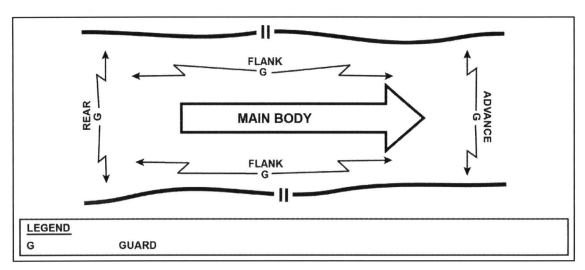

Figure 7-1. Guard operations

COVER

7-47. The covering force's distance forward of the main body depends on the intentions and instructions of the main body commander, the terrain, the location and strength of the enemy, and the rates of march of the main body and the covering force. The width of the covering force area is the same as the AO of the main body.

7-48. The covering force is a force conducting the cover mission. The covering force, or portions of it, often becomes decisively engaged with enemy forces. Therefore, the covering force must have substantial combat power to engage the enemy and accomplish its mission. The company team may participate in covering force operations but does not conduct them on its own. The covering force develops the situation earlier than a screen or a guard force. It fights longer and more often and defeats larger enemy forces.

7-49. While the covering force provides more security than a screen or guard force, it requires more resources. Before assigning a cover mission, the main body commander must determine if there is sufficient combat power to resource the covering force and the main effort. When the commander lacks the resources to support both, the main body commander must assign the security force a less resource-intensive security mission, either a screen or a guard.

7-50. The covering force accomplishes all the tasks of screening and guard forces. The covering force for a stationary force performs a defensive mission, while the covering force for a moving force generally conducts offensive actions. The covering force normally operates forward of the main body in the offense or defense, or to the rear for a retrograde operation. Unusual circumstances could dictate a flank covering force, but this is normally a screen or guard mission.

AREA SECURITY

7-51. Area security operations may be offensive or defensive in nature. They focus on the protected force, installation, route, or area. Area security operations protect range from echelon HQ artillery and reserves to the sustaining base. Protected installations can be part of the sustaining base, or they can constitute part of the area's infrastructure. Areas to secure range from specific points (bridges and defiles) and terrain features (ridgelines and hills) to large population centers and their adjacent areas. The company team can conduct an area security operation independently or as part of a CAB operation.

7-52. Area security operations can require the execution of a wide variety of supporting efforts and tasks. Depending on mission variables, the company team might require augmentation to conduct area security effectively. Infantry units can expect to provide personnel augmentation to armored units to offset the limited personnel in those formations.

7-53. When conducting an area security mission, the company team prevents threat ground reconnaissance elements from directly observing friendly activities within the area being secured. It prevents threat ground maneuver forces from penetrating the defensive perimeters established by the commander. The commander may direct subordinate platoons to employ a variety of techniques such as OPs, BPs, ambushes, and combat outposts to accomplish this security mission. A reserve or quick reaction force enables the commander to react to unforeseen contingencies. Using the assigned information collection assets available to the CAB, the company team can execute ambushes and preemptive strikes proactively and with greater precision.

7-54. An analysis of mission variables enables the commander to determine the augmentation for the company team, with consideration given to the need for aviation, engineers, and artillery. Early warning of threat activity is paramount when conducting area security missions and provides the commander with time and space to react to threats. Proper intelligence analysis and reconnaissance planning, coupled with dismounted and mounted patrols and aerial reconnaissance, is essential to successful operations, especially when securing fixed sites. Failure to conduct continuous reconnaissance can create a vulnerable seam through which the enemy can execute an infiltration or attack.

7-55. Most circumstances do not permit establishment of defined, neat perimeters. When a perimeter is not feasible, the company team secures the area by establishing a presence and conducting operations throughout the area. Company teams establish perimeters around base camps, critical infrastructure, and high-value assets, while other units conduct operations to establish presence, provide security, assist humanitarian operations, and conduct other stability operations. The company can position a reaction force between several secured perimeters. Other missions or tasks in support of area security can include the following:
- Screens along zones of separation or other designated areas.
- Route or convoy security of critical lines of communication.
- Checkpoint operations to monitor or control movement.
- Demonstrations to maintain an observable presence.

LOCAL SECURITY

7-56. Local security includes measures taken by units to prevent surprise by the enemy. It involves avoiding detection by the enemy or deceiving the enemy about friendly positions and intentions. Local security is an important part of maintaining the initiative. The requirement for maintaining local security is an inherent part of all operations. Units use active and passive measures to provide local security. Active measures include OPs, patrols, and conducting stand-to. Passive measures include camouflage, noise and light discipline, and sensors to maintain surveillance over the area immediately around the unit.

7-57. The company team is responsible for always maintaining its own security. It does this by deploying mounted and dismounted patrols and establishing OPs to maintain surveillance and by employing appropriate OPSEC measures. Besides maintaining security for its own elements, the company team may implement local security for other units as directed by the CAB commander. Examples of such situations include, but are not limited to, the following:
- Provide security for engineers as they emplace/clear obstacles or construct survivability positions in the company team's BP.
- Secure a landing zone.
- Establish mounted and dismounted OPs to maintain surveillance of enemy infiltration and reconnaissance routes.
- Conduct patrols to cover gaps in observation and to clear possible enemy OPs from surrounding areas.
- Provide security for human intelligence collection teams, when attached.
- Secure nongovernmental organizations delivering supplies.

SECTION III – RELIEF IN PLACE

7-58. A *relief in place* is an operation in which, by the direction of higher authority, all or part of a unit is replaced in an area by the incoming unit and the responsibilities of the replaced elements for the mission and the assigned zone of operations are transferred to the incoming unit (JP 3-07.3). The responsibilities of the replaced elements for the mission and the assigned AO are transferred to the incoming unit. The incoming unit continues the operations as ordered. A commander conducts a relief in place as part of a larger operation, primarily to maintain the combat effectiveness of committed units. The higher HQ directs when and where to conduct the relief and establishes the appropriate control measures. Normally, the unit relieved is defending. However, a relief may set the stage for resuming offensive operations. (See FM 3-96 for more information.)

7-59. A relief may serve to free the relieved unit for other tasks (such as decontamination, reconstitution, routine rest, resupply, maintenance, or specialized training). Sometimes, as part of a larger operation, a commander wants the enemy force to discover the relief, because that discovery might cause it to do something in response that is prejudicial to its interest (such as move reserves from an area where the friendly commander wants to conduct a penetration).

7-60. The three variations for conducting a relief are sequential, simultaneous, and staggered. These three relief variations can occur regardless of the operational theme in which the unit is participating. Sequential or staggered reliefs can take place over a significant amount of time. Simultaneous relief in place takes the least time to execute but is easily detected by the enemy. The variations of reliefs are defined as follows:

- A sequential relief in place occurs when each element within the relieved unit is relieved in succession, from right to left or left to right, depending on how it is deployed.
- A simultaneous relief in place occurs when all elements are relieved at the same time.
- A staggered relief in place occurs when a commander relieves each element in a sequence determined by the tactical situation, not its geographical orientation.

7-61. A relief can be characterized as either deliberate or hasty, depending on the amount of planning and preparations associated with the relief. The major differences are the depth and detail of planning and, potentially, the execution time. Detailed planning generally facilitates shorter execution time by determining exactly what the commander believes needs to be done and the resources needed to accomplish the mission. Deliberate planning allows the commander and staff to identify, develop, and coordinate solutions to most potential problems before they occur and to ensure the availability of resources when and where they are needed.

PLANNING

7-62. Once ordered to conduct a relief in place, the commander of the relieving unit contacts the commander of the unit to be relieved. The collocation of unit CPs helps achieve the level of coordination required. If the relieved unit's forward elements can defend the AO, the relieving unit executes the relief in place from the rear to the front. This facilitates movement and terrain management.

7-63. When planning for a relief in place, the company commander takes the following actions:

- Issues an order immediately.
- Sends an advance party of key leaders to conduct detailed reconnaissance and coordination.
- Ensures the relieving unit adopts the outgoing unit's normal pattern of activity as much as possible.
- Ensures the relieving unit determines when the company team assumes responsibility for the outgoing unit's position.
- Collocates team HQ, as the relieving unit, with the relieved unit's HQ.
- Maximizes OPSEC to prevent the enemy from detecting the relief operation.
- Plans for relief of sustainment elements after combat elements are relieved.
- Plans, as the unit being relieved, for transfer of excess ammunition, wire, petroleum, oils, lubricants, and other material of tactical value to the incoming unit.
- Controls movement by reconnoitering, designating, and marking routes, and providing guides.

Note. Whenever possible, the commander conducts the relief at night or under other limited-visibility conditions.

COORDINATION

7-64. Incoming and outgoing commanders meet to exchange tactical information, conduct a joint reconnaissance of the area, and complete other required coordination. The two commanders carefully address passage of command and jointly develop contingency actions to deal with enemy contact during the relief. This process usually includes coordination of the following information:

- Location of vehicle and individual positions (to include hide, alternate, and supplementary positions). Leaders should verify positions by conventional map and on digital command and control system.
- The enemy situation.
- The outgoing unit's tactical plan, including graphics, company team and platoon fire plans, and individual vehicles' sector sketches.
- Fire support coordination, including indirect fire plans and the time of relief for supporting artillery and mortar units.
- Types of weapons systems being replaced.
- Time, sequence, and method of relief.
- Location and disposition of obstacles, and the time when commanders will transfer responsibility.
- Supplies and equipment to be transferred.
- Movement control, route priority, and placement of guides.
- Command and signal information.
- Maintenance and logistical support for disabled vehicles.
- Visibility considerations.

Note. Units conduct relief on the radio or digital nets of the outgoing unit.

CONDUCTING THE RELIEF

7-65. When conducting the relief, the outgoing commander retains responsibility for the AO and the mission. The outgoing commander exercises operational control over all subordinate elements of the incoming unit that have completed their portion of the relief. Responsibility passes to the incoming commander when all elements of the outgoing unit are relieved and adequate communications are established.

SEQUENTIAL RELIEF

7-66. Sequential relief is the most time-consuming relief method. The relieving unit moves to an AA to the rear of the unit to be relieved. Subordinate elements are relieved one at a time. This can occur in any order, with the relief following this general sequence:

- The outgoing and incoming units collocate their HQ and trains elements to facilitate mission command and transfer of equipment, ammunition, fuel, water, and medical supplies.
- The first element being relieved (such as a platoon) moves to its alternate positions or BPs while the relieving element moves into the outgoing element's primary positions. The incoming element occupies vehicle and individual positions as appropriate.
- Incoming and outgoing elements complete the transfer of equipment and supplies.
- The relieved element moves to the designated AA behind its position.
- Once each outgoing element clears the rally point en route to its AA, the next relieving element moves forward.

SIMULTANEOUS RELIEF

7-67. Simultaneous relief is the fastest, but least secure, method. All outgoing elements are relieved at once, with the incoming unit usually occupying existing positions, including BPs, and vehicle and individual positions. The relief takes place in the following general sequence:

- Outgoing elements move to their alternate BPs and vehicle and individual positions.
- Incoming elements move along designated routes to the outgoing elements' primary positions.
- The units complete the transfer of equipment and supplies.
- Relieved elements move to the designated unit's AA.

STAGGERED RELIEF

7-68. Staggered relief is the same as the sequential relief, but the sequence is determined by the tactical situation, not its geographical orientation.

SECTION IV – PASSAGE OF LINES

7-69. *Passage of lines* is an operation in which a force moves forward or rearward through another force's combat positions with the intention of moving into or out of contact with the enemy (JP 3-18). A passage may be designated as a forward or rearward passage of lines. (See FM 3-90 for more information.)

- A *forward passage of lines* occurs when a unit passes through another unit's positions while moving toward the enemy (ADP 3-90).
- A *rearward passage of lines* occurs when a unit passes through another unit's positions while moving away from the enemy (ADP 3-90).

7-70. A commander conducts a passage of lines to continue an attack or conduct a counterattack, retrograde, or security operation when one unit cannot bypass another unit's position. A passage of lines is a complex operation requiring close supervision and detailed planning, coordination, and synchronization between the commanders of the unit conducting the passage and the unit being passed. The primary purpose of a passage of lines is to transfer responsibility (forward or rearward) for an area from one unit to another. Units must consider the location for conducting forward passage of lines/rearward passage of lines in order to prevent compromising the passing unit's EA and reduce chances of fratricide.

PLANNING CONSIDERATIONS

7-71. The controlling CAB is responsible for planning and coordinating a passage of lines involving the company team. In some situations, such as the company team using multiple passage routes (such as, a separate route for each platoon), the company commander takes responsibility for planning and coordinating each phase of the operation.

7-72. When planning a passage of lines, the commander considers the following tactical factors and procedures:

- Assigned area.
- Attack positions.
- BHL.
- Contact points.
- Passage points.
- Passage lanes.
- Routes.
- Gaps.
- Phase lines.
- Recognition signals.
- The CAB HQ directing the passage of lines designates or recommends:
    - Routes.
    - Start and end times for the passage of lines.

FORWARD PASSAGE OF LINES

7-73. In a forward passage, the passing unit first moves to an AA or an attack position behind the stationary unit. Designated liaison personnel move forward to linkup with guides and confirm coordination information with the stationary unit. Guides then lead the passing elements through the passage lane.

7-74. The company conducts a forward passage by employing tactical movement. It moves quickly, using appropriate dispersal and formations whenever possible, and keeps radio traffic to a minimum. It bypasses disabled vehicles as needed. The team holds its fire until it passes the BHL or the designated fire control measure unless the commander has coordinated fire control with the stationary unit. Once clear of passage lane restrictions, the unit consolidates at a rally point or attack position, and then conducts tactical movement according to its orders. (See figure 7-2.)

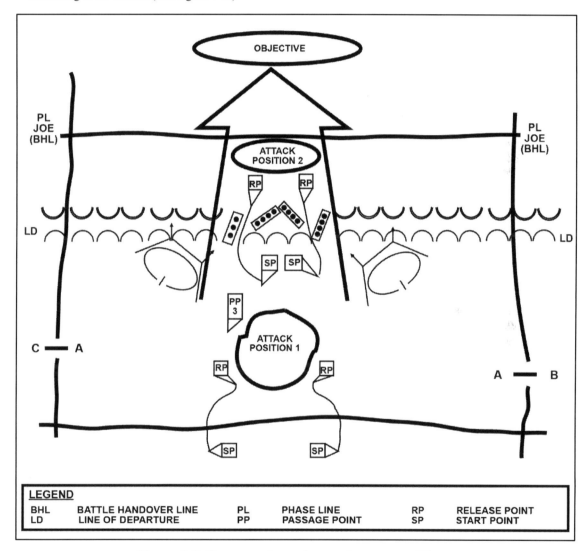

Figure 7-2. Company team forward passage of lines

REARWARD PASSAGE OF LINES

7-75. Because of the increased chance of fratricide during a rearward passage, coordination of recognition signals and direct fire restrictions is critical. The passing unit contacts the stationary unit while it is still beyond direct fire range and conducts coordination as discussed previously. Near recognition signals and location of the BHL are emphasized. Both the passing unit and the stationary unit can employ additional fire control measures, such as RFLs, to minimize the risk of fratricide. (See figure 7-3.)

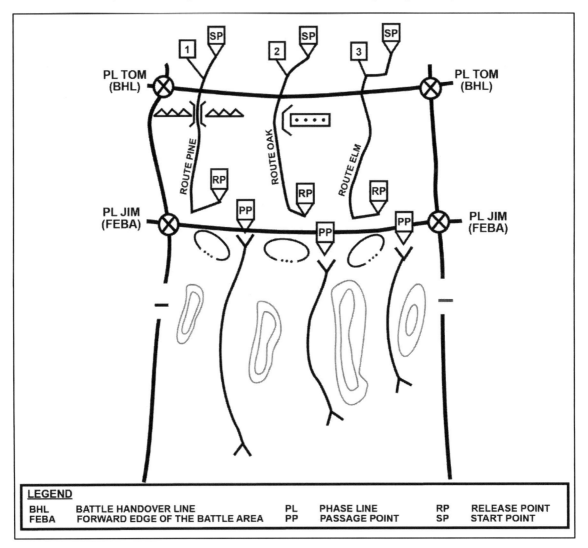

Figure 7-3. Company team rearward passage of lines

7-76. Following coordination, the passing unit continues tactical movement toward the passage lane. Gun tubes are oriented on the enemy, and the passing unit is responsible for its security until it passes the BHL. If the stationary unit provides guides, the passing unit can conduct a short halt to linkup and coordinate with them. The passing unit moves quickly through the passage lane to a designated location behind the stationary unit. (See table 7-1.)

Table 7-1. Stationary and passing unit responsibilities

Stationary Unit	Passing Unit
Clears lanes or reduces obstacles along routes.	May assist with reducing obstacles.
Provides obstacle and friendly units' locations.	Provides order of movement and scheme of maneuver.
Clears and maintains routes up to the battle handover line (BHL).	May assist with maintaining routes.
Provides traffic control for use of routes and lanes.	Augments the traffic control capability of the stationary unit as required.
Provides security for the passage up to the BHL.	Maintains protection measures.
Identifies locations for the passing unit to use as assembly areas (AAs) and attack positions.	Reconnoiters from its current location to its designated AAs and attack positions.
Provides the passing unit any previously coordinated or emergency logistics assistance within its capability.	Assumes full responsibility for its own sustainment support forward of the BHL.
Controls all fires in support of the passage.	Positions artillery to support the passage.

SECTION V – LINKUP

7-77. A *linkup* is a type of enabling operation that involves the meeting of friendly ground forces, which occurs in a variety of circumstances (FM 3-90). Linkup may occur in, but is not limited to, the following situations:

- Advancing forces reaching an objective area previously secured by air assault, Airborne, or infiltrating forces.
- Units coordinating a relief in place.
- Cross attached units moving to join their new organization.
- A unit moving forward with a fixing force during a follow and support mission.
- A unit moving to assist an encircled force, or when a unit exfiltrates towards.
- Units converging on the same objective during the attack.
- Units conducting both rearward and forward passage of lines.

7-78. The HQ ordering the linkup establishes the following:

- Common operational picture.
- Command relationship and responsibilities of each force before, during, and after linkup.
- Coordination of fire support before, during, and after linkup, including control measures.
- Linkup method.
- Recognition signals and communication procedures to use including pyrotechnics, armbands, vehicle markings, gun-tube orientation, panels, colored smoke, lights, and challenge and passwords.
- Operations to conduct following linkup.

TWO LINKUP METHODS

7-79. There are two linkup methods. The preferred method is when the moving force has an assigned LOA near the other force and conducts the linkup at predetermined contact points. Units then coordinate further operations.

7-80. The least preferred method of linkup a commander can use during highly mobile, or fluid operations is when the enemy force escapes from a potential encirclement or when one of the linkup forces is at risk and requires immediate reinforcement. In this method, the moving force continues to move and conduct long-range recognition via radio or other measures, stopping only when it makes physical contact with the other force.

PHASES OF LINKUP

7-81. The company team conducts linkup activities independently or as part of a larger force. Within a larger unit, the team may lead the linkup force. The linkup consists of three phases. The following actions are critical to the execution of a successful linkup operation.

PHASE 1—FAR RECOGNITION SIGNAL

7-82. During this phase, the forces conducting a linkup establish FM radio and digital communications before reaching direct fire range. The lead element of each linkup force should monitor the radio frequency and the digital command and control system messages of the other friendly force.

PHASE 2—COORDINATION

7-83. Before initiating movement to the linkup point, the forces must coordinate necessary tactical information that includes the following:

- Known enemy situation.
- Number and type of friendly units or personnel.
- Disposition of stationary forces if either unit is stationary.
- Routes to linkup and rally points, if used.
- Fire control measures.
- Near recognition signal(s).
- Combat support coverage.
- Sustainment responsibilities and procedure.
- Final location of the linkup point and rally point, if used.
- Any special coordination such as maneuver instructions or requests for medical support.

PHASE 3—MOVEMENT TO LINKUP POINT AND LINKUP

7-84. All units or elements involved in the linkup enforce strict fire control measures to help prevent fratricide. Linkup points and RFLs must be easily recognizable by moving and converging forces. Linkup elements take the following actions:

- Conduct far recognition by radio or digital means.
- Conduct short-range (near) recognition using designated signal(s).
- Complete movement to the linkup point.
- Establish local security at the linkup point.
- Conduct additional coordination and linkup activities as needed.

SECTION VI – TACTICAL DECEPTION

7-85. Deception is a low cost and effective way to cause the enemy to waste their efforts. Deception enhances the conditions that allow friendly units to concentrate forces at decisive times and locations. *Tactical deception* is a friendly activity that causes enemy commanders to take action or cause inaction detrimental to their objectives (FM 3-90). The purpose of tactical deception is to—

- Gain the initiative.
- Reduce overall operational risk.
- Preserve combat power.

7-86. While tactical deception is not decisive by itself, it may be the main effort during some point of the operation. Tactical deception can be employed in both offensive and defensive operations. It is an effective way to deceive the enemy into squander time and resources on irrelevant objectives.

TACTICAL DECEPTION MEANS

7-87. Tactical deception means provide the signatures, associations, and profiles of friendly alleged activities to the enemy. Physical means are resources, methods, and techniques used to convey information normally derived from direct observation or active sensors by the deception target. Most physical means also have technical signatures visible to sensors that collect scientifically or electronically. Planners typically evaluate physical means using characteristics such as shape, size, function, quantity, movement pattern, location, activity, and association with the surroundings. Examples might include—

- Movement of forces.
- Decoy equipment and devices.
- Security measures.
- Tactical actions, such as feints and demonstrations.
- Reconnaissance, security, and surveillance activities.

VARIATIONS OF TACTICAL DECEPTION

7-88. There are two variations of tactical deception, feints, and demonstrations. (See FM 3-90 for more information.) Feints and demonstrations are specific tactical deceptions, units can use variations of offensive and defensive operations to deceive.

FEINT

7-89. A *feint* is a variation of tactical deception that makes contact solely to deceive the adversary as to the location, time of attack or both (FM 3-90). Units conduct a feint deceive the enemy into erroneous conclusions about friendly dispositions. Feints are usually offensive in nature and closely resemble an attack; however, they can be executed during other operations. A feint requires engagement with the enemy to give the appearance of the main attack.

DEMONSTRATION

7-90. A *demonstration* is a variation of tactical deception used as a show of force in an area where a unit does not seek a decision and attempts to mislead an adversary (FM 3-90). The demonstration is similar to the faint but contact, direct or indirect, with the enemy is not intended. A demonstration tries to get an enemy to respond to the friendly forces that are displayed.

SECTION VII – PATROLS

7-91. A *patrol* is a detachment sent out by a larger unit to conduct a specific mission that operates semi-independently and return to the main body upon completion of mission (ATP 3-21.8). The missions that a patrol can conduct are a combat, reconnaissance, or security. A patrol's organization is temporary and specifically matched to the immediate task.

7-92. A patrol can consist of a unit as small as a fire team. Squad and platoon-size patrols are normal. Sometimes, for larger combat tasks, normally for a raid, the patrol can be a company. (See ATP 3-21.8 for more information.)

TYPES OF PATROLS

7-93. The planned action determines the type of patrol. The two main types of patrols are combat and reconnaissance. Regardless of the type of patrol, the unit needs a clear task and purpose. The leader of any patrol, regardless of the type or the tactical task assigned, has an inherent responsibility to prepare and plan for possible enemy contact while on the mission. Patrols are never administrative as they are always assigned a tactical mission.

COMBAT PATROL

7-94. A *combat patrol* is a patrol that provides security and harasses, destroys, or captures enemy troops, equipment, or installations (ATP 3-21.8). When the commander gives a unit the mission to send out a combat patrol, the intent for the patrol is to make contact with the enemy and engage in close combat. A combat patrol always tries to escape detection while moving, but when it discloses its location to the enemy in a sudden, violent attack. For this reason, the patrol normally carries a significant number of weapons and ammunition. It may carry specialized munitions.

7-95. A combat patrol collects and reports any information gathered during the mission, whether related to the combat task or not. The three types of combat patrols are—

- Raid.
- Ambush.
- Security.

RECONNAISSANCE PATROL

7-96. A reconnaissance patrol collects information or confirms or disproves the accuracy of information previously gained. (See ATP 3-21.8 for more information.) The intent for this patrol is to avoid enemy contact and accomplish its tactical task without engaging in close combat. With one exception (reconnaissance in force patrol), reconnaissance patrols always try to accomplish their mission without being detected or observed. Because detection cannot always be avoided, a reconnaissance patrol carries the necessary arms and equipment to protect itself and break contact with the enemy. A reconnaissance patrol travels light, that is, with as few personnel and as little arms, ammunition, and equipment as possible. This increases stealth and cross-country mobility in close terrain. Regardless of how the patrol is armed and equipped, the leader always plans for contact.

PLANNING CONSIDERATIONS FOR MOUNTED PATROLS

7-97. To help maintain Soldier strength and energy, units often use vehicle transportation to move up to or closer to the actual targeted patrol area. Usually this is where the vehicles can no longer effectively travel or that best accommodates the intended mission. At that point, the unit dismounts and continues with the mission. Dismounted Infantry units may be augmented with military vehicles, allowing them to conduct mounted patrolling. They may procure other types of vehicles.

7-98. Mounted patrolling principles include the following actions:

- Ensure mutual support and depth by maintaining constant observation among vehicles.
- Coordinate a supporting fire plan with any dismounted units in the area.
- Use a form of overwatch whenever possible to maintain 360-degree security.
- Develop a reliable communications plan for mounted and dismounted elements.
- Develop vehicle recovery and CASEVAC plans.
- Adjust patrol routes and speed to promote deception, OPSEC, and avoid repetitive patterns.
- Maintain SA.
- Adjust formations and vehicle separation distance based on METT-TC (I) to maintain mutual visibility.
- Length of patrol.

7-99. Mounted patrols never enter an area via the route they will use to exit unless another viable route does not exist. Vehicles should travel at moderate speeds, with the lead vehicle stopping only to investigate those areas that pose a potential threat or support the essential tasks of the patrol. A vehicle speed of 15 to 20 miles per hour allows for adequate observation and quick reaction. Slower speeds may allow noncombatants or the enemy to impede movement. On the other hand, vehicles should move at high speeds only when responding to an incident or contact. Equipment and weapons stored externally should be secured high enough on the vehicle to prevent locals from snatching these items.

7-100. When vehicles must stop, designated personnel dismount to provide security. The vehicle gunner is at the ready, and the driver remains in the driver's seat at the ready. Units must maintain SA during patrols; this includes orientation on other patrols in the urban area. If an element takes fire, it should be capable of communicating with other patrols to obtain assistance and support.

PLANNING CONSIDERATIONS FOR DISMOUNTED PATROLS

7-101. Dismounted patrolling often begins with movement by some means of transportation to or near the area to be patrolled. If vehicles are used to transport personnel to a dismount location, leaders have two options when considering what to do with the vehicles after dropping off. The first option is to send the vehicles to another more secure staging area or back to the area they departed from (such as a combat outpost or other base, until needed for pick-up of personnel). The second option is to leave the vehicles in or near the drop off location. The decision on what to do with the vehicles relies on many factors with some of the main considerations being—

- Duration of the patrol.
- Use of available covering artillery or mortar fires.
- Security of the vehicles and personnel remaining with the vehicles.
- CASEVAC or MEDEVAC procedures.

7-102. Leaders should determine what their Soldiers carry with them on a dismounted patrol. Leaders should ensure Soldiers only carry what is necessary for the duration of the mission. Body armor, weapons, and ammunition all weigh the Soldier down. Assault packs often consist of little more than water, food, additional ammunition, a lightweight blanket, survival gear, and some medical supplies. If resupply is needed for the patrol, it will often come by way of air since travel back to a resupply pick up location is often exhausting and time consuming.

SECTION VIII – ASSEMBLY AREAS

7-103. An *assembly area* is an area a unit occupies to prepare for an operation (FM 3-90). Certain tasks are associated with planning, occupying, and operating an AA, largely as a matter of tactical SOPs. The circumstances in which the AA is occupied dictate to what extent these tasks are performed. AA tasks include—

- Site selection.
- Quartering party.
- Occupation.
- Security.
- Departure.

SITE SELECTION

7-104. Although AAs are generally secure from enemy interference, commanders must consider the possibility of enemy attacks or observation. AAs should provide the following:

- Concealment from air and ground observation.
- Cover from direct fire.
- Terrain masking of electromagnetic signal signature.
- Sufficient area for the dispersion of subunits and their vehicles consistent with the enemy and friendly tactical situation.
- Areas for unit trains, maintenance operations, and CPs.
- Suitable entrances, exits, and internal routes.
- Terrain allowing the observation of ground and air avenues of approach into the AA.
- Good drainage and soil conditions that support unit vehicle movement.

7-105.   The proper location of AAs contributes significantly to security and flexibility. It should facilitate future operations so movement to subsequent positions can take place smoothly and quickly by concealed routes. The tactical mobility of the company allows it to occupy AAs at greater distances from the LD.

QUARTERING PARTY OPERATIONS

7-106.   A *quartering party* is a group dispatched to a new assigned area in advance of the main body (FM 3-90). Quartering parties have four responsibilities: conducting reconnaissance (if reconnaissance parties are not used), securing the area, organizing the area, and guiding arriving units.

7-107.   During tactical unit movement, the reconnaissance party can perform area reconnaissance as a follow-on mission. An area reconnaissance is performed to determine suitability of the area. The quartering party provides initial security of the area until the main body arrives. Aerial reconnaissance, such as UAS, can help the quartering party secure the AA by conducting screening missions and surveillance of possible threat avenues of approach.

7-108.   The company team establishes the quartering party according to its SOPs. For example, the quartering party could consist of one vehicle per platoon and a vehicle from the HQ's section. The company XO, first sergeant, or senior NCO usually leads the quartering party. The quartering party's actions at the AA include the following:

- Reconnoiter for enemy forces and CBRN contamination.
- Evaluate the condition of the route leading into the AA and the suitability of the area (drainage, space, internal routes).
- Organize the area based on the commander's guidance; designate and mark tentative locations for platoons' vehicles, CP vehicles, and trains.
- Improve and mark entrances, exits, and internal routes.
- Mark bypasses or removes obstacles (within the party's capabilities).
- Develop digital AA overlay and send overlays to company team main body.

OCCUPATION OF ASSEMBLY AREA

7-109.   Once the quartering party finishes preparing the AA, it awaits the arrival of the company team main body, maintaining surveillance and providing security of the area within its capabilities. The *main body* is the principal part of a tactical command or formation. It does not include detached elements of the command, such as advance guards, flank guards, and covering forces (ADP 3-90). SOPs and guides assist vehicle commanders to find their positions quickly, clear the route, and assume designated positions in the AA. Once in position, units and vehicles make adjustments. Positioning considerations are as follows:

- Locations selected to afford dispersion and hide positions.
- Vehicles oriented or positioned to facilitate defense.
- CPs and trains centrally located for security, ease of support, and road access.
- OPs established to provide security.
- Communications by wire or messenger established between vehicle, OPs, and the CP.

7-110.   The company team may occupy the AA as an independent element or as part of the CAB. In either situation, the company team occupies its positions upon arrival using the procedures for hasty occupation of a BP. The commander establishes local security and coordinates with adjacent units. The commander also assigns weapons orientation and a sector of responsibility for each platoon and subordinate element. If the company team occupies the AA alone, it establishes a perimeter defense. (See figure 7-4.)

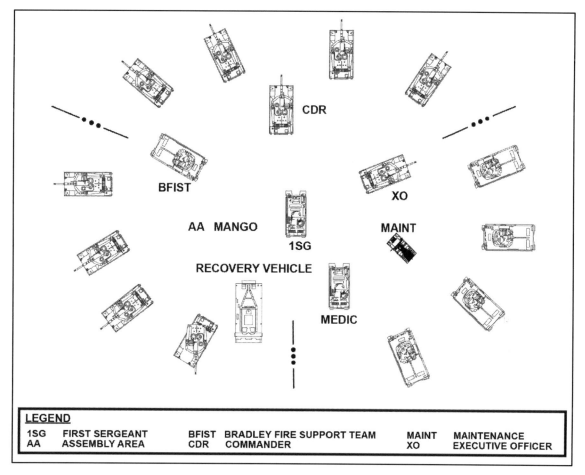

Figure 7-4. Company team assembly area, example

ACTIONS AND SECURITY IN ASSEMBLY AREA

7-111.   An AA is not designated as a defensive position, but the company organizes it so that a threat ground attack could be detected and defeated. Security against air attack is best provided by passive measures designed to conceal the unit from detection. Additional security considerations include the following:

- Guards at all entrances and exits control the flow of traffic.
- OPs cover key terrain features and likely avenues of approach.
- Platoons prepare fire plans and coordinate on the flanks.
- Fire support plans are prepared by the FIST and commander.
- Patrols, sensors, and surveillance devices augment security.
- Contact points for units assist in coordination.
- Roads are the specific responsibility of subordinate units.
- Movement is confined to roads to preclude needless surface disruption that could leave a visible aerial indicator.
- Unnecessary vehicle movement is restricted.
- Minimal use of radios reduces electronic signature.
- Noise and light discipline are strictly enforced.
- Readiness condition level is established and adjusted based on METT-TC (I).
- Units must consider the location and activities of other units within the AO and coordinate with those assets for mutual security.

7-112. Following occupation of the AA, the company team prepares for future operations by conducting TLP and priorities of work according to the CAB and company team OPORDs. These preparations include the following:

- Establish and maintain security.
- Develop a defensive fire plan and forward it to the CAB's main CP via digital command and control system if equipped.
- Emplace OPs.
- Emplace CBRN alarms.
- Prepare range cards and fire plans.
- Establish wire communication (if directed by unit SOP).
- Camouflage vehicles.
- Select alternate, supplementary positions, and rally points.
- Develop an obstacle plan.
- Conduct TLP.
- Perform maintenance activities on vehicles, communications equipment, and weapon systems.
- Verify weapons system status, conduct boresighting, prepare-to-fire checks, test-firing, and other necessary preparations.
- Account for company team personnel and sensitive items.
- Conduct resupply, refueling, and rearming operations.
- Conduct rehearsals and other training for upcoming operations.
- Conduct PCCs and PCIs based on time available.
- Conduct personal care and hygiene activities.
- Reestablish vehicle load plans, as needed.
- Adjust task organization as necessary.

Note. The company usually coordinates test-firing with its higher HQ.

DEPARTURE

7-113. Departing the AA is the first step of a mission. Uncoiling from the AA must be planned for and rehearsed by key leaders at a minimum. Leaders must understand the sequence and timing of the departure as the large number of vehicles, moving in a potentially relatively confined area may result in confusion, congestion, and loss of tempo. A progressive system of increasing readiness ensures that units are ready to move when required without needlessly tiring Soldiers and wasting fuel during long waits. The AA is occupied with the follow-on mission in mind to preclude congestion on departure. Routes from subordinate unit locations are reconnoitered and timed. Subordinate units designate a linkup point, and units move to and through that point based on their reconnaissance. Depending on threat capabilities, departure may be conducted under radio listening silence.

LAAGER FORMATION

7-114. The Laager formation affords the company team some advantages in an open terrain, rolling hills or grassland. (See figure 7-5.) The following considerations apply when using the Laager formation:

- Optics and weapons stand-off are maximized and the need for dismounted OPs is minimized.
- In the event the company team receives indirect fire, displacement to an alternate location is efficient because all vehicles are oriented in the same direction and platoon formations are contiguous.
- Light-skinned vehicles are protected inside the formation.

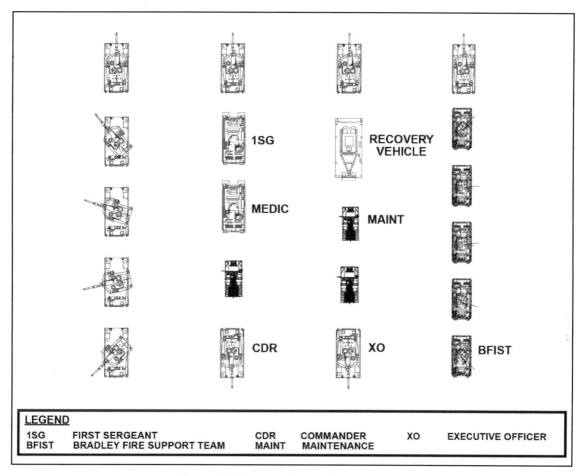

Figure 7-5. Laager formation, example

TROOP MOVEMENT

7-115. *Troop movement* is the movement of Soldiers and units from one place to another by any available means (FM 3-90). The ability of a commander to posture friendly forces for a decisive or shaping operation depends on the commander's ability to move those forces. The essence of battlefield agility is the capability to conduct rapid and orderly movement to concentrate the effects of combat power at decisive points and times. Successful movement places troops and equipment at their destination at the proper time, ready for combat. The two types of troop movement are nontactical movement and tactical movement.

NONTACTICAL MOVEMENT

7-116. *Nontactical movement* is a movement in which troops and vehicles are arranged to expedite their movement and conserve time and energy when no enemy ground interference is anticipated (FM 3-90). The commander conducts nontactical movements in secure areas. Examples of nontactical movements include rail and highway movement in the continental United States and normally does not employ administrative movements once the units deploy into combat operations.

TACTICAL MOVEMENT

7-117. A *tactical movement* is a movement in which troops and vehicles are arranged to protect combat forces during movement when a threat of enemy interference is possible (FM 3-90). The company team must maintain security against enemy attacks from both the air and ground and prepare to take immediate action against enemy ambushes. During a tactical movement, units are always prepared to take immediate action.

There are three methods of a tactical movements that units of all types can conduct: approach march, forced march, and tactical road march.

Approach March

7-118.   An *approach march* is the advance of a combat unit when direct contact with the enemy is intended (FM 3-90). However, it emphasizes speed over tactical deployment. Both heavy and light forces conduct tactical road marches and approach marches.

7-119.   The commander employs an approach march when the enemy's approximate location is known, since it allows the force to move with greater speed and less physical security or dispersion. Units conducting an approach march are task-organized before the march begins to allow them to transition to an on-order or a be-prepared mission without making major adjustments in organization.

7-120.   The approach march terminates in a march objective, such as an attack position, AA, or assault position, or can be used to transition to an attack. Follow-and-assume and reserve forces may conduct an approach march forward of an LD.

Forced March

7-121.   A *forced march* is a march longer or faster than usual or in adverse conditions (FM 3-90). Forced marches require speed, exertion, and an increase in the number of hours marched each day beyond normal standards. Soldiers cannot sustain forced marches for more than a short period. Leaders must understand that immediately following a long and fast march, Soldiers experience a temporary deterioration in their physical condition. The combat effectiveness and cohesion of the unit also temporarily decreases.

Tactical Road Marches

7-122.   A *tactical road march* is a rapid movement used to relocate units within an assigned area to prepare for combat operations (FM 3-90). Security against enemy air attack is maintained and the unit is prepared to take immediate action against an enemy ambush, although contact with enemy ground forces is not expected.

7-123.   The primary consideration of the tactical road march is rapid movement. However, the moving force employs security measures, even when contact with enemy ground forces is not expected. Units conducting road marches may or may not be organized into a combined arms formation. During a tactical road march, the commander is always prepared to take immediate action if the enemy attacks.

7-124.   The organization for a tactical road march is the march column. A *march column* consists of all march serials using the same route for a single movement under control of a single commander (FM 3-90). The commander organizes a march column into four elements:

- Reconnaissance.
- Quartering party.
- Main body.
- Trail party.

7-125.   Units conducting tactical road marches employ three tactical march techniques: open column, close column, and infiltration. Each of these techniques uses scheduled halts to control and sustain the road march. Mission variables require adjustments in the standard distances between vehicles and Soldiers. During movement, elements within a column of any length may encounter many different types of routes and obstacles simultaneously. Consequently, parts of the column may be moving at different speeds, which can produce an undesirable accordion-like effect. The movement order establishes the order of march, rate of march, interval or time gaps between units, column gap, and maximum catch-up speed. Unless the commander directs them not to do so for security reasons, march units report when they have crossed each control point.

SECTION IX – GAP CROSSING OPERATIONS

7-126.   There are three gap crossings: deliberate, hasty, and covert. Each has a general list of conditions that define their category. As with the categories of breaching operations, all other labels placed upon a crossing are a variation of a deliberate, hasty, or covert gap crossing. The planning requirements for each gap crossing are similar. However, the required degree of detail and necessary conditions for a high degree of success varies based on the type and the unique features associated with a given crossing operation.

7-127.   Operational considerations for a company hasty gap crossing are like those for a breach, with the company team task organized into support, breach, and assault forces. The primary crossing means in the company team hasty gap crossing is the Wolverine or joint assault bridge (known as JAB), which moves as part of the breach force. Without a vehicle launched bridge, the company team employs an armored combat earthmover team to fill in or breach through the obstacle. Additionally, if the mechanical method is unavailable, the company team may employ a field expedient method, such as explosives, to facilitate the crossing.

DELIBERATE GAP CROSSING

7-128.   A *deliberate crossing* is the crossing of an inland water obstacle or other gap that requires extensive planning and detailed preparations (ATP 3-90.4). A deliberate gap crossing is classified as wet or dry, and it is usually accomplished with one or more bridge companies in support of combat maneuver. It is normally accomplished when a hasty crossing is not feasible or has failed. Any deliberate crossing requires detailed reconnaissance, detailed planning, coordination of fire plans, extensive preparations and rehearsals, and significant engineer assets. This type of crossing normally requires a higher HQ to assist in planning and command and control since it generally involves brigade or higher to execute. (See ATP 3-90.4 for more information.)

HASTY GAP CROSSING

7-129.   A hasty gap crossing (wet or dry) is conducted to maintain the momentum of the maneuver force by quickly massing combat power on the far side of the gap with no intentional pause. To do this, it is critical in the planning process to identify gap locations and their dimensions, and then request and/or allocate the necessary assets to ensure unimpeded movement. Hasty gap crossings are typically for, but are not limited to, gaps 20 meters or less in width and can be overcome by self-bridging assets (organic or augmented). Planned, organized, and executed much like a hasty breaching operation, the unit must consider the integration of the crossing assets (Wolverine or JAB) in their movement formation; redundancy in crossing means; traffic flow across the gap; and the recovery of the crossing assets. Despite use of the term "hasty," the commander must use all available time and assets to ensure that the conditions are set for the crossing. The crossing is like a breach in that suppression and obscuration normally precede any attempt to cross the obstruction.

HASTY (WET) GAP CROSSING

7-130.   The depth and width of the wet gap, bank conditions, and current velocity are major factors in determining the maneuver unit's ability to conduct a hasty (wet) gap crossing. These factors determine if the maneuver force can cross by fording or swimming, if expedient materials can be used, or if specific bridging assets are required. Identifying wet gaps early and deploying the required resources allow hasty crossings of known or anticipated gaps to occur. Hasty (wet) gap crossings are decentralized operations to cross inland bodies of water such as canals, creeks, or streams. These operations include crossing by tactical bridging or fording operations.

HASTY (DRY) GAP CROSSING

7-131.   Typical dry gap obstacles that maneuver forces encounter include AT ditches, craters, dry riverbeds, partially blown bridges, and similar obstacles. Maneuver forces can leverage engineer horizontal assets to push down the sides of ditches or fill in craters. Substantial fill material placed in dry gaps allows the passage of tracked vehicles. The crossing site can be improved and maintained for wheeled traffic use by follow-on forces. The Wolverine, JAB, or rapidly Emplace Bridge System are also well-suited for hasty (dry) gap crossings. As with any hasty crossing, consideration must be given to the need for replacement bridging so that the maneuver unit can maintain its assets for follow-on, gap-crossing requirements. Operational considerations for a company team hasty gap crossing are like those for a breach, with the company team task organized into support, breach, and assault forces.

ASSAULT FORCE

7-132. The assault force conducts the initial assault across gap (wet or dry). Assault boats or air assault aircraft transport the assault force across the body of water. There, the assault force usually seizes immediate objectives on the far side to secure the crossing site for other elements. If it has the capability, the assault force then continues the advance from the exit bank to the final objective. Infantry elements establish local security on the exit bank to permit development of the crossing site. Engineers move with the assault force to breach obstacles and open or improve trails.

SUPPORT FORCE

7-133. The support force usually consists of engineer elements and command elements from the controlling HQ. It develops the crossing site, emplaces the crossing means (if applicable), and controls units moving into and away from the crossing site. The controlling commander may position the support force where it can assist the assault force in the direct assault on the crossing site. The engineers provide these types of support for crossing operations—

- Improve mobility and reduce obstacles at the entrance and exit to the crossing site.
- Improve fording sites.
- Emplace assault boats, rafts, ferries, or bridges as the means of crossing the body of water. Bridges used by supporting engineers include the JAB, Wolverine, and ribbon or medium girder bridges. In addition, engineers might repair an existing bridge so that it can support the crossing operation.

FOLLOW AND SUPPORT FORCE

7-134. As the follow and support force, the company team's primary mission is to provide OPSEC as the assault force moves to the far side of the water obstacle and seizes its immediate objectives. The company team does this mainly by suppressing defending enemy elements with direct and indirect fires, and by firing or calling for smoke to screen the crossing site from enemy observation. It prepares to take over the assault force's mission.

COVERT GAP CROSSING

7-135. A *covert crossing* is a planned crossing of an inland water obstacle or other gap in which the crossing is intended to be undetected (ATP 3-90.4). The covert gap crossing applies the same gap-crossing fundamentals as the other gap-crossing types; however, it is focused on the crossing fundamental of surprise. Surprise is the primary element of the covert crossing. The requirement to execute the crossing without enemy detection is the element that distinguishes it from the other types of crossings. It can be used in a variety of situations to support various operations but should be considered (as opposed to deliberate or hasty) only when there is a need or opportunity to cross a gap without being discovered.

7-136. Common crossing means to facilitate a covert crossing include the use of rope bridges, Infantry foot bridges, assault boats, rigid inflatable boats, fording, swimming, or aerial insertion. Consideration must be given to recovering the crossing assets no matter which means is used.

Chapter 8

Augmenting Combat Power

For the Armor and mechanized Infantry company team to achieve its full combat potential, the commander must understand the capabilities and how to integrate and synchronize assets effectively. This chapter focuses on those elements with which the company team is most likely to work: fires, aviation, and protection.

SECTION I – FIRES

8-1. *Fires* are the use of weapon systems or other actions to create specific lethal or nonlethal effects on a target (JP 3-09). Lethal fire support comes from ABCT organic indirect fires assets, Army artillery and aviation assets, and joint and multinational artillery and aviation assets. Nonlethal effects can come from a wide range of military, civilian, joint, and multinational partners. This section provides a brief overview on fire support for CAB operations, but primarily focuses on the organization and employment of fires in support of the company team. (See ATP 3-90.5 for more information.)

FIRE SUPPORT

8-2. *Fire support* are fires that directly support land, maritime, amphibious, space, cyberspace, and special operations forces to engage enemy forces, combat formations, and facilities in pursuit of tactical and operational objectives (JP 3-09). Fire support is the collective and coordinated use of indirect fire weapons and armed aircraft in support of the commander's scheme of maneuver. Fire support planning is the process of analyzing, allocating, and scheduling fire support assets. Fire support assets available, dependent upon the mission variables of METT-TC (I), to the company team may include mortars, FA cannons and rockets, Army attack aviation, CAS, naval gunfire, and electromagnetic attacks.

8-3. Lethal fire support systems consist of indirect fire weapons and armed aircraft to include FA, mortars, naval surface fire support, and air-delivered munitions from fixed-wing and rotary-wing aircraft. Nonlethal capabilities include cyberspace electromagnetic activities, information related activities, space, and munitions such as illumination and smoke. Fires are the use of weapons systems to create a specific lethal or nonlethal effect on a target.

FIRE SUPPORT SYSTEM

8-4. The fire support system acquires and tracks targets, delivers timely and accurate lethal fires, provides counterfire, and plans, coordinates, and orchestrates fire support. The fire support system achieves desired effects (lethal and nonlethal means) through a combination of fire support assets. The integration of fire support assets is critical regardless of which element of decisive action currently dominants. For example, in the defense, fire support systems support security forces by using precision and area munitions to destroy enemy reconnaissance and high-payoff targets, and by delivering on-call fires at appropriate times and places. Fire support facilitates the withdrawal of security forces at the completion of their mission. Fire support systems cover barriers, gaps, and open areas within the defense. Disruptive means to deny, degrade, deceive, delay, or neutralize enemy aircraft systems temporarily and can include an electromagnetic attack during an area defense.

PLANNING AND COORDINATION PRINCIPLES

8-5. In advising commanders on the application of fire support, FSOs review fire support requirements against basic fire support planning principle during the development of the fire support plan. (See FM 3-09 for more information on planning principles.) Fire support planning and coordination principles include the following:

- Plan early and continuously.
- Ensure the continuous flow of target information.
- Consider the use of all capabilities.
- Use the lowest echelon capable of furnishing effective support.
- Furnish the support requested.
- Use the most effective fire support means.
- Avoid unnecessary duplication.
- Consider airspace coordination.
- Provide adequate support.
- Provide for rapid coordination.
- Protect the force.
- Provide for flexibility.
- Use fire support coordination measures.

PLANNING AND THE INTEGRATION OF FIRES

8-6.   *Fire support planning* is the continuous process of analyzing, allocating, integrating, synchronizing, and scheduling fires to describe how the effects of fires facilitate maneuver force actions (FM 3-09). Fire support planning is focused on using the timely and effective delivery of fires to enhance the actions of the maneuver force. Fire support planning involves the assignment of command or support relationships and positioning of fire support systems. Planning identifies the types of targets to attack and the collection assets that acquire and track the targets, specifies the fire support assets to attack each identified target, and establishes the criteria for target defeat. Fire support planning considers existing limitations on the employment of fires, such as ROE and positive identification requirements, weather effects on fires assets, the presence of special operations forces within the AO, desired conditions of subsequent phases, and requirements for collateral damage avoidance.

8-7.   Fire support planning includes developing fire plans. A *fire plan* is a tactical plan for using the weapons of a unit or formation so that their fire will be coordinated (FM 3-09), for example, target lists and overlays. Fire support planning determines forward observer control options to ensure fire support is integrated into the commander's scheme of maneuver and can be executed quickly. (See ATP 3-09.42 for more information.)

Fire Support Plan

8-8.   The *fire support plan* is a plan that addresses each means of fire support available and describes how Army indirect fires, joint fires, and target acquisition are integrated with maneuver to facilitate operational success (FM 3-09). An effective fire support plan clearly defines fire support requirements, focuses on the tasks and their resulting effects, uses all available acquisition and attack assets, and applies the best combination of fire support assets against high-payoff targets. The fire support plan identifies critical times and places where the commander anticipates the need to maximize effects from fire support assets. (See ATP 3-09.42 for more information.)

Commander's Guidance

8-9.   The purpose of commander's guidance is to focus staff activities in planning an operation. The ABCT commander's guidance for fires provides subordinates with the general guidelines and restrictions for the employment of fires and their desired effects. The guidance emphasizes in broad terms when, where, and how the commander intends to synchronize the effects of fires with the other elements of combat power to accomplish the mission. Commander's guidance should include priorities and how the commander envisions the operation unfolding and the impact that fires will have on its success. Priority of fires is the commander's guidance to the subordinate commanders, fires planners, and supporting agencies to organize and employ fires per the relative importance of the unit's mission. (See FM 3-96 for more information.)

8-10. The CAB typically uses top-down fire support planning, with bottom-up refinement of the plans. The CAB commander develops guidance for fire support in terms of task, purpose, and effect. In turn, the CAB's FSO, in conjunction with the CAB operations staff officer, determines the method used to accomplish each task. Subordinate company teams then incorporate assigned tasks into their fire support plans. Units tasked to initiate fires refine and rehearse their assigned tasks. The CAB commander refines the CAB's fire support plan, ensuring that designated targets achieve the intended purpose. The commander conducts rehearsals to prepare for the mission and, as specified in the plan, directs subordinate units to rehearse their assigned targets. (See ATP 3-90.5 for more information.)

Fire Support Tasks

8-11. A fire support task is a task that a FIST, fire support unit, or organization must accomplish to support a combined-arms operation. Failure to achieve a fire support task may require the commander to alter the unit's scheme of maneuver. A fully developed fire support task must be clear, concise, and include the elements of task, purpose, and effect. The task describes what targeting objective fires, such as delay, disrupt, limit, or destroy, must achieve on an enemy formation's function or capability. The purpose describes why the task contributes to maneuver. The opposite quantifies successful accomplishment of the task. (See ATP 3-09.42 for more information.)

COMPANY TEAM FIRE SUPPORT

8-12. The company team FSO is with the commander when the commander develops the company's maneuver plan. The FSO plans company fire support, and the commander approves the plan. The FSO coordinates, synchronizes, and executes fire support in the plan. The FSO identifies observer (including joint fires observer) requirements in the commander's observation plan and integrates them into the company rehearsal.

ROLE OF THE COMMANDER AND THE FIRE SUPPORT OFFICER

8-13. The company commander ensures the FSO clearly understands the intent and desired effects for the company's scheme of fires and scheme of movement and maneuver. The scheme of fires paragraph together with the scheme of movement and maneuver, describes how the company will accomplish the mission and meet the CAB commander's intent. The scheme of fires provides the sequence of fire support tasks and outlines the who, what, where, when, and why for each fire support task needed for the operation.

8-14. While the company commander develops and refines the tactical plan, the commander and FSO concurrently develop and refine the fire support plan. Once determined, the fire support task is placed in the fire support planning channels as soon as possible to be processed at the CAB fire support cell or FA battalion's FDC. Regardless of the planning method used, the company fire support plan includes—

- Target number and location.
- Description of the expected target.
- Primary and alternate persons responsible for shooting each target.
- Amount of effect required and purpose.
- Radio frequency and call sign to use in requesting fires.
- When to engage the target.
- Priority of fires and shifting of priority.
- Size, location, code word, and emergency signal to begin FPFs.

8-15. The FSO does most of the technical aspects of the company's fire support plan; however, the FSO may receive targets and target information from PLs and the CAB's FSO. The company commander and FSO should not plan too many targets. The number of targets planned by the company and included in the formal fire support plan depends upon the company's priority for fire support and the number of targets allocated to them. The total number of targets in the fire support plan or the CAB mortar plan might be constrained. An excessive number of targets tends to dilute the focus of fire planning and can lead to increases in response time.

8-16. Informal planning continues with target locations being recorded on terrain sketches or the FSO's map or being stored in Advanced FA Tactical Data System for quick reference and transmission. Care must be taken to ensure that planning focuses on the critical fire support requirements identified by the company commander.

8-17. The company FSO completes the indirect fire plan and briefs the company commander on any updates. The company commander may alter the plan or approve it as is, but the commander makes the final decision. After the company commander approves the plan, the FSO makes sure the targets are passed to the CAB fire support cell where the fire plans are integrated into the CAB scheme of fires.

8-18. The commander and the FSO ensure PLs are thoroughly familiar with the indirect fire plan. The FSO provides target overlays to the PLs, forward observers, and the commander. The FSO may disseminate the company fire support plan as a target list and an FSEM. The FSO does this in sufficient time to allow subordinates to brief their platoons and sections. A good plan given with the company order is better than a perfect plan handed out at the LD.

PLANNING

8-19. The company FSO (as does the CAB's FSO) uses fire support planning questions to determine the commander's intent. The answers to these questions help the FSO prepare fire support plans and briefings. The FSO assists the commander in estimating the situation and in war-gaming to develop the commander's concept of the operation. The FSO aggressively inputs fire planning as the scheme of maneuver is being developed to help achieve synchronization. The FSO does this by mentally employing all fire support assets along a proposed COA in concert with the company commander's other resources. While the commander fights through each action in the war-gaming process to determine factors critical to success, the FSO, in coordination with the CAB's FSO, mentally considers the following factors:

- Attack emerging targets with the most effective system.
- Determine the tasks and requirements for all fire support resources.
- Consider proper distribution of assets (focused mainly at ABCT and CAB echelon) for close support of maneuver elements, for counterfire, for interdiction, and for suppression of enemy air defenses.
- Visualize fire support unit movements required to follow the battle flow.
- Consider fire support sustainment needs and their impact on the battle.
- Consider the use of fire support coordination measures and airspace coordinating measures.

Fire Support Planning Questions

8-20. Fire support planning questions are answered to ensure that fire support is coordinated with maneuver. Some questions are answered by the commander, however, most of the information will come from the CAB staff, the FA or mortar unit in support, or the FSO's own expertise and experience. The following are some questions to determine the commander's intent for fire support:

Note. Many of the questions should be submitted to the commander in the form of recommendations for approval.

- What is the task, for example, offensive defensive, or stability operation?
- What is the commander's concept of operation and intent?
- What is the company/CAB's AO?
- How are firing units to maneuver within the supported unit's AO?
- What is the enemy situation?
- Where are the known and suspected enemy locations?
- What is the most likely avenue(s) of approach?
- Where are the designated EAs?
- What is the priority of fires?

- What fire support assets provide the priority fires?
- Is there a shift in priority of fires planned?
- What are the priority targets?
- When is priority shifted to the next priority target?
- Where are special fires to be planned (obscurant, illumination, and scatterable mines)?
- Is there a requirement to adjust obscurant or illumination targets?
- Is there a requirement to register fire support assets?
- How are fire support vehicles to be used?
- What are the laser locator range finder and designator codes?
- What are the signals or events to commence special fires?
- What maneuver control measures have been established?
- Are any restrictive fire support coordination measures required?
- What additional fire support assets have been allocated (attached or in support) such as CAS, naval gunfire, or Army aviation?
- Are there any peculiar communications requirements?
- Are security forces forward? What are the fire support requirements for security forces?
- What are the future fire support plans?
- What is the succession of command?
- How much time is available?
- When and where is the rehearsal(s)?
- What type and how much mortar ammunition is available?
- What is the plan for ammunition resupply?
- For automated fire directions systems, what are the defeat criteria for different targets?
- What are the high-payoff target priorities for fire support?
- Where are the obstacles? How are they to be covered?
- What is the breaching plan?
- Have FPFs been allocated? Where are they to be planned? Are they to be adjusted?
- What are the primary and alternate signals to fire the FPFs?
- How will logistical support for mortars be accomplished?
- Who will control and position CAB mortars?

Fire Support Plan

8-21. The CAB scheme of fires states the fire support tasks and the purpose of each task, and the priorities for, allocation of, and the restrictions on these fires to subordinate units. The scheme of fires paragraph should include a subparagraph for each type of fire support involved. Appropriate fire support liaison representatives (if available) prepare their respective paragraphs in the CAB order. The scheme of fires paragraphs and the supporting annex (if any), target lists, schedules, matrices, or other documents within the CAB's OPORD (or overlay with written instructions, an FSEM, and a target list) make up the fire support plan for the CAB.

8-22. The company FSO extracts information from the CAB's fire support plan to develop the company's fire support plan per the commander's concept of the operation and intent. During planning and the refinement of the company fire support plan, the FSO:

- Begins fire planning on receipt of the company's mission and before the FSO's briefing to the platoon forward observers or the submission of targets by the platoon forward observers.
- Plans targets in-depth and other targets that were not planned by platoons but are required and within the company's AO.
- Coordinates with the CAB's FSO and S-2 on all known, suspected, or likely enemy locations, and advises the commander on enemy indirect-fire support capabilities and limitations.
- Consolidates target lists from the platoon forward observers, resolves duplications, and forwards the target lists to the CAB's FSO. (Note. The target lists from the company should consist of not

more than three to five targets. When the number of targets is limited, the fire support plan is more manageable and can be better supported than a fire support plan with a lengthy target list.)
- Distributes the consolidated target list to all forward observers.
- Coordinates requests for additional fire support when the fire support means available at company level are inadequate.
- Develops the company fire support plan and briefs the commander to obtain approval or further planning guidance.
- Keeps the fire support plan current. Adjusts the fire support plan as required when intelligence and SPOTREPs are received.
- Keeps the commander informed of the capabilities and limitations of all fire support assets that may be made available to the company and advises the commander on all fire support matters.
- Serves as the FA liaison officer from the company and the representative to the CAB's FSO and fire support cell. (Note. The absence of other liaison or staff officers does not relieve the FSO of the responsibility to keep the maneuver commander informed of all available fire support assets and to keep the FA units informed of the CAB's plans and requirements.)
- Advises and consults with other forward observer representatives, for example, joint fire observers.
- Collects information from the various liaison officers, correlates that information, and informs the commander. (Note. As a minimum, this information should include the availability of fire support assets [command or support relationship], suitability, response time, and assigned priorities.)

Observer Positions

8-23. To ensure that indirect fire can be called on a specific target, observers are designated and in the proper position. As the company plans indirect fire targets to support the mission and passes these down to the platoon, specific observers are positioned to observe the target and the associated trigger line or TRP. Any Soldier can perform this function if the Soldier understands the mission and has the communications capability and training. Once the target has been passed to the platoon or included by the platoon in the fire support plan, the PL must position the observer and make sure the observer understands the following:
- The nature and description of the target that the observer is expected to engage.
- The terminal effects required (destroy, delay, disrupt, limit, and so on) and purpose.
- The communications means, radio net, call signs, and FDC to be called.
- When or under what circumstances targets are to be engaged.
- The relative priority of targets.
- The method of engagement and method of control to be used in the call for fire.
- Purpose and location of target, observers (primary and alternate), trigger, communications, and the resource providing the fires.

Linking Tasks to Purpose

8-24. A clearly defined purpose enables the company commander to articulate precisely how fires are to affect the enemy during different phases of the battle. This, in turn, allows the FSO to develop a fire support plan that effectively supports the intended purpose. The FSO can determine each required task (in terms of effects on target), the best method for accomplishing each task (in terms of a fire support asset and its fire capabilities), and a means of quantifying accomplishment. A carefully developed method of fire is equally valuable during execution of the fire support mission; it helps not only the firing elements but also the observers who are responsible for monitoring the effects of the indirect fires. With a clear understanding of the intended target effects, fire support assets and observers can work together effectively, planning and adjusting the fires as necessary to achieve the desired effects on the enemy. The following bullets describe several types of targeting objectives associated with fire support tasks and provide examples of how the company commander might link a target task to a specific maneuver purpose in their order.
- Delay. Friendly forces use indirect fires to cause a function or action to occur later than the enemy desires.

- Disrupt. Disrupting fires are employed to break apart the enemy's formation; to interrupt or delay their tempo and operational timetable; to cause premature commitment of their forces; or to force them to stage their attack piecemeal.
- Limit. Indirect fires help prevent the enemy from executing an action or function where they want it to occur.
- Destroy. Friendly forces use indirect fires to render an enemy formation ineffective.
- Divert. Diverting fires are used to cause the enemy to modify their course or route of attack.
- Screen. Screening fires entail the use of smoke to mask friendly installations, positions, or maneuver.
- Obscure. Obscurant is placed between enemy forces and friendly forces or directly on enemy positions to confuse and disorient the enemy's direct fire gunners and artillery forward observers.

Final Protective Fire

8-25. *Final protective fire* is an immediately available prearranged barrier of fire designed to impede enemy movement across defensive lines or areas (JP 3-09.3). An FPF is a special type of priority target. Normally, an FPF target is assigned to the company or platoon that is covering the most dangerous avenue of approach or covering the most vital area. Most often this company or platoon also has priority of fire. This prevents conflict of missions. In some situations, however, one commander may have priority of fires while another has the FPF. This could occur when a security force has priority of fires initially, but the FPF target is assigned to a defending company. This requires close coordination between maneuver commanders, CAB and company FSOs, and the FA or mortar unit responsible for the fires. A specific amount of ammunition is always designated, prepared, and set aside for use with the FPF target. FPF ammunition may not be used on any other mission without specific authorization from the commander.

Field Artillery and Mortar Fires

8-26. In the fire support plan, an FPF is continuous artillery or mortar fires:
- Fired on a predetermined target.
- Fired at the maximum rate of fire until the firing unit is requested to stop, ammunition is exhausted, or the firing unit is forced to move.
- Allocated FA FPF, normally from the ABCT to the CAB level, which may allocate to the company level.
- Allocated mortar platoon FPF, normally from CAB to the company level.
- Authorized to shoot at the lowest maneuver commander's level in whose area the FPF is placed or that commander's authorized representative.

8-27. The FIST has the responsibility to adjust in the FPF when the tactical situation dictates. The FIST may adjust one gun or all guns designated to fire the FPF and cancel the FPF when it is no longer needed.

8-28. The CAB mortar platoons normally have a single four-mortar FPF, but commanders may direct the platoons to prepare two two-mortar FPFs. This should be done only if terrain dictates the need for more FPFs than has been allocated and only after seeking additional FA allocations.

8-29. Table 8-1 on page 8-8 provides fire planning data for FA and mortar FPFs. The FPF approximate widths in the table are neither precise nor restrictive. The sheaf can be opened or closed to cover the specific terrain on which the FPF is located. The FPF approximate depths in the table are derived from data on the bursting diameter of rounds. (See ATP 3-09.32 for more information.) The bursting diameter of a high-explosive round is generally considered to be twice the distance from the point of impact at which the round will reliably place one lethal fragment per square meter of target.

Table 8-1. Field artillery and mortar final protective fire planning data

Size	Number of Mortars or Guns	*Approximate Width (meters)	*Approximate Depth (meters)
120 mm	4	280	70
120 mm	2	140	70
155 mm	3	150	50
155 mm	6	300	50
Legend: mm – millimeter			
*measurements are approximate			

Priority Target Versus Final Protective Fire

8-30. A *priority target* is a target, based on either time or importance, on which delivery of fires takes precedence over all the fires for the designated firing unit or element (FM 3-09). FPF differ from standard priority target in that an FPF is fired at the maximum rate of fire until mortars are ordered to stop or until all ammunition is expended. The RED for a given delivery system (see ATP 3-09.32) is a factor in how close the FPF can be placed in front of friendly front lines. Closer FPFs are easier to integrate into direct-fire FPLs. The high rate of fire achievable by mortars creates effective barriers of fire. The normal allocation of FPFs is identical to the allocation of priority targets (one for each battery/platoon and one for each mortar platoon). While firing FPFs, mortar sections are not normally allowed to cease fire and displace. Due to countermortar fires, they must take precautions to avoid or withstand countermortar fire when firing an FPF.

8-31. When an FPF is allocated to a company, the commander designates the precise FPF location to best augment direct-fire weapons and obstacles. Figure 8-1 shows how mortar FPFs are positioned to integrate them into the direct-fire weapons and obstacles in the final protective lines of the defender.

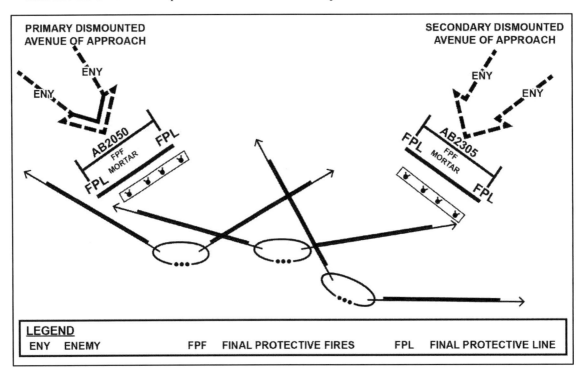

Figure 8-1. Final protective line integration of fires and obstacles

8-32. As illustrated in figure 8-1 mortar FPFs are normally targeted on an avenue of likely dismounted attack. FPFs can be any distance from the friendly position that fits into the commander's subordinate form of the defense (for example, a defense of a linear obstacle, perimeter defense, or reverse-slope defense) but are always within the range of organic direct-fire weapons, normally within 100 to 400 meters of friendly troops. The importance of accurate defensive fires and the proximity of friendly troops means that each mortar firing an FPF should be individually adjusted into place, normally using delay fuse settings and the creeping method of adjustment.

8-33. The company commander retains the authority to call for the mortar FPF to be fired or may delegate it to a subordinate. If the decision is delegated to a forward PL, the leader directs the platoon's forward observer to transmit the request to fire the FPF directly to the FDC or through the company's FSO. When the request is transmitted directly to the FDC, the PL must inform the company commander that the FPF is initiated. The mortar section or PL always informs the commander when the firing of the FPF is initiated.

8-34. As with any operation, the commander ensures alternate means of communication are established to support the execution of FPFs. Alternate means are established in addition to standard voice messages such as wire, runner, or visual signal. Once begun, FPFs are fired until ordered to terminate or until all mortar ammunition is gone.

8-35. High-explosive ammunition with point detonating fuses is normally used in firing the FPF. When planning FPFs, the mortar section leader, in coordination with the FSO, decides how many rounds to prepare based on ammunition available and the control supply rate and sets them aside for immediate use. This allows mortars to begin the FPF quickly and maintain it without pausing to prepare rounds when the call for fire is received. Additional rounds can be prepared during the firing of FPFs if the ammunition requirement exceeds the quantity prepared.

Target Refinement

8-36. The commander is responsible for the employment of lethal and nonlethal indirect fires within the company's assigned AO. A critical aspect of this responsibility is target refinement, in which the commander makes necessary changes to the fire support plan to ensure that targets accomplish the commander's intended battlefield purpose. Rather than merely executing targets without regard to the actual enemy situation, the company commander and FSO adjust existing targets or nominate new targets that allow engagement of specific enemy forces.

8-37. Necessary refinements usually emerge when the commander war-games as part of Step 6 (complete the plan) of the TLP. The war-gaming process enables the commander to identify required additions, deletions, and adjustments to the CAB's fire support plan. The company FSO then submits refinements to the CAB's FSO for inclusion in the scheme of fires for the mission. (This is normally only the first step of target refinement, with the commander and FSO making further adjustments as the enemy situation becomes clearer.)

8-38. As a specific requirement in defensive planning, the commander focuses on target refinement for within the company's AO. This usually takes place as part of EA development. The commander makes appropriate adjustments to the targets based on refinements to the situation template such as the actual positions of obstacles and enemy direct fire systems.

8-39. Because fire support is planned from the top down, cutoff times for target nomination and target refinement are normally specified in the CAB's OPORD. Commanders must ensure that nominations and refinements meet these deadlines to provide fire support planners with sufficient time to develop execution plans.

Tactical and Technical Triggers

8-40. The two types of triggers associated with a target are tactical and technical. The commander develops a tactical trigger for each target, then develops (or the FSO develops) the technical trigger. A tactical trigger is the maneuver related event or action that causes the commander to initiate fires. This event can be friendly or enemy based. The tactical trigger is usually determined during COA development.

Note. The commander must ensure that tactical and technical triggers are developed, understood, and rehearsed. Ineffective, or nonexistent technical triggers, therefore, can result in significant delays in firing priority targets.

8-41. When selecting the tactical trigger, the commander, or designated observer, must be able to observe the enemy force or the event that is the tactical trigger if it is enemy driven; for example, when enemy forces occupy their defensive positions via Objective Brown. The tactical trigger may also be friendly event or time driven; for example, when Company C crosses Phase Line Bowen.

8-42. The technical trigger is the mathematically derived solution for firing the indirect fires based on the tactical trigger to ensure that the indirect fires arrive at the correct time and location to achieve the desired effects. Sometimes conditions for the technical trigger might occur before the tactical trigger, and the technical trigger may also serve as WARNORD to the firing unit of a pending mission. Several factors govern the selection and positioning of the technical trigger.

8-43. Critical factors are the enemy's likely locations or rate of travel, and the time required for the enemy force to move from the technical trigger to the target area. Using this information, the commander can then select the technical trigger location based on the following considerations:

- The amount of time required to initiate the call for fire.
- The time needed by the fire support element to prepare for and fire the mission.
- The time required to clear the fires.
- Any built-in or planned delays in the firing sequence.
- The time of flight of the indirect fire rounds.
- Possible adjustment times.

8-44. The commander can use an estimated rate of enemy movement, along with the information in table 8-2, to complete the process of determining the location of the technical trigger in relation to the target area. Table 8-2 lists the response time required by FA assets to prepare for and fire various types of support missions. Trigger lines or points (used in this method) are usually employed as technical triggers to synchronize the effects of direct fires, countermobility efforts, and indirect fires in time and space, rather than try to engage moving targets based on mathematical calculations. (See ATP 3-09.42 for more information.)

Table 8-2. Artillery response times

Support Mission	*Response Time
Grid or polar mission (unplanned)	5 to 7 minutes
Preplanned mission	3 minutes
Planned priority mission	1 to 2 minutes
Note: *These are approximate times needed to process and execute calls for fire on normal artillery targets. Special missions may take longer.	

Ceasing or Shifting Fires

8-45. The commander establishes triggers for ceasing or shifting fires based on battlefield events such as the movement of enemy or friendly forces. One technique is the use of a minimum safe line when a friendly element, such as a breach force, is moving toward an area of indirect fires. As the element approaches the minimum safe line, observers call for fires shift or cease, allowing the friendly force to move safely in the danger area.

Clearance of Fire

8-46. The commander is responsible to approve (clear) fires and their effects within the company's AO. Although the commander may delegate authority to coordinate and clear fires to the FSO, the ultimate responsibility belongs to the commander. Normally, the FSO helps the commander by making recommendations on the clearance of fires.

8-47. When the higher commander establishes ROE within the company's AO, the commander ensures they are followed through the operations process. ROE, especially during stability, often place limitations or prohibit the firing of certain types of indirect fires within the company's AO.

Preparation

8-48. Although the CAB commander normally establishes most target tasks, purposes, and effects, and allocatees appropriate fire support assets, the company commander is responsible to ensure assigned targets are executed successfully. In turn, successful execution demands thorough preparation at the company level. The commander's fire support preparation responsibilities, although not inclusive, include:

- Involving company FIST in company- and CAB-level rehearsals.
- Making the company available for any separate fire support rehearsals.
- Rehearsing the company's forward observers in the execution of targets.
- Using rehearsals to ensure primary and backup communications systems adequately support the plan.

8-49. Once the company develops and coordinates the fire support plan, it rehearses the plan. As the company rehearses the maneuver, it rehearses the fire plan. The target list is executed as the maneuver is conducted during rehearsal; fires are requested (though not actually executed by the firing units) just as they would be during the mission. Additional considerations include:

- If time or conditions do not permit full-scale rehearsals, key leaders can meet, preferably at a good vantage point, and backbrief the plan.
- Rehearsals on like terrain can reveal any problems in visibility, communications, and coordination of the fire support plan.
- Under ideal circumstances, an FPF can be adjusted during the rehearsal.
- Conduct rehearsals under degraded conditions (for example, at night, in mission oriented protective posture [MOPP] 4, with degraded or no communications) to make sure the company can execute the plan under different conditions.
- Conduct a rock drill or use a sand table to:
  - Show the plan with each participant, to include the FSO, explaining what they do, where they do it, and how they plan to overcome key-leader casualties.
  - Execute the fire plan as the company walks through/conducts the mission.
  - Fire targets as required and adjust based on the anticipated enemy reactions.
  - Cancel targets as friendly units pass them or they are no longer relevant to the maneuver.

SCHEME OF FIRES

8-50. The scheme of fires describes what fire support must accomplish to support the company's operation and describes the logical sequence of fire support tasks and how each task contributes to the execution of the operation. The overall scheme of fires subparagraph mirrors that of the scheme of move and maneuver subparagraph. When the scheme of movement and maneuver is phased or otherwise organized, the scheme of fires takes on the same organization.

Company Fire Support Task

8-51. A company fire support task is a task given to a fire support unit or organization that supports the commander's scheme of movement and maneuver. One or more fire support tasks may be developed for each phase of an OPORD. Taken together and considered sequentially the fire support tasks represent a summary of the scheme of fires supporting the OPORD. The scheme of fires paragraph in the OPORD must be concise but specific enough to state what fires are to accomplish in the operation clearly.

Scheme of Fire Format

8-52. The scheme of fires subparagraph format includes the elements of task, purpose, and effect. (See table 8-3 on page 8-12.) The task states the supported company task and the type(s) of effects the firing unit must provide for that phase of the operation. The task describes what fire support must accomplish to support the mission. The effect identifies the desired result or outcome the delivered fires are to achieve. (See FM 3-60 for more information.) The purpose states the supported company commander's purpose and the desired end state for the targeted enemy formation, function, or capability. The purpose describes the why of the fire support task. In this case why is to disrupt the enemy's ability to affect the breach force. (See appendix C for a detailed discussion on breaching operations.)

Table 8-3. Scheme of fires subparagraph format, example

Example, Company Task			
When	**Who**	**Where**	**What/Task and Desired Effect, When**
0400	Company A	AB00054	Disrupt the ability of the enemy motorized Infantry platoon at point of penetration to place effective direct fire against the breach force.
Why/Purpose			
To allow the company team to breach the obstacle without becoming decisively engaged by the motorized Infantry platoon at the point of penetration.			

Observation Plan

8-53. In developing the observation plan to support the scheme of fires, the company commander and FSO ensures that primary and alternate observers cover all targets and determine whether the desired target effects have been achieved. The plan provides clear, precise guidance for the observers. Perhaps the most important aspect of the plan is positioning. An observer's position must allow them to see the trigger for initiating fires as well as the target area and the enemy force on which the target is oriented; this is done to help the observer determine if the target effects have been achieved. The commander must also consider the observer capabilities, including any available systems. The observation plan must also include contingency plans that cover limited-visibility conditions and backup communications.

Company Fire Support Execution Matrix

8-54. The FSEM for a company may be as simple as a hand-drawn matrix listing the platoons, phase lines, and minimal necessary information. Table 8-4 is an example of FSEMs for a company. Using these types of formats, the FSO can depict fire-support-related information for an operation together with the matrix. A format of these type might be used if a formal written OPORD or separate fire support annex were not prepared. The FSEM example in table 8-4 is illustrative only. Tailor the matrix preparation, format, and content to unit needs. Identify the FSEM preparation steps in local SOPs.

Table 8-4. Fire support execution matrix, example

Event	Event I	Event II	Event III	Event IV
SUPPORT DATA/ CONSIDERATIONS	**LD to 3d Platoon SBF 01**	**LD to 3d Platoon SBF 01**	**LD to 3d Platoon SBF 01**	**LD to 3d Platoon SBF 01**
TARGET/GRID	AE0001 (PK 10184938)	AE0002 (PK09005031)	O/O shift AE0001 to AE0003 (PK10204810) and lift AE0002	O/O lift AE0003
DELIVERY SYSTEM	120-mm HE	120-mm obscurant	120-mm	120-mm
OBSERVER/BACKUP	3d platoon will initially call for and adjust fires; FSO adjusts upon arrival at SBF; 3d platoon leader is backup	FSO (primary)/3d platoon leader (backup)	AE0003; FSO (primary)/3d platoon leader (backup)	FSO (primary)/3d platoon leader (backup)
TRIGGER	3d platoon crosses PL Lynx	On-call at SBF	1st platoon crosses PL Lion	2d platoon completes consolidation on OBJ Bob
COMMUNICATIONS	Primary: CAB FS NET FH800 Alternate: ABCT FS NET FH700	Primary: Company fire control NET FH800 Alternate: CAB FS NET FH800	Primary: CAB FS NET FH800 Alternate: ABCT FS NET FH700	Primary: CAB FS NET FH800 Alternate: ABCT FS NET FH700
PURPOSE	Disrupt enemy on OBJ Bob to facilitate maneuver of 3d platoon to SBF position	Obscure enemy to prevent interference with 1st platoon's breach	Disrupt reserve to protect the assault force (2d platoon)	Protect the assault force (2d platoon)

LEGEND: ABCT – Armored brigade combat team; CAB – combined arms battalion; FS – fire support; FSO – fire support officer; HE – high explosive; LD – line of departure; MM – millimeter; NET– network; OBJ – objective; O/O – on-order; PL – phase line; SBF – support by fire

8-55. The advantage of the matrix is that it reduces the plan to one page and simplifies execution. The company FSEM also directs execution responsibilities and reduces the possibility that planned fires will not be executed. The company commander is responsible for disseminating the FSEM. The commander and key subordinate leaders must understand the categories of targets and how to engage those targets to create the desired result.

MORTARS

8-56. Mortars are high-angle, relatively short-range, high rate-of-fire, area fire weapons. Their mobility makes them well-suited for close support of maneuver and can rapidly be brought into action. Mortars are ideal weapons for attacking targets on reverse slopes, in gullies, in ditches, in built-up areas, and in other areas that are difficult to reach with low-angle fire. The proliferation of handheld GPS devices and the fielding of the new mortar fire control system partially compensate for the fact that mortar positions are seldom surveyed. The commander may specify mortar support for subordinate units by changing the command or support relationship, by assigning priority of fires or by assigning priority targets such as FPFs.

MORTAR EMPLOYMENT

8-57. Mortars act as a killer of enemy forces and as an enhancer of friendly mobility. They provide commanders with responsive, organic indirect-fire support at a higher rate of fire than FA units. Using mortars to suppress the enemy inhibits their fire and movement while allowing friendly forces to gain a tactical mobility advantage. The CAB mortar PL works closely with commanders and FSOs to maximize mortar fires and ensures the mortars are integrated into the echelonment of fires. (See ATP 3-21.90 for more information.) Additional employment considerations include:

- Mortars provide the maneuver commander with immediately available, responsive indirect fires in support of combat missions, and reinforce direct fires during close combat.
- Mortars are integrated with FA assets in an echelonment of fires.
- In the offense, mortars establish conditions for the maneuver elements in conducting their combat missions by:
  - Assisting in suppressing and fixing the enemy and providing close support fires during the assault.
  - Providing obscurants for screening and friendly movements.
  - Using heavy mortars to penetrate buildings and destroy enemy field fortifications.
- In the defense, mortars can—
  - Force the enemy in armored vehicles to button up.
  - Obscure their ability to employ supporting fires.
  - Deny use of defilade terrain.
  - Break up enemy concentrations and formations.
  - Separate enemy dismounted infantry from their armored PCs and accompanying tanks.
  - Destroy synchronization, reduce enemy mobility, and canalize enemy units into EAs.

ECHELONMENT OF FIRES

8-58. Echelonment of fires is critical for the fire support plan to be synchronized effectively with the maneuver plan. The purpose of echeloning fires is to maintain constant and overlapping fires on an objective while using the optimum delivery system up to the point of its RED in combat operations or minimum safe distance in training. RED is the minimum distance friendly troops can approach the effects of friendly fires without suffering appreciable casualties. Echeloning fires provides protection for friendly forces as they move to and assault an objective, which allows them to get in close with minimal casualties. It prevents the enemy from observing and engaging the assault by forcing the enemy to take cover, which allows the friendly force to continue the advance unimpeded. (See ATP 3-90.5 for more information on the echelonment of fires.)

CONCEPT OF ECHELONING FIRES

8-59. The concept of echeloning fires begins with attacking targets on or around the objective using the weapons system with the largest RED. As the maneuver unit closes the distance en route to the objective, the fires cease or shift. This triggers the engagement of the targets by the delivery system with the next largest RED. The length of time to engage the targets is based on the rate of the friendly force's movement between the RED trigger lines. The process continues until the system with the smallest RED ceases or shifts fires and the maneuver unit is close enough to eliminate the enemy with direct fires or make its final assault and clear the objective.

8-60. The RED considers the bursting radius of munitions and the characteristics of the delivery system and associates this combination with a percentage for the probability of incapacitation of Soldiers at a given range. The munitions delivery systems include mortars, FA, helicopter, and fixed-wing aircraft. The RED is defined as the minimum distance friendly Soldiers can approach the effects of friendly fires without suffering appreciable casualties of 0.1 percent or higher probability of incapacitation. Commanders may maneuver their units within the RED area based on the mission; however, in doing so, they are making a deliberate decision to accept the additional risk to friendly forces. Before the commander accepts this risk, the commander should try to mitigate the probability of incapacitation. For example, maneuvering units in a defilade that provides some protection from the effects of exploding munitions.

> **WARNING**
>
> **REDs are for combat use and do not represent the maximum fragmentation envelopes of the weapons listed. REDs are not minimum safe distances for peacetime training use.**

8-61. Using echelonment of fires within the specified RED for a delivery system requires the unit to assume some risks. The maneuver commander determines, by delivery system, how close fire will be delivered in proximity to forces. The maneuver commander makes the decision for this risk level but relies heavily on the FSO's expertise. While this planning normally is accomplished at the CAB level, the company FSO has input and should be familiar with the process because the FSO must execute the same process with the company mortars. (See ATP 3-09.32, appendix H for information on REDs and appendix I for information on minimum safe distances.)

SECTION II – AVIATION

8-62. Army aviation uses maneuver to concentrate and sustain combat power at critical times and places to find, fix, and destroy threat forces. Aviation units design, tailor, and configure their assets to support the company team for specific operational support based on mission guidance and the specific area of responsibility in which the units operate. The organization could be a combination of attack reconnaissance, assault, lift, and maintenance units. (See FM 3-04 for more information.)

AIR-GROUND OPERATIONS

8-63. *Air-ground operations* are the simultaneous or synchronized employment of ground forces with aviation maneuver and fires to seize, retain, and exploit the initiative (FM 3-04). Employing the combined and complimentary effects of air and ground maneuver and fires through air-ground operations presents the enemy with multiple dilemmas and ensures that aviation assets are position to support ground maneuver. Air-ground operations increase the overall combat power, mission effectiveness, agility, flexibility, and survivability of the entire combined arms team.

8-64. Air-ground operations ensure that all members of the combined arms team, whether on the ground or in the air, work toward common and mutually supporting objectives to meet the higher commander's intent. The likelihood of the company commander receiving attack and utility aviation for support is ever increasing. The following are some considerations for the company commander when receiving aviation assets:
- Exchange of frequencies, call signs, and FM check-in times.
- Terrain model and radio rehearsals.
- Location of air corridors and air control points.
- Location of aerial attack by fire, SBF, or BPs.
- Identification method for marking ground targets.
- Aircraft weapons configuration and station times.
- Friendly recognition symbols for aircraft and ground vehicles.
- Fire coordination measures.
- Location and marking of landing zones and pickup zones for MEDEVAC, CASEVAC, and aerial resupply.

8-65. Ground maneuver commanders understand that aviation forces can provide a significant advantage during operations. The company commander understands that the unique capabilities of Army aviation require specific planning and coordination. Direct fire aviation missions in the close fight differ greatly from engagements forward of the line of own troops operation.

8-66. In engagements forward of the line of own troops operation, attack aircraft can benefit from deliberate planning and freely engaging at maximum ranges with minimal concern of fratricide. Engagements in the close fight, on the other hand, often result in engagements within enemy direct fire weapons system ranges that are close to friendly units. TLP need to integrate Army aviation forces to ensure effective combined arms employment. Effective combined arms employment requires that aviation and ground maneuver forces synchronize their operations by operating from a common perspective.

ARMY ATTACK AVIATION

8-67. During the planning process, Army aviation attack and reconnaissance units are integrated into the company's scheme of maneuver to ensure responsiveness, synergy, and agility during actions on the objective or upon contact with the enemy. Pre-mission development of control measures provides a foundation for the successful integration of Army aviation into company operations. Among these control measures are engagement criteria; the triggers and conditions for execution; fire support coordination measures, such as TRPs; EAs and TRPs; and airspace coordinating measures, such as aerial ingress and egress routes and restricted operations zone, which is airspace reserved for specific activities in which the operations of one or more airspace users is restricted. (See JP 3-52 for more information.)

CALL FOR FIRE

8-68. *Call for fire* is a standardized request for fire containing data necessary for obtaining the required fire on a target (FM 3-09). Army attack aviation targets are planned on probable enemy locations. Army attack aviation call for fire is a coordinated attack by Army attack aircraft against enemy forces near friendly units. Army attack aviation call for fire (see figure 8-2) is not synonymous with CAS flown by joint and multinational aircraft. Terminal control from ground units or controllers is not required due to aircraft capabilities and enhanced situational understanding of the aircrew. Depending on the enemy situation, Army attack aviation can be on station during times when contact is most likely to occur. Air-ground integration ensures frequencies are known and markings are standardized to prevent fratricide. (See ATP 3-04.1 for more information.)

```
┌─────────────────────────────────────────────────────────────────────────┐
│ 1. Observer and Warning Order                                             │
│    "        J27          , this is        041        , fire mission, over"│
│          (aircraft call sign)          (observer call sign)               │
│                                                                           │
│ 2. Friendly Location and Mark                                             │
│    "My position  AL78241638  , marked by      Strobe           "          │
│              (TRP, grid, etc.)          (strobe, beacon, IR strobe, etc.) │
│                                                                           │
│ 3. Target Location                                                        │
│    "Target Location             AL82781942                      "         │
│              (bearing [magnetic] and range [meters], TRP, grid, etc.)     │
│                                                                           │
│ 4. Target Description and Mark                                            │
│    " Dismounted Infantry       , marked by     Tracer          "          │
│          (target description)           (IR pointer, tracer, etc.)        │
│                                                                           │
│ 5. Remarks: "              At my command              , over"             │
│        (threats, danger close clearance, restriction, at my command, etc.)│
├───────────────────────────────────────────────────────────────────────────┤
│ Notes:                                                                    │
│ 1. Clearance: If airspace has been cleared between the employing aircraft │
│    and the target, transmission of this brief is clearance to fire unless │
│    "danger close" or "at my command" is stated.                           │
│ 2. Danger Close: For danger close fire, the observer or commander must    │
│    accept responsibility for increased risk. State "cleared danger close" │
│    in line 5 and pass the initials of the on-scene ground commander. This │
│    clearance may be preplanned.                                           │
│ 3. At My Command: For positive control of the aircraft, state "at my      │
│    command" on line 5. The aircraft will call "ready to fire" when ready. │
├───────────────────────────────────────────────────────────────────────────┤
│ LEGEND                                                                    │
│ IR    INFRARED                      TRP   TARGET REFERENCE POINT          │
└───────────────────────────────────────────────────────────────────────────┘
```

Figure 8-2. Army attack aviation call for fire format

8-69. During call for fire, the flight lead must have direct communication with the on-scene ground commander to provide direct-fire support. After receiving the call for fire brief from ground forces, pilots must be able to positively identify friendly location before engagement. Once the crew has identified enemy and friendly locations, flight leads formulate an attack plan and brief the supported commander and their other attack team members.

CLOSE AIR SUPPORT

8-70. The CAS sorties allocated to the CAB can be passed down to the company teams. *Close air support* is air action by aircraft against hostile targets that are in close proximity to friendly forces and that require detailed integration of each air mission with the fire and movement of those forces (JP 3-09.3). CAS can be employed to blunt an enemy attack; to support the momentum of the ground attack; to help set conditions for CAB and company team operations as part of the overall counterfire fight; to disrupt, delay, and destroy enemy second echelon forces and reserves; and to provide cover for friendly movements. The effectiveness of CAS is related directly to the degree of local air superiority attained. Until air superiority is achieved, competing demands between CAS and counterair operations may limit sorties apportioned for the CAS role. CAS is the primary support given to committed forces by Air Force, Navy, and Marine aircraft. CABs can request air reconnaissance and battlefield air interdiction missions through the next higher HQ, but these missions normally are planned and executed at that higher-unit level, with the results provided to the CAB commander and staff.

8-71. The BCT normally plans and controls CAS. However, this does not preclude the CAB from requesting CAS, receiving immediate CAS to support company-level operation, or accepting execution responsibility for a planned CAS mission. CAS is another means of indirect-fire support available to the CAB. In planning CAS missions, the commander must understand the capabilities and limitations of CAS and synchronize CAS missions with the CAB fire plan and scheme of maneuver. CAS capabilities and limitations such as windows for use, targets, observers, and airspace coordination present some unique challenges, but the commander must plan CAS with maneuver the same way indirect artillery and mortar fires are planned. When executing a CAS mission, the CAB must have a plan that synchronizes CAS with maneuver and the scheme of fires of maneuver companies.

SECTION III – PROTECTION

8-72. *Protection* is the preservation of the effectiveness and survivability of mission-related military and nonmilitary personnel, equipment, facilities, information, and infrastructure deployed or located within or outside the boundaries of a given operational area (JP 3-0). Protection preserves capability, momentum, and tempo, which are important contributors to operational reach. Protection is an enduring quality that differentiates it from defense and specific security operations. It is not a linear activity, but a continuous activity.

PROTECTION PRINCIPLES

8-73. The five principles of protection summarize the characteristics of successful protection integration and practice are comprehensive, integrated, redundant, and enduring. (See ADP 3-37 for more information.) They provide Army professionals with a context for implementing protection tasks, developing schemes of protection, and allocating resources:

- Comprehensive. Protection is an all-inclusive utilization of complementary and reinforcing protection tasks and systems available to commanders and incorporated into the plan to preserve the force.
- Integrated. Protection is unified with other activities, systems, efforts, and capabilities associated with the conduct of operations within one of three strategic contexts: competition below armed conflict, crisis, and armed conflict. Integration must occur vertically and horizontally with unified action partners throughout the operations process.
- Layered. Protection capabilities are deliberately sequenced across multiple domains to eliminate, mitigate, or assume the risk of threat effects.
- Redundant. Protection efforts for identified critical vulnerabilities require dedicated primary and alternate protection capabilities.
- Enduring. Protection is a continuous activity. Commanders and leaders preserve combat power and reduce the risk of loss, damage, or injury to their formations.

PROTECTION TASKS

8-74. Commanders incorporate protection tasks when they understand and visualize available protection capabilities, the threats, and hazards within the OE. Commanders develop protection strategies for each phase of the operation. Units must consider all protection tasks and systems and apply them as appropriate. (See ADP 3-37 for more information on protection tasks.) The primary protection tasks are:

- Conduct survivability operations.
- Provide force health protection (see FM 4-02).
- Conduct CBRN operations (see appendix D).
- Report explosive hazards and request explosive ordnance disposal support (see ATP 4-32.1).
- Coordinate air and missile defense support.
- Conduct personnel recovery (see FM 3-50).
- Conduct detention operations (see FM 3-63).
- Conduct risk management (see ATP 5-19).

- Implement physical security procedures (see ATP 3-39.32).
- Apply antiterrorism measures (see ATP 3-37.2).
- Conduct police operations (see ATP 3-39.10).
- Conduct populace and resources control (see ATP 3-39.30 and ATP 3-57.10).
- Conduct area security.
- Preform cyberspace security and defense (see ATP 6-02.71).
- Conduct electromagnetic protection.
- Implement OPSEC.

8-75. The commander integrates and synchronize protection tasks and systems to reduce risk, mitigate identified vulnerabilities, and act on opportunity. When properly integrated and synchronized, the tasks and systems that comprise the protection warfighting function effectively protect the force, enhance the preservation of combat power, and increase the probability of mission success.

CONDUCT SURVIVABILITY OPERATIONS

8-76. *Survivability* is a quality or capability of military forces which permits them to avoid or withstand hostile actions or environmental conditions while retaining the ability to fulfill their primary mission (ATP 3-37.34). Survivability and survivability operations are not interchangeable. Survivability refers to a quality or capability, while survivability operations are a specific group of tasks that enhance survivability.

8-77. Company teams conduct survivability within the limits of their capabilities. When existing terrain features offer insufficient cover and concealment, altering the physical environment to provide or improve cover and concealment enhances survivability. Similarly, using natural or artificial materials such as camouflage may confuse or mislead the enemy or adversary. Together, these are called survivability operations—those protection activities that alter the physical environment by providing or improving camouflage, cover, and concealment.

8-78. Movement, such as rapid dispersal, is used with cover and concealment to enhance protection. Survivability operations enhance the ability to avoid or withstand hostile actions by altering the physical environment. They accomplish this by providing or improving camouflage, cover, and concealment.

8-79. Units at all echelons have an inherent responsibility to improve their positions, whether a BP, bunker, or forward operating base. Survivability comprises four tasks that are designed to focus efforts on mitigating friendly losses to hostile actions or environments. The four tasks are as follows:

- Fighting positions. The fighting position is a place on the battlefield from which troops engage the enemy with direct and indirect fire weapons. The positions provide necessary protection for personnel yet allow for fields of fire and maneuver.
- Protective positions. A protective position protects the personnel and material not directly involved with fighting the enemy from attack or environmental extremes.
- Hardened positions. Hardening is the act of using natural or man-made materials to protect personnel, equipment, or facilities. Hardened positions protect resources from blast, direct and indirect fire, heat, radiation, or electromagnetic warfare. Hardening is accomplished by using barriers, walls, shields, berms, or other types of physical protection. It is intended to defeat or negate the effects of an attack and includes BPs, protective positions, armored vehicles, Soldiers, and information systems.
- Camouflage and concealment. Camouflage and concealment use materials and techniques to hide, blend, disguise, decoy, or disrupt the appearance of military targets and their backgrounds to prevent visual and electronic detection of friendly forces. Camouflage and concealment help prevent an enemy from detecting or identifying friendly troops, equipment, activities, or installations and include battlefield obscuration capabilities to obscure, screen, or mark. Battlefield obscuration is a major supporting task of camouflage and concealment and is typically provided by specialized fires.

COORDINATE AIR AND MISSILE DEFENSE SUPPORT

8-80. Air and missile defense include active and passive defense actions taken to destroy, nullify, or reduce the effectiveness of hostile air and ballistic missile threats against friendly forces and assets. The company commander and subordinate leaders ensure all passive and active air defense measures are well-planned and implemented. Passive measures include use of concealed routes and AAs, movement on secure routes, marches at night, increased intervals between elements of the columns, and dispersion. Active measures include use of organic and attached weapons according to the OPORD and unit SOP. Air guard duties assigned to specific Soldiers during mounted (or dismounted) movements and marches give each a specific search area. For movements and marches, seeing the enemy first gives the unit time to react. Leaders understand that scanning for long periods decreases the Soldier's ability to identify enemy aircraft. During extended or long movements and marches, Soldiers are assigned air guard duties in shifts.

8-81. Offensive and defensive air defense planning considerations apply in every type of operation the company conducts. The air threat trends toward Group 1 and 2 UASs (see ATP 3-01.81) employed by enemy forces opposing the company's effort to plan, prepare, and execute operations. Air and missile defense sensors and command and control systems elements external to the CAB provide early warning against aerial attack and populate the CAB and company common operational picture. Soldiers train in aircraft recognition and on ROE due to multiple factions using the same or similar aircraft, to include international and private organizations employing their own or charter civilian aircraft.

8-82. Counterrocket, artillery, and mortar batteries may be in or near the company's AO to support its operation. Battery sensors detect incoming rockets, artillery, and mortar shells and may be used to detect Group 1 and 2 UASs. The battery's fire control system predicts the flight path of incoming rockets and shells, prioritizes targets, and activates the supported AO's warning system according to established ROE. The CAB commander clearly defines command and support relationships between counterrocket, artillery, and mortar elements and the company during planning. (See ATP 3-01.60 for more information.)

Counter-Unmanned Aircraft Systems

8-83. The company team should assume they are being observed by enemy and not assume they are under an umbrella of air and missile defense units. UAS are everywhere. While not all hostile air threats require engagement using air defense measures from air and missile defense units, there is still a requirement to detect, identify and be prepared to defeat all classes of UASs.

8-84. The adversary's use of commercial-off-the-shelf technology to gain a tactical advantage compromises the company team's ability to conduct operations without revealing their intentions and making themselves vulnerable to attack. Not all encounters with unknown UAS means your unit is at risk or under attack. However, spotting unidentified UAS operating approximately in the unit's location may be a precursor to an imminent attack. The company team must react quickly and appropriately respond and report when recognizing signs of possible enemy observation or attack. Whether a counter response is available or not units must implement passive air defense measures to include camouflage, cover, concealment, and hardening to protect lives and equipment.

Counter-Unmanned Aircraft Systems Planning

8-85. Commanders must plan for the threat environment in which where the units will conduct operations. Passive air defense, combined arms for air defense and counterreconnaissance tasks training should be an integral part of the units' counter-unmanned aircraft system (C-UAS) practices. The unit should develop and refine C-UAS planning and tailored to the expected threat environment. The company team must plan and execute operations as an integrated combined arms team employing all forms of passive air defense techniques when active air defense is limited or not available IPB provides the commander and staff with specific threat information on known enemy locations, tactics, and threat capabilities.

8-86. For any mission, any adversary, and any environment, the company team must ruthlessly reduce its signature. While the company team can reduce, it will never completely mask its signature. BPs and operating bases must be small, dispersed, well-camouflaged, and temporary.

8-87. When exercising mission command, the company commander assisted by the PLs may use a variety of techniques to prepare for missions, employ the company, communicate, and issue orders. Company commanders must understand the tasks relative to C-UAS operations. This understanding should translate into a quick reference guide or precombat checklist to focus the company on C-UAS. The purpose of C-UAS planning is to reduce the physical signature (visual, IR thermal, and radar) of company team in order to avoid being observed and targeted by the adversary.

Techniques for conducting Counter-Unmanned Aircraft System Air Guard

8-88. Company level security operations are complemented by employing air guard techniques. An air guard may assist with mitigating the threat UAS' capability to conduct reconnaissance, surveillance and intelligence gathering operations and execute attacks on friendly forces. Air guards need to be vigilant, eyes on the horizon. Air guards will perform actions such as search and scan techniques for approaching threat UASs while observing their assigned sectors. Identify likely launch points and patterns of UAS traffic. Terrain features and locations UAS could be launched from. Early warning is the key for air guards since it is their job to alert the formation of any possible air threats. Reporting threat UAS activity should include an estimate of the threat location from the air guard position. The air guard reports the approximate distance, time, duration, size, estimated elevation, and direction the UAS was heading when detected. Reporting of a threat UAS should utilize a standard reporting format. See table 8-5 for an example reporting format.

Table 8-5. Counter-unmanned aircraft system reporting format, example

Line	Information Example	Example
1	Unit call sign and frequency	Red 1, FHXXXX
2	Unit location	NV1234598765
3	Location of threat unmanned aircraft system (UAS)	NV1345287659, headed northeast
4	Time threat UAS asset spotted or detected	DTG: 252355ZDEC23
5	Estimated time on site	32 minutes
6	Flight characteristics	Flight pattern in figure 8 formation
7	Estimated size, elevation, and physical description	12-inch wingspan, 200 meters above ground level, gray with three red dots on side

Passive Defense

8-89. Companies and platoons should be ready to employ passive defense measures to protect themselves from detection, observation, and attack. Passive defense measures decrease the effectiveness of enemy attacks using UAS. Damage-limiting and attack avoidance measures are passive defense measures that are used to avoid detection from aerial threats and limit damage if attacked. Company teams must use caution when exercising C-UAS passive measures. Commanders should select positions of advantage that provide concealment for Soldiers, equipment, and unit activities. When planning damage-limiting and attack avoidance measures the commander should consider their forces on the following passive defense tasks:

- Operate at night or during limited visibility. Practice light restrictions and discipline during times of limited visibility and night operations.
- Disseminating early warning of air threats to the lowest echelon. Early warning to the lowest echelons is essential to countering the UAS threat.
- Practice good OPSEC. OPSEC is essential part of the planning process. Commanders and leaders must always enforce their units' OPSEC measures.
- Use emission control to limit electromagnetic and acoustic footprint. The selective and controlled use of electromagnetic, acoustic, or other emitters to optimize mission command systems and controlling capabilities while minimizing OPSEC.
- Use camouflage and concealment. Camouflage is the use of natural or artificial materials to disguise personnel and/or equipment. Concealment is used to reduce the factors of recognition. Hiding, blending, and disguising are some techniques of concealment.

- Use decoys and deception. Using such things as decoys to set up false locations, with smoke to draw attention away from an operation, or emitters and emulators to confuse collection activities can conceal unit activities from enemy detection.
- Hardening. Use protective construction and overhead cover to provide damage-limiting cover for friendly forces and equipment. The hardening and fortifying of cover will limits the threat UAS's ability to visually see and limit the damaging effects of an aerial attack.
- Use of obscurants. Use optical and noise reducing measures to limit the glare or noise of equipment. Placing mud on headlights and using camouflage nets to obscure the glare of windshields prevents drawing attention to their position.
- Unit dispersion. Disperse assets to minimize detection and damage if attacked. Dispersion may be your best damage-limiting measure. Proper dispersion of units and equipment lessens target density and reduces the lethal effects of threat ordnance.
- Find a concealed site. Conform to terrain by finding low dead ground and micro-terrain, behind hills, tucked against the shadows of buildings, or under trees. In the city, move inside a building.
- Maintain vigilance. Company team must assume they are always vulnerable to enemy targeting attempts. This is especially true when conducting troop movements or performing supply actions or move through open areas or concentrate at choke points.
- Establish early warning network. Establish an air defense early warning network using the radios and digital networks.

Active Defense

8-90. Commanders have the responsibility to take whatever action is necessary to protect their forces and equipment against attack and ensure their Soldiers operate in accordance with established ROE. Soldiers encountering groups 1 and 2 UAS should consider these as threats eligible for engagement unless positively identified as nonthreatening. Active measures for the company team must include basic rules that assist in the identification and defeat process for threat UASs. For example, establish SOPs for disseminating WCS and hostile criteria. The commander should consider training their forces on the following active measures:

- Define characteristics for threat UAS. Factors for defining the characteristics of threat UASs are speed, altitude, location, and heading.
- Develop and transmit weapon control status. Weapon control status is a control measure designed to establish procedures for forces using surface-to-air weapons (including small arms weapons) to engage threats. Weapon control statuses can apply to weapon systems, volumes of airspace, or types of air platforms. This includes established restricted and engagement zones. Categories of WCS are:
  - Weapons-Free. Indicates that weapons systems may fire at any target not positively identified as friendly. This is the least restrictive weapon control status.
  - Weapons-Tight. Indicates that weapons systems may only fire at targets identified as hostile in accordance with current ROE.
  - Weapons-Hold. Indicates that weapons systems may only fire in self-defense or in response to a formal order. This is the most restrictive weapon control status.
- Use air guard: Designate air guards for every vehicle and position to establish 360-degree security.
  - React to threat UASs by determining distance and bearing to the threat and take pictures if possible.
  - Immediately report sightings of threat UAS SPOTREP as prescribed by the SOPs.
  - If the air guards' position and personnel become threatened, respond in accordance with established unit SOP that could include moving to alternate positions, engaging the threat UAS with small arms using combined arms for air defense firing techniques, and requesting engagement support with air and missile defense weapon systems and aviation assets.

CONDUCT AREA SECURITY

8-91. Area security is a type of security operation conducted to protect friendly forces, lines of communications, installation routes and actions within a specific area. Area security operations may be offensive or defensive in nature and require the execution of a wide variety of supporting efforts and tasks.

8-92. When conducting an area security operation, the company team prevents threat ground reconnaissance elements from directly observing friendly activities within the area being secured. It prevents threat ground maneuver forces from penetrating the defensive perimeters established by the commander. The commander may direct subordinate platoons to employ a variety of techniques (such as OPs, BPs, ambushes, sniper employment, and combat outposts) to accomplish this. A reserve or quick reaction force enables the commander to react to unforeseen contingencies.

8-93. During area security operations civilians will be present. Therefore, leaders ensure Soldiers understand the current ROE, with regards to protection of civilians and noncombatants on the battlefield, balancing judicious use of lethal force with mission accomplishment and the moral principles of the Army Ethic to accomplish the mission in the right way. However, leaders are always responsible for protecting their forces and consider this responsibility when applying the ROE. Restrictions on conducting operations and using force need to be explained clearly and understood by everyone. Soldiers need to understand their actions, no matter how minor, may have far-reaching positive or negative effects.

CONDUCT ELECTROMAGNETIC PROTECTION

8-94. *Electromagnetic protection* is the division of electromagnetic warfare involving the actions taken to protect personnel, facilities, and equipment from any effects of friendly or enemy use of the electromagnetic spectrum that degrade, neutralize, or destroy friendly combat capability (JP 3-85). For example, electromagnetic protection includes actions taken by the commander to ensure friendly use of the electromagnetic spectrum, such as frequency agility in a radio or variable pulse repetition frequency in radar. The commander avoids confusing electromagnetic protection with self-protection. However, electromagnetic protection protects from the effects of electromagnetic attack (friendly and enemy) and electromagnetic interference, while defensive electromagnetic attack primarily protects against lethal attacks by denying enemy use of the electromagnetic spectrum to guide or trigger weapons.

8-95. Electromagnetic protection is a command responsibility. The more emphasis the commander places on electromagnetic protection, the greater the benefits, in terms of casualty reduction and combat survivability, in a hostile environment or degraded information environment. The commander ensures the company team trains on and practices sound electromagnetic protection techniques and procedures. The commander continually measures the effectiveness of electromagnetic protection techniques and procedures used throughout the operations process.

EMISSION CONTROL

8-96. Units should use proactive techniques to avoid jamming, including minimizing radio transmissions. Minimizing transmissions is the most basic technique to avoid enemy jamming and direction finding. Radio transmissions should never exceed six seconds in duration (see ATP 6-02.53 for more information).

8-97. *Emission control* is the selective and controlled use of electromagnetic, acoustic, or other emitters to optimize command and control capabilities while minimizing, for operations security (JP 3-85):

- Detection by enemy sensors.
- Mutual interference among friendly systems.
- Enemy interference with the ability to execute a military deception plan.

8-98. In large-scale combat operations against near-peer competitors, the enemy is expected to use electronic warfare capabilities to detect, intercept, deny, degrade, disrupt, destroy, or manipulate friendly communications, command and control, and intelligence capabilities. These considerations for planning are designed to help commanders develop SOPs and battle drills for their unit's unique suite of emitters using an appropriate mix of the practices such as:

- Minimize length and frequency of radio transmissions.

- Use appropriate power settings.
- Plan radio messages.
- Establish and enforce a primary, alternate, contingency, and emergency communication plan.
- Use brevity codes and proword execution matrixes.
- Train while employing radio silence.
- Use encrypted GPS.
- Train on land navigation (without GPS).
- Execute survivability moves.
- Mask with camouflage netting.
- Understand the impact of terrain composition on emissions.
- Recognize communications jamming (reporting criteria).
- Recognize GPS jamming (reporting criteria).
- Recognize radar jamming (reporting criteria).
- Recognize satellite jamming (reporting criteria).

8-99. Electromagnetic protection and emission control are an integral part of all operations. The establishment of emission control levels is an effective tool in developing the unit SOP. Table 8-6 is a sample of emission control status levels.

Table 8-6. Emission control status levels

EMCON Status	Description
EMCON 5 (Green)	Describes a situation where there is no apparent hostile activity against friendly emitter operations. Operational performance of all EMS-dependent systems is monitored, and password/encryption-enabled systems are used as a layer of protection.
EMCON 4 (Yellow)	Describes an increased risk of attack after detection. Increased monitoring of all EMS activities is mandated, and all units must make sure their systems are secured and encrypted, power levels are monitored, and transmissions are limited. Electromagnetic spectrum usage may be restricted to certain emitters, and rehearsals for elevated EMCON is ideal.
EMCON 3 (Amber)	Describes when a risk has been identified. Electronic counter-countermeasures (encryption/frequency hop (FH)/directional antennas) on important systems is a priority, and the CEWOs alertness is increased. All unencrypted systems are disconnected.
EMCON 2 (Red)	Describes when an attack has taken place, but the EMCON system is not at its highest alertness. Nonessential emitters may be taken offline, alternate methods of communication may be implemented, and modifications are made to standard lower EMCON configurations (power levels and antenna types).
EMCON 1 (Black)	Describes when attacks are taking place based on the use of the EMS. The most restrictive methods of electromagnetic protection are enforced (blackout transmissions, use couriers and wire). Isolate compromised systems from the network.
Legend: CEWO – cyber and electromagnetic warfare officer; EMCON – emission control; EMS – electromagnetic spectrum	

IMPLEMENT OPERATIONS SECURITY

8-100. OPSEC is the process of identifying essential elements of friendly information and subsequently analyzing friendly actions attendant to military operations and other activities to—

- Identify those actions that can be observed by threat intelligence systems.
- Determine indicators hostile intelligence systems might obtain that could be interpreted or pieced together to derive critical information in time to be useful to adversaries.
- Select and execute measures that eliminate or reduce to an acceptable level the vulnerabilities of friendly actions to threat exploitation.

8-101.   OPSEC applies to all military operations. All units conduct OPSEC to preserve essential secrecy. Good field craft and the disciplined enforcement of camouflage and concealment are essential to OPSEC. Commanders establish routine OPSEC measures in unit SOPs.

This page intentionally left blank.

Appendix A

Command Post Operations and Organization

The Armor and mechanized Infantry company team is not resourced for a CP by the modified table of organization and equipment. It is generally limited to a tent or one of its organic HQ's vehicles as the CP. It consists of the commanding officer and other personnel and equipment required to support company command and control. The CP is located where the commander determines it is best able to support the mission and execute command and control. Its purpose is to provide communications with higher, lower, adjacent, and supporting units; to assist the commander in planning, coordinating, and issuing company orders; and to support continuous operations by the company. Often the CP is required to provide its own security but is able to locate with subordinate elements on the move or stationary when necessary. (See ATP 6-0.5 for more information on CP operations.)

COMPANY COMMAND POST

A-1. Armor company team options include the first sergeant's armored vehicle or the Bradley fire support vehicle. The first sergeant's vehicle is organic to the team and thus is more likely to be available during the preparation phase. The Bradley fire support vehicle is large enough to serve as the CP, but it may be retained by the CAB and, therefore, would not be available to the company. The mechanized Infantry team may use one of its HQ's IFVs, the first sergeant's armored vehicle, or the Bradley fire support vehicle. Disadvantages in using an IFV are that it may be required for a mounted rehearsal and is required for boresighting.

A-2. Although the company team is not resourced to operate a functional CP, not establishing a CP may have an impact on the company team's day-to-day performance, particularly during sustained operations. The CP is a combat multiplier especially during the planning and preparation phases of an operation. This in turn frees company leaders to focus their attention on more important matters. However, the CP is not designed to act as a battle tracking platform during execution of an operation. Vehicles that comprise the CP revert to their primary purposes once the LD is crossed or the not later than defend time has arrived.

A-3. Normally the CP consists of the radiotelephone operators (RTOs), FIST HQ, and the senior RTO. The XO, first sergeant, signal support NCO, armorer, CBRN NCO, and the leaders of attached or supporting elements may also locate with the CP. When positioning the CP, the commander considers communication requirements, the security needs for the CP, and above all, the location where the commander is best able to fight the company.

A-4. The commander organizes and mans the CP to conduct continuous operations. Techniques the commander considers ensuring continuous operations include the following:

- Cross train personnel within the CP.
- Ensure the XO and first sergeant are aware of critical decisions in the commander's absence.
- Establish a rest plan and ensure compliance.
- Ensure key decision makers get rest.

A-5. CP personnel support the commander by—

- Establishing command and control systems (antennas, radios, tracking mechanisms).
- Assisting in preparation of the company OPORD.
- Providing recommendations or input during planning.
- Receiving and sending required reports and updated information to the CAB and subordinates.

COMMAND POST LOCATIONS WITHIN THE COMPANY TEAM

A-6. The commander establishes a CP to command and control operations. The commander organizes a CP to control the battle and an alternate CP that can assume command of the company if the primary CP is destroyed or unable to communicate. The commander considers security and communications requirements when positioning the primary and alternate CPs on the move and stationary.

A-7. When moving, the commander designates where the CP is positioned in the formation. At times, the commander may move away from the CP, for example, to better control the company's maneuver, in this instance the commander may move with the lead platoon or during the attack locate with the main effort. In these situations, the commander may designate a part of the CP (the FSO) to move with the commander.

A-8. In static positions (AAs, BPs), a stationary CP location may be designated by the commander where field expedient antennas are employed to allow communications to be established with the CAB and subordinate units within the company. The stationary CP provides a designated location whereby messengers and leaders can report to conduct face-to-face interaction. The CP should be in defilade with covered and concealed routes to and from its location. The CP should be off natural lines of drift and key terrain features. It must be well-camouflaged from ground and air observation. Local security is provided by either its relation to platoons, by collocating with the company reserve element, or using its own organic HQ's personnel. When the commander leaves the primary CP, the XO or the first sergeant assumes control of CP operations or when an alternate CP is established and assumes control of CP operations from that location.

RESOURCING THE COMMAND POST

A-9. Perhaps the most critical decision in establishing a company CP is committing resources. The level of dedicated resources, personnel, and equipment to the company CP has a direct correlation to the effectiveness of the fusion between operations and locally developed intelligence.

A-10. Several options are available for manning a company team CP. A basic manning requirement is for two NCOs to serve as NCOICs. One NCO is in charge during the day shift and the other during the night shift. These NCOs must be able to perform their duties with little or no supervision. Several members of the company can meet this manning requirement. They include, but are not limited to:

- Company master gunner.
- XO's gunner.
- Signal support specialist.
- Separate HQ's PSG (if available).

A-11. Members of the HQ section or other attached elements can man other positions in the CP (for example, RTO) on a rotating basis. These members include the crews of HQ tanks or IFVs and the company command group drivers. At a minimum, there should be two RTOs. One RTO supports the day shift and the other the night shift. The RTO assists the NCOIC as needed to accomplish the mission.

A-12. The Soldiers manning the company CP assist the commander by reducing the number of items the commander must personally track and report. This frees the commander to focus on and conduct TLP during planning. Key tasks performed by the Soldiers manning the CP include—

- Record incoming information such as status reports, WARNORD, and fragmentary orders.
- Continuously refine the situation template using the latest intelligence and distribute the updated situation template to all company elements.
- Post current guidance, timelines, and overlays.
- Pass required reports to the CAB and subordinate units.
- Track unit preparations and logistical status.
- Conduct required coordination with adjacent and flank units.
- Facilitate bottom-up refinement of planning and preparation.
- Battle track.

A-13. Attached or operational control units can use the CP as the point of contact. The units can further assist the commander in the TLP by supervising and enforcing the timeline and reproducing overlays and constructing sand tables for company and platoon rehearsals. The company CP is an information management center during the plan and preparation phase of a mission and battle tracking during mission execution. Additional tasks performed by the Soldiers manning the CP include—

- Track and provide situational updates of current missions.
- Alert the command group or subordinate elements.
- Coordinate with higher and subordinate units to receive, send, and track daily and reoccurring information requirements.
- Track friendly unit locations.
- Track times for planned patrols or upcoming combat missions.
- Track current manning status and task organization of unit.
- Track status of key weapons systems, vehicles, and equipment.
- Record and verify any messages needing the attention of the commanding officer, first sergeant, or XO when they are not available.
- Update to the commanding officer to include tracking charts, maps, troop movements, personnel accountability, and other products as specified by the commander.
- Track company significant activities in a staff journal, such as, a DA Form 1594 (*Daily Staff Journal or Duty Officer's Log*), when able.
- Act as a communications retransmitting site to higher HQ when necessary.

This page intentionally left blank.

Appendix B

Planning and Preparation

The company commander is the primary planner that receives the OPORD, WARNORD, and fragmentary order from the CAB and develops the company plan to complete assigned missions. The XO, first sergeant, FSO, and other personnel may assist the company commander. The company commander employs TLP to develop the plan and prepare for the mission.

SECTION I – PLANNING

B-1. Planning is the process by which the company commander translates visualization into a specific COA for preparation and execution, focusing on the expected results. Planning helps the commander create and communicate a common vision and a shared understanding between subordinate leaders and unified action partners. Planning results in an order that synchronizes the action of forces in time, space, and purpose to achieve objectives and accomplish missions. The commander relies on intuitive decision making and direct contact with subordinate leaders to integrate activities when circumstances are not suited for TLP.

ORDERS

B-2. Planning at the company team level can start when the CAB shares information continuously on future missions with subordinate units. Rather than waiting until the CAB commander and staff finish planning, the company commander starts to develop the company's mission as information becomes available (typically through WARNORDs). The commander develops an initial intent, ensuring that the commander's intent reflects the intent and concept of operation of the two higher commanders. The commander identifies tasks most likely to be assigned to the company, then develops an initial mission statement based on the information received. The commander's visualization of the initial plan will require ongoing clarification to ensure a shared understanding among subordinate leaders.

B-3. The company commander cannot finalize the company order until the CAB completes its order. If each successive WARNORD contains enough information, the CAB's final order will confirm what the company commander has already analyzed and put into an initial plan. In other cases, the CAB's order may change or modify the company's tasks enough that additional planning and reconnaissance are required. As the next higher commander's concept of operation continues to mature, planning continues, and the company plan adjusts. Figure B-1 on page B-2 illustrates the parallel sequences of the military decision-making process and the TLP.

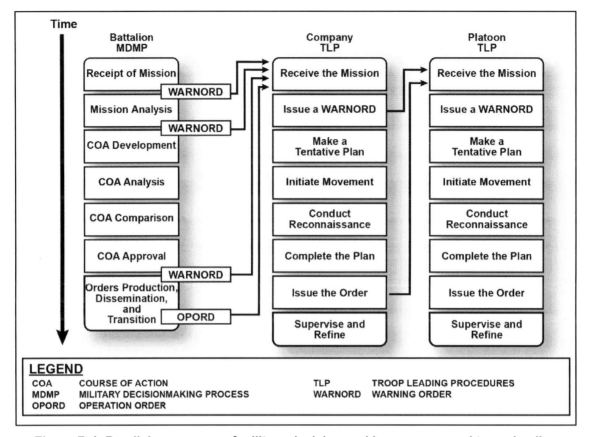

Figure B-1. Parallel sequences of military decision-making process and troop leading procedures

TROOP LEADING PROCEDURES

B-4. *Troop leading procedures* are a dynamic process used by small-unit leaders to analyze a mission, develop a plan, and prepare for an operation (ADP 5-0). TLP extend the military decision-making process to the company level. These procedures enable company-level leaders to maximize available planning time while developing effective plans and preparing the company for a mission. TLP consist of eight steps. TLP are also supported by risk management. The sequencing of the steps to the TLP is not always rigid. The commander modifies the sequence to meet the mission, situation, and available time. Some steps are done concurrently while others may go on continuously throughout the mission. The TLP procedure steps are as follows:

- Step 1. Receive the mission.
- Step 2. Issue a WARNORD.
- Step 3. Make a tentative plan.
- Step 4. Initiate movement.
- Step 5. Conduct reconnaissance.
- Step 6. Complete the plan.
- Step 7. Issue the order.
- Step 8. Supervise and refine.

B-5. TLP begin when the company commander receives the first indication of an upcoming mission and continues throughout the operational process (plan, prepare, execute, and assess). TLP comprise a sequence of actions to help the commander use available time effectively and efficiently to issue orders and execute operations. Normally, the first three steps (receive the mission, issue a WARNORD, and make a tentative plan) of TLP occur in order. The tasks involved in some actions (such as initiate movement, issue the WARNORD, and conduct reconnaissance) may recur several times during the process. The last step, supervise and refine, occurs throughout.

B-6.   A tension exists between executing current missions and planning for future missions. The company commander must balance both. If the company is engaged in a current mission, there is less time for TLP. If in a lull, transition, or an AA, the commander has more time to conduct TLP. In some situations, time constraints or other factors may prevent the commander from performing each step of TLP as thoroughly as possible. For example, during the step, make a tentative plan; the commander often develops only one acceptable COA vice multiple COAs. The commander may develop, compare, and analyze several COAs before arriving at a decision on which one to execute if time permits.

B-7.   The commander and subordinate leaders begin TLP when they receive an initial written or verbal WARNORD or receive a new mission. It is critical to understand that during regular updates to the CAB commander the initial WARNORD may come verbally as part of the commander 's discussion. It benefits the company commander for the CAB to provide verbal WARNORDs as it receives new information so subordinate elements can proactively prepare for the next mission. As each subsequent order arrives, the commander modifies assessments, updates tentative plans, and continues to supervise and assess preparations. In some situations, the commander may not receive or be issued the full sequence of WARNORDs; security considerations or tempo may make it impractical. The commander carefully considers decisions to eliminate WARNORDs. Subordinates always need to have enough information to plan and prepare for their mission. In other cases, TLP are started before receiving a WARNORD based on existing plans and orders (contingency plans or be-prepared missions) and on subordinate leader's understanding of the situation.

B-8.   The commander uses TLP when working alone or with a small group to solve tactical problems. For example, the company commander may use the XO, first sergeant, and FSO to assist during TLP. The type, amount, and timeliness of information passed from the CAB to the company directly impacts the company commander's TLP.

B-9.   Risk management occurs continuously throughout TLP, with varying emphasis on different steps at different times. The supervision (during operations) and evaluation (during and after operations) must feed back into the system (see figure B-2 on page B-4). Through feedback, leaders ensure corrections are made during the current operation and in future operations.

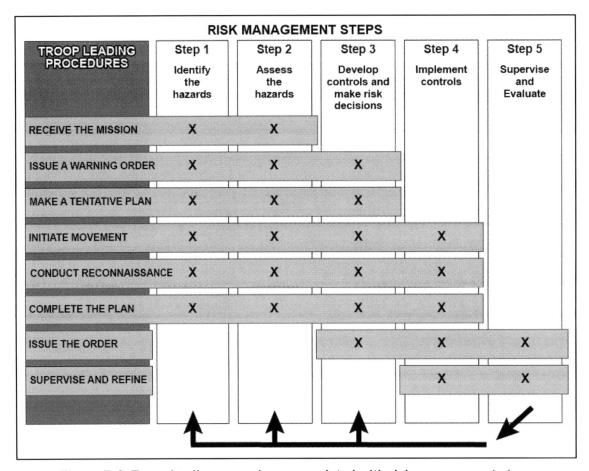

Figure B-2. Troop leading procedures correlated with risk management steps

B-10. The type, amount, and timeliness of risk management information passed from higher to lower levels of command may have a significant effect on the level of detail used by lower unit leaders. The time between receiving the mission from higher HQ and initiating the company WARNORD can significantly affect the time available for a subordinate unit to conduct risk assessments and implement appropriate controls. While CAB- and higher-level HQ have specialized staff sections conducting risk assessments, companies and platoons may have only one or two individuals performing assessments. Higher-level leaders should provide subordinates sufficient time and details to conduct each of the five steps of risk management. Particular attention should be given to Step 4 of risk management (implement controls). Aligning CAB and company SOPs and ensuring regular use may reduce the time needed for planning at each level. A key part of risk assessment is identifying tactical risk associated with the COA, once the scheme of maneuver is prepared. Commanders and the CAB staff act on requests for information as quickly as possible to minimize planning delays at subordinate units. (See ATP 5-19 for a detailed discussion on the analysis of risk.)

> ***Notes.*** DD Form 2977 (*Deliberate Risk Assessment Worksheet*) is the Army's standard form for deliberate risk assessment. (See ATP 5-19, appendix A.) DD Form 2977 captures the information analyzed during the five steps of risk management and TLP.

B-11. TLP are not a hard and fast set of rules. Some actions may be performed in an order different than shown in figure B-3. TLP are a guide that must be applied consistently with the situation and the experience of the commander and subordinate leaders. The following information concerning the TLP assumes that the company will plan in a time-constrained environment. All steps should be done, even if done in abbreviated fashion. As such, the suggested techniques are provided to help the commander quickly develop and issue an order. (See FM 5-0 for more information.)

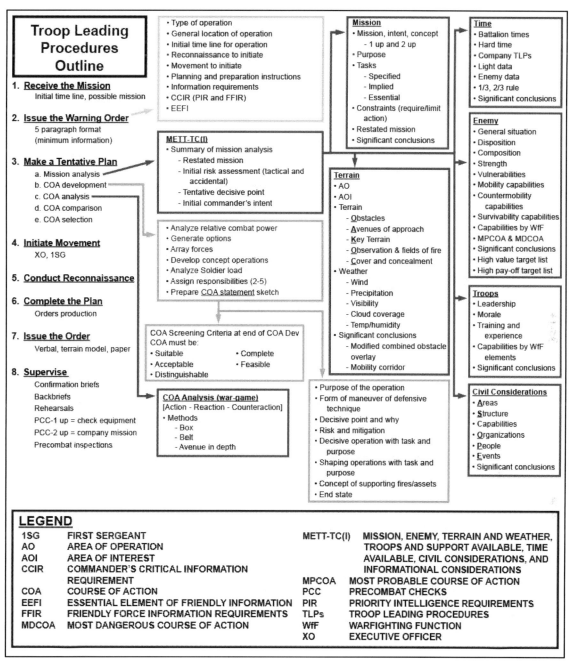

Figure B-3. Troop leading procedures outline

STEP 1, RECEIVE THE MISSION

B-12. In Step 1 of TLP, the commander determines the company's mission and assesses the time available to accomplish the mission. The commander can conduct an initial analysis of the order using METT-TC (I). The commander conducts detailed METT-TC (I) analysis only after the first WARNORD is issued (Step 2). Rarely will the company receive its missions until after the CAB issues the third WARNORD or the OPORD itself. However, during parallel planning, the commander already will have deduced a tentative mission.

B-13. The company can receive the mission in several ways. The company can receive the mission in the form of WARNORDs or, if the CAB chooses to wait for more information, an actual OPORD. Sometimes the CAB chooses not to send WARNORDs, opting instead to wait and send a full OPORD. Worst case, the company receives a new mission due to situational changes occurring during the execution of a prior mission. In addition to receiving (or deducing) the mission during this step, the commander also—

- Conducts a confirmation brief to the CAB commander to verify an understanding of the CAB commander's intent and concept of operation.
- Analyze total time available based off higher HQ's planning and operational timeline.
- Analyze the total time the company team must conduct mission planning and preparation.
- Analyze risk to that mission planning and preparation as the commander attempts to adhere to the one-thirds, two-thirds rule (see the following note).
- Prepares an initial timeline.

Note. The "one-third/two-thirds" technique to give subordinates sufficient time to prepare at their level. One-third of the time available remains set aside for the company commander to prepare and issue an order, while the remaining two-thirds of the time is for subordinate leaders to disseminate the order to their units and prepare for the mission.

B-14. The most important element of the company's WARNORD is the initial timeline for planning. The commander does timeline analysis to determine available time (day and night), identify probable enemy timeline, and plan initial timeline accounting for when to give the company OPORD. The WARNORD may convey other instructions or information that the commander thinks will help subordinate leaders prepare for the upcoming mission.

STEP 2, ISSUE WARNING ORDER

B-15. A *warning order* is a preliminary notice of an order or action that is to follow (JP 5-0). Though less detailed than a complete OPORD—a directive issued by a commander to subordinate commanders for the purpose of effecting the coordinated execution of an operation. A WARNORD aids in parallel planning. After the commander receives the new mission and assesses the time available for planning, preparing, and executing the mission, the commander immediately issues a WARNORD to subordinates. The commander should receive up to three WARNORDs from higher and begin to develop the company WARNORDs from them by filling in the details on the required elements. If the commander does not receive these, the commander needs to figure out nature of pending mission and associated CAB timeline, issue nature of mission, timeline, rehearsal guidance, and so forth. Then, upon receipt of CAB's OPORD, the commander must issue a WARNORD before jumping into writing the OPORD.

B-16. By issuing the initial WARNORD as quickly as possible, the commander enables subordinates to begin their own planning and preparation (parallel planning) while they begin to develop OPORDs. Based off the amount of information given by the higher HQ, this WARNORD can be verbally or in written format and communicated to the company commander's subordinates verbally or in written format. When the commander obtains more information, the commander issues an updated WARNORD, giving subordinates a shared understanding of what the commander knows.

B-17. The commander can issue a WARNORD to subordinates right after receiving the CAB's initial WARNORD. Subordinate leaders include the same elements given in the company's initial WARNORD. If practical, the commander briefs subordinate leaders within the company face-to-face. In the defense, ideally the commander briefs subordinates on the actual ground to defend. Otherwise, the commander uses a terrain model, sketch, or map. (See figure B-4 for an example of a WARNORD format.)

Warning Order #   **to Operations Order #**
Initial Task Organization:
Effective Date/Time:

1. **Situation:**
    General Enemy Overview:
      - Area of Operation (AO)
      - Area of Interest (AOI)
      - Who the Company/Team is fighting
      - Brigade Combat Team Mission
      - Brigade Combat Team Commander Intent
      - Battalion/Task Force Mission
      - Battalion/Task Force Commander Intent

2. **Mission:**
    Upcoming Task and Purpose or Type of Operational/
    General Location:

3. **Execution:**
    Movement Instructions/Movement to Initiate:
      - Our Current Location
      - Our Next Location:
      - Objective Location:
    Reconnaissance Tasks/Reconnaissance to Initiate:
      - Reconnaissance Team:
    Information Requirements:
    Coordinated Instructions:
      - Mission-Oriented Protective Posture (MOPP)
      - Collection Operations Management (COM)
      - Route
      - Zero/Boresight
      - Precombat Checks (PCC)
      - Commander's Critical Information Requirement (CCIR)
      - Priority Intelligence Requirement (PIR)
      - Friendly Force Information Requirement (FFIR)
      - Priorities of Work
      - Priorities of Rehearsals
    Initial Operational/Planning Timeline:
      - Battalion
      - Company/Platoon Planning/Operational
      - Enemy
      - Weather (WX)/Light Data

4. **Sustainment:**
    Planning/Preparation Instructions:
    Combat Trains Command Post (CTCP)
    Unit Maintenance Collection Point (UMCP)
    Logistics Release Point (LRP) Grid
    Ambulance Exchange Point (AXP) Grid
    Casualty Collection Point (CCP) Grid
    Company Trains Grid
    Class of Supply:
      - Class I
      - Class III
      - Class IV
      - Class V
      - Others

5. **Command and Signal:**
    Company Command Post (CP):
      - Primary CP
      - Alternate CP
    Succession of Command
    Battalion Grid
    Tactical Command Post Grid
    Main Command Post Grid

Figure B-4. Warning order format, example

B-18. The commander issues the WARNORD to subordinates immediately after the initial assessment, which includes the—

- Mission or nature of the operation.
- Time and place for issuing the OPORD.
- Task organize units or elements participating in the operation.
- Reconnaissance to initiate.
- Security missions to initiate.
- Movement to initiate.
- Information requirements.
- CCIR (PIR and friendly force information requirement).
- Essential element of friendly information.
- Planning and preparation instructions.
- Specific tasks not addressed by unit SOPs.
- Timeline for the operation.

B-19. During hasty operations, the intelligence process must respond rapidly to the CCIRs. PIRs are information the commander needs to know about the terrain or enemy to make a critical decision. PIRs are best expressed in a question not answered by a yes or no response. The commander uses WARNORDs to modify PIRs based on current mission parameters. Friendly force information requirements will include information the commander needs to know about the company or about adjacent units to make critical decisions. Although essential elements of friendly information are not part of the CCIR, they still become priorities when the commander states them. Essential elements of friendly information are the critical aspects of a friendly operation, if known by the enemy, that subsequently would compromise or lead to failure of the operation. Consequently, this information must be protected from identification by the enemy.

> *Note.* The commander issues additional WARNORDs throughout the TLP as necessary when new information is available. A technique is to use a WARNORD format like the one in example figure B-4 on page B-7 to fill in gaps and refine the plan with new information. Once the commander has delivered the WARNORD, subordinate leaders should initiate preparation to issue their WARNORDs.

STEP 3, MAKE A TENTATIVE PLAN

B-20. In a time-constrained environment, the commander typically develops only one COA. However, as time permits, the commander can develop additional COAs for comparison purposes. The commander begins Step 3 after the issuant of the company WARNORD, and generally after receiving the CAB's third WARNORD, or until the commander has enough information to proceed. The commander does not wait for a complete OPORD before starting to develop a tentative plan. Once subordinate leaders receive the company WARNORD they begin to develop their tentative plan and adjust as more information becomes available.

Mission Analysis

B-21. The commander conducts mission analysis to develop *situational understanding*—the product of applying analysis and judgment to relevant information to determine the relationship among the operational and mission variables (ADP 6-0) and to confirm what the company must do to accomplish the mission. At lower levels, the company commander and subordinate leaders conduct mission analysis by evaluating the mission variables of METT-TC (I). Mission analysis has no time standard. The commander takes as much time as needed within the constraints of the mission and while still adhering to the one-third, two-thirds rule.

B-22. Within mission analysis the commander makes significant deductions about the enemy, terrain, and own forces affecting the mission. These significant deductions drive the planning process, preparation activities, and the execution of the mission. During the planning process the commander conveys to subordinates the importance of these deductions, and the effects they will have on the unit's mission.

B-23. Mission analysis answers four questions that become inputs into developing a COA. These questions are—

- What is the company's mission?
- What is the current situation?
- How does the company accomplish the mission?
- What are the risks?

B-24. Analyzing the mission variables of METT-TC (I) is a continuous process. The commander constantly receives information, from the time planning begins through execution. During execution analysis continues, enabling the commander to issue a well-developed fragmentary order—an abbreviated OPORD issued as needed to change or modify an order. The commander assesses new information to determine the effect on the mission and future plans. If determined to be an effect on the mission, the commander must decide how to adjust the plan to meet the new situation. The commander need not analyze METT-TC (I) in a particular order. How and when to do so depends on when the information is received as well as on the experience and preferences of the commander. One technique is to parallel the TLP based on the products received from higher.

B-25. During Step 3, the commander and subordinate leaders begin their mission analysis. During mission analysis, the commander—

- Restates the mission.
- Conducts an initial risk assessment.
- Identifies a tentative decisive point.
- Develops initial commander's intent.

Conduct Initial Risk Assessment

B-26. Risk assessment is the identification and assessment of hazards allowing the commander to implement measures to control hazards (risk management, fratricide avoidance, and effects of continuous operations). The commander's risk assessment to protect the force aids in mission accomplishment. The commander considers tactical risk and accident risk during planning.

B-27. Tactical risk is associated with hazards existing due to the enemy's presence. The consequences of tactical risk take two major forms, which are described in the following bullets:

- Enemy action where the commander has accepted risk such as an enemy attack where the friendly commander has chosen to conduct an economy of force.
- Lost opportunity, such as movement across terrain that severely restricts speed to traverse the terrain. This then would restrict the unit's ability to mass the effects of combat power.

B-28. Accident risk includes all operational risk other than tactical risk and can include hazards concerning friendly personnel, equipment readiness, and the environment. Fratricide is an example of an accident risk.

B-29. The commander identifies risks based on the results of mission analysis. Once identified, risk must be reduced through controls. For example, fratricide is a hazard categorized as an accident risk; surface danger zones and RED are used to identify the controls, such as TRPs and phase lines, to reduce this accidental risk. When the commander decides what risks to accept, the commander must decide in a COA how to reduce risk to an acceptable level. (See ATP 5-19 for information on making informed decisions to reduce or offset risk.)

Identify Tentative Decisive Point

B-30. Identifying a tentative decisive point and verifying it during COA development is the most important aspect of the TLP. The commander visualizes a valid decisive point to determine how to achieve success and accomplish the mission's purpose. The commander develops the entire COA from the decisive point. Without determining a valid decisive point, the commander cannot begin to develop an appropriate COA. The commander, based on the initial analysis of METT-TC (I), SA, visualization, and insight into how such factors can affect the unit's mission, visualizes where, when, and how the company's ability to generate combat power can overwhelm the enemy's abilities to generate combat power. The decisive point might orient on terrain, enemy, time, or a combination of these. The decisive point might be where, how, or from where the company will combine the effects of combat power against the enemy. The decisive point might be the event or action (with respect to terrain, enemy, or time, and generation of combat power) that will ultimately and irreversibly lead to the company achieving its purpose.

B-31. The decisive point does not simply restate the unit's essential task or purpose; it defines how, where, or when the unit will accomplish its purpose. The company's main effort always focuses on the decisive point and always ensures the accomplishment of the company's purpose. Designating a decisive point is critical to the commander's visualization of how to use combat power to achieve the company's purpose, how to task organize the company and how shaping operations will support the main effort, and how the main effort will accomplish the company's purpose. This tentative decisive point forms the basis for planning and COA development; it also forms the basis of communicating the COA to subordinates. The commander clearly explains what the decisive point is to subordinate leaders and why it is decisive; this objective, in conjunction with their commander's intent, facilitates subordinate initiative. A valid decisive point enables the commander to clearly and logically link how the application of combat power with respect to terrain, enemy, and time allows the company to accomplish its purpose. If the commander determines a tentative decisive point is not valid during COA development or analysis, the commander determines another decisive point and restarts COA development.

Develop Initial Commander's Intent

B-32. The *commander's intent* is a clear and concise expression of the purpose of the operation and the desired objectives and military end state (JP 3-0). The commander's intent provides the link between mission and concept of operation by stating key tasks or conditions existing to achieve the stated purpose of the operation. The intent and mission statement forms the basis for subordinates to exercise disciplined initiative and judgment in the face of new opportunities, or whenever the concept of operation ceases to apply. The commander's intent continuously evolves throughout the planning and preparation for the operation as the commander becomes more attuned to what the company must do to accomplish the mission.

B-33. The key tasks and conditions specified in the commander's intent are not tied to a specific COA. Essential tasks are not limited to tactical tasks. The operation's tempo, duration, and effect on the enemy, and terrain being controlled are examples of essential tasks or conditions.

B-34. The commander's intent does not include the method by which the force will get from its current state to the end state. The method is the concept of operation. Nor does the intent contain acceptable risk. Risk is addressed in the COA. The final commander's intent included in the OPORD is based on the sum of all the analysis conducted during the TLP. This final intent can be provided after the commander understands the end state of the mission.

Analysis of the Mission

B-35. A mission is task and purpose clearly indicating the action to be taken and reason for the action. In common usage, especially when applied to the company and below, a mission is a duty or task assigned to an individual or unit. The commander analyzes the CAB's WARNORD, OPORD, and mission to determine how the company contributes to the CAB's mission.

B-36. The mission is always the first factor the commander considers and the most basic question: What has the company been told to do and why?

B-37. The commander must understand the mission, intent, and concept of operation one and two levels higher. This understanding makes it possible to exercise disciplined initiative. The commander captures understanding of what the company is to accomplish in the revised mission statement. The commander uses five steps to analyze the company's assigned mission fully as directed from—

- Higher HQs' (one and two levels up) mission, commander's intent, and concept of operation.
- Company's purpose.
- Constraints.
- Specified, implied, and essential tasks.
- Restated mission.

Higher Headquarters' (One and Two Levels Up) Mission, Commander's Intent, and Concept of Operation

B-38. The commander understands the higher HQs', one and two levels up, mission, commander's intent, and concepts of operation. The commander identifies the higher HQ's tasks and purposes, and how they contribute to the fight. This understanding is required for all adjacent units to the company.

Company's Purpose

B-39. The commander identifies the company's purpose from the CAB's OPORD. The company's purpose generally matches or achieves the purpose of the CAB. Similarly, the purpose of shaping operations relates directly to those of the main effort. The purpose of sustaining operations relates directly to those of the main effort and shaping operations. The commander ensures the company's purpose relates directly to the CAB's purpose.

Constraints

B-40. A *constraint* is a restriction placed on the command by a higher command. A constraint dictates an action or inaction, thus restricting the freedom of action of a subordinate commander (FM 5-0). The commander determines all constraints the CAB's OPORD places on the company's ability to execute the mission. Annexes to the order may also include constraints. The operation overlay, for example, may contain an RFL or a no-fire area. Constraints may also be issued verbally, in WARNORDs, or in policy memoranda. Constraints may also be based on resource limitations within the command, such as organic fuel transport capacity or physical characteristics of the OE.

Specified Tasks, Implied Tasks, and Essential Tasks

B-41. A *task* is a clearly defined action or activity specifically assigned to an individual or organization, or derived during mission analysis, that must be done as it is imposed by an appropriate authority (JP 1, Vol 1). The commander must identify and understand tasks required to accomplish a given mission. The three types of tasks (specified, implied, and essential) are discussed in the following three paragraphs.

B-42. A *specified task* is a task specifically assigned to a unit by its higher headquarters (FM 5-0)—are found throughout the OPORD. Specified tasks also may be found in annexes and overlays, for example: seize Objective Cow; reconnoiter Route Red; assist the forward passage of First Platoon, B Company; send two Soldiers to assist in the loading of ammunition.

B-43. An *implied task* is a task that must be performed to accomplish a specified task or mission but is not stated in the higher headquarters' order (FM 5-0). Implied tasks derive from a detailed analysis of the CAB's order, from the enemy situation and COA, from the terrain, and from knowledge of doctrine and history. Analyzing the company's current location in relation to future AO as well as the doctrinal requirements for each specified task might reveal the implied tasks. Only those requiring resources should be used. For example, if the specified task is seize Objective Cow and new intelligence has Objective Cow surrounded by reinforcing obstacles, this intelligence would drive the implied task of breach reinforcing obstacles in the vicinity of Objective Cow.

B-44. An *essential task* is a specified or implied task that must be executed to accomplish the mission (FM 5-0). An essential task, along with the company's purpose, is usually assigned by the CAB's OPORD in the concept of operation or tasks to subordinate units. For offensive and defensive operations, since the purpose is the same nested concept, the essential task accomplishes the CAB's purpose. For shaping operations, it accomplishes the assigned purpose, which shapes the main effort. For sustaining operations, it accomplishes the assigned purpose, which enables the shaping operation and main effort (again, nested concept).

Restated Mission

B-45. The commander concludes mission analysis by restating the mission. A *mission statement* is a short sentence or paragraph that describes the organization's essential task(s), purpose, and action containing the elements of who, what, when, where, and why (JP 5-0). The five elements of a mission statement answer these questions, commonly referred to as the five Ws:
- Who will execute the operation (unit or organization)?
- What is the unit's essential task (tactical mission task)?
- When will the operation begin (by time or event) or what is the duration of the operation?
- Where will the operation occur (AO, objective, grid coordinates)?
- Why will the force conduct the operations (for what purpose)?

Analysis of Terrain and Weather

B-46. Terrain and weather are key aspects to mission analysis. When analyzing terrain, the commander considers man-made features and effects on natural terrain features and climate. The commander also considers the effects of man-made and natural terrain in conjunction with the weather on friendly and enemy operations. In general, terrain and weather do not favor one side over the other unless one is better prepared to operate in the environment or is more familiar with it. The terrain, however, may favor defending or attacking. Analysis of terrain answers the question: What is the terrain's effect on the operation? The commander analyzes terrain using the five military aspects of terrain.

B-47. From the modified combined obstacle overlay developed by CAB, the commander already understands the general nature of the ground and effects of weather. However, the commander must conduct a detailed analysis to determine how terrain and weather uniquely affects the company's mission and the enemy. The commander must go beyond merely passing along the modified combined obstacle overlay to subordinate leaders and making general observations of the terrain such as, this is high ground, or this is a stream. The commander must determine how the terrain and weather will affect the enemy and the units. Additionally, the commander applies these conclusions when developing a COA for enemy forces and the company.

B-48. At company level and below, the commander and subordinate leaders develop a graphic terrain analysis overlay. With the reduced time to conduct that same level of analysis, and the lack of expertise and capability to produce the same detail as a modified combined obstacle overlay, the company commander builds a graphical terrain analysis overlay to show the critical military aspects of terrain. This allows them to brief the five military aspects of terrain (OAKOC). Not only does it facilitate planning, but it also aids in briefing subordinates.

B-49. For the commander to have a starting point for the company's terrain analysis, the commander must first define the OE. The commander must understand the company's AO and areas of interest, which are—

- AO. The CAB commander use boundaries to define a company's AO. Assigning an AO to companies lets subordinate commanders use their initiative and supports decentralized execution.
- Area of interest. An area of interest is a geographical area, usually larger than the commander's AO. The area of interest includes threat forces or other elements characterizing the OE that can greatly influencing the accomplishment of the mission.

B-50. Limited planning time forces the commander to prioritize portions of terrain analysis. For example, in the conduct of an attack, the commander might prioritize the areas immediately around the objective for analysis, followed the lead platoon's axis of advance leading to the objective. Given more time, the commander might analyze the remainder of the company's AO and area of interest.

B-51. The commander prepares a graphical depiction of terrain (graphical terrain analysis overlay) to help explain findings about the effects of terrain and weather on the mission. The graphic depiction of terrain can be a photograph, overlay for a map sheet, or a terrain model. In it, the commander shows terrain mobility classifications, key terrain, intervisibility lines, known obstacles, avenues of approach, and mobility corridors.

Five Military Aspects of Terrain

B-52. The commander analyzes terrain using the five military aspects of terrain (OAKOC). (See ATP 2-01.3 and ATP 3-34.80 for information on analyzing the military aspects of terrain.) Military aspects of terrain are used to analyze the ground. The sequence can vary. The leader determines the effects of each aspect of terrain on friendly and enemy forces. These effects translate directly into conclusions applying to friendly or enemy COA. Even if time is tight, the commander should allocate as much time as possible to factor, starting at the objective area, and analyzing other aspects of key terrain. Analyzing the five military aspects of terrain assists the commander in drawing conclusions about how the enemy and friendly forces are affected by that terrain. These conclusions include (but are not limited to):

- Templating of enemy forces and essential weapon systems.
- Potential positioning of own assets.
- Understanding of time and space in relationship to movement and sequencing of events, leading to thorough contingency plans.
- Echeloning and identifying of enemy observation and indirect fires.
- Selecting of movement techniques and formations, to include when to transition to tactical maneuver.

Obstacles

B-53. The commander identifies existing (inherent to terrain and either natural or man-made) and reinforcing (tactical or protective) obstacles that limit mobility in an AO. Reinforcing obstacles are constructed, emplaced, or detonated by military force as follows:

- Existing obstacles, natural include rivers; forests; mountains; ravines; gaps and ditches more than three meters wide; tree stumps and large rocks more than 18-inches high; forests with trees 8 inches or more in diameter, with less than 4 meters between trees.
- Existing obstacles, man-made include towns, canals, railroad embankments, buildings, power lines, and telephone lines.
- Reinforcing obstacles, tactical. Tactical (reinforcing) obstacles inhibit the ability of the opposing force to move, mass, and reinforce. Examples include minefields (conventional and situational), AT ditches, and wire obstacles.
- Reinforcing obstacles, protective (reinforcing) obstacles offer close-in protection and are important to survivability.
- Offensive considerations when analyzing obstacles and restricted terrain:
  - How is the enemy using obstacles and restricted terrain features?
  - What is the composition of the enemy's reinforcing obstacles?
  - How will obstacles and terrain affect the movement or maneuver of the unit?
  - If necessary, how can I avoid such features?
  - How do I detect and, if desired, bypass the obstacles?
  - Where has the enemy positioned weapons to cover the obstacles, and what type of weapons are they using?
  - If I must support a breach, where is the expected breach area and where will the enemy be overwatching the obstacle?
  - How will the terrain affect the employment of mortars, medium machine guns, and Javelin missiles?
- Defensive considerations when analyzing obstacles and restricted terrain:
  - Where does the enemy want to go? Where can I kill the enemy? How do I get the enemy to go there?
  - How will existing obstacles and restricted terrain affect the enemy?
  - How can I use these features to force the enemy into its EA, deny them an avenue, or disrupt their movement?
  - How will the terrain affect the employment of mortars, medium machine guns, and Javelin missiles?
- Categories of terrain:
  - Unrestricted. Terrain free of restrictions to movement, so no actions are needed to enhance mobility. For armored forces, unrestricted terrain typically is flat or moderately sloped, with scattered or widely spaced obstacles such as trees or rocks. This terrain generally allows wide maneuver and offers unlimited travel over well-developed road networks. It allows the platoon and squads to move with little hindrance.
  - Restricted. Terrain hindering movement somewhat. Little effort is needed to enhance mobility, but units might have to zigzag or make frequent detours. They could have a hard time maintaining optimum speed, moving in some types of combat formations, or transitioning from one formation to another. For armored forces, restricted terrain typically means moderate to steep slopes or moderate to dense spacing of obstacles such as trees, rocks, or buildings. Swamps and rugged ground are two examples of restricted terrain for Infantry forces. Poorly developed road systems may hamper logistical or rear area movement.
  - Severely restricted. Terrain that severely hinders or slows movement in combat formations unless some effort is made to enhance mobility. Engineer forces might be needed to improve mobility or platoon and squads might have to deviate from doctrinal tactics. For example, they might have to move in columns rather than in lines. Or, they might have to move much more slowly than they would like. For armored forces, steep slopes, densely spaced obstacles, and absence of a developed road system characterize severely restricted terrain.

> *Note.* Terrain categorization is especially important to armored forces and reinforces the need to conduct additional analysis at the company level despite being provided a modified combined obstacle overlay from the CAB.

Avenues of Approach

B-54. An avenue of approach is an air or ground route leading to an objective (or to key terrain in its path) that an attacking force can use. Avenues of approach are classified by type (mounted, dismounted, air, or subterranean), formation, and speed of the largest unit traveling on it.

B-55. The commander groups mutually supporting mobility corridors to form an avenue of approach. If the commander has no mutually supporting mobility corridors, then a single mobility corridor might become an avenue of approach. Avenues of approach are classified the same as mobility corridors. After identifying these avenues, the commander evaluates each and determines its importance.

B-56. The commander can include the following offensive considerations in evaluation of avenues of approach:
- How can I use each avenue of approach to support the company's movement and maneuver?
- How will each avenue support movement techniques, formations and, once the company makes enemy contact, maneuver?
- Will variations in trafficability force changes in formations or movement techniques, or require clearance of restricted terrain?
- What are the advantages and disadvantages of each avenue?
- What are the enemy's likely counterattack routes?
- What lateral routes could we use to shift to other axes, and which could the enemy use to threaten the company's flanks?
- How will each avenue of approach affect the rate of movement of each type of force?

B-57. The commander can include the following defensive considerations in evaluation of avenues of approach:
- What are all likely enemy avenues into the company's AO?
- How can the enemy use each avenue of approach?
- What lateral routes could the enemy use to threaten the company's flanks?
- What avenues would support a friendly counterattack or repositioning of forces?

Key Terrain

B-58. Key terrain is locations or areas whose seizure, retention, or control gives a marked advantage to either combatant. It is a conclusion, usually arrived at after enemy analysis and COA development, rather than an observation.

B-59. A prominent hilltop overlooking an avenue of approach might or might not be key terrain. Even if it offers clear observation and fields of fire, it offers nothing if the enemy can easily bypass it, or if the selected COA involves maneuver on a different avenue of approach. However, if it offers cover and concealment, observation, and good fields of fire on multiple avenues of approach, or on the only avenue of approach, then it offers a definite advantage to whoever controls it.

B-60. The commander must assess what terrain is essential to mission accomplishment. Another example of essential terrain for a platoon and squad in the attack is high ground overlooking the enemy's reverse-slope defense. Controlling this area could prove critical in establishing an SBF position to protect a breach force.

B-61. Leaders also must determine if terrain is decisive. Decisive terrain is key terrain which seizure, retention, or control is necessary for mission accomplishment. Some situations have no decisive terrain. If the commander identifies terrain as decisive, this means seizing or retaining it is necessary to accomplish the mission and should be achieved as part of the friendly COA.

B-62. There are tactical considerations in analyzing key terrain. Terrain is important for friendly observation, for commanding and controlling and for calling for fire? What terrain is important to the enemy and why?

B-63. Is it important to the company? What terrain has higher HQ named as key? Is this terrain also important to the enemy? Is the enemy controlling this key terrain? How do I gain or maintain control of key terrain? What terrain is essential for communications nodes dictating the employment of digital communications equipment?

Observation and Fields of Fire

B-64. The commander identifies locations along each avenue of approach providing clear observation and fields of fire for the attacker and defender. The commander analyzes the area surrounding key terrain, objectives, EA, and obstacles. The commander locates intervisibility lines (ridges or horizons which can hide equipment or personnel from observation). The commander assesses the ability of the attacking force to overwatch or support movement (with direct fire). Intervisibility line analysis enables the leader to visualize the profile view of terrain when only a topographic product (map) is provided.

B-65. In analyzing fields of fire, the commander considers the friendly and enemy potential to cover avenues of approach and key terrain with direct fires. The commander identifies positions where artillery observers can call for indirect fire. The observer must observe the impact and effects of indirect fires. The observer analyzes if vegetation will affect the employment or trajectory of the Javelin or 60-mm mortars. Vegetation can do this by masking the target or by reducing overhead clearance. When possible, the observer conducts a ground reconnaissance from enemy and friendly perspectives. The observer might do it personally, by map, or with the subordinate units, or the observer can use the assets and information provided by the CAB scout platoon. This reconnaissance helps the commander to see the ground objectively and to see how it will affect both forces.

B-66. Offensive considerations in analyzing observation and fields of fire include the following:
- Where do enemy observers and weapon systems have clear observation and fields of fire available on or near the objective?
- Where can the enemy concentrate fires?
- Where will the enemy be unable to concentrate fires?
- Where is the enemy vulnerable?
- Where can the company support the movement of a friendly force with mortar, medium machine gun, or Javelin?
- Where can friendly forces conduct SBF or assault by fire?
- Where are the natural target registration points?
- Where does the commander position indirect fire observers?

B-67. Defensive considerations in analyzing observation and fields of fire:
- What locations have clear observation and fields of fire along enemy avenues of approach?
- Where will the enemy establish firing lines or SBF positions?
- Where will the company be unable to mass fires?
- Where is the dead space in company's AO? Where is the company vulnerable?
- Where are the natural target registration points?
- Where can the commander destroy the enemy? Can the company observe and fire on enemy locations with at least two-thirds of the company's combat power?
- How obvious are these positions to the enemy?
- Where do the commander position indirect fire observers?

Cover and Concealment

B-68. Commanders look at the terrain, foliage, structures, and other features along avenues of approach (and on objectives or key terrain) to identify sites offering cover (protection from the effects of direct and indirect fire) and concealment (protection from observation). In the defense, weapon positions must be lethal to the enemy and survivable to the Soldier. Cover and concealment is just as vital as clear fields of fire. Cover and concealment can be either part of the environment or something brought in by the unit to create the desired effect. Both offensive and defensive considerations must be made:

- Offensive considerations include—
  - What axes afford clear fields of fire and cover and concealment?
  - Which terrain provides bounding elements with cover and concealment while increasing lethality?
- Defensive considerations include—
  - What locations afford cover and concealment as well as good observation and fields of fire?
  - How can friendly and enemy forces use the available cover and concealment?

Conclusions from Terrain Analysis

B-69. Terrain analysis should produce several specific conclusions as listed in the following bullets:

- Potential locations for battle, SBF, and assault by fire positions.
- Potential locations that support EAs and ambush sites.
- Immediate and intermediate objectives.
- Potential asset locations such as enemy CPs or ammunition caches.
- Potential AAs for friendly or threat forces.
- Potential OPs.
- Likely location for artillery firing positions.
- Likely locations for air defense artillery system positions.
- Locations that enable reconnaissance, surveillance, and target-acquisition positions.
- Locations for forward area arming and refueling points.
- Suitable landing and drop zones.
- Potential breach locations.
- Optimized infiltration lanes.

Five Military Aspects of Weather

B-70. The five military aspects of weather are visibility, winds, precipitation, cloud cover, and temperature and humidity. Consideration of the weather's effects is an essential part of the commander's mission analysis. The commander goes past observing to application. The commander determines how the weather will affect the visibility, mobility, and survivability of the company and that of the enemy. The commander applies the results to the friendly and enemy COA during development. The subordinate leaders within the company review their commander's conclusions and identify their own.

Visibility

B-71. The commander identifies critical conclusions about visibility factors such as light data, fog, and smog; and about battlefield obscurants such as smoke and dust. The commander considers light data and identifies critical conclusions about begin morning nautical twilight, sunrise, sunset, end evening nautical twilight, moonrise, moonset, and percentage of illumination. Some additional visibility considerations include:

- Will the sun rise behind the attacker or in the attacker's eyes? Will the attack be in the direction of the sunrise?
- How can the commander take advantage of the limited illumination?
- How will this affect friendly and enemy target acquisition?
- Will the current weather favor the use of obscurants during breaching?
- When are night vision devices effective?

Winds

B-72. Winds of sufficient speed can reduce the combat effectiveness of a force downwind as the result of blowing dust, obscurants, sand, or precipitation. The upwind force usually has better visibility. CBRN operations usually favor the upwind force. Windblown sand, dust, rain, or snow can reduce the effectiveness of radar and other communications systems. Strong winds also can hamper the efficiency of directional antenna systems by inducing antenna wobble. Strong winds and wind turbulence limit Airborne, air assault, and aviation operations.

B-73. Evaluation of weather in support of operations requires information on surface winds at the surface as well as at varying altitudes. Near the ground, high winds increase turbulence and may inhibit maneuver. At higher altitudes, it can increase or reduce fuel consumption. Wind always is described as "from…to" as in winds are from the east moving to the west. The commander must answer these questions:

- Will wind speed cause obscurants to dissipate quickly?
- Will wind speed and direction favor enemy use of obscurants?
- Will wind speed and direction affect the employment of available mortars?
- How will the downwind spread of CBRN contamination impact operations?
- Will the wind increase weathering and mitigate the hazard?

Precipitation

B-74. Precipitation affects soil trafficability, visibility, and functioning of many electro-optical systems. Heavy precipitation can reduce the quality of supplies in storage. Heavy snow cover can reduce the efficiency of many communications systems as well as degrade the effects of many munitions and air operations. The commander identifies critical factors such as type, amount, and duration of precipitation. Some precipitation questions to answer include:

- How will precipitation (or lack of it) affect the mobility of the unit or of enemy forces?
- How can precipitation (or lack of it) add to the unit achieving surprise?
- How will precipitation affect CBRN contamination?

Cloud Cover

B-75. Cloud cover affects ground operations by limiting illumination and solar heating of targets. Heavy cloud cover can degrade many target acquisition systems, IR guided munitions, and general aviation operations. Heavy cloud cover often canalizes aircraft within air avenues of approach and on the final approach to the target. Partial cloud cover can cause glare, a condition attacking aircraft might use to conceal their approach to the target. Some types of clouds reduce the effectiveness of radar systems. The commander identifies critical factors about cloud cover, including limits on illumination and solar heating of targets. Some cloud cover questions include the following:

- How will cloud cover affect unit operations at night? How will it affect the enemy?
- How will cloud cover affect the target acquisition of the command launch unit?
- How will cloud cover affect Army aviation (attack reconnaissance and lift) and Air Force CAS?

Temperature and Humidity

B-76. Extremes of temperature and humidity reduce personnel and equipment capabilities and may require the use of special shelter or equipment. Air density decreases as temperature and humidity increase. This can require reduced aircraft payloads. Temperature crossovers, which occur when target and background temperatures are nearly equal, degrade thermal target acquisition systems. The length of crossover time depends on air temperature, soil and vegetation types, amount of cloud cover, and other factors. The commander identifies critical factors about temperature, including high and low temperatures, IR crossover times, and effects of obscurants and CBRN. Some temperature considerations include:

- How will temperature and humidity affect the unit's rate of march?
- How will temperature and humidity affect the Soldiers and equipment?
- Will temperatures and humidity favor the use of chemical and biological threat capabilities?

Analysis of Enemy

B-77. The commander's analysis of assumptions is made from the CAB regarding the enemy and the enemy's doctrine, compositions, dispositions, strengths, capabilities, vulnerabilities, probable COA, and recent activities. The commander is aware the line between enemy combatants and civilian noncombatants is sometimes unclear. This requires the commander to understand the laws of war, the ROE, and the local situation.

B-78. Analyzing the enemy answers the question, what is the enemy doing and why? The commander answers the following:

- What is the composition and strength of the enemy?
- What are the capabilities of their weapons? Other systems?
- What is the location of current and probable enemy positions?
- What is the enemy's most probable COA? (Defend, reinforce, attack, withdraw, or delay.)

Assumptions

B-79. The commander must understand assumptions the CAB's S-2 uses to portray the enemy's COA. Furthermore, the commander's own assumptions about the enemy must be consistent with those of the higher commander. The commander must continually improve situational understanding of the enemy and update enemy templates as new information or trends become available. Deviations or significant conclusions reached during enemy analysis could positively or negatively affect the CAB and company plans and should be shared immediately between the CAB commander and staff and the commander and subordinate leaders of the company.

B-80. In analyzing the enemy, the commander must understand the IPB. Though the company commander usually does not prepare IPB products for subordinates, the commander utilizes the IPB products from the CAB to ensure subordinates have a shared understanding of the current situation.

Doctrinal Analysis (How the Enemy Will Fight)

B-81. The commander must know more than just the enemy's number and types of vehicles, troops, and weapons. The commander must understand when, where, and how the enemy prefers or tends to use assets. A threat template is a visual illustration of how the enemy force might look and act without the effects of weather and terrain. The commander looks at specific enemy actions during a given operation and uses the appropriate threat template to gain insights into how the enemy may fight. Likewise, the commander must understand enemy doctrinal objectives. In doctrinal terms, the commander asks, "Is the enemy oriented on the terrain, example, a reconnaissance force, their own force (assault force, terrorists, or insurgent forces), civilian forces or critical infrastructure (terrorist or insurgent forces, sabotage), or other supporting or adjacent friendly forces (as in a disruption zone)? What effect will this have on the way the enemy fights?"

B-82. In such a situation, the commander must rely on information provided by CAB or higher echelon reconnaissance and surveillance assets and, most importantly, the higher HQ's pattern analysis and deductions about the enemy in its AO. The commander may also make logical assumptions about the enemy, human nature, and the local culture.

Disposition

B-83. The commander determines how the enemy is (or might be) arrayed using information from the CAB. From this information the commander determines the echelon from where the enemy force originated. The commander determines the disposition of the next two higher enemy elements. From this analysis, the commander might be able to determine patterns in the enemy's employment or troops and equipment.

Composition

B-84. The commander's analysis must determine the types of vehicles, troops, and equipment the enemy could use against the company. The commander must be familiar with the basic characteristics of the enemy units and platforms identified.

Strength

B-85. The commander identifies the enemy's strength by unit. The commander obtains this information by translating percentages given from the CAB to the actual numbers in each enemy element or from information provided by the common operational picture.

Capabilities

B-86. Based on the CAB S-2's assessment and the enemy's doctrine and current location, the commander must determine the enemy's capabilities. This includes studying the maximum effective range for each weapon system, the doctrinal rates of march, and timelines associated with the performance of certain tasks. One technique is to use the warfighting functions as a checklist to address every significant element the enemy brings to the fight.

B-87. The commander determines the capabilities of the next higher enemy element. These capabilities should include reasonable assets the next higher element, or other higher enemy HQ, may provide. This includes the employment of enemy reserves, CBRN weapons, artillery or mortar locations and ranges, reconnaissance and surveillance, and security operations.

Recent Activities

B-88. Gaining complete understanding of the enemy's intentions can be difficult when the enemy's situation templates, composition, and disposition are unclear. The enemy's recent activities must be understood because they can provide insight into future activities and intentions. When time permits, the commander conducts a pattern analysis of the enemy's actions to predict future actions. In the OE, this might be the most important analysis the commander conducts and is likely to yield the most useful information to the commander.

Enemy Situation Template

B-89. The commander weighs the result of the analysis of terrain and weather against the CAB's situation template to identify how the enemy may potentially fight. The refined product is an enemy situation template, a graphic showing how the commander believes the enemy will fight under specific conditions. The situation template portrays one echelon lower than developed by the CAB's S-2. For example, if a CAB's situation template identifies a platoon-size enemy element on the company's objective and squad-size enemy elements on the platoon's objective, the commander, using knowledge of the enemy's doctrine and terrain, develops a situation template positioning squad-size BPs, crew-served weapons positions, key enablers, or defensive trenches.

B-90. The commander includes in the situation template the likely sectors of fire of the enemy weapons and tactical and protective obstacles, either identified or merely template, which support defensive operations. Table B-1 on page B-20 shows recommended situation template items. (See ATP 2-01.3 for more information.)

Table B-1. Recommended enemy situation template items

Defense	Offense
Primary, alternate, subsequent positions.	Attack formations.
Engagement area(s).	Axes of advance.
Individual vehicles.	Firing lines.
Crew-served weapons.	Objectives.
Tactical and protective obstacles.	Reserve force commitment.
Trenches.	Planned indirect-fire targets.
Planned indirect-fire targets.	Situational obstacles.
Observation posts.	Reconnaissance objectives.
Command and control positions.	Reconnaissance force routes.
Final protective fires and final protective line.	Phase lines.
Locations of reserves.	Planned point of penetration.
Routes for reserve commitment.	
Travel time for reserve commitment.	
Battle positions, strong point, area of operation.	
Sectors of fire.	

B-91. The commander avoids developing a situation template independently of the CAB commander's guidance and S-2's products. The template reflects the results of reconnaissance and surveillance and shared understanding. Differences between the situation templates are resolved before the commander can continue analyzing the enemy. Given the scale with which the commander often develops the situation template, on a 1:50,000 map, the situation template is transferred to a graphic depiction of terrain for briefing purposes, as the situation allows. This is not for analysis but use as a briefing tool to show subordinates the details of the anticipated enemy COA and create a shared visualization and understanding of how the enemy will fight. Once the commander briefs the enemy analysis to subordinates, the commander must ensure a shared understanding of the differences between what is known, what is suspected, and what is just templated (estimated). Unless given the benefit of information collection, the situation template is only an estimate of how the enemy might be disposed. The commander must not take these as facts. Therefore, the commander develops a tactically prudent and flexible plan and clearly explains commander's intent to subordinates. A clearly understood commander's intent allows subordinates to exercise initiative and judgment to accomplish the company's purpose. Information collection (reconnaissance, surveillance, security operations, and intelligence operations) is critical in developing the best possible enemy scenario.

Initial Priority Intelligence Requirements

B-92. The commander defines critical information about the enemy leading to a decision and develops a PIR for each situation. Answering the PIR questions lets the commander confirm or deny assumptions made during planning. Although doing this helps to clarify the enemy situation, it usually leads to answering the PIRs of the CAB and next higher level. The commander must understand the higher HQ's collection plan and how the company assists in answering PIRs.

Analysis of Civil Considerations

B-93. Civil considerations include the influences of man-made infrastructure, civilian institutions, and attitudes, activities of civilian leaders, populations, and organizations within the AO (to include informational aspects for each), about the conduct of military operations. Civil considerations generally focus on the immediate impact of civilians on operations in progress. Civil considerations of the environment can either help or hinder friendly or enemy forces; the difference lies in the commander taking time to learn the situation and its possible effects on the operation. Analysis of civil considerations answers two critical questions:
- How do civilian considerations affect the operation?
- How does the operation affect civilians?

B-94. The CAB provides the commander with civil considerations affecting the next echelon's mission. The memory aid: areas, structures, capabilities, organizations, people, and events (ASCOPE) is used to analyze and describe these civil considerations. (See ATP 2-01.3 for more information.)

Areas

B-95. The population within a prescribed AO comprises several different groups, ethnically and politically. The commander must understand each group's perception about the United States, the Army, and specific units operating within that area. Population statuses overlays can best describe groups and define what feelings the group has toward American forces. This is extremely important in understanding when and where to commit combat power, what relationships can be reinforced with certain groups versus what relationships need to start or cease, and ultimately what second and third order effects our actions will have in the AO. Information related capabilities also can be properly focused with a healthy understanding of the perceptions of the civilian population.

B-96. The commander addresses terrain analysis from a civilian perspective and analyzes how vital civilian areas affect the mission of respective forces and how military operations affect these areas. Factors to consider include political boundaries, locations of government centers, by-type enclaves, special regions such as mining or agricultural, trade routes, and possible settlement sites.

Structures

B-97. Structures include traditional high-payoff targets, protected cultural sites, and facilities with practical applications. The commander's analysis is a comparison of how a structure's location, functions, and capabilities as compared to costs and consequences of such use.

Capabilities

B-98. The commander assesses capabilities in terms of those required to save, sustain, or enhance life, in that order. Capabilities can refer to the ability of local authorities to provide essential functions and services. These can include areas needed after combat operations and contracted resources and services.

Organizations

B-99. The commander considers all nonmilitary groups or institutions in the AO. These may be indigenous, come from a third country or U.S. agencies. They influence and interact with the populace, force, and each other. Current activities, capabilities, and limitations are some of the information necessary to build situational understanding. This often becomes a union of resources and specialized capabilities.

People

B-100. This consideration is a general term describing all nonmilitary personnel military forces encountered in the AO. This includes those personnel outside the AO whose actions, opinions, or political influence can affect the mission. The commander identifies the essential communicators and formal and informal processes used to influence people. Additionally, the commander identifies how historical, cultural, and social factors shape public perceptions, beliefs, goals, and expectations.

Events

B-101. Events are routine, cyclical, planned, or spontaneous activities which significantly affect organizations, people, and military operations, including seasons, festivals, holidays, funerals, political rallies, and agricultural crops and livestock and market cycles and paydays. Other events, such as disasters and those precipitated by military forces, stress and affect the attitudes and activities of the populace and include a moral responsibility to protect displaced civilians. The commander templates events and analyzes them for the political, economic, psychological, environmental, and legal implications.

B-102. The commander identifies civil considerations affecting the mission. Civil considerations are important when conducting operations against terrorist or insurgent forces in urban areas. Most terrorists and insurgents depend on the support or neutrality of the civilian population to camouflage them. The commander must understand the impact of the actions as well as the subordinate's actions on the civilian population and effects the commander will have on current and future operations. Considerations may include—

- Ethnic dynamics.
- Organizations of influence.
- Patterns.
- Leaders and influencers.
- Economic environment.

Ethnic Dynamics

B-103. Ethnic dynamics include religion, cultural mores, gender roles, customs, superstitions, and values certain ethnic groups hold dear which differ from other groups. The commander analyzes the ethnic dynamics within the company's AO to best apply combat power, shape maneuver with information related capabilities, and ultimately find the common denominator all ethnic varieties have in common. The commander then focuses the company's efforts at that common denominator. The commander gains local support by demonstrating dignity and respect to the civilian population the commander has been charged to protect and train.

Organizations of Influence

B-104. Organizations of influence force the commander to look beyond preexisting civilian hierarchical arrangements. By defining organizations within the community, the commander understands what groups have power and influence over their own smaller communities and what groups can assist our forces. Once the organizations are defined, the commander analyzes them to determine their contributions or resistance to friendly operations. Many Eastern cultures rely upon religious organizations as their centers of power and influence, whereas Western cultures' power comes from political institutions by elected officials. Defining other influential organizations or groups of influence enables information collection.

Patterns

B-105. Every culture and every group of people has patterns of behavior. Whether it is set times for prayer, shopping, or commuting people follow patterns. Understanding these patterns helps the commander plan and execute information collection, combat operations, and logistical resupply. Studying the history of civic culture helps the commander understand and explain to others how and why the people have fought previous wars and conflicts. Starting with a baseline pattern and keeping an analysis on how the population is responding or has responded in the past under similar circumstances assists the commander in using patterns to the company's advantage.

Leaders and Influencers

B-106. Know who is in charge and who can influence and enable unit leaders to exercise governance and monitor security within a prescribed area. Many times, the spiritual leader is not necessarily the decision maker for a community, but the spiritual leader must approve the decision maker's actions. The CAB provides the commander with a link-diagram of leaders including religious, political, and criminal personnel to focus planning and decentralized execution to bolster legitimacy within the population. Using the targeting methodology of decide, detect, deliver, and assess may prove useful in determining whether a leader or influencer would best facilitate an operation, when to engage them, and what to expect.

Economic Environment

B-107. Money and resources drive prosperity and stability. The commander identifies the economic production base within the AO that bolsters the economic welfare of the people. Economic considerations include infrastructure rebuild projects, creation of labor opportunities, and education. By focusing on the motivations for civilian labor and creating essential services and prosperity where there was none, the commander and subordinate leaders win the support of the civilian who now can feed and clothe their families and now has clean running water. This aspect of civil considerations reinforces the security of the community against poverty and other enablers to instability.

Analysis of Troops and Support Available

B-108. The commander reviews the company's task organization to determine the number, type, capabilities, and condition of available friendly troops and other support. Analysis of troops follows the same logic as analyzing the enemy by identifying capabilities, vulnerabilities, and strengths. The commander should know the disposition, composition, strength, and capabilities of the forces one and two levels down. This information can be maintained in a checkbook-style matrix for use during COA development (specifically array forces). The commander maintains an understanding of subordinate readiness, including maintenance, training, strengths and weaknesses, leaders, and logistics status. Analysis of troops and support available answers the question: What assets are available to accomplish the mission? Additional questions the commander answers include:

- What are the strengths and weaknesses of subordinate leaders?
- What is the supply status of ammunition, water, fuel (if required), and other necessary items?
- What is the present physical condition of Soldiers (morale, sleep)?
- What is the condition of equipment?
- What is the unit's training status and experience relative to the mission?
- What additional attachments will accompany?
- What additional assets are required to accomplish the mission?

B-109. Perhaps the most critical aspect of mission analysis is determining the combat potential of one's own force. The commander realistically and unemotionally determines all available resources and new limitations based on level of training or recent fighting. This includes troops who are either attached to or in direct support of the company. It also includes understanding the full array of assets in support of the company. The commander must know how much indirect fire by type is available and when it will become available.

B-110. Throughout planning and preparation for an operation the commander continually assesses the company's combat effectiveness—the ability of a unit to perform its mission. Factors such as ammunition, personnel, fuel status, and weapon systems are evaluated and rated by the commander. The ratings used by the commander are—

- Fully operational – green (85 percent or greater).
- Substantially operational – amber (70 to 84 percent).
- Marginally operational – red (50 to 69 percent).
- Not operational – black (less than 50 percent).

B-111. The commander cannot be expected to think of everything during mission analysis because of the constant uncertainty present in operations at the small-unit level. This fact forces the commander to determine how to get assistance when the situation exceeds the company's capabilities. Therefore, a secondary product of analysis of troops and support available should be an answer to the question, "how do I get help?"

Analysis of Time Available

B-112. Time available refers to many factors during the operations process (plan, prepare, execute, and assess). The four categories the commander considers include—

- Next higher echelon's timeline.
- Operations.
- Planning and preparation.
- Enemy timeline.

B-113. During all phases, the commanders consider critical times, unusable time, the time it takes to accomplish activities, the time it takes to move, priorities of work, and tempo of operations. Other critical conditions to consider include visibility and weather data, and events such as higher HQ's tasks and required rehearsals. Implied in the analysis of time is the commander's prioritization of events and sequencing of activities.

B-114. As addressed in Step 1 of the TLP, time analysis is a critical aspect to planning, preparation, and execution. Time analysis is often the first thing the commander does. The commander must not only appreciate how much time is available but be able to appreciate the time and space aspects of preparing, moving, fighting, and sustaining. The commander must be able to see the company's tasks and enemy actions in relation to time. Most importantly, as events occur, the commander must adjust the time available to them and assess its impact on what the commander wants to accomplish. Finally, the commander updates previous timelines for subordinates, listing all events affecting the platoon and its subordinate elements.

Course of Action Development

B-115. The purpose of COA development is to determine one or more ways to accomplish the mission consistent with the CAB commander's intent. A COA describes how the unit might generate the effects of overwhelming combat power against the enemy at the decisive point with the least friendly casualties. Each COA the commander develops must be detailed enough to clearly describe how the commander envisions using all of the assets and combat multipliers to achieve the company's task and purpose.

B-116. To develop a COA, the commander focuses on the actions the company must take at the decisive point and work backward to the start point. The commander focuses company efforts to develop at least one well-synchronized COA; if time permits, additional COAs are developed. The result of the COA development process is paragraph 3 of the OPORD. A COA should position the unit for future operations and provide flexibility to meet unforeseen events during execution. COAs should give subordinates the maximum latitude for initiative. From developing a strategy to analyzing, refining, and rehearsing the plan, the commander must be knowledgeable in the following areas detailed under this subheading to construct a solid COA. Once a commander has worked backwards from the decisive point to "now" the commander must plan from the decisive point forward to the point where the company will receive its change of mission. This allows the commander to account for all the resources necessary to achieve the decisive point and reach mission accomplishment.

Screening Criteria

B-117. A COA should be suitable, feasible, acceptable, distinguishable, and complete. These elements are defined in the following bullets:

- Suitable. If executed, the COA accomplishes the mission legally and ethically while consistent with the CAB commander's concept and intent.
- Feasible. The company has the technical and tactical skills and resources to accomplish the COA, with available time, space, resources, and available capabilities.
- Acceptable. The military advantage gained by executing the COA must justify the cost in resources, especially casualties. This assessment is largely subjective and asks the following question: Is it worth the cost or risk? If it is illegal, immoral, or unethical, it is not acceptable.
- Distinguishable. If more than one COA is developed, does it differ significantly from the other solutions? Each COA must differ significantly from the others (such as scheme of maneuver, lines of effort, phasing, use of the reserve, and task organization).
- Complete. The COA covers the operational factors of who, what, when, where, and why, and must show from start to finish how the company will accomplish the mission. The COA must address the doctrinal aspects of the mission. For example, in an attack against a defending enemy, the COA must address the movement to, deployment against, assault of, and consolidation upon the objective. A plan that only achieves the decisive point is not a complete plan.

Note. Leaders assess risk continuously throughout COA development.

Actions

B-118. Next, the commander analyzes relative combat power, generates options, arrays forces, develops concept of operation, analyzes Soldier load, assigns responsibility, and prepares a COA statement and sketch. The following paragraphs describe the process that must be taken when developing a COA.

Analyze Relative Combat Power

B-119. During the first step of COA development, analyzing relative combat power, leaders compare and contrast friendly combat power with the enemy. The commander determines where, when, and how friendly forces can overwhelm the enemy by reviewing the dynamics of combat power, specifically by warfighting function. The six functions include:

- Intelligence.
- Movement and maneuver.
- Fires.
- Sustainment.
- Protection.
- Command and control.

B-120. The purpose of this step is to compare the combat power of friendly and enemy forces, by analyzing troop to tasks to determine if the company has enough combat power to accomplish its assigned task. It is not merely a calculation and comparison of friendly and enemy weapons numbers or units with the aim of gaining a numerical advantage. Using the results of all previous analysis done during mission analysis, the commander compares the company's combat power strengths and weaknesses with those of the enemy. The commander seeks to calculate the time and way the company (and enemy) can maximize the effects of maneuver, firepower, protection, leadership, and information in relation to the specific terrain, disposition, and composition of each force. The commander determines how to avoid enemy strengths or advantages in combat power. In short, the commander strives to determine where, when, and how the company's combat power can overwhelm the enemy's ability to generate combat power. An analysis of the ability to generate combat power will help the commander confirm or deny tentative decisive point. Additionally, the CCIRs (PIRs and friendly force information requirements) and essential elements of friendly information are identified.

Generate Options

B-121. Most missions and tasks can be accomplished in more than one way. The goal of this step, generating options, is to determine one or more of those ways quickly. First, the commander considers tactics, techniques, and procedures from doctrine, unit SOPs, history, or other resources to determine if a solution to a similar tactical problem exists already. If it does, the commander's job is to take the existing solution and modify it to the company's unique situation. If a solution does not exist, the commander must develop one. Second, the commander confirms the mission's decisive point. Then, using doctrinal requirements as a guide, the commander assigns purposes to the tactical tasks involved. The commander adheres to the doctrinal requirement for the mission including all tactical tasks normally assigned to subordinates. By defining the decisive point, the commander understands where and when the company can mass overwhelming combat power to achieve a specific result that accomplishes the mission's purpose with respect to the enemy, terrain, time, or civil considerations. The commander considers enemy and friendly decisive and decision points that lead to the desired mission end state when generating options.

Array Forces

B-122. Using the product from generating options, the commander determines what combinations of Soldiers, weapons, and other systems are needed to accomplish each task. This is known as arraying forces or assigning troops to task. This judgment call is unique to the specific METT-TC (I) conditions the commander faces. The commander then task organizes the company specific to the respective essential tactical tasks and purposes assigned to subordinate elements. The commander determines the specific quantity of squads, weapons (by type), and fire support necessary to accomplish each task against the enemy array of forces. The commander allocates resources required for the main effort's success first, and determines the resources needed for shaping operations in descending order of importance.

Develop a Concept of Operations

B-123. The concept of operation describes how the commander envisions the operation unfolding, from its start to its conclusion or end state. Operations and actions consist of numerous activities, events, and tasks.

The concept of operation describes the relationships between activities, events, and tasks, and explains how the tasks will lead to accomplishing the mission. The concept of operation is a framework to assist leaders, not a script. The normal cycle for an offensive mission is tactical movement, actions on the objective, and consolidation and reorganization. The normal cycle for defensive missions is EA development and preparation of the BPs, actions in the EA, counterattack, and consolidation and reorganization. In developing the concept of operation, the commander clarifies the best ways to use the available terrain and to employ the company's strengths against the enemy's weaknesses. The commander includes the requirements of indirect fire to support the maneuver. The commander then develops the maneuver control measures necessary to convey commander's intent, enhance the understanding of the schemes of maneuver, prevent fratricide, and clarify the tasks and purposes of the decisive, shaping and sustaining operations. The commander determines the sustainment aspects of the COA.

Assign Responsibilities

B-124. The commander assigns responsibility for each task to a subordinate. Whenever possible and depending on the existing chain of command, the commander avoids fracturing unit integrity. The commander attempts to keep the span of control between two to five subordinate elements. The commander ensures every subordinate unit is employed, every asset is attached, and adequate command and control is provided for each element. The commander must avoid unnecessary complicated command structures and maintain unit integrity where feasible.

Prepare a Course of Action Statement and Sketch

B-125. The company commander primarily uses the COA statement and COA sketch to describe the concept of operation. These two products are the basis for paragraph 3 of the OPORD. The COA statement specifies how the company will accomplish the mission. The first three steps of COA development provide the bulk of the COA statement. The COA statement details how the company's operation supports the CAB commander's operation, the decisive point and why it is decisive, the form of maneuver or type of defensive mission, and operational framework. The COA sketch is a drawing or series of drawings to assist the commander in describing how the operation will unfold. The sketch provides a picture of the maneuver aspects of the concept. The commander uses tactical mission task graphics and control measures (see FM 1-02.2) to convey the operation in a doctrinal context. Both the COA statement and sketch focus at the decisive point. The COA statement should identify—

- Decisive point and what makes it decisive.
- Form of maneuver or form of the defense.
- Tasks and purposes of the decisive, shaping, and sustaining operations (or main and supporting efforts).
- Reserve planning priorities.
- Purposes of critical warfighting functions.
- End state.

B-126. The COA sketch should identify how the company intends to focus the effects of overwhelming combat power at the decisive point. When integrated with terrain, the refined product becomes the company's operations overlay. The COA sketch is used to help the commander during planning and during briefing to the subordinates and to visualize the sequence of events as an operation unfolds.

Course of Action Analysis

B-127. COA analysis begins with friendly and enemy COA and, using a method of action-reaction-counteraction war-game, results in a synchronized friendly plan, identified strengths and weaknesses, and updated risk assessment. After developing the COA, the commander analyzes it to determine its strengths and weaknesses, visualizes the flow of the battle, identifies the conditions or requirements necessary to enhance synchronization, and gains insights into actions at the decisive point of the mission. During the war-game, the commander visualizes a set of enemy and friendly actions and reactions. War-gaming is the process of determining "what if?" factors of the overall operations. The object is to determine what can go wrong and what decision the commander likely will have to make as a result. COA analysis allows the commander to synchronize assets, identify potential hazards, and develop a better understanding of the upcoming operation. The COA enables the commander to—

- Determine how to maximize the effects of combat power while protecting friendly forces and minimizing collateral damage.
- Anticipate events within the AO.
- Determine conditions and resources required for success.
- Identify additional control requirements.
- Identify friendly coordination requirements.

B-128. COA analysis (war-gaming) brings together friendly and enemy forces on the actual terrain to visualize how the operation will unfold. It is a continuous cycle of action, reaction, and counteraction. This process highlights critical tasks, stimulates ideas, and provides insights rarely gained through mission analysis and COA development alone. War-gaming helps the commander fully synchronize friendly actions, while considering the likely reactions of the enemy. The product of this process is the synchronization matrix. War-gaming, depending on how much time is devoted to planning, provides—

- An appreciation for time, space, and triggers needed to integrate direct- and indirect-fire support, obscurants, engineers, air defense artillery, and CBRN enablers with maneuver platoons to support the company's tasks and purposes identified in the scheme of maneuver.
- Flexibility built into the plan by gaining insights into possible branches to the basic plan.
- The need for control measures, such as checkpoints, contact points, and target registration points, aid in control, flexibility, and synchronization.
- Coordinating instructions to enhance execution and unity of effort, and to ease confusion between subordinate elements.
- Information needed to complete paragraphs 3, 4, and 5 of the OPORD. Assessments regarding on order and be-prepared missions.
- Projected sustainment expenditures, friendly casualties, and resulting medical requirements.

B-129. The best way for the commander to war-game is to start at the company's current location and go through the mission from start to finish, or start at a critical point such as the objective or EA. Using the action-reaction method, the commander can think through the engagement beforehand. As war-gaming proceeds, the commander can either record observations into a matrix or keep notes in a notebook. The most important aspect of this process is not the method but the output, meaning a more in-depth understanding of the operation. At the conclusion of the war-game, the commander fully understands the potential tactical risk associated with the plan. It is here that the commander may refine the plan to mitigate those risks internally or present them to the CAB staff and commander for assistance.

Course of Action Comparison and Selection

B-130. If the commander has developed more than one COA, the commander must compare them by weighing the specific advantages, disadvantages, strengths, and weaknesses of each as noted during the war-game. These attributes may pertain to the accomplishment of the company's purpose, the use of terrain, the destruction of the enemy or other aspect of the operation the commander believes is important. The commander uses these factors, gained from the relational combat power analysis matrix, as the frame of reference when tentatively selecting the best COA. The commander makes the final selection of a COA based on own judgment, the start time of the operation, the AO, the scheme of maneuver, and subordinate unit tasks and purposes. The right decision must be ethical (consistent with the moral principles of the Army Ethic), effective (likely to accomplish its purpose), and efficient (makes the disciplined use of resources).

B-131. The CCIR identifies and filters information needed by commander to support the commander's vision and to make critical decisions, especially to determine or validate COA. CCIRs help the commander determine what is relevant to mission accomplishment. In one technique, the commander writes the desired question, the quantified answer, and reaction (critical decision to make). CCIRs help focus the efforts of subordinates and aids in the allocation of resources. The commander limits CCIRs to essential information.

STEP 4, INITIATE MOVEMENT

B-132. The commander initiates movement necessary to continue mission preparation or to posture the company for starting the mission. This step can be executed anytime throughout the sequence of the TLP. The step can include movement to an AA, BP, a new AO, or the movement of guides or quartering parties.

STEP 5, CONDUCT RECONNAISSANCE

B-133. To exploit the principles of speed and surprise, the commander weighs the advantages of reconnoitering personally against the combat multiplier in the form of supplied information from CAB information collection efforts. The commander realistically considers the dangers of reconnoitering personally and the time required to conduct them. The commander might be able to plan the company's operation using the unprecedented amount of combat information provided by the higher echelon information collection assets. However, if time permits, the commander verifies higher HQ's intelligence by reconnoitering visually. The commander seeks to confirm the PIR supporting tentative plans. PIR usually consists of assumptions or critical facts about the enemy. This can include strength and location, especially at templated positions. It also can include information about the terrain. For example, verification of a tentative SBF position can suppress the enemy or see if an avenue of approach is useable.

B-134. If possible, the commander includes subordinate leaders in the company's reconnaissance efforts. This allows subordinates to see as much of the terrain and enemy as possible. Reconnaissance helps subordinate leaders gain insight into the commander's vision of the operation. This is most critical when executing a defense. It is during this step that commanders and subordinate leaders conduct their leaders' reconnaissance in support of EA development.

B-135. The commander's reconnaissance might include moving to or beyond the LD, reconnaissance of an AO, or walking from the FEBA back to and through the platoon AO or BP along likely enemy avenues of approach. If possible, the commander selects a vantage point(s) with the best possible view of the decisive point. In addition to the commander's reconnaissance efforts, subordinate units can conduct additional reconnaissance operations. Examples include surveillance of an area by subordinate elements, patrols to determine enemy locations, and establishment of OPs to gain additional information. Subordinate leaders can incorporate Javelin command launch units as surveillance tools (day or night), based on an analysis of METT-TC (I).

B-136. The nature of the reconnaissance, including what it covers and how long it lasts, depends on the tactical situation and time available. The commander uses the results of the COA development process to identify information and security requirements of the company's reconnaissance missions.

B-137. The commander includes disseminating results and conclusions arrived from reconnaissance into the commander's time analysis. The commander must consider how to communicate changes in the COA to subordinates and how these changes affect the plan, actions of the subordinates, and other supporting elements.

STEP 6, COMPLETE THE PLAN

B-138. During this step, the commander expands the selected (or refined) COA in to complete OPORD. The commander prepares overlays, refines the indirect fire list, completes sustainment and command and control requirements and, of course, updates the tentative plan based on the latest reconnaissance or information. The commander prepares briefing sites and other briefing materials needed to present the OPORD directly to subordinates. The commander conducts final coordination with other units and CAB staff members before issuing the order to subordinates.

B-139. Using the five-paragraph OPORD format helps the commander explain all aspects of the operation: terrain, enemy, higher and adjacent friendly units, unit mission, execution, support, and command and control. The format serves as a checklist to ensure the commander covers all relevant details of the operation and gives subordinates a smooth flow of information from beginning to end.

STEP 7, ISSUE OPERATION ORDER

B-140. The OPORD precisely and concisely explains the commander's intent and concept of how the commander envisions the company accomplishing the mission. The order does not contain unnecessary information. The OPORD is delivered quickly and in a manner allowing subordinates to concentrate on understanding the commander's vision and not just copying what the commander says verbatim. The commander must prepare adequately and deliver the OPORD confidently and quickly to build and sustain confidence in the subordinates.

B-141. When issuing the OPORD, the commander must ensure the subordinates understand and share the vision of what must be done and when and how it must be done. Subordinate leaders must understand how all platoons and elements work together to accomplish the company's mission. They also must understand how platoons and the company's mission supports the intentions of the immediate higher commander. When the commander finishes issuing the order, subordinate leaders should leave with a clear understanding of what the commander expects their elements to do. The commander is responsible for ensuring subordinate leaders understand what is to be expected. This common visualization and understanding is translated into execution through operational graphics. These graphics are necessary to ensure synchronization of the plan (and most likely higher HQ) while maximizing effects on the enemy and preventing fratricide.

B-142. In many respects, the commander must issue the order in a manner that instills subordinates with confidence in the plan and a commitment to do their best to achieve the plan. Whenever possible, the commander issues the order in person. The commander looks into the eyes of subordinate leaders to ensure each one understands the mission and what the element must achieve.

B-143. The commander completes the order with a confirmation brief. At a minimum, each subordinate leader should be able to backbrief the company's mission and commander's intent, the immediate higher commander's intent, the tasks and purpose, and time the subordinate leader will issue the unit's OPORD. Each subordinate confirms understanding of the commander's vision and how the mission is accomplished with respect to the decisive point. This confirmation brief provides an opportunity to highlight issues or concerns.

B-144. The five-paragraph OPORD format (see figure B-5 on page B-30), helps the commander paint a picture of all aspects of the operation, from the terrain to the enemy, and finally to the company's own actions from higher to lower. The format helps the commander decide what relevant details are included and provides subordinates with a smooth flow of information from beginning to end. At the same time, the commander ensures the order is not only clear and complete but also as brief as possible. If the commander has already addressed an item adequately in a previous WARNORD, the commander can simply state, "No change," or provide necessary updates. The commander is free to brief the OPORD in the most effective manner to convey information to subordinate leaders.

```
┌─────────────────────────────────────────────────────────────────────────────┐
│  1. SITUATION                          3. EXECUTION (continued)                │
│      • Area of Interest                    • Coordinating Instructions         │
│      • Area of Operations                      - Time Schedule                 │
│          - Terrain                             - CCIR, PIR, FFIR, EEFI         │
│          - Weather                             - Risk Reduction Control Measures│
│      • Enemy Forces (Latest Intelligence)      - Rules of Engagement           │
│      • Friendly Forces                         - Environment Considerations    │
│          - Two Levels up                       - Protection                    │
│          - One Level up                        - Handling of EPW               │
│          - Adjacent Units                                                      │
│      • Attachments and Detachments     4. SUSTAINMENT                          │
│          - Who                             • Logistic                          │
│          - Why                                 - Maintenance                   │
│                                                - Transportation                │
│  2. MISSION                                    - Field Services                │
│      • Who                                 • Personnel Services Support         │
│      • What                                • Army Health Systems Support        │
│      • When                                    - Casualty Care                 │
│      • Where                                   - Medical / Casualty Evacuations │
│      • Why                                     - Preventive Medicine           │
│                                                                                │
│  3. EXECUTION                          5. COMMAND AND SIGNAL                    │
│      • Commander's Intent                  • Command (Location of Leaders)      │
│      • Concept of Operations               • Control (Command Post Location)    │
│      • Scheme of Movement and Maneuver     • Signal                            │
│          (Explain from Start to Finish)        - Radio Frequencies             │
│      • Tasks to Subordinate Units              - Passwords / Running Passwords  │
│                                                - Pyrotechnic Signals            │
├─────────────────────────────────────────────────────────────────────────────┤
│  LEGEND                                                                         │
│  CCIR   COMMANDER'S CRITICAL INFORMATION    EPW    ENEMY PRISONER OF WAR        │
│         REQUIREMENT                         FFIR   FRIENDLY FORCE INFORMATION REQUIREMENT│
│  EEFI   ESSENTIAL ELEMENTS OF FRIENDLY INFORMATION  PIR   PRIORITY INTELLIGENCE REQUIREMENT│
└─────────────────────────────────────────────────────────────────────────────┘
```

Figure B-5. Operation order format

STEP 8, SUPERVISE AND REFINE

B-145. This final step of the TLP is crucial. After issuing the OPORD, the commander and subordinate leaders ensure the required activities and tasks are completed promptly prior to mission execution. Supervision is the primary responsibility of all leaders. Both officers and NCOs must check everything important for mission accomplishment. This includes, but is not limited to—

- Conducting numerous backbriefs on all aspects of the platoon and subordinate unit operations.
- Ensuring the second in command in each element is prepared to execute in the leaders' absence.
- Listening to subordinates' OPORD.
- Observing rehearsals of subordinate units.
- Checking load plans to ensure they are carrying only what is necessary for the mission or what the OPORD specified.
- Checking the status and serviceability of weapons.
- Checking on maintenance activities of subordinate units.
- Ensuring local security is maintained.

SECTION II – PREPARATIONS

B-146. Preparation consists of activities performed by the company to improve its ability to execute a mission. Preparation includes but is not limited to plan refinement, rehearsals, information collection, coordination, inspections, and movements. Thorough backbriefs and comprehensive rehearsals are important keys to refining a plan. Preparation activities play a critical role in ensuring that the company can execute its mission effectively. These activities allow the commander, subordinate leaders, and each team or crewman to discover potential problem areas and to develop contingency plans to avoid unforeseen difficulties.

B-147.   Since time is a factor in all operations, the commander conducts a time analysis early in the planning process to determine what preparation activities need to take place and when to begin those activities to ensure forces are ready and in position before execution. The plan may require the commander to direct subordinates to start necessary movements; conduct task organization changes; begin reconnaissance, surveillance, and security operations; and execute other preparation activities before completing the plan.

B-148.   Commander-driven key preparation activities (although not inclusive) are addressed in the following paragraphs. (See ADP 5-0 for a complete listing of preparation activities.)

REHEARSALS

B-149.   Rehearsals are practice sessions conducted to prepare units for an upcoming operation or event. They are essential in ensuring thorough preparation, coordination, and understanding of the commander's plan and intent. Leaders should never underestimate the value of rehearsals.

B-150.   Rehearsals require subordinate leaders and, when time permits, other platoon Soldiers to perform required tasks, ideally under conditions as close as possible to those expected for the actual operation. At their best, rehearsals are interactive; participants maneuver their actual vehicles or use vehicle models or simulations while verbalizing their elements' actions. During every rehearsal, the focus is on the how element, allowing subordinates to practice the actions called for in their individual scheme of maneuver.

> *Note.* Rehearsals are different from a discussion of what is supposed to happen during the actual event. The commander can test subordinates' understanding of the plan by ensuring they push the rehearsal forward rather than waiting to dictate each step of the operation. A technique for rehearsing is send real SPOTREPs when reporting enemy contact, rather than just saying, "I would send a SPOTREP now."

B-151.   The commander uses well-planned, efficiently run rehearsals to accomplish the following:
- Reinforce training and increase proficiency in critical tasks.
- Reveal weaknesses or problems in the plan, leading to more refinement of the plan or development of additional branch plans.
- Integrate the actions of subordinate elements.
- Confirm coordination requirements between the platoon and adjacent units.
- Improve each Soldier's understanding of the concept of the operation, the direct fire plan, anticipated contingencies, and possible actions and reactions for various situations may arise during the operation.
- Ensure seconds-in-command are prepared to execute in their leaders' absence.

REHEARSAL TYPES

B-152.   The commander may use several types of rehearsals, which include:
- Backbrief.
- Combined arms rehearsal.
- Support rehearsal.
- Battle drill or SOP rehearsal.

Backbrief

B-153.   A backbrief is a briefing by subordinates to the commander to review how subordinates intend to accomplish their mission. Normally, subordinates perform backbriefs throughout preparation. These briefs allow the commander to clarify the commander's intent early in subordinate planning. The commander uses the backbrief to identify problems in the concept of operation.

Combined Arms Rehearsal

B-154. A combined arms rehearsal is a rehearsal in which subordinate units synchronize their plans with each other. A maneuver unit HQ normally executes a combined arms rehearsal after subordinate units issue their OPORD. This rehearsal type helps ensure subordinate commanders' plans achieve the higher commander's intent.

Support Rehearsal

B-155. The support rehearsal helps synchronize each warfighting function with the overall operation. This rehearsal supports the operation so units can accomplish their missions. Throughout preparation, units conduct support rehearsals within the framework of a single or limited number of warfighting functions. These rehearsals typically involve coordination and procedure drills for aviation, fires, engineer support, or CASEVAC. Support rehearsals and combined arms rehearsals complement preparations for the operation. Units may conduct rehearsals separately or combine them into full-dress rehearsals. Although these rehearsals differ slightly by warfighting function, they achieve similar results.

Battle Drill or Standard Operating Procedure Rehearsal

B-156. A battle drill or SOP rehearsal ensures all participants understand a technique or a specific set of procedures. Throughout preparation, subordinate units and staffs rehearse battle drills and SOPs. These rehearsals do not need a completed order from higher HQ. The commander places priority on those drills or actions that are anticipated occurring during the operation. All echelons use these rehearsal types; however, they are most common for platoons, squads, and sections. They are conducted throughout preparation and are not limited to published battle drills.

REHEARSAL TECHNIQUES

B-157. Rehearsals should follow the crawl-walk-run training methodology whenever possible. This prepares the platoons and subordinate elements for increasingly difficult conditions. (See FM 6-0 for more information.) Resources required for each technique range from broad to narrow and each rehearsal technique imparts a different level of understanding to participants (see figure B-6). Units can conduct these forms of rehearsals if mission variables permit—

- Full-dress rehearsal.
- Key-leader rehearsal.
- Terrain-model rehearsal.
- Digital terrain-model rehearsal.
- Sketch-map rehearsal.
- Map rehearsal.
- Network rehearsal.

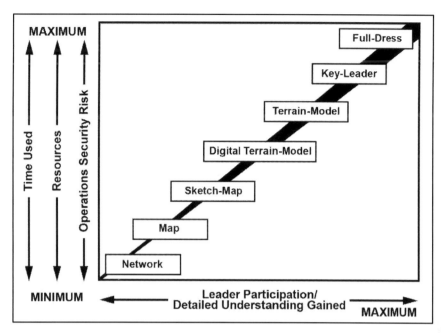

Figure B-6. Methods of rehearsals

Full-Dress Rehearsal

B-158. A full-dress rehearsal produces the most detailed understanding of the operation. It includes every participating Soldier and system. The commander rehearses subordinates on terrain like the AO, initially under good light conditions, and then in limited visibility. Subordinate leaders repeat small-unit actions until executed to standard. Full-dress rehearsals help Soldiers clearly understand what the commander expects of them. It helps them gain confidence in their ability to accomplish the mission. Supporting elements, such as aviation crews, meet and rehearse with Soldiers to synchronize the operation.

Key-Leader Rehearsal

B-159. Circumstances may prohibit a rehearsal with all members of the company. A key-leader rehearsal involves only select individuals of the organization and its subordinate units. It normally takes fewer resources than a full-dress rehearsal. Terrain requirements mirror those of a full-dress rehearsal, even though fewer Soldiers participate. The commander first decides the level of leader involvement. Then selected leaders rehearse the plan while traversing actual or similar terrain. Often the commander uses this technique to rehearse fire control measures for an EA during defensive operations. The commander often uses a key-leader rehearsal to prepare key leaders for a full-dress rehearsal. It may require developing a rehearsal plan mirroring the actual plan but fits the rehearsal terrain.

Terrain-Model Rehearsal

B-160. The terrain-model rehearsal is the most popular rehearsal technique. It takes less time and fewer resources than a full-dress or reduced-force rehearsal. (A terrain-model rehearsal takes a platoon between 1 to 2 hours to execute to standard.) An accurately constructed terrain model helps subordinate leaders visualize the commander's intent and concept of operation. When possible, the commander places the terrain model where it overlooks the actual terrain of the AO. However, if the situation requires more security, the commander places the terrain model on a reverse slope within walking distance of a point overlooking the AO. The model's orientation coincides with the terrain. The size of the terrain model can vary from small (using markers to represent units) to large (on which the participants can walk). A large model helps reinforce the participants' perception of unit positions on the terrain.

Digital Terrain-Model Rehearsal

B-161. With today's digital capabilities, users can construct terrain models in virtual space. Units drape high-resolution imagery over elevation data thereby creating a fly-through or walk-through. Holographic imagery produces views in three dimensions. Often, the model hot links graphics, detailed information, UASs, and ground imagery to key points providing accurate insight to the plan. Digital terrain models reduce the OPSEC risk because they do not use real terrain. Geospatial engineers or imagery analysts from the ABCT HQ can assist in digital model creation. Detailed city models exist for many world cities.

Sketch-Map Rehearsal

B-162. The commander can use the sketch-map technique almost anywhere, day or night. The procedures are like a terrain-model rehearsal except the commander uses a sketch map in place of a terrain model. Large sketches ensure all participants can see as each participant walks through execution of the operation. Participants move markers on the sketch to represent unit locations and maneuvers. Sketch-map rehearsals take less time than terrain-model rehearsals and more time than map rehearsals.

Map Rehearsal

B-163. A map rehearsal is like a sketch-map rehearsal except the commander uses a map and operation overlay of the same scale used to plan the operation. The map rehearsal itself consumes the most time. A map rehearsal is normally the easiest technique to set up since it requires only maps and graphics for current operations. Units gear a map rehearsal's operation overlay to the echelon conducting the rehearsal. Multi-echelon rehearsals using this technique are difficult. This rehearsal can present OPSEC risks if the area around the rehearsal site is not secured. This technique requires the least terrain of all rehearsals. A good site ensures participants can easily find it yet stay concealed from the enemy. An optimal location overlooks the terrain where the unit will execute the operation.

Network Rehearsal

B-164. The company conducts network rehearsals over wide-area networks or local area networks. The commander practices these rehearsals by talking through critical portions of the operation over communications networks in a sequence the commander establishes. The company rehearses only critical parts of the operation. These rehearsals require all information systems needed to execute portions of the operation. All participants require working information systems, OPORD, and overlays. CPs, when established, can rehearse battle tracking during network rehearsals.

PRECOMBAT CHECKS AND PRECOMBAT INSPECTIONS

B-165. PCCs and PCIs are critical to the success of missions. These checks and inspections are leader tasks and cannot be delegated below the team-leader level. They ensure the Soldier is prepared to execute the required individual and collective tasks supporting the mission. Checks and inspections are part of the TLP protecting against shortfalls endangering Soldiers' lives and jeopardizing the execution of a mission.

B-166. PCCs and PCIs must be tailored to the specific unit and mission requirements. Each mission may require a separate set of checklists. Each element will have its own established set of PCCs and PCIs, but each platoon within its element should have identical checklists. Mounted elements and the dismounted Infantry squads will have a different checklist than the tank platoons.

B-167. One of the best ways to ensure PCCs and PCIs are complete and thorough is with full-dress rehearsals. These rehearsals, run at combat speed with communication and full-battle equipment, allow the commander and subordinate leaders to envision minute details, as they will occur in the AO. If the operation is to be conducted at night, Soldiers should conduct full-dress rehearsals at night as well. PCCs and PCIs should include backbriefs on the mission, the task and purpose of the mission, and how the Soldiers' role fits into the scheme of maneuver. The Soldiers should know the latest intelligence updates, ROE, be versed in casualty response, evacuation procedures, and sustainment requirements.

Appendix C

Combined Arms Breach

A combined arms breach is a complex operation which requires detailed planning, preparation, and execution, and continuous assessment throughout the operations process. Effective breaching operations allow the company to maneuver in the face of obstacles. This appendix provides a brief overview of combined arms breaching operation types, areas, and tenets, and includes a discussion on deliberate and hasty breaching operations. (See ATP 3-90.4 for more information.)

SECTION I – OVERVIEW

C-1. A *breach* is a tactical mission task in which a unit breaks through or establishes a passage through an enemy obstacle (FM 3-90). As a tactical mission task, a breach is an action by a friendly force conducted to allow maneuver despite the presence of obstacles. During maneuver, the commander attempts to bypass and avoid obstacles and enemy defensive positions to the maximum extent possible to maintain tempo and momentum. Breaching enemy defenses and obstacle systems is normally the last choice. The breach begins when friendly forces detect an obstacle and begin to apply the breaching fundamentals and ends when battle handover has occurred between follow-on forces and a unit conducting the breach.

C-2. The breaching tenets are essential when planning breaching operations in support of an attack. Breaching activities include the reduction of minefields, other explosive hazards, and other obstacles. Breaching at CAB and above (and to a lesser degree at company level) requires significant combat engineering support to accomplish.

C-3. *Reduction* is the creation of lanes through a minefield or obstacle to enable passage of the attacking ground force (JP 3-15). A *lane* is a route through, over, or around an enemy or friendly obstacle that provides passage of a force (ATP 3-90.4). The lane may be reduced and proofed as part of breaching, constructed as part of the obstacle, or marked as a bypass. The number and width of lanes vary depending on the enemy situation, the size and composition of the assaulting force and the scheme of movement and maneuver.

C-4. *Proof* is the verification that a lane is free of mines or explosive hazards and that the width and trafficability at the point of breach are suitable for the passing force (ATP 3-90.4). Proofing can be conducted visually, electronically, or mechanically. Some mines are resistant to reduction assets and may require a combination of breaching techniques; for example, magnetic and double impulse mines may resist a mine clearing line charge (known as MICLIC) blast. Proofing is an important component of breaching considering the wide variety of explosive obstacle threats in use today.

C-5. Most combined arms breaching is conducted by an ABCT or a CAB as a tactical mission, but higher echelons may also execute operational-level combined arms breaching tasks. Significant engineer augmentation from echelons above brigade is typically required to enable an ABCT breach or a CAB deliberate or hasty breach. (See ATP 3-90.4 for more information.)

TYPES OF BREACH

C-6. Maneuver forces are task organized specifically for an operation to provide a fully synchronized combined arms team. Most operations lie somewhere along a continuum between two extremes—deliberate operations and hasty operations. Attacks take place along this continuum (commonly referred to as a deliberate attack or hasty attack) based on the knowledge of enemy capability and disposition and the intentions and details of friendly force planning and preparation. Deliberate attack and hasty attack refer to the opposite ends of that continuum and describe characteristics of the attack. Breaching may be required to support an attack anywhere along this continuum. Breaching activities must be adapted to exploit the situation. The level and type of planning distinguish which of the three general types of breaching (deliberate, hasty, and covert) are used to meet mission variables.

DELIBERATE BREACH

C-7. A deliberate breach is the creation of a lane through a minefield or a clear lane through a barrier or fortification, which is systematically planned and carried out. A deliberate breach is used against a strong defense or complex obstacle system. (See JP 3-15 for more information.) It is like a deliberate attack, requiring detailed knowledge of the defense and obstacle systems. It is characterized by the planning, preparation, and buildup of combat power on the near side of obstacles. Subordinates are task-organized to accomplish the breach. The breach often requires securing the far side of the obstacle with an assault force before or during reduction. Amphibious breaching is an adaptation of the deliberate breach intended to overcome antilanding defenses to allow a successful amphibious landing.

HASTY BREACH

C-8. *Hasty breach* is the creation of lanes through enemy obstacles by expedient methods such as blasting with demolitions, pushing rollers or disabled vehicles through the minefields when the time factor does not permit detailed reconnaissance, deliberate breaching, or bypassing the obstacle (JP 3-15). It may be conducted during a deliberate or hasty attack due to lack of clarity on enemy obstacles or changing enemy situations, to include the emplacement of scatterable mines.

COVERT BREACH

C-9. A covert breach is the creation of lanes through minefields or other obstacles that is planned and intended to be executed without detection by an adversary. (See JP 3-15 for more information.) Its primary purpose is to reduce obstacles in an undetected fashion to facilitate the passage of maneuver forces. A covert breach is conducted when surprise is necessary or desirable and when limited visibility and terrain present the opportunity to reduce enemy obstacles without being seen. A covert breach uses elements of deliberate and hasty breaching, as required.

C-10. A covert breach is characterized by using stealth to reduce obstacles, with support and assault forces executing their mission only if reduction is detected. Through surprise, the commander conceals the capabilities and intentions and creates the opportunity to position support and assault forces to strike the enemy while unaware or unprepared. The support force does not usually provide suppressive fire until the initiation of the assault or if the breach force is detected. Covert breaches are usually conducted during periods of limited visibility.

IN-STRIDE BREACH

C-11. An in-stride breach is a breach conducted by forces organic to (or task organized with) the attacking force. It is enabled by preplanned, well-trained, and well-rehearsed breaching battle drills and execution of the unit's SOPs. The in-stride breach takes advantage of surprise and momentum to breach obstacles. In-stride breaches are effective against either weak defenders or very simple obstacles when joint forces can execute battle drills on the move. Attacking forces are generally configured to execute an in-stride breach except when a deliberate breach is planned.

BREACH AREA

C-12. The *breach area* is a defined area where a breach occurs (ATP 3-90.4). It is established and fully defined by the higher HQ of the unit conducting the breach. Within the breach area is the POB, the reduction area, the far side objective, and the point of penetration. Their definitions follow:

- *Point of breach* is the location at an obstacle where the creation of a lane is being attempted (ATP 3-90.4). Initially, POBs are planned locations only. Normally, the breach force determines the actual POBs during the breach.

- *Reduction area* is a number of adjacent points of breach that are under the control of the breaching commander (ATP 3-90.4). The commander conducting the attack determines the size and location of the reduction area that supports the seizure of a point of penetration. The reduction area is indicated by the area located between the arms of the control graphic for breach. (See figure C-1 on page C-4.) The length and width of the arms extend to include the entire depth of the area that must be reduced.

- *Far side objective* is a defined location oriented on the terrain or on an enemy force that an assaulting force seizes to eliminate enemy direct fires to prevent the enemy from interfering with the reduction of the obstacles and allows follow-on forces to move securely through created lanes (ATP 3-90.4). A far side objective can be oriented on the terrain or on an enemy force. The higher HQ assigns the objective; however, the attacking unit normally subdivides the objective into smaller objectives to assign responsibilities and to control and focus the assault of subordinate forces. When breaching as part of a larger force, seizing the far side objective provides the necessary maneuver space for the higher unit follow-on forces to move securely through the lanes, assemble or deploy, and continue the attack without enemy interference.

- *Point of penetration* is the location, identified on the ground, where the commanders concentrates their efforts to seize a foothold on the far side objective (ATP 3-90.4). This is achieved along a narrow front through maneuver and direct and indirect fires that are accurately placed against enemy forces. A commander conducting a breach establishes a point of penetration that supports planning locations for the reduction area and the seizure of the far side objective.

C-13. The breach area must be large enough to provide sufficient cover and concealment to the attacking unit's assault and breach elements. The area must allow the support force to deploy on the near side of the obstacle and extend far enough on the far side of the obstacle to allow follow-on forces to deploy before leaving the breach area. One technique is to establish the breach area using phase lines or unit boundaries. The phase line defining the far side of the breach area may be established as a BHL (see figure C-1 on page C-4).

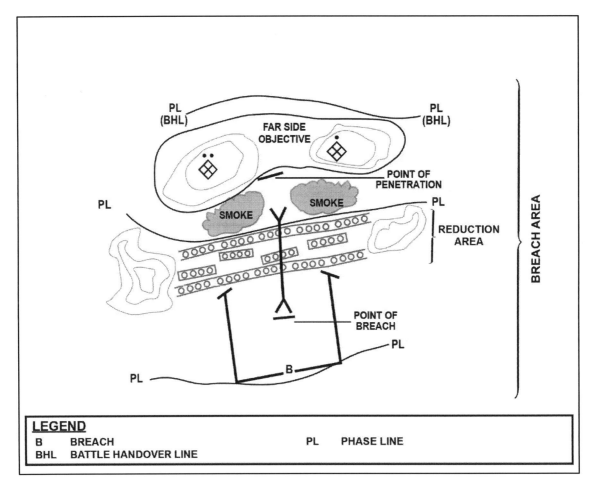

Figure C-1. Breach area

SECTION II – BREACHING TENETS

C-14. The commander applies the tenets of breaching when planning breaching operations. Breaching tenets apply whenever an obstacle is encountered, whether friendly forces are conducting an attack or route clearance operations. These tenets are integrated during planning. (See ATP 3-90.4, table 3-1 for a detailed listing of planning actions within each breaching tenet.) The tenets are—

- Intelligence.
- Breaching fundamentals suppress, obscure, secure, reduce, and assault (known as SOSRA).
- Breaching organization.
- Mass.
- Synchronization.

INTELLIGENCE

C-15. When the company team conducts a breach as part of a CAB attack, the ability to identify how the enemy applies obstacles to the terrain is critical to the company team's success. The CAB conducts its IPB process, which facilitates the company commander's IPB to develop initial situational templates. Information collected by the CAB reconnaissance forces and assets above the CAB, is essential to developing a finalized enemy situation template and final POB locations. Enemy situation templates may cause the company team to deploy to reduce obstacles early, waste time trying to locate nonexistent obstacles, develop COAs using ineffective obstacle reduction methods, and fail to locate bypasses or become surprised by an obstacle.

TEMPLATED ENEMY OBSTACLES

C-16. Templated enemy obstacles on the situation templates provided to the company team are based on—
- Threat patterns based on past operations and emerging tactics, techniques, and procedures.
- Enemy countermobility capabilities (based on manpower, equipment, materials, and time available), including scatterable mines.
- Terrain and weather effects.
- The range of enemy weapon systems covering obstacles and emplacing scatterable mines.

REQUIRED OBSTACLE INFORMATION

C-17. Augmentation of reconnaissance forces by engineer squads or sections may be used as part of the CAB's information collection effort. Information used to produce enemy obstacle overlays include—
- Location of existing or reinforcing obstacles.
- Composition of obstacles: mine, wire, AT ditch, or a combination.
- Orientation of long axis of obstacles.
- Width and depth of obstacles (in meters), particularly obstacle belts.
- Soil conditions. (Determines ability to use mine plows and their appropriate depth settings.)
- Potential breach lane locations, with depth at those points.
- Potential bypass locations.
- Composition of minefields (buried or surface laid AT and antipersonnel mines).
- Types of mines and fuses. (Determines effectiveness of mechanical or explosive reduction techniques.)
- Composition of complex obstacles (combination of wire, mines, and tank ditches).
- Location of direct and indirect fire systems overwatching obstacle.
- Estimate of likely planned obstacle effect.

BREACHING FUNDAMENTALS

C-18. Breaching fundamentals are integrated into the planning process and always apply when reducing a defended obstacle. This includes breaching, gap crossing, and route clearance missions. The breach fundamentals of SOSRA.

SUPPRESS

C-19. Suppression protects friendly forces reducing and maneuvering through an obstacle. Suppression must occur from a position that can array enemy forces in-depth, which may mean planning an SBF that is close to enemy forces. Successful suppression generally triggers subsequent actions in the breach area. Fire control measures ensure that all fires are synchronized with other actions at the POB. The mission of the support force is to suppress the enemy overwatching the obstacle. The breach force also provides additional suppressive fires as the situation dictates; however, its primary focus is on reducing the obstacle.

OBSCURE

C-20. Obscuration degrades observation and target acquisition by enemy forces while concealing friendly force reduction and assault activities. Obscuration planning factors include the length and duration of required obscuration, plus the weather and environment. In urban areas, indirect delivered obscuration and suppressive fires will be more restricted. In some situations, using mortars (because of the ability to fire high-level trajectory), smoke pots, and smoke grenades rather than artillery-fired obscurants may be more effective. Normally, obscuration starts with smoke delivered by indirect fire that builds quickly, followed by mechanical or smoke pots that have a longer duration but take more time to place and build. Typically, the most effective placement of obscuration is between the obstacle and the overwatching enemy forces. (See ATP 3-11.50 for more information on obscuration.)

SECURE

C-21. *Secure* is a tactical mission task in which a unit prevents the enemy from damaging or destroying a force, facility, or geographical location (FM 3-90). Identifying the extent of the enemy defense is critical in selecting the appropriate technique to secure the POB. The POB must be secured before reducing the obstacle. Friendly forces secure the POB to prevent enemy forces from interfering with the reduction of lanes and passage of assault forces. The breach force must be resourced with sufficient maneuver assets to provide local security against the enemy that the support force cannot adequately engage. Elements within the breach force that secure the reduction area may also be used to suppress the enemy once reduction is complete.

REDUCE

C-22. *Reduce* is a tactical mission task in which a unit destroys an encircled or bypassed enemy force (FM 3-90). Reduction cannot be accomplished until effective suppression and obscuration is achieved and the POB secured. The breach force will reduce, proof, and mark the required number of lanes to pass the assault force through the obstacle. The number and width of lanes needed depend on the enemy situation, terrain, size and composition of the assault force, and scheme of movement and maneuver. Follow-on forces will continue to improve and reduce the obstacle when required. When possible, the breach force also should try to secure a foothold to assist in the passage of the assault force.

ASSAULT

C-23. The assault force's primary mission is to seize the far side of the breach lane(s) to enable the attacking force to build combat power on the far side of the breach. The assault force may also be tasked to continue the attack to the POB or even to seize the far side objective. If planned, the battle handover with follow-on forces occurs.

BREACHING ORGANIZATION

C-24. Establishing the breach organization facilitates the application of the breaching fundamentals. Commanders develop COAs that organize friendly forces into a support force, a breach force, and an assault force to execute the breach fundamentals quickly and effectively. Table C-1 shows the relationship between the breach organization as well as the responsibilities of each force.

Table C-1. Breaching organization and responsibilities

Breach Organization	Responsibilities
Support Force	Suppress enemy forces capable of placing direct fires on the reduction area.
	Prevent the enemy from repositioning or counterattacking to place direct fires on breach force.
	Control indirect fires and obscuration within the breach area.
Breach Force	Reduce, proof, and mark the necessary number of lanes through the obstacle.
	Report the status and location of created lanes.
	Provide local security on the near side and far side of the obstacle.
	Provide additional suppression of enemy overwatching the obstacle.
	Assumes control of obscuration upon commitment to breach.
	Assist the passage of the assault force through created lanes.
Assault Force	Seize the far side objective.
	Reduce the enemy protective obstacles.
	Provide clear lanes from the reduction area to the battle handover line for follow-on forces.
	Prevent the enemy from placing direct fires on follow-on forces as they pass through the created lanes.
	Conduct battle handover with follow-on forces.
	Provide reinforcing fires for the support force.
	Destroy the enemy on the obstacle far side that is capable of placing direct fires on the reduction area.

Support Force

C-25. Support force responsibilities are to isolate the reduction area with direct and indirect fires and suppress the enemy's direct and indirect fire at the POB. The support force initially obscures the reduction area to set the conditions for the breach, controls friendly direct and indirect fires within the breach area. The support force is responsible for assessing when sufficient suppression of enemy forces has been achieved to commit the breach force.

Breach Force

C-26. The breach force must have sufficient combat power to secure the POB as well as sufficient reduction assets to reduce the required number of lanes through the obstacle. Critical friendly zones should be activated at the POB before commitment of the breach force to protect it from enemy indirect fires. When conditions are set, the breach force moves rapidly from covered positions to reduce, proof, and emplace initial markings in the lane. Because of the proximity to the POB, once committed, the breach force assumes responsibility for control of obscuration in support of the breach. The breach force is responsible to ensure that all elements within the breach area are aware of explosive hazards (for example, MICLIC) and assume a covered posture prior to detonation.

Assault Force

C-27. The assault force's primary mission is the destruction of enemy forces on the far side of the obstacle to prevent the enemy from placing direct fires on the breach lanes. In complex or restrictive terrain, the assault force may be constrained to a single lane and the assault force commander must ensure that the sequencing of forces through the lane is appropriate to achieve the mission. To maintain tempo, the commander may creep the assault force forward to a last covered position before commitment. The commander must commit the assault force before the engineers block the whole lane by going through it and putting the final markings in. Once committed, the assault force rapidly assaults using all available lanes. The assault force must be prepared to react to the loss of a vehicle in a lane by pushing it aside and continuing the assault.

Mass

C-28. Breaching is conducted by rapidly applying concentrated efforts at a point to reduce obstacles and penetrate the defense. Massed combat power is directed against the enemy's weakness. The location selected for breaching depends largely on the weakness in the enemy's defense, where its covering fires are minimized. If friendly forces cannot find a natural weakness, they create one by fixing most of the enemy force and isolating a small portion of it for attack.

Synchronization

C-29. Breaching operations elements that require precise synchronization are the timing of suppression, time available for obscuration, compared to how much obscuration is necessary (derived from: time to adjust mission, build smoke, how long to get breach force from assault positions to POB, time to reduce, time to proof, time to initially mark, time to get assault force through). Do we have enough smoke available to get this done? Synch buttoning up, commitment of assault force, and so forth. What signals and what triggers are necessary?

C-30. Failure to synchronize effective suppression and obscuration with obstacle reduction and assault can result in rapid, devastating losses of friendly troops at the obstacle or enemy EA. The commander must employ obscuration at the right time and place to maximize its effectiveness or risk hampering target acquisition and command and control. The breach force must be task-organized with the necessary reduction assets (based on the composition and location of obstacles) and have them properly sequenced in the movement formation. Commanders must ensure that they do not prematurely exhaust their reduction assets needed to reduce subsequent obstacles.

C-31. The company team achieves synchronization in a breaching operation best by using detailed reverse planning, clear instructions to subordinate elements, effective command and control, and extensive rehearsals. The emphasis is on the steps of SOSRA. Planning considerations for synchronization during breaching, listed in reverse order, include the following:
- Reverse planning starts with actions on the objective.
- The planned actions on the objective influence the size and composition of the assault force, and the number and location of lanes the team must create.
- Lane requirements, topography, and the type and depth of obstacles determine the type and number of reduction assets task organized to the breach force to include redundancy in breach assets.
- The ability of the enemy's infantry to interfere with the breach through ATGMs drives the nature of security at the breach.
- The enemy's ability to mass fires at the breach site dictates the nature of the required suppression fires (including the composition of the support force and the type and amount of supporting fires).
- The location of the enemy and the availability of clear fields of fire determine the location of the support force and its SBF position.
- Availability of cover and concealment within the breach area inform the locations for the assault positions for the assault and breach forces and their routes to the POB.

Reverse Planning

C-32. The size and composition of the support, breach, and assault forces (breach organization) are determined during COA development using reverse planning. Reverse planning begins with actions on the objective and moves backward to the LD, since seizing an objective is typically the decisive point and directly tied to mission accomplishment. Using reverse planning and force ratios, the commander determines the size and composition of the force(s) that will perform the tasks that support the main and supporting efforts for each COA. Reverse planning for breaching is performed using the following steps:
- Step 1. Identify available reduction assets.
- Step 2. Template enemy obstacles.
- Step 3. Understand the scheme of movement and maneuver.
- Step 4. Identify the number of required breach lanes.

- Step 5. Identify the assets required to reduce, proof, and mark lanes.
- Step 6. Task-organize reduction assets within the maneuver force.

C-33. When the company is part of the CAB's combined arms breaching operation, detailed reverse planning initiates during the IPB and the development of enemy situation template (see figure C-2 on page C-10). The scheme of maneuver, engineer operations, fires, air defense, and actions at the obstacle are based upon this common situation template. The situation template, developed by the S-2 depicting enemy direct- and indirect-fire coverage of templated enemy obstacles, determines the size and composition of the support forces.

C-34. The enemy's ability to interfere with the breach force at the POB determines size and composition of the security element within the breach force. The enemy's ability to mass fires on the POB determines the amount of suppression required as well as the size and composition of the breach force. Lane requirements and the composition of obstacles drive the amount and type of reduction assets needed by the breach force. The engineer staff planner focuses on the allocation of reduction assets.

C-35. Actions on the objective drive the size and composition of the force that conducts the final assault onto the objective as part of an attack, which dictates lane requirements (the number and location of required lanes). The engineer staff planner for the CAB and other planners determine how best to allocate reduction assets within the arrayed forces to facilitate the scheme of movement and maneuver for each COA.

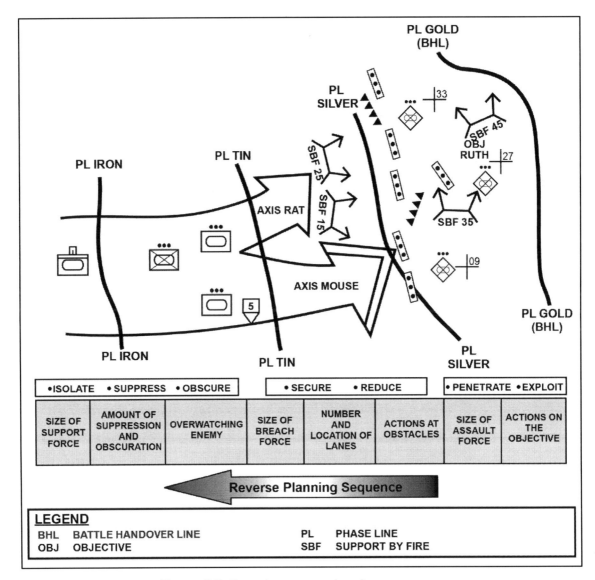

Figure C-2. Breach reverse planning sequence

C-36. Breaching activities are planned by incorporating the breaching tenets within the planning steps of TLP. The need to conduct a breach is determined based on the identification of specified, implied, and essential tasks for mobility as part of mission analysis, within Step 3–Make a Tentative Plan of TLP at the company level. The company may be tasked to conduct a breach in support of the CAB's mission, the commander's intent, and the scheme of movement and maneuver; or it may be implied based on the enemy situation, the terrain (mobility corridors), and the commander's intent. Table C-2 provides a listing of breach planning considerations in relation to TLP at the company level.

Table C-2. Breaching considerations within troop leading procedures

Steps to Troop Leading Procedures	Breach Planning Considerations	
Step 1 – Receive the Mission	Gather geospatial information and products (mobility corridors and combined obstacle overlays) for the area operation.	
	Gather intelligence products on threat countermobility capabilities and patterns.	
	Determine the availability of information on obstacles within the company propose area of operation.	
	Determine status of breaching assets available to the company.	
Step 2 – Issue a Warning		
Step 3 – Make a Tentative Plan	*Mission Analysis*	Understand the mission, commander's intent, and scheme of movement and maneuver (two levels up).
		Complete the following as part of the initial intelligence preparation of the battlefield—
		Develop terrain products (mobility corridor and combined obstacle overlay).
		Evaluate the effects of terrain and weather on friendly mobility and enemy countermobility and survivability capabilities.
		Assess enemy countermobility capabilities (manpower, equipment, and materials), and template enemy obstacles based on threat patterns, terrain, and time available.
		Identify specified and implied mobility (breaching) tasks and determine any obvious shortfalls in breaching assets engineer forces and special equipment and initiate requests for augmentation as early as possible.
		Develop information requirements related to breaching (terrain restrictions and mobility restraints, necessary or desired obstacle information, enemy countermobility and survivability efforts), and draft requirements as possible commander's critical information requirements.
		Integrate information collection tasks and engineer or other necessary specialized reconnaissance capabilities into the information collection plans.
	Course of Action (COA) Development	Identify the need to conduct a breach for each course of action based on mobility corridors and template enemy obstacles.
		Allocate reduction assets (engineer units and breaching equipment) based on the results of reverse planning.
		Develop tasks that implement the breaching fundamentals suppress, obscure, secure, reduce, and assault.
		Determine breach organization requirements (support, breach, assault force) and ensure that arrayed forces have been adequately resourced.
	COA Analysis	War-game the breach organization—
		Force ratios against variances in the enemy disposition.
		Array of breach assets based on losses or variances in the composition of obstacles.
		War-game changes in the planned point of breach, locations of support by fire positions, and wind effects on obscuration.
		War-game friendly reactions to enemy counterattacks within the breach area and enemy use of scatterable mines to isolate forces and repair breached obstacles.
		Refine the plan based on results of war-gaming.

Table C-2. Breaching considerations within troop leading procedures (continued)

Steps to Troop Leading Procedures	Breach Planning Considerations	
Step 3 – Make a Tentative Plan (continued)	COA Comparison	Analyze and evaluate the advantages and disadvantages for each COA in relation to the ability to execute the breaching:
		Ability (time-distance) to shift breaching assets between units beyond the line of departure.
		Ability to reinforce the breaching forces or respond to enemy counterattacks within the breach area (use of a reserve).
	COA Selection	Gain approval for any changes to the essential tasks for mobility.
		Gain approval for recommended priorities of effort and support.
		Gain approval for requests for engineer augmentation to be sent to higher headquarters.
Step 4 – Initiate Movement	Ensure that the task organization of engineer forces and critical breach equipment is accurate and clear, to include the necessary instructions for effecting linkup (linkup should be as early as possible in the planning process).	
Step 5 – Conduct Reconnaissance		
Step 6 – Complete the Plan	Ensure the quality and completeness of subunit instructions for performing breaching.	
Step 7 – Issue the Order		
Step 8 – Supervise and Refine		

BREACH IN SUPPORT OF AN ATTACK

C-37. The following example provides information that a company team commander should consider when conducting a breach in support of an attack:

- The commander for Alpha Company receives a specified task from the CAB's OPORD to secure the CAB's objective and deny the enemy's ability to reposition forces against Bravo Company.
- The enemy force on the objective have been in position for 24 to 36 hours by the time friendly forces cross the LD. Enemy vehicles have hull down fighting positions; and Infantry squads have prepared fighting positions. Protective obstacles consisting of triple-strand concertina wire and single-impulse fuse antipersonnel mines are located 25 to 50 meters in front of the vehicle and Infantry squad positions. The enemy has emplaced a fixing obstacle that is approximately 120 to 150 meters in-depth. This obstacle consists of triple-strand concertina wire and mixed single impulse fuse antipersonnel and AT mines. These mines may be buried 6 to 8 inches deep in the first row.
- Alpha Company is task organized with two tank platoons (1st platoon has a plow and roller, 2d platoon has one plow tank), one mechanized Infantry platoon, and one engineer platoon. The engineer platoon consists of three engineer squads with four Bradley fighting vehicles and one assault breacher vehicle (known as ABV).

C-38. The Alpha Company commander and engineer PL conduct a mission analysis and reverse planning to develop a COA. The key elements of the breach tenets to consider during reverse planning are as follows:

- The CAB's scout platoon has been assigned responsibility for collecting information on a named area of interest. Specific information to report includes confirming the location, composition, disposition, and orientation of the obstacles.
- Enemy vehicle and squad positions on the objective are destroyed sequentially from East to West. Breaching the protective obstacles in front of these enemy positions requires the assault force to have mobility assets (tank plow).
- The breach force creates one breach lane through the enemy's fixing obstacle. The obstacle composition favors the use of MICLICs as the primary breach method. The soil conditions favor the use of tank plows or rollers as a proofing method. The depth of the obstacle requires a minimum of two MICLICs to create one lane.

- Alpha Company has priority of fires during this phase of the CAB's operation. The breach force plans to use self-obscuration with smoke pots and vehicle smoke grenades while ensuring the breach force will not silhouette vehicles or personnel later. The company rehearses the mission to develop accurate triggers to initiate, build, and sustain obscuration throughout the reduction of the obstacle by the breach force.
- The enemy positions are approximately 800 to 1,100 meters from the far side of the obstacle with infantry squads located 400 meters from the left and right limits of the obstacle. A friendly platoon-sized maneuver element and the engineer platoon provide adequate near and far side security at the POB.
- Effective suppression requires a platoon-sized element and indirect fire to prevent the enemy vehicles and squads from repositioning and massing of fires on the breach force.

C-39. The Alpha Company commander completes analysis of the COA and issues the OPORD. Initially, the commander and XO are located with the support force. Once the assault is initiated, the commander will follow the assault element through the lane and the XO will move with the support force. The breach organization and key tasks to subordinate units are as follows:

C-40. The 1st tank platoon (+) — Breach force. The breach force consists of a tank platoon with plow and roller and the engineer platoon. The breach force accomplishes the following:

- Confirms the POB.
- Confirms the location, composition, and disposition of the obstacle.
- Identifies the leading edge of the obstacles.
- Adjusts obscuration if required.
- Breaches, proofs, and emplaces entry point and initial markings in accordance with the SOP for one lane through the obstacle.
- Secures near and far side of the POB to protect the assault force.
- Emplaces/improves final lane markings in accordance with the SOP.
- Prepares to support assault breach of protective obstacles.

C-41. The 2d tank platoon — Assault force. The assault force is equipped with four tanks with one tank plow. The assault force accomplishes the following:

- Secures the far side of the obstacle.
- Transits breach lanes rapidly.
- Prepares to react to loss of vehicle in lane.
- Prepares to breach protective obstacles.
- Destroys the remaining elements of the enemy platoon and seizes the objective.

C-42. The 3d mechanized Infantry platoon — Support force. The support force accomplishes the following:
- Initiates/adjusts obscuration.
- Suppresses enemy platoon on the objective to protect the breach force.
- Assesses effectiveness of suppression and level of isolation of objective.
- Follows behind 2d platoon and clears enemy dismounted positions on the objective.

C-43. Figures C-3 through figure C-7 on pages C-14 through C-18, illustrate a company team breaching an obstacle during an attack.

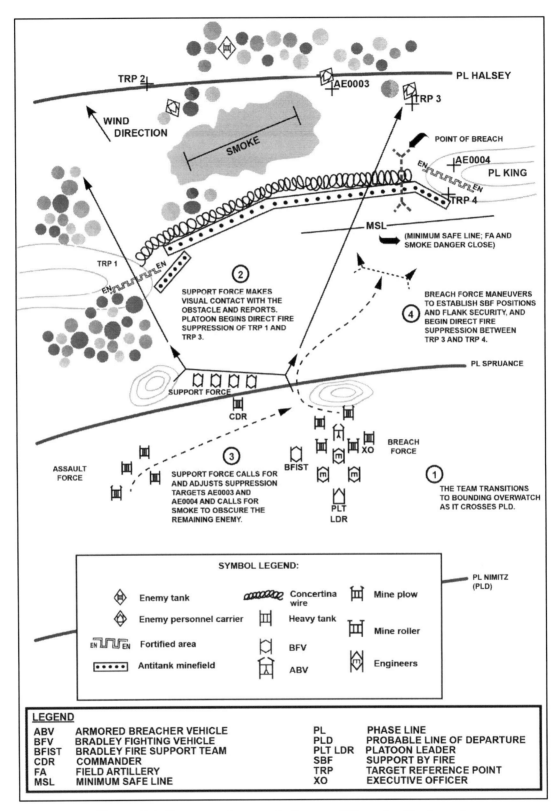

Figure C-3. Company team sets the conditions for the breach

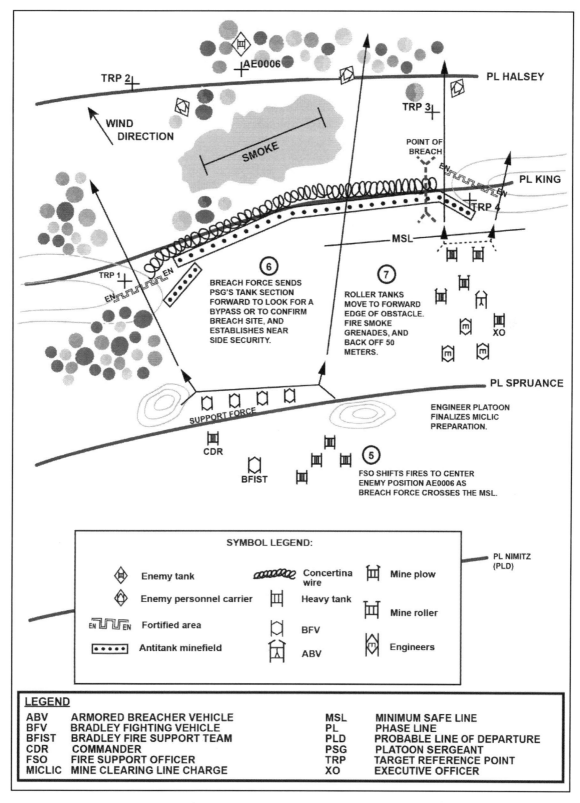

Figure C-4. Company team establishes security

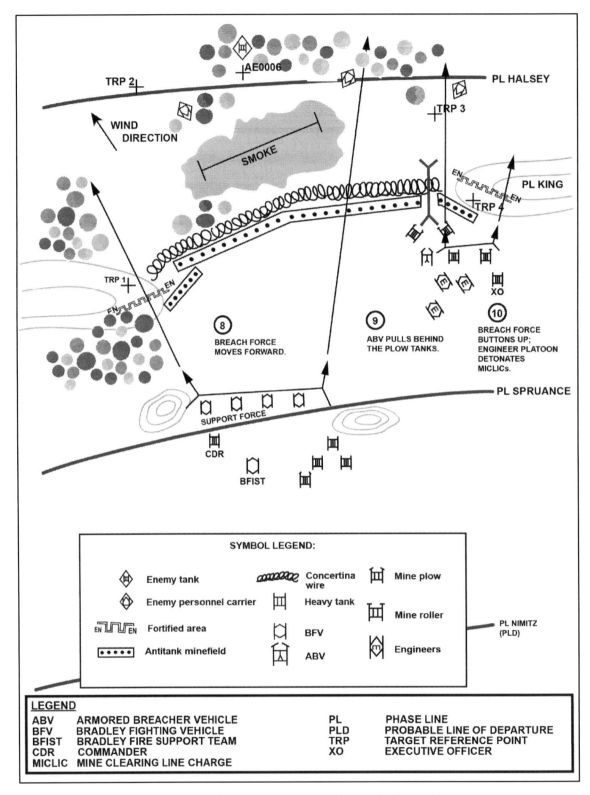

Figure C-5. Breach force conducts the breach

ATP 3-90.1

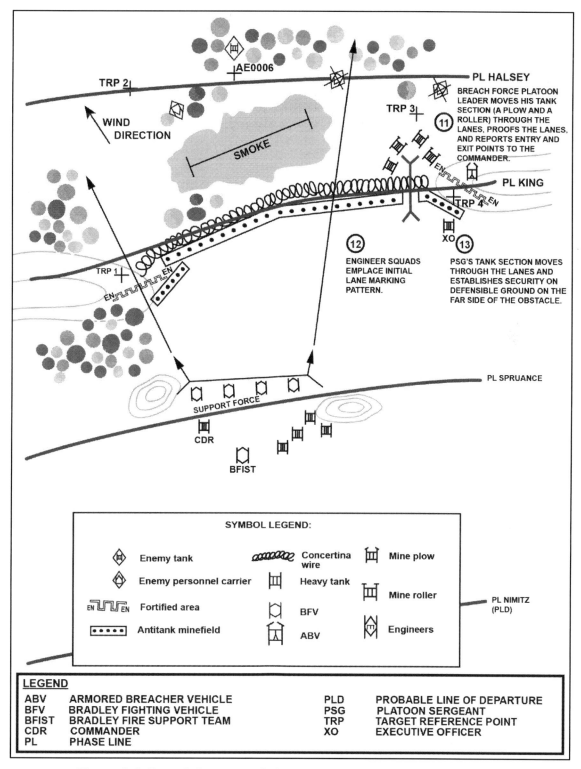

Figure C-6. Breach force proofs lane and establishes far side security

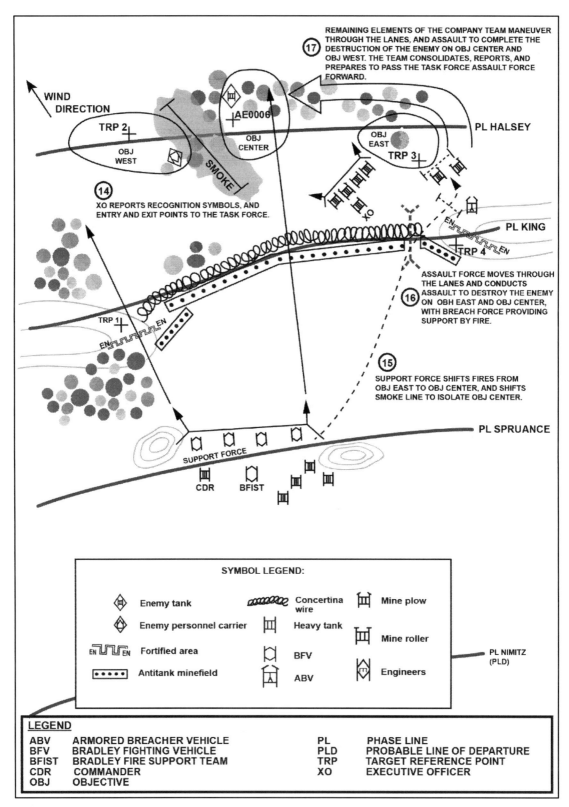

Figure C-7. Assault force conducts assault and secures the objective

BREACHING METHODS

C-44. The company team can create a lane by itself if it is equipped with the assets required to breach the type of obstacle encountered. If the company team does not have this capability, it may be required to provide close-in protection for attached engineers with breaching assets. Three breaching methods are as follows:

- Mechanical. This breaching usually occurs with mine plows or mine rakes.
- Explosive. This breaching employs such means as the MICLIC, M173 line charge, or hand-placed 1/4-pound blocks of trinitrotoluene.
- Manual. This breaching occurs with Soldiers probing by hand or using such items as grappling hooks, shovels, picks, axes, and chain saws. Manual breaching is the least preferred method.

CREATING AND PROOFING LANE

C-45. For complex obstacles, or obstacles with significant depth, the preferred mechanism is to use an ABV with MICLC. However, given the unpredictable nature of threat obstacle employment, the company team may often resort to the use of mine plows as the primary breaching tool. The CAB or company commander may allocate one to three plows per tank platoon. When properly equipped and supported, the tank platoon can create up to two lanes through an obstacle.

C-46. Plow tanks lead the breach force. Immediately following them are vehicles that proof the lane; these are usually tanks equipped with mine rollers. This process ensures that the lane is clear.

C-47. If the location and dimensions of the obstacle are unknown, the breach element may choose to lead with tanks equipped with mine rollers to identify the beginning of the obstacle. The processes of locating the leading edge of an obstacle, positioning plows, building up sufficient spoil, the slow rate of movement, and the time required to dump spoil mean that the breach element is exposed. The lack of survivability (plows and rollers can survive minimal mine strikes), combined with the gun tube being over the side during a breach, place the crews in high risk. It is imperative that the company team commander ensures a high volume of fires prior to, during, and after the breach occurs.

LANE MARKING

C-48. After the lane is created and proofed, it can be marked to ensure safe movement by vehicles and personnel; this is critical for follow-on forces that may not know the exact location of the cleared lane. A distinctive marker shows where drivers should move to then move into the entry point to the lane. From there, additional markings must show where the lane begins and ends. (See ATP 3-90.4 for more information.)

C-49. Entrance markers indicate the start of a lane through an obstacle. They signify the friendly-side boundary of the obstacle and the point at which movement is restricted by the lane width and path. Entrance markers also indicate the lane width. The distance between entrance markers must be the same as the width of the created lane.

C-50. To minimize the necessary breaching time, the proofing vehicle may simultaneously mark the lane. Unit SOPs dictate marking methods and materials, which commonly include the following:

- Cleared lane mechanical marking system.
- Traffic cones.
- Hand Emplaceable Minefield Marking Set.
- U-shaped picket stakes with tape.
- Mounted guides.
- Chemical lights.
- Expended shell casings.
- End connectors (tank track) with engineer tape and chemical light sticks.

C-51. Whatever markings are established, they must be visible from within a buttoned-up vehicle and commonly understood by everybody in the organization. (See ATP 3-90.4 for more information.) Units must conduct extensive lane marking rehearsals so that each subelement understands the marking system and what the markings looks like under combat conditions.

COMPLETING BREACH

C-52. Throughout the operation, the breach element provides continuous updates of the breach force's progress to higher HQ and other elements involved in the breach. It coordinates with the support force for suppressive fires. In particular, the assault force closely monitors percent-proofed and is prepared to assault immediately upon reaching 100 percent.

C-53. After initial marking is complete, the breach element uses voice and digital systems to report the lane's entry and exit points and confirms the method of marking to expedite the movement of the assault force. Digital overlays enable units to move quickly to the breach lanes using the position navigation or GPS. The assault force often moves behind the breach force and closely follows the breach vehicles through the new lane.

ATTACHMENTS

C-54. The types and quantities of these attachments depend on the commander, the mission and the number, size, and type of organizations requiring support. These attachments and assets are used to breach and reduce obstacles.

COMBAT ENGINEERS

C-55. The most versatile of all breaching assets, combat engineers can conduct explosive or manual breaches, proof and mark lanes through an obstacle, and provide guides during breaching operations. While it conducts breaching and proofing operations, however, the squad is vulnerable to enemy direct and indirect fires and must be secured by tanks or other IFVs. The engineer squad is equipped with a Bradley fighting vehicle and organic weapons that provide flexibility and safety.

MECHANIZED INFANTRY PLATOON OR TANK PLATOON

C-56. If other breaching assets are unavailable, a mechanized Infantry or tank platoon can conduct explosive breaches (with hand-emplaced charges) or use manual breaching kits (usually consisting of grappling hooks, gloves, and wire cutters). At the same time, however, employment of either type of platoon organization in breaching operations has distinct disadvantages. The pace of the breach is slow, and the operation leaves the platoon vulnerable to enemy attack.

ARMORED VEHICLE LAUNCHED BRIDGE

C-57. Units employ the armored vehicle launched bridge/Wolverine primarily to cross short gaps, such as narrow streams, AT ditches, craters, canals, or partially blown bridges. Its span is 18.3 meters using prepared abutments and 17 meters (57 feet) with unprepared abutments. The capacity of the armored vehicle launched bridge is one military load class 60 (70 with improved bridge) vehicle. The capacity of the Wolverine bridge is military load class 70 traffic over gaps of up to 24 meters (57 feet).

JOINT ASSAULT BRIDGE

C-58. The JAB is based off the M1-series Abrams tank chassis and modified to transport, launch, and retrieve a military load class 70 bridge that can be retrieved from either end. The JAB can hold a class 70 vehicle across a 60-foot gap. Because the bridge is mounted on the M1 chassis, the JAB can maintain the tempo of combat maneuver organizations.

ASSAULT BREACHER VEHICLE

C-59. The ABV is a single-platform minefield breaching, clearing, proofing, and marking system built on an M1A1 tank chassis that provides explosive and mechanical reduction capabilities. It weighs approximately 63 tons and has a cruising speed of 29 miles per hour (47 kilometers per hour), which is comparable with the M1A1 tank. The ABV is operated by a vehicle commander and driver. A .50-caliber machine gun is externally mounted at the commander's weapon station. The ABV is configured with two MK-155 linear demolition charge launchers (two M58 linear demolition charges); an integrated lane-marking system; a full-width mine plow; and combat bulldozer blade, surface mine plow, and rapid ordnance removal system attachments. The linear demolition charge system contains two single-shot launchers.

C-60. The MICLIC is fired 62 meters from the obstacle to get the full 100 meters of depth. The charge creates two skip zones, where the mines are not detonated, on the right and left side of the center line of the cleared lane. The skip zones, which are about 1.5 meters wide, necessitate the proofing of all MICLIC lanes. (See ATP 3-90.4 for more information.)

C-61. The MICLIC is effective against pressure-activated AT mines and against mechanically activated antipersonnel mines. Effectiveness is limited against magnetically activated mines, including scatterable mines, and those with multi-impulse (double-impact) or time-delay fuse. The MICLIC is not effective on severely broken ground where the line charge cannot lay flat. When detonated, the MICLIC has a danger area with a radius of 1,600 meters. While the ABV can proof its own lane, commanders should consider the risk in losing ABVs during proofing rather than using their organic tank plows.

MINE PLOW

C-62. The company team uses the mine plow (also known as the mine-clearing blade) to breach and proof minefields. The system affords good survivability and, when fully operational, a tank equipped with a mine plow can quickly clear two 68-inch-wide lanes, one in front of each track.

> *Note.* The plow's dog-bone assembly detonates the tilt rods of mines in the area between the two plowed lanes; however, only plows equipped with the improved dog-bone assembly project a magnetic signature and defeat tilt-rod and magnetic mines.

C-63. To build up sufficient spoil, the plow is dropped at least 100 meters before the tank reaches the minefield. It is not lifted until the tank is at least 100 meters past the far edge of the minefield. The plow needs 18 inches of soil depth to be effective, limiting the tank's speed to 10 miles per hour or less in the lane. The mine plow is used only in a straight line; it does not work well on hard, rocky, or uneven ground where it cannot maintain adequate spoil. Mine detonation can cause violent upward movement of the blade; the tank's main gun is traversed to the side during plowing to prevent damage to the gun tube. The plow's lifting straps can become entangled in wire obstacles. Manual lifting of the plow takes at least 10 minutes. It is essential that the mine plow only be operated with the mold board extensions installed to ensure displaced mines do not fall into the path of the tank's tracks.

MINE ROLLER

C-64. If breaching is anticipated, the company mounts and employs rollers. Because the mine rollers are normally kept in the CAB's trains, anticipated use must be forecast, and the rollers brought forward to be mounted in a covered and concealed position. Once installed, that tank's cross-country mobility and speed are severely limited. Units use the mine roller to identify the forward edges of a minefield and to proof lanes. The roller sweeps a 44-inch path in front of each track and is equipped with an improved dog-bone assembly. It is effective in breaching wire obstacles.

C-65. The roller, however, is not effective on broken or uneven ground. The mine roller, like the mine plow, does not defeat magnetic fuse mines unless the mine roller is equipped with the improved dog-bone assembly. The main gun is traversed to the side or rear when contact with a mine is possible or imminent; detonation can throw the roller (or pieces of it) violently upward, possibly damaging the tube.

This page intentionally left blank.

Appendix D

Chemical, Biological, Radiological, and Nuclear Defense

Chemical, biological, radiological, and nuclear operations include the employment of capabilities that assess, protect against, and mitigate the entire range of chemical, biological, radiological, and nuclear incidents to enable freedom of action (FM 3-11). The commander integrates CBRN considerations into mission planning depending on the CBRN threat. This appendix provides guidance for planning and providing tactical response to assess, protect, and mitigate CBRN threats and hazards.

OVERVIEW

D-1. The proliferation of WMD (to include the constant pursuit of the materials, expertise, and technology required to employ WMD) will increase in the future. Adversaries may create novel chemical warfare agents. The anticipated OE will contain restrictive terrain when CBRN hazards are employed to disrupt operations. Industrial facilities have the potential risk of causing exposure to agents or toxic industrial materials (TIMs). The likelihood of the enemy's use of WMD increases during large-scale combat operations, particularly against command and control systems, massed formations, and critical infrastructure.

D-2. The commander must anticipate and plan for CBRN defense. To accomplish the mission, commanders must balance the inherent risks of CBRN environments with mission accomplishment. This is accomplished through assessing CBRN threats and hazards, providing protection in and against CBRN environments, and mitigating CBRN incidents.

CHEMICAL, BIOLOGICAL, RADIOLOGICAL, AND NUCLEAR ENVIRONMENT

D-3. *Chemical, biological, radiological, and nuclear environment* is an operational environment that includes chemical, biological, radiological, and nuclear threats and hazards and their potential resulting effects (JP 3-11). CBRN environment conditions can be the result of deliberate enemy or terrorist actions or the result of an industrial accident. CBRN threats include the intentional employment of, or intent to employ, weapons or improvised devices to produce CBRN hazards. CBRN hazards may result from WMD employment or include those created from accidental or intentional releases of TIMs, biological pathogens, or radioactive matter. TIM is a generic term for toxic or radioactive substances in solid, liquid, aerosolized, or gaseous form that may be used or stored for industrial, commercial, medical, military, or domestic purposes. TIM may be chemical, biological, or radiological. (See FM 3-11 for more information on CBRN hazards.)

D-4. Brigade and battalion CBRN staffs maintain situational understanding of CBRN or TIM hazards and advise the commander on the proper detection, identification, and follow-on tactical decisions that must be made when friendly forces encounter CBRN threats and hazards. CBRN staff down to the company level support assessment of CBRN hazards by ensuring that CBRN teams are trained and equipped with the correct gear to detect and identify hazards. The initial detection and presumptive identification of CBRN hazards provides enough information to commanders for immediate tactical decisions, such as MOPP level increase, increased tactical dispersion, or repositioning units.

CHEMICAL HAZARDS

D-5. A *chemical hazard* is any chemical manufactured, used, transported, or stored that can cause death or other harm through toxic properties of those materials, including chemical agents and chemical weapons prohibited under the Chemical Weapons Convention as well as toxic industrial chemicals (JP 3-11). This includes—

- Chemical weapons—toxic chemicals specifically designed as a weapon.
- Chemical agents—chemical substance that is intended for use in military operations to kill, seriously injure, or incapacitate, mainly through physiological effects.
- Fourth generation agents—are unique organophosphorus nerve agents that are more persistent than and at least as toxic as traditional nerve agents.
- Toxic industrial chemicals—chemicals that are developed or manufactured for use in industrial operations or research.

D-6. Chemical agents cause casualties, degrade performance, slow maneuver, restrict terrain, and disrupt operations. They can cover large areas and may be delivered as liquid, vapor, or aerosol. Chemical agents can be delivered by artillery, mortars, rockets, missiles, aircraft spray, bombs, land mines, and covert means.

D-7. Against chemical attacks, friendly units increase tactical dispersion and frequently reposition AAs, CPs, and sustainment nodes to prevent effective enemy targeting and contamination of larger formations. Advance understanding of chemical threats in the OE will enable rapid response. Company teams are trained to recognize hazard indicators, utilize detection, implement collective protection, and mitigate the hazard. See table D-1 for more characteristics of chemical agents.

Table D-1. Characteristics of chemical agents

Agent	Nerve	Blister	Blood	Incapacitating
Protection	Mask and IPE	Mask and IPE	Mask and IPE	Mask
Detection	JCAD, M256A2, CAM, and M8 and M9 paper	JCAD, M256A2, CAM, and M8 and M9 paper	JCAD, M256A2	Technical equipment available to CBRN forces
Symptoms	Difficulty breathing, drooling, nausea, vomiting, convulsions, and blurred vision	Burning eyes, stinging skin, irritated nose	At high concentrations: seizures, respiratory and cardiac arrest	Coughing, nausea, choking, headache, and tight chest Fentanyl derivatives: dizziness, sleepiness, rapid unconsciousness
Effects	Incapacitates	Blisters skin, damages respiratory tract	Incapacitates	Incapacitates
First Aid	ATNAA and CANA DECON	As for second- and third-degree burns	Medical support	Medical support
Decontamination	RSDL and flush eyes with water	RSDL and flush eyes with water	RSDL	RSDL
Legend: ATNAA – antidote treatment nerve agent auto-injector; CAM – chemical agent monitor; CANA – convulsive antidote nerve agent; CBRN – chemical, biological, radiological, and nuclear; DECON – decontamination; IPE – individual protective equipment; JCAD – joint chemical agent detector; RSDL – reactive skin decontamination lotion			

BIOLOGICAL HAZARDS

D-8. *Biological hazard* is an organism, or substance derived from an organism, that poses a threat to human or animal health (JP 3-11). This can include medical waste or samples of a microorganism, virus, or toxin from a biological source that can impact human health. Biological hazards are difficult to detect initially as most symptoms, upon onset, may mimic cold and flu symptoms. Pathogens require an incubation period to establish themselves in the body of a host to produce symptoms. Commanders may establish illness thresholds by percentage that trigger increased separation. Formations use aerosolized vapor protection (such as plastic sheeting, facemasks, and ultraviolet lamps) and increased field sanitation with leader oversight as an incremental step to increase the protective posture.

D-9. Leaders provide vigilant oversight on field hygiene, sleeping areas, and potentially sick personnel to prevent the spread of biological agents as well as limit the effects on personnel. Soldier readiness prior to deployments is crucial in setting conditions for successful biological protection. Medical screening provides immunizations and identifies Soldiers with compromised immune systems before deployments to minimize vulnerability.

RADIOLOGICAL HAZARDS

D-10. Radiological hazards include any electromagnetic or particulate radiation that is capable of producing ions to cause damage, injury, or destruction. Radiological hazards also include TIMs. Enemies could disperse radioactive material in several ways, such as—

- Targeting a research or power-generating nuclear reactor with conventional munitions to release nuclear/radiological material.
- Adding radioactive material to a munition.
- Release of low-level radioactive material intended for use in industry or medicine.

D-11. Depending on the radioactive particle, the hazard may be more internal than external. Protecting personnel against alpha particles includes inhalation and ingestion while beta, gamma, and neutron radiation require external protection. Efforts should be made to minimize particle dispersion by wearing masks and minimizing movement that raises dust into the air.

NUCLEAR HAZARDS

D-12. Nuclear weapon effects are qualitatively different from biological or chemical weapon effects. The nature and intensity of nuclear detonation effects are determined by the type of weapon, its yield, and the physical medium in which the detonation occurs. The effects of a nuclear detonation include—

- Blast produces shockwaves that can cause critical injuries to personnel and destroy material.
- Thermal radiation causes severe burns and secondary fires.
- Electromagnetic pulse can cause widespread disruption of electrical and electronic equipment.
- Ionizing radiation is a significant threat to personnel and materiel.
- Fallout is residual radiation and may be a lingering, widespread hazard that limits military operations.

D-13. Time, cover, and shielding offer the best protection from the immediate effects of a nuclear detonation; this includes avoiding a contaminated area until radiation levels lower, covering fighting positions with 18 inches overhead cover, or shielding by using sandbags to line the floor of armored vehicles. Soldiers should cover exposed skin and stay down until the blast wave passes and debris stops falling. Immediately after a nuclear detonation, continuous radiation monitoring should begin.

D-14. Operations in a nuclear environment are complicated by the necessity to control exposure of personnel to nuclear radiation. An operation exposure guide determines the maximum radiation dose to which units may be exposed and still accomplish a mission. Determination of this dose is based on the accumulated dose or radiation history of the unit.

CHEMICAL, BIOLOGICAL, RADIOLOGICAL, AND NUCLEAR PASSIVE DEFENSE

D-15. The core CBRN functions (assess, protect, and mitigate) support all CBRN defense tasks and communicate the tasks that provide units the means to accomplish its mission in a CBRN environment. These functions also define the contribution CBRN units and staffs provide. These functions provide a focus for task and unit training, leader development, and force design. The CBRN core functions are assess threats and hazards, provide protection in and against CBRN environments, and mitigate CBRN incidents. The application of CBRN defense tasks address the hazards created by CBRN incidents or accidents and help minimize vulnerabilities, protect friendly forces, and maintain the company team's operating tempo.

Assessing Chemical, Biological, Radiological, and Nuclear Hazards

D-16. CBRN staffs, by design, support commander's decision-making and risk decisions when facing potential CBRN threats and hazards. Assessment of CBRN hazards, when integrated into the IPB, provides commanders with a clear understanding of how to protect freedom of action and preserve combat power. Intelligence and CBRN staffs ensure that they account for CBRN and TIM, named areas of interest, and known WMD targeted areas of interest during IPB, war-gaming, and information collection planning.

Chemical, Biological, Radiological, and Nuclear Protection

D-17. CBRN protection measures are taken to keep CBRN threats and hazards from having an adverse effect on personnel, equipment, and facilities. Tasks that enable CBRN protection include the following:

- Employ individual protective equipment and other CBRN protective equipment.
- Establish CBRN alarm conditions.
- Exercise personal hygiene and force health protection programs.
- Utilizing shielding or protective cover.

D-18. CBRN protection is an integral part of all operations. Techniques that work for avoidance also work for protection such as shielding Soldiers and units and shaping the battlefield. Other forms of protection involve sealing or hardening positions, protecting Soldiers, assuming appropriate MOPP (see table D-2), reacting to the attack, and using collective protection. Individual protective items include the protective mask, joint service lightweight integrated suit technology, overboots, and gloves. The higher-level commander above the ABCT establishes the minimum level of protection. Subordinate units may increase this level as necessary but may not decrease it. The joint service lightweight integrated suit technology may be worn for 45 days with up to six launderings or up to 120 days with no launderings. The joint service lightweight integrated suit technology can be worn for 24 hours once contaminated. The overboots provide 60 days of durability and 24 hours of protection against liquid chemical agents.

Table D-2. Mission oriented protective posture levels

Level/Equipment	MOPP Ready	MOPP-0	MOPP-1	MOPP-2	MOPP-3	MOPP-4	Mask Only
Mask	Carried	Carried	Carried	Carried	Worn	Worn	***Worn
JSLIST	*Ready	**Available	Worn	Worn	Worn	Worn	
Overboots	*Ready	**Available	**Available	Worn	Worn	Worn	
Gloves	*Ready	**Available	**Available	**Available	**Available	Worn	
Helmet Cover	*Ready	**Available	**Available	Worn	Worn	Worn	
Notes:							
* Items available to the Soldier within 2 hours with replacement available within 6 hours							
** Items must be positioned within arms-reach of the Soldier							
*** Never "mask only" if nerve or blister agent is used in the area of operation							
Legend:							
JSLIST – joint service lightweight integrated suit technology; MOPP – mission oriented protective posture							

D-19. Passive measures can be used to monitor for the presence of CBRN hazards. Depending on the threat and probability of use, periodic or continuous techniques are used. An area array of CBRN detectors and/or monitors can be positioned within a given area for detection and early warning of a CBRN incident. ATP 3-11.32 describes specific techniques for monitoring radiological exposure including determining correlation factor data, radiation exposure status, and recording exposure. All units initiate continuous monitoring when they receive a fallout warning, when a unit is on an administrative or tactical move, when a nuclear burst occurs, when radiation levels above one centigray per hour are detected by periodic monitoring, and on order of the commander. Except for units on the move, continuous monitoring stops on instructions from the commander or higher HQ or when the dose rate falls below one centigray per hour.

MITIGATING CHEMICAL, BIOLOGICAL, RADIOLOGICAL, AND NUCLEAR HAZARDS

D-20. Mitigating a CBRN incident encompasses a range of tasks to mitigate hazard effects after a CBRN incident. A CBRN incident can include deliberate attacks or accidental releases from technological or natural disasters. It includes all efforts to respond to CBRN incidents and reduce hazard effects on forces and equipment. Tasks for mitigating CBRN hazards include—

- Marking contaminated areas.
- Establishing control zones.
- Conducting decontamination.
- Controlling run off contamination.
- Implementing warning and reporting.
- Documenting exposures.

D-21. Use of CBRN weapons creates unique residual hazards that may require decontamination. In addition to the deliberate use of these weapons, collateral damage, natural disasters, and industrial emitters may require decontamination. Contamination forces units into protective equipment that degrades performance of individual and collective tasks. Decontamination restores combat power and reduces casualties that may result from exposure, allowing the commander to sustain combat operations. Use the three principles of decontamination listed in the following when planning decontamination operations:

- Decontaminate as soon as possible.
- Decontaminate only what is necessary.
- Decontaminate as far forward as possible, which is METT-TC (I) dependent.

D-22. When a CBRN incident occurs, the CAB quickly responds to and initially mitigates the effects of contamination. The company team performs only those actions required to allow continuation of the mission and, within mission constraints, save lives. To recover, the commander decides whether decontamination is required to restore combat power, and if so, what level of decontamination is required. The levels of decontamination are immediate, operational, thorough, and clearance. (See ATP 3-11.32 for a detailed discussion of decontamination levels.)

D-23. Immediate decontamination minimizes casualties and limits the spread or transfer of contamination. The contaminated individual to save lives and reduce penetration of agent into surfaces carries out immediate decontamination. This may include decontamination of personnel, clothing, and equipment. Immediate decontamination should help prevent casualties limit the spread or transfer of contamination and permit the use of individual equipment and key systems.

D-24. Operational decontamination sustains operations by reducing the contact hazard, limiting the spread of contamination, and eliminating or reducing the duration that MOPP equipment should be used. The contaminated unit carries out operational decontamination with possible assistance from an organic decontamination organization. Operational decontamination is restricted to the specific parts of contaminated, operationally essential equipment, material, and work areas to minimize contact and transfer hazards and to sustain operations. This may include individual decontamination beyond the scope of immediate decontamination, MOPP gear exchange, and vehicle wash-down. Operational decontamination reduces the level of contamination, thus lessening the chance of spread and transfer.

D-25. Thorough decontamination reduces contamination to the lowest detectable level using tactical-level capabilities. The intent of thorough decontamination is to reduce or eliminate the level of MOPP. This is accomplished by units (with or without external support) when operations and resources permit. Detailed equipment decontamination, detailed troop decontamination, and detailed aircraft decontamination are conducted as part of a reconstitution effort during breaks in combat operations. These operations require immense logistics support and are manpower intensive. Thorough decontamination is carried out to reduce contamination on personnel, equipment, materiel, and work areas. This permits the partial or total removal of individual protective equipment and maintains operations with minimum degradation. While conducting thorough decontamination, contaminated units are not mission capable. The resulting decrease in MOPP should allow the unit to operate with restored effectiveness.

D-26. Clearance decontamination provides decontamination to a level that allows unrestricted transportation, maintenance, employment, and disposal. CBRN forces may be called on to advise a commander on support to clearance decontamination. Current U.S. Army CBRN structures are unable to conduct clearance decontamination to DOD policy standards. Outside agencies are needed to support clearance decontamination. CBRN forces may be called on to advise a commander on support to clearance decontamination.

D-27. Additional decontamination considerations include the following:

- Plan decontamination sites throughout the width and depth of the AO.
- Tie decontamination sites to the scheme of maneuver and templated CBRN incidents.
- Plan for contaminated routes.
- Plan logistics and resupply of MOPP, mask parts, vehicle filters, water, and decontamination supplies.
- Consider medical concerns, including treatment and evacuation of contaminated casualties.
- Plan for site security.

Glossary

The glossary lists acronyms and terms with Army or joint definitions. Where Army and joint definitions differ, (Army) precedes the definition. ATP 3-90.1 is not the proponent publication (the authority) for any operational term or definition. The proponent publication for other terms is listed in parentheses after the definition.

SECTION I – ACRONYMS AND ABBREVIATIONS

AA	assembly area
ABCT	Armored brigade combat team
ABV	assault breacher vehicle
ADP	Army doctrine publication
AFTTP	Air Force tactics, techniques, and procedures
AO	area of operations
ASCOPE	areas, structures, capabilities, organizations, people, and events
AT	antitank
ATGM	antitank guided missile
ATP	Army techniques publication
BAS	battalion aid station
BCT	brigade combat team
BHL	battle handover line
BP	battle position
C-UAS	counter-unmanned aircraft system
CAB	combined arms battalion
CAS	close air support
CASEVAC	casualty evacuation
CBRN	chemical, biological, radiological, and nuclear
CCIR	commander's critical information requirement
CCP	casualty collection point
class I	rations and gratuitous issue of health, morale, and welfare items
class II	clothing, individual equipment, tentage, tool sets, and administrative and housekeeping supplies and equipment
class III	petroleum, oil, and lubricants
class IV	construction materials
class V	ammunition
class VI	personal demand items
class VII	major end items, including tanks, helicopters, and radios
class VIII	medical
class IX	repair parts and components for equipment maintenance

CLS	combat lifesaver
COA	course of action
CP	command post
DA	Department of the Army
DD	Department of Defense Form
DFCM	direct fire control measure
DLIC	detachment left in contact
DOD	Department of Defense
EA	engagement area
FA	field artillery
FDC	fire direction center
FEBA	forward edge of the battle area
FIST	fire support team
FM	field manual, frequency modulation
FMT	field maintenance team
FPF	final protective fire
FSC	forward support company
FSEM	fire support execution matrix
FSF	foreign security forces
FSO	fire support officer
GPS	Global Positioning System
HN	host nation
HQ	headquarters
IFV	Infantry fighting vehicle
IPB	intelligence preparation of the battlefield
IR	infrared
JAB	joint assault bridge
JP	joint publication
LD	line of departure
LOA	limit of advance
LOGPAC	logistics package
LRP	logistics release point
MBA	main battle area
MCP	maintenance collection point
MCRP	Marine Corps reference publication
MCTP	Marine Corps training publication
MCWP	Marine Corps warfighting publication
MEDEVAC	medical evacuation
METT-TC (I)	mission, enemy, terrain and weather, troops and support available, time available, civil considerations, and informational considerations
MICLIC	mine clearing line charge
mm	millimeter

MOPP	mission oriented protective posture
MTC	movement to contact
MTF	medical treatment facility
NCO	noncommissioned officer
NCOIC	noncommissioned officer in charge
NTTP	Navy tactics, techniques, and procedures
OAKOC	obstacles, avenues of approach, key terrain, observation and fields of fire, and cover and concealment
OE	operational environment
OP	observation post
OPORD	operation order
OPSEC	operations security
OTERA-A	organize, train, equip, rebuild and build, advise and assist, and assess
PC	personnel carrier
PCC	precombat check
PCI	precombat inspection
PIR	priority intelligence requirement
PL	platoon leader
PLD	probable line of deployment
PMESII-PT	political, military, economic, social, information, infrastructure, physical environment, and time
POB	point of breach
PSG	platoon sergeant
RED	risk estimate distance
RFL	restrictive fire line
ROE	rules of engagement
RTO	radiotelephone operator
S-1	battalion or brigade personnel staff officer
S-2	battalion or brigade intelligence staff officer
SA	situational awareness
SBF	support by fire
SFA	security force assistance
SOP	standard operating procedure
SOSRA	suppress, obscure, secure, reduce, and assault
SPOTREP	spot report
SWEAT-MSO	sewage, water, electricity, academics, trash, medical, security, other considerations
TC	training circular
TIM	toxic industrial material
TLP	troop leading procedures
TOA	transfer of authority
TOW	tube launched, optically tracked, wire guided

TRP	target reference point
UAS	unmanned aircraft system
U.S.	United States
WARNORD	warning order
WCS	weapons control status
WMD	weapons of mass destruction
XO	executive officer

SECTION II – TERMS

actions on contact

A process to help leaders understand what is happening and to take action. (FM 3-90)

air-ground operations

The simultaneous or synchronized employment of ground forces with aviation maneuver and fires to seize, retain, and exploit the initiative. (FM 3-04)

alternate position

A defensive position that the commander assigns to a unit or weapon system for occupation when the primary position becomes untenable or unsuitable for carrying out the assigned task. (FM 3-90)

ambush

A variation of attack from concealed positions against a moving or temporarily halted enemy. (FM 3-90)

approach march

The advance of a combat unit when direct contact with the enemy is intended. (FM 3-90)

area defense

A type of defensive operation that concentrates on denying enemy forces access to designated terrain for a specific time rather than destroying the enemy outright. (ADP 3-90)

area of influence

An area inclusive of and extending beyond an operational area wherein a commander is capable of direct influence by maneuver, fire support, and information normally under the commander's command or control. (JP 3-0)

area of interest

That area of concern to the commander, including the area of influence, areas adjacent to it, and extending into enemy territory. (JP 3-0)

area of operations

An operational area defined by a commander for the land or maritime force commander to accomplish their missions and protect their forces. (JP 3-0)

area reconnaissance

A form of reconnaissance operation that focuses on obtaining detailed information about the terrain or enemy activity within a prescribed area. (FM 3-90)

area security

A type of security operation conducted to protect friendly forces, lines of communications, installation routes and actions within a specific area. (FM 3-90)

assembly area

An area a unit occupies to prepare for an operation. (FM 3-90)

attack

A type of offensive operation that defeats enemy forces, seizes terrain, or secures terrain. (FM 3-90)

basic load

The quantity of supplies required to be on hand within, and moved by a unit or formation, expressed according to the wartime organization of the unit or formation and maintained at the prescribed levels. (JP 4-09)

battle position

A defensive location oriented on a likely enemy avenue of approach. (ADP 3-90)

biological hazard

An organism, or substance derived from an organism, that poses a threat to human or animal health. (JP 3-11)

block

A tactical mission task that denies the enemy access to an area or an avenue of approach. (FM 3-90)

bonding overwatch

A movement technique used when contact with enemy forces is expected. (FM 3-90)

breach

A tactical mission task in which a unit breaks through or establishes a passage through an enemy obstacle. (FM 3-90)

breach area

A defined area where a breach occurs. (ATP 3-90.4)

call for fire

A standardized request for fire containing data necessary for obtaining the required fire on a target. (FM 3-09)

casualty evacuation

(Army) The movement of casualties aboard nonmedical vehicles or aircraft without en route medical care. (FM 4-02)

chemical, biological, radiological, and nuclear environment

An operational environment that includes chemical, biological, radiological, and nuclear threats and hazards and their potential resulting effects. (JP 3-11)

chemical, biological, radiological, and nuclear operations

Chemical, biological, radiological, and nuclear operations include the employment of capabilities that assess, protect against, and mitigate the entire range of chemical, biological, radiological, and nuclear incidents to enable freedom of action. (FM 3-11)

chemical hazard

Any chemical manufactured, used, transported, or stored that can cause death or other harm through toxic properties of those materials, including chemical agents and chemical weapons prohibited under the Chemical Weapons Convention as well as toxic industrial chemicals. (JP 3-11)

close air support

Air action by aircraft against hostile targets that are in close proximity to friendly forces and that require detailed integration of each air mission with the fire and movement of those forces. (JP 3-09.3)

column formation

A movement formation with elements arranged one behind another. (FM 3-90)

combat lifesaver

A nonmedical Soldier of a unit trained to provide enhanced first aid as a secondary mission. (FM 4-02)

combat load

The minimum mission-essential equipment and supplies as determined by the commander responsible for carrying out the mission, required for Soldiers to fight and survive immediate combat operations. (FM 4-40)

combat patrol

A patrol that provides security and harasses, destroys, or captures enemy troops, equipment, or installations. (ATP 3-21.8)

combat power

The total means of destructive and disruptive force that a military unit/formation can apply against an enemy at a given time. (JP 3-0)

combined arms

The synchronized and simultaneous application of arms to achieve an effect greater than if each arm was used separately or sequentially. (ADP 3-0)

command and control warfighting function

The related tasks and a system that enable commanders to synchronize and converge all elements of power. (ADP 3-0)

commander's critical information requirement

Specific information identified by the commander as being essential to facilitate timely decision making. (JP 3-0)

commander's intent

A clear and concise expression of the purpose of the operation and the desired objectives and military end state. (JP 3-0)

constraint

(Army) A restriction placed on the command by a higher command. A constraint dictates an action or inaction, thus restricting the freedom of action of a subordinate commander. (FM 5-0)

contain

A tactical mission task in which a unit stops, holds, or surrounds an enemy force. (FM 3-90)

control measure

A means of regulating forces or warfighting functions. (ADP 6-0)

cordon and search

A variation of movement to contact where a friendly force isolates and searches a target area. (FM 3-90)

counterattack

A variation of attack by a defending force against an attacking enemy force. (FM 3-90)

countermobility

(Army/Marine Corps) A set of combined arms activities that use or enhance the effects of natural and man-made obstacles to prevent the enemy freedom of movement and maneuver. (ATP 3-90.8)

cover

(Army) A type of security operation done independent of the main body to protect them by fighting to gain time while preventing enemy ground observation of and direct fire against the main body. (ADP 3-90)

covert crossing

A planned crossing of an inland water obstacle or other gap in which the crossing is intended to be undetected. (ATP 3-90.4)

defensive operation

An operation to defeat an enemy attack, gain time, economize forces, and develop conditions favorable for offensive or stability operations. (ADP 3-0)

delay

When a force under pressure trades space for time by slowing down the enemy's momentum and inflicting maximum damage on enemy forces without becoming decisively engaged. (ADP 3-90)

deliberate crossing

The crossing of an inland water obstacle or other gap that requires extensive planning and detailed preparations. (ATP 3-90.4)

deliberate operation

An operation in which the tactical situation allows the development and coordination of detailed plans, including multiple branches and sequels. (ADP 3-90)

demonstration

A variation of tactical deception used as a show of force in an area where a unit does not seek a decision and attempts to mislead an adversary. (FM 3-90)

deny

A task to hinder or prevent the enemy from using terrain, space, personnel, supplies, or facilities. (ATP 3-21.20)

directed obstacle

An obstacle directed by a higher commander as a specified task to a subordinate unit. (ATP 3-90.8)

disengagement line

A phase line located on identifiable terrain that, when crossed by the enemy, signals to defending elements that it is time to displace to their next position. (ADP 3-90)

double envelopment

A variation of envelopment where forces simultaneously attack along both flanks of an enemy force. (FM 3-90)

echelon formation

A movement formation with elements arranged on an angle to the left or to the right of the direction of attack (echelon left, echelon right). (FM 3-90)

electromagnetic protection

Division of electromagnetic warfare involving the actions taken to protect personnel, facilities, and equipment from any effects of friendly or enemy use of the electromagnetic spectrum that degrade, neutralize, or destroy friendly combat capability. (JP 3-85)

emission control

The selective and controlled use of electromagnetic, acoustic, or other emitters to optimize command and control capabilities while minimizing, for operations security: a. detection by enemy sensors, b. mutual interference among friendly systems, and/or c. enemy interference with the ability to execute a military deception plan. (JP 3-85)

enabling operation

An operation that sets the friendly conditions required for mission accomplishment. (FM 3-90)

enemy

A party identified as hostile against which the use of force is authorized. (ADP 3-0)

engagement area

An area where the commander masses effects to contain and destroy an enemy force. (FM 3-90)

engagement criteria

Protocols that specify those circumstances for initiating engagement with an enemy force. (FM 3-90)

engagement priority

Identifies the order in which the unit engages enemy systems or functions. (FM 3-90)

envelopment

A form of maneuver in which an attacking force avoids an enemy's principal defense by attacking along an assailable flank. (FM 3-90)

essential task

(Army) A specified or implied task that must be executed to accomplish the mission. (FM 5-0)

exploitation

(Army) A type of offensive operation following a successful attack to disorganize the enemy in depth. (FM 3-90)

far side objective

A defined location oriented on the terrain or on an enemy force that an assaulting force seizes to eliminate enemy direct fires to prevent the enemy from interfering with the reduction of the obstacles and allows follow-on forces to move securely through created lanes. (ATP 3-90.4)

feint

A variation of tactical deception that makes contact solely to deceive the adversary as to the location, time of attack or both. (FM 3-90)

final protective fire

An immediately available prearranged barrier of fire designed to impede enemy movement across defensive lines or areas. (JP 3-09.3)

final protective line

A selected line of fire where an enemy assault is to be checked by interlocking fire from all available weapons and obstacles. (FM 3-90)

fire plan

A tactical plan for using the weapons of a unit or formation so that their fire will be coordinated. (FM 3-09)

fires

The use of weapon systems or other actions to create specific lethal or nonlethal effects on a target. (JP 3-09)

fire support

Fires that directly support land, maritime, amphibious, space, cyberspace, and special operations forces to engage enemy forces, combat formations, and facilities in pursuit of tactical and operational objectives. (JP 3-09)

fire support plan

A plan that addresses each means of fire support available and describes how Army indirect fires, joint fires, and target acquisition are integrated with maneuver to facilitate operational success. (FM 3-09)

fire support planning

The continuous process of analyzing, allocating, integrating, synchronizing, and scheduling fires to describe how the effects of fires facilitate maneuver force actions. (FM 3-09)

fires warfighting function

The related tasks and systems that create and converge effects in all domains against the adversary or enemy to enable operations across the range of military operations. (ADP 3-0)

fix

A tactical mission task in which a unit prevents the enemy from moving from a specific location for a specific period. (FM 3-90)

fixing force

A force designed to supplement the striking force by preventing the enemy from moving from a specific area for a specific time. (ADP 3-90)

follow and assume

A tactical mission task in which a committed force follows and supports a lead force conducting an offensive operation and continues mission if lead force cannot continue. (FM 3-90)

follow and support

A tactical mission task in which a committed force follows and supports a lead force conducting an offensive operation. (FM 3-90)

forced march

A march longer or faster than usual or in adverse conditions. (FM 3-90)

forward passage of lines

Occurs when a unit passes through another unit's positions while moving toward the enemy. (ADP 3-90)

frontal attack

A form of maneuver in which the attacking force seeks to destroy a weaker enemy force or fix a larger enemy force in place over a broad front. (FM 3-90)

guard

A type of security operation done to protect the main body by fighting to gain time while preventing enemy ground observation of and direct fire against the main body. (ADP 3-90)

hasty breach

The creation of lanes through enemy obstacles by expedient methods such as blasting with demolitions, pushing rollers or disabled vehicles through the minefields when the time factor does not permit detailed reconnaissance, deliberate breaching, or bypassing the obstacle. (JP 3-15)

hasty operation

An operation in which a commander directs immediately available forces, using fragmentary orders, to perform tasks with minimal preparation, trading planning and preparation time for speed of execution. (ADP 3-90)

health service support

(Army) Health service support is support and services performed, provided, and arranged by the Army Medicine to promote, improve, conserve, or restore the behavioral and physical well-being of personnel by providing direct patient care that include medical treatment (organic and area support) and hospitalization, medical evacuation to include medical regulating, and medical logistics to include blood management. (FM 4-02)

implied task

(Army) A task that must be performed to accomplish a specified task or mission but is not stated in the higher headquarters' order. (FM 5-0)

infiltration

A form of maneuver in which an attacking force conducts undetected movement through or into an area occupied by enemy forces. (FM 3-90)

informational considerations

Those aspects of the human, information, and physical dimensions that affect how humans and automated systems derive meaning from, use, act upon, and are impacted by information. (FM 3-0)

intelligence warfighting function

The related tasks and systems that facilitate understanding the enemy, terrain, weather, civil considerations, and other significant aspects of the operational environment. (ADP 3-0)

interdict

A tactical mission task in which a unit prevents, disrupts, or delays the enemy's use of an area or route in any domain. (FM 3-90)

kill zone

The location where fires are concentrated in an ambush. (FM 3-90)

lane

A route through, over, or around an enemy or friendly obstacle that provides passage of a force. (ATP 3-90.4)

large-scale combat operations

Extensive joint combat operations in terms of scope and size of forces committed, conducted as a campaign aimed at achieving operational and strategic objectives. (ADP 3-0)

line formation

A movement formation in which elements move abreast of each other. (FM 3-90)

linkup

A type of enabling operation that involves the meeting of friendly ground forces, which occurs in a variety of circumstances. (FM 3-90)

main body

The principal part of a tactical command or formation. It does not include detached elements of the command, such as advance guards, flank guards, and covering forces. (ADP 3-90)

main effort

A designated subordinate unit whose mission at a given point in time is most critical to overall mission success. (ADP 3-0)

march column

All march serials using the same route for a single movement under control of a single commander. (FM 3-90)

medical evacuation

The timely and effective movement of the wounded, injured, or ill to and between medical treatment facilities on dedicated and properly marked medical platforms with en route care provided by medical personnel. (ATP 4-02.2)

meeting engagement

A combat action that occurs when a moving force engages an enemy at an unexpected time and place. (FM 3-90)

mission statement

A short sentence or paragraph that describes the organization's essential task(s), purpose, and action containing the elements of who, what, when, where, and why. (JP 5-0)

mobile defense

A type of defensive operation that concentrates on the destruction or defeat of the enemy through a decisive attack by a striking force. (ADP 3-90)

movement and maneuver warfighting function

The related tasks and systems that move and employ forces to achieve a position of relative advantage over the enemy and other threats. (ADP 3-0)

movement formation

An ordered arrangement of forces for a specific purpose and describes the general configuration of a unit on the ground. (ADP 3-90)

movement to contact

(Army) A type of offensive operation designed to establish or regain contact to develop the situation. (FM 3-90)

multidomain operations

The combined armed employment of joint and Army capabilities to create and exploit relative advantages to achieve objectives, defeat enemy forces, and consolidate gains on behalf of joint force commanders. (FM 3-0)

neutral

In combat and combat support operations, an identity applied to a track whose characteristics, behavior, origin, or nationality indicate that it is neither supporting nor opposing friendly force. (JP 3-0)

nontactical movement

A movement in which troops and vehicles are arranged to expedite their movement and conserve time and energy when no enemy ground interference is anticipated. (FM 3-90)

obstacle

Any barrier designed or employed to disrupt, fix, turn, or block the movement and maneuver, and to impose additional losses in personnel, time, and equipment. (JP 3-15)

offensive operation

An operation to defeat or destroy enemy forces and gain control of terrain, resources, and population centers. (ADP 3-0)

operation

A sequence of tactical actions with a common purpose or unifying theme. (JP 1, Vol 1)

operational environment

The aggregate of the conditions, circumstances, and influences that affect the employment of capabilities and bear on the decisions of the commander. (JP 3-0)

operational framework

A cognitive tool used to assist commanders and staffs in clearly visualizing and describing the application of combat power in time, space, purpose, and resources in the concept of operations. (ADP 1-01)

operational variables

A comprehensive set of information categories used to describe an operational environment. (ADP 1-01)

overwatch

A task that positions an element to support the movement of another element with immediate fire. (ATP 3-21.10)

passage of lines

An operation in which a force moves forward or rearward through another force's combat positions with the intention of moving into or out of contact with the enemy. (JP 3-18)

patrol

A detachment sent out by a larger unit to conduct a specific mission that operates semi-independently and return to the main body upon completion of mission. (ATP 3-21.8)

penetration

A form of maneuver in which a force attacks on a narrow front. (FM 3-90)

point of breach

The location at an obstacle where the creation of a lane is being attempted. (ATP 3-90.4)

point of penetration

(Army) Point of penetration is the location, identified on the ground, where the commanders concentrates their efforts to seize a foothold on the far side objective. (ATP 3-90.4)

primary position

The position that covers the enemy's most likely avenue of approach into the assigned area. (FM 3-90)

priority of support

A priority set by the commander to ensure a subordinate unit has support in accordance with its relative importance to accomplish the mission. (ADP 5-0)

priority target

A target, based on either time or importance, on which delivery of fires takes precedence over all the fires for the designated firing unit or element. (FM 3-09)

proof

The verification that a lane is free of mines or explosive hazards and that the width and trafficability at the point of breach are suitable for the passing force. (ATP 3-90.4)

protection

Preservation of the effectiveness and survivability of mission-related military and nonmilitary personnel, equipment, facilities, information, and infrastructure deployed or located within or outside the boundaries of a given operational area. (JP 3-0)

protection warfighting function

The related tasks, systems, and methods that prevent or mitigate detection, threat effects, and hazards to preserve combat power and enable freedom of action. (FM 3-0)

pursuit

A type of offensive operation to catch or cut off a disorganized hostile force attempting to escape, with the aim of destroying it. (FM 3-90)

quartering party

A group dispatched to a new assigned area in advance of the main body. (FM 3-90)

raid

(Army) A variation of attack to temporarily seize an objective with a planned withdrawal. (FM 3-90)

rearward passage of lines

Occurs when a unit passes through another unit's positions while moving away from the enemy. (ADP 3-90)

reconnaissance

A mission undertaken to obtain information about the activities and resources of an enemy or adversary, or to secure data concerning the meteorological, hydrographic, geographic, or other characteristics of a particular area, by visual observation or other detection methods. (JP 2-0)

reconnaissance by fire

A technique in which a unit fires on a suspected enemy position. (FM 3-90)

reconnaissance in force

A form of reconnaissance operation designed to discover or test the enemy's strength, dispositions, and reactions or to obtain other information. (FM 3-90)

reduce

A tactical mission task in which a unit destroys an encircled or bypassed enemy force. (FM 3-90)

reduction

The creation of lanes through a minefield or obstacle to enable passage of the attacking ground force. (JP 3-15)

reduction area

A number of adjacent points of breach that are under the control of the breaching commander. (ATP 3-90.4)

relief in place

An operation in which, by the direction of higher authority, all or part of a unit is replaced in an area by the incoming unit and the responsibilities of the replaced elements for the mission and the assigned zone of operations are transferred to the incoming unit. (JP 3-07.3)

reorganization

All measures taken by the commander to maintain unit combat effectiveness or return it to a specified level of combat capability. (ATP 3-94.4)

reserve

(Army) That portion of a body of troops that is withheld from action at the beginning of an engagement to be available for a decisive movement. (ADP 3-90)

reserved obstacle

(Army) Obstacles of any type, for which the commander restricts execution authority. (ATP 3-90.8)

restrictive fire line

A specific boundary established between converging, friendly surface forces that prohibits fires or their effects from crossing. (JP 3-09)

retirement

When a force out of contact moves away from the enemy. (ADP 3-90)

retrograde

(Army) A type of defensive operation that involves organized movement away from the enemy. (ADP 3-90)

retrograde movement

Any movement to the rear or away from the enemy. (FM 3-90)

route reconnaissance

A form of reconnaissance operation to obtain detailed information of a specified route and all terrain from which the enemy could influence movement along that route. (FM 3-90)

screen

A type of security operation that primarily provides early warning to the protected force. (ADP 3-90)

search and attack

A variation of a movement to contact where a friendly force conducts coordinated attacks to defeat a distributed enemy force. (FM 3-90)

sector

An operational area assigned to a unit in the defense that has rear and lateral boundaries and interlocking fires. (FM 3-0)

sector of fire

That area assigned to a unit or weapon system in which it will engage the enemy according to the established engagement priorities. (FM 3-90)

secure

A tactical mission task in which a unit prevents the enemy from damaging or destroying a force, facility, or geographical location. (FM 3-90)

security cooperation

Department of Defense interactions with foreign security establishments to build security relationships that promote specific United States security interests, develop allied and partner military and security capabilities for self-defense and multinational operations, and provide United States forces with peacetime and contingency access to allies and partners. (JP 3-20)

security operations

Those operations performed by commanders to provide early and accurate warning of enemy operations, to provide the force being protected with time and maneuver space within which to react to the enemy, and to develop the situation to allow commanders to effectively use their protected forces. (ADP 3-90)

single envelopment

A variation of envelopment where a force attacks along one flank of an enemy force. (FM 3-90)

situational understanding

The product of applying analysis and judgment to relevant information to determine the relationship among the operational and mission variables. (ADP 6-0)

specified task

(Army) A task specifically assigned to a unit by its higher headquarters. (FM 5-0)

spoiling attack

A variation of an attack employed against an enemy preparing for an attack. (FM 3-90)

stability operation

An operation conducted outside the United States in coordination with other instruments of national power to establish or maintain a secure environment and provide essential governmental services, emergency infrastructure reconstruction, and humanitarian relief. (ADP 3-0)

striking force

A dedicated counterattack force in a mobile defense constituted with the bulk of available combat power. (ADP 3-90)

strong point

A heavily fortified battle position tied to a natural or reinforcing obstacle to create an anchor for the defense or to deny the enemy decisive or key terrain. (ADP 3-90)

subsequent position

A position that a unit expects to move to during the course of battle. (ADP 3-90)

supplementary position

A defensive position located within a unit's assigned area that provides the best sectors of fire and defensive terrain along an avenue of approach that is not the primary avenue where the enemy is expected to attack. (FM 3-90)

supporting effort

A designated unit with a mission that supports the success of the main effort. (ADP 3-0)

suppress

A tactical mission task in which a unit temporarily degrades a force or weapon system from accomplishing its mission. (FM 3-90)

survivability

(Army/Marine Corps) A quality or capability of military forces which permits them to avoid or withstand hostile actions or environmental conditions while retaining the ability to fulfill their primary mission. (ATP 3-37.34)

survivability operations

(Army/Marine Corps) Those protection activities that alter the physical environment by providing or improving cover, camouflage, and concealment. (ATP 3-37.34)

sustainment

(Army) The provision of the logistics, financial management, personnel services, and health service support necessary to maintain operations until successful mission completion. (ADP 4-0)

sustainment warfighting function

The related tasks and systems that provide support and services to ensure freedom of action, extend operational reach, and prolong endurance. (ADP 3-0)

tactical deception

A friendly activity that causes enemy commanders to take action or cause inaction detrimental to their objectives. (FM 3-90)

tactical movement

A movement in which troops and vehicles are arranged to protect combat forces during movement when a threat of enemy interference is possible. (FM 3-90)

tactical road march

A rapid movement used to relocate units within an assigned area to prepare for combat operations. (FM 3-90)

target acquisition

The detection, identification, and location of a target in sufficient detail to permit the effective employment of capabilities that create the required effects. (JP 3-60)

target reference point

A predetermined point of reference, normally a permanent structure or terrain feature that can be used when describing a target location. (JP 3-09.3)

task

A clearly defined action or activity specifically assigned to an individual or organization, or derived during mission analysis, that must be done as it is imposed by an appropriate authority. (JP 1, Vol 1)

threat

Any combination of actors, entities, or forces that have the capability and intent to harm United States forces, United States national interests, or the homeland. (ADP 3-0)

traveling

A movement technique used when speed is necessary and contact with enemy forces is not likely. (FM 3-90)

traveling overwatch

A movement technique used when contact with enemy forces is possible. (FM 3-90)

trigger line

A phase line located on identifiable terrain used to initiate and mass fires into an engagement area at a predetermined range. (FM 3-90)

troop leading procedures

A dynamic process used by small-unit leaders to analyze a mission, develop a plan, and prepare for an operation. (ADP 5-0)

troop movement

The movement of Soldiers and units from one place to another by any available means. (FM 3-90)

turning movement

(Army) A form of maneuver in which the attacking force seeks to avoid the enemy's principal defensive positions by attacking to the rear of their current positions forcing them to move or divert forces to meet the threat. (FM 3-90)

unity of effort

Coordination and cooperation toward common objectives, even if the participants are not necessarily part of the same command or organization that is the product of successful unified action. (JP 1, Vol 2)

vee formation

A movement formation with two elements abreast and one or more elements trailing. (FM 3-90)

vertical envelopment

A variation of envelopment where air-dropped or airlanded troops attack an enemy forces rear, flank, or both. (FM 3-90)

warfighting function

A group of tasks and systems united by a common purpose that commanders use to accomplish missions and training objectives. (ADP 3-0)

warning order

A preliminary notice of an order or action that is to follow. (JP 5-0)

wedge formation

A movement formation with one lead element and the trail elements are paired off abreast of each other on the flanks. (FM 3-90)

withdraw

To disengage from an enemy force and move in a direction away from the enemy. (ADP 3-90)

zone

An operational area assigned to a unit in the offense that only has rear and lateral boundaries. (FM 3-0)

zone reconnaissance

A form of reconnaissance operation that involves a directed effort to obtain detailed information on all routes, obstacles, terrain, and enemy forces within a zone defined by boundaries. (FM 3-90)

References

All websites accessed on 23 October 2023.

REQUIRED PUBLICATIONS

These documents must be available to intended users of this publication.

DOD Dictionary of Military and Associated Terms. September 24 October 2023. FM 1-02.1. *Operational Terms*. 9 March 2021.

FM 1-02.2. *Military Symbols*. 18 May 2022.

RELATED PUBLICATIONS

These documents are cited in this publication.

JOINT PUBLICATIONS

Most joint publications are available online: https://www.jcs.mil/Doctrine.

JP 1 Volume 1. *Joint Warfighting*. 27 August 2023.

JP 1 Volume 2. *The Joint Force*. 19 June 2020.

JP 2-0. *Joint Intelligence*. 26 May 2022.

JP 3-0. *Joint Campaigns and Operations*. 18 June 2022.

JP 3-07.3. *Peace Operations*. 1 March 2018.

JP 3-09. *Joint Fire Support*. 10 April 2019.

JP 3-09.3. *Joint Close Air Support*. 10 June 2019.

JP 3-11. *Operations in Chemical, Biological, Radiological, and Nuclear Environments*. 29 October 2018.

JP 3-15. *Barriers, Obstacles, and Mines in Joint Operations*. 26 May 2022.

JP 3-18. *Joint Forcible Entry Operations*. 27 June 2018.

JP 3-20. *Security Cooperation*. 9 September 2022.

JP 3-52. *Joint Airspace Control*. 22 October 2022.

JP 3-60. *Joint Targeting*. 28 September 2018.

JP 3-85. *Joint Electromagnetic Spectrum Operations*. 22 May 2020.

JP 4-09. *Distribution Operations*. 14 March 2019.

JP 5-0. *Joint Planning*. 1 December 2020.

ARMY PUBLICATIONS

Most Army doctrinal publications are available online: https://armypubs.army.mil.

ADP 1-01. *Doctrine Primer*. 31 July 2019.

ADP 2-0. *Intelligence*. 31 July 2019.

ADP 3-0. *Operations*. 31 July 2019.

ADP 3-07. *Stability*. 31 July 2019.

ADP 3-19. *Fires*. 31 July 2019.

ADP 3-37. *Protection*. 31 July 2019.

ADP 3-90. *Offense and Defense*. 31 July 2019.

ADP 4-0. *Sustainment.* 31 July 2019.

ADP 5-0. *The Operations Process.* 31 July 2019.

ADP 6-0. *Mission Command: Command and Control of Army Forces.* 31 July 2019.

ATP 2-01.3. *Intelligence Preparation of the Battlefield.* 1 March 2019.

ATP 3-01.60. *Counter-rocket, Artillery, and Mortar Operations.* 10 May 2013.

ATP 3-01.81. *Counter-Unmanned Aircraft System Techniques.* 11 August 2023.

ATP 3-04.1. *Aviation Tactical Employment.* 7 May 2020.

ATP 3-07.5. *Stability Techniques.* 31 August 2012.

ATP 3-07.10/MCRP 3-03D.1/NTTP 3-07.5/AFTTP 3-2.76. *Advising. Multi-service Tactics, Techniques, and Procedures for Advising Foreign Security Forces.* 15 June 2023.

ATP 3-09.30. *Observed Fires.* 28 September 2017.

ATP 3-09.32/MCRP 3-31.6/NTTP 3-09.2/AFTTP 3-2.6. *JFIRE. Multi-service Tactics, Techniques, and Procedures for Joint Application of Firepower.* 18 October 2019.

ATP 3-09.42. *Fire Support for the Brigade Combat Team.* 1 March 2016.

ATP 3-11.32/MCWP 10-10E.8/NTTP 3-11.37/AFTTP 3-2.46. *Multi-service Tactics, Techniques, and Procedures for Chemical, Biological, Radiological, and Nuclear Passive Defense.* 13 May 2016.

ATP 3-11.50. *Battlefield Obscuration.* 15 May 2014.

ATP 3-13.5. *Soldier and Leader Engagement.* 21 December 2021.

ATP 3-20.15/MCRP 3-10B1. *Tank Platoon.* 3 July 2019.

ATP 3-21.8. *Infantry Platoon and Squad.* 12 April 2016.

ATP 3-21.10. *Infantry Rifle Company.* 14 May 2018.

ATP 3-21.20. *Infantry Battalion.* 28 December 2017.

ATP 3-21.90/MCTP 3-01D. *Tactical Employment of Mortars.* 9 October 2019.

ATP 3-34.22. *Engineer Operations—Brigade Combat Team and Below.* 14 April 2021.

ATP 3-34.80. *Geospatial Engineering.* 22 February 2017.

ATP 3-37.2. *Antiterrorism.* 19 July 2021.

ATP 3-37.34/MCTP 3-34C. *Survivability Operations.* 16 April 2018.

ATP 3-39.10. *Police Operations.* 24 August 2021.

ATP 3-39.30. *Security and Mobility Support.* 21 May 2020.

ATP 3-39.32. *Physical Security.* 8 March 2022.

ATP 3-57.10. *Civil Affairs Support to Populace and Resources Control.* 6 August 2013.

ATP 3-90.4/MCTP 3-34A (MCWP 3-17.8). *Combined Arms Mobility.* 10 June 2022.

ATP 3-90.5. *Combined Arms Battalion.* 15 July 2021.

ATP 3-90.8/MCTP 3-34B. *Combined Arms Countermobility.* 30 November 2021.

ATP 3-94.4. *Reconstitution Operations.* 5 May 2021.

ATP 4-02.2. *Medical Evacuation.* 12 July 2019.

ATP 4-02.4. *Medical Platoon.* 12 May 2021.

ATP 4-31/MCRP 3-40E.1. *Recovery and Battle Damage Assessment and Repair (BDAR).* 18 November 2020.

ATP 4-32.1. *Explosive Ordnance Disposal (EOD) Group and Battalion Headquarters Operations.* 24 January 2017.

ATP 4-35. *Munitions Operations.* 31 January 2023.

ATP 4-43. *Petroleum Supply Operations.* 18 April 2022.

ATP 5-19. *Risk Management.* 9 November 2021.

ATP 6-0.5. *Command Post Organization and Operations.* 1 March 2017.

ATP 6-02.53. *Techniques for Tactical Radio Operations.* 13 February 2020.

ATP 6-02.71. *Techniques for Department of Defense Information Network Operations.* 30 April 2019.

FM 2-0. *Intelligence.* 1 October 2023.

FM 3-0. *Operations.* 1 October 2022.

FM 3-04. *Army Aviation.* 6 April 2020.

FM 3-07. *Stability.* 2 June 2014.

FM 3-09. *Fire Support and Field Artillery Operations.* 30 April 2020.

FM 3-11. *Chemical, Biological, Radiological, and Nuclear Operations.* 23 May 2019.

FM 3-22. *Army Support to Security Cooperation.* 1 July 2023.

FM 3-34. *Engineer Operations.* 18 December 2020.

FM 3-50. *Army Personnel Recovery.* 2 September 2014.

FM 3-60. *Army Targeting.* 11 August 2023.

FM 3-63. *Detainee Operations.* 2 January 2020.

FM 3-90. *Tactics.* 1 May 2023.

FM 3-96. *Brigade Combat Team.* 19 January 2021.

FM 3-98. *Reconnaissance and Security Operations.* 10 January 2023.

FM 4-0. *Sustainment Operations.* 31 July 2019.

FM 4-02. *Army Health System.* 17 November 2020.

FM 4-40. *Quartermaster Operations.* 22 October 2013.

FM 5-0. *Planning and Orders Production.* 16 May 2022.

FM 6-0. *Command and Staff Organization and Operations.* 16 May 2022.

FM 6-27/MCTP 11-10C. *The Commander's Handbook on the Law of Land Warfare.* 7 August 2019.

TC 3-20.31-4. *Direct Fire Engagement Process (DIDEA).* 23 July 2015.

PRESCRIBED FORMS

This section contains no entries.

REFERENCED FORMS

Unless otherwise indicated, DA forms are available online: https://armypubs.army.mil.

DD forms are available online: https://www.esd.whs.mil/Directives/forms.

DA Form 1156. *Casualty Feeder Card.*

DA Form 1594. *Daily Staff Journal or Duty Officer's Log.*

DA Form 2028. *Recommended Changes to Publications and Blank Forms.*

DA Form 5988-E. *Equipment Maintenance and Inspection Worksheet.* (Available from Global Combat Support System-Army [GCSS-A].)

DD Form 1380. *Tactical Combat Casualty Care (TCCC) Card.* (Available through normal publications supply channels.)

DD Form 2977. *Deliberate Risk Assessment Worksheet.*

Index

Entries are by paragraph number.

Made in the USA
Columbia, SC
25 September 2024

b3525179-c7e3-4eb9-82d7-a0ccff02f393R01